A Concise
Legal History of
South-East Asia

A CONCISE LEGAL HISTORY OF SOUTH-EAST ASIA

M. B. Hooker

Clarendon Press · Oxford
1978

Oxford University Press, Walton Street, Oxford OX2 6DP

OXFORD LONDON GLASGOW
NEW YORK TORONTO MELBOURNE WELLINGTON
IBADAN NAIROBI DAR ES SALAAM LUSAKA CAPE TOWN
KUALA LUMPUR SINGAPORE JAKARTA HONG KONG TOKYO
DELHI BOMBAY CALCUTTA MADRAS KARACHI

© *M. B. Hooker 1978*

All rights reserved. No part of this publication may be reproduced, stored in a retrieval system, or transmitted, in any form or by any means, electronic, mechanical, photocopying, recording, or otherwise, without the prior permission of Oxford University Press

British Library Cataloguing in Publication Data

Hooker, Michael Barry
A concise legal history of South-east Asia.
1. Law—Asia, Southeastern
I. Title
340'.0959   [Law]   77-30245

ISBN 0-19-825344-3

*Printed in Great Britain by
William Clowes & Sons Limited
London, Beccles and Colchester*

Preface

SOUTH-EAST Asia is an area of special interest for the legal historian because it has been a meeting-place for almost all of the world's great legal systems. But they never survived long in their original form. The peculiarly South-East Asian genius has always shown itself in the ability to absorb and transform foreign elements and this has been as true of law as of any other aspect of culture. Moreover, the laws in the area have always interacted with each other and with indigenous elements, producing a *mélange* unique in legal history. These characteristics pose serious methodological problems which I have tried to deal with in the Introduction as well as throughout the text. I should emphasize that this book is not in any way a narrative or chronological history, nor is it more than a bare outline compressed and perhaps over-simplified in some parts. There are considerable lacunae in the legal history of the area—for example, the Portuguese legal administration in Malacca, Vietnamese administrative regulations, and Javanese inscriptions, to name only the most obvious. However, there is sufficient material for an outline of the history of South-East Asian legal thought, and it is with this fundamental aspect that I have been concerned.

In writing this outline I have had the immense advantage of earlier work on particular South-East Asian laws and I acknowledge an obvious debt to scholars such as Emil Forchhammer and D. Richardson (Burma), W. E. Maxwell and J. W. Norton Kyshe (Malaysia), Robert Lingat (Burma, Thailand, and Indo-China), Ph. Philastre and G. H. Camerlynck (Indo-China), Cornelis van Vollenhoven and J. C. G. Jonker (Indonesia), and Juan Plasencia (Philippines). It is also pleasing to record that modern scholars are showing an increasing interest in South-East Asian legal history in such diverse subjects as Thai law, late medieval Javanese law, and the classical laws of Malacca, to mention only those with which

I am personally acquainted. It is also important to acknowledge that much material is being made available by historians and social scientists, and here I would like to enter a plea for more co-operative effort in writing South-East Asian law, both historical and modern.

It is very pleasant to pay tribute to the efficiency and patience of the staff of the Clarendon Press in seeing this book through the press.

My wife, yet again, typed a disorganized draft and by her patient criticism helped immeasurably. She also bore cheerfully the disruptions to normal life which were inflicted upon her.

Eliot College   M. B. HOOKER
University of Kent at Canterbury
May 1977

Contents

TABLE OF CODES AND STATUTES	ix
TABLE OF CASES	xiii
Introduction A Historical Jurisprudence of South-East Asia	1

PART I: STATUS

1. The Indian Legal World: The Law Texts of Burma, Thailand, Champā and Cambodia, and Java — 17
2. The Islamic Legal World: The Law Texts of Island South-East Asia — 48
3. The Chinese Legal World: The Vietnamese Texts — 73
4. The South-East Asian Law Texts: Cultural Borrowing and the Concept of Law — 95

PART II: CONTRACT

5. The English Legal World: The Straits Settlements, Federated and Unfederated Malay States, British Borneo, and Burma — 123
6. The French Legal World: French Indo-China and Thailand (Siam) — 153
7. The Dutch Legal World: The Netherlands East Indies — 187
8. The Spanish-American Legal World: The Philippines — 214

BIBLIOGRAPHY — 239

INDEX — 267

Table of Codes and Statutes

Burma
Buddhist Women's Special Marriage and Succession Act (XXIV of 1939), 152.
Buddhist Women's Special Marriage and Succession Act, 1954, 152.
Burma Laws Act, 1898, 143–4, 147, 150–1.
Christian Marriage Act (XV of 1872), 151.

Cambodia
Civil Code, 1912, 166, 168.
Civil Code, 1920, 167, 177, 181.
Code of Criminal Instruction and Judicial Organization, 1912, 166.
Law on Control of the Judiciary, 1922, 167.
Law on Judicial Organization, 1922, 167.
Penal Code, 1912, 166.
Penal Code, 1924, 167.
Statut Personnel, 1922, 167.

China
Ch'ing Code (*Ta Ch'ing Lü Li*), 76, 80–9, 106, 114, 115, 116–17, 118.
Ming Code (*Ta Ming Lü*), 74, 76.
T'ang Code, 74, 78, 80.

Cochin-China
Civil Law Précis, 1883, 159, 177, 179.
Code of Civil Procedure, 1924, 156.
Code of Commerce, 1919, 158.

Federated Malay States
Christian Marriage Enactment (c. 109 of revised laws, 1935), 149.
Civil Law Enactment, 141.
Civil Law Ordinance, 1956, 141.
Courts Enactment, 1905, 139.
Regulations and Orders in Council for Appointment of a Judicial Commission, 1896, 139.

France
Civil Code, 158, 159–60, 179, 183.
Code Napoléon, 155.
Code of Civil Procedure, 158.
Code of Criminal Investigation, 159.
Commercial Code, 158.
Law of 20 April 1810, 155.
Organic Decree of 16 February 1921, 156.
Penal Code, 158, 161, 165, 167.
Royal Ordinance of 9 February 1827, 155.

India
Act XVI of 1839, 137.
Act XXVI of 1854, 134.
Act XXVI of 1861, 137.
Indian Contract Act, 146–7.

Laos
Civil and Commercial Code, 164–5.
Code of Civil and Commercial Procedure, 165–6.
Code of Criminal Procedure, 165–6.
Penal Code, 165.

x Table of Codes and Statutes

Negri Sembilan
Customary Tenure Enactment, 140.
Muhammadan Marriage and Divorce Registration Enactment, 1900, 140

Netherlands East Indies and Indonesia
Agrarian Act, 1870, 188, 206–7.
Basic Agrarian Law, 1960, 199, 207, 213.
Civil Code, 189, 195, 206, 207, 208–9, 210, 213.
Civil Code (draft), 189, 190–1.
Commercial Code, 189, 195.
Constitution, 1847, 194.
Constitution, 1854, 190.
Constitution, 1925, 190–1.
Marriage Law, 1 of 1874, 213.
Marriage Ordinance for Christian Indonesians (*Staatsblad* 84 of 1933), 195, 212.
Organic Act, 1870, 206.
Penal Code, 1918, 189.
Regulations—
Algemene Bapalingen van Wetgeving, 1847 (*Staatsblad* 23 of 1847), 194.
Constitutional Regulations, 1815 and 1858, 188.
Indische Staats regeling, 1854, 198.
Indische Staats regeling, 1926 (*Staatsblad* 415 of 1925), 195.
Regeling op de Gemengde Huwelijken, 1896 (*Staatsblad* 158 of 1898), 199, 200–1, 211–12.
Regeringsreglement (*Staatsblad* 2 of 1855), 194–5.
Regulation on Mortgages (*Staatsblad* 542 of 1909), 196.
Regulation on Mortgages (*Staatsblad* 584 of 1909), 196.
Regulation on Native Associations (*Staatsblad* 570 and 571 of 1939), 196.
Regulation on Native Corporations (*Staatsblad* 569 of 1939), 196.
Regulation on Religious Courts (*Staatsblad* 51 of 1933), 195.
Royal Decree of 1870 (implementing Agrarian Act) (*Staatsblad* 118 of 1870), 206–7.
Royal Decree on Choice of Law, 1916 (*Staatsblad* 12 of 1917), 190, 198.

North Borneo
Application of Law Ordinance, 1951, 143.
Civil Law Ordinance, 1938, 141–2.

Pahang
Muhammadan Marriage and Divorce Registration Enactment, 1900, 140.

Penang
Regulation, 1800, 125.

Perak
Distribution Enactment, 1929, 140.
Order in Council, 23 of 1893, 140.
Registration of Muhammadan Marriages and Divorce Enactment, 1885, 140.

Philippines
Cattle Registration Act, 235.
Civil Code (Act 368 of 1949), 224, 225, 228, 229, 230, 231, 232, 233–5, 237, 238.
Code of Civil Procedure (Act 190 of 1901), 225, 232, 233.
Code of Civil Procedure, 1950, 232.
Code of Criminal Procedure General Order 58 of 1900), 225.
Code of Muslim Personal Law (Presidential Decree 1083 of 1977), 238.

Table of Codes and Statutes

Commercial Code, 238.
Constitution, 237.
Corporation Law, 236.
Divorce Law (Act 2710 of 1917), 225–6, 230.
Judiciary Act (Act 136 of 1901), 228.
Land Reform Code (Act 3844 of 1963), 238.
Land Registration Law (Act 496 of 1902), 226.
Penal Code (Act 3815 of 1932), 226.
Revised Marriage Law (Act 3613 of 1929), 225, 229.
Rules of Court, 1940, 225, 226, 232, 237, 238.

Sarawak
Application of Laws Ordinance, 1949 (c. 2 of revised laws, 1958), 143.
Chinese Marriage Ordinance, 1933 (c. 74 of revised laws, 1946), 142.
Courts Order, 1922, 142.
Native Customary Laws Ordinance (c. 51 of revised laws, 1958), 143.
Order IX of 1911, 142.

Selangor
Muhammadan Marriage and Divorce Registration Enactment, 1900, 140.

Singapore
Regulations III and IV of 1823, 126.
Women's Charter (Ordinance 18 of 1961, amended by Ordinance 9 of 1967), 148–9.

Spain
Civil Procedure Code, 226.
Code of Commerce, 236.
Codigo Civil, 1889, 222, 228–9, 230, 231–2, 235, 236.

El Ordenamiento de Alcalá, 1348, 220.
Fuero Juzgo, 650, 220.
Fuero Partidas (*Las Siete Partidas*), 1256–65, 220, 225, 226.
Fuero Real, 1254, 220.
Leyes de Toro, 1502–5, 220, 221.
Marriage Law, 1870, 225, 229.
Penal Code, 1870, 226.

Straits Settlements
Mahomedan Marriage (Amendment) Ordinances, 1894, 1902, 1908, 1909 and 1917, 132–3.
Mahomedan Marriage Ordinance, 5 of 1880, 132–3, 134.
Mahomedans Ordinance, 26 of 1933 (c. 57 of revised laws, 1936), 133–4.
Malacca Lands Customary Rights Ordinance, 1886 (c. 125 of revised laws, 1936), 137.
Malacca Lands Ordinance, 1861 (c. 127 of revised laws, 1936), 137.
Malacca Regulation IX of 1830, 137.
Married Women's Property Ordinance, 1902, 134.
Regulations of P.O.W.I., Singapore and Malacca, 1825–33, 128.

Thailand
Civil and Commercial Code, 1935, 184–5.
Civil Code, 184–5.
Code of Civil Procedure, 1908, 183, 184, 185.
Constitution, 1932, 185.
Criminal Code, 1908, 183–4, 185.
Land Code, 1954, 185.
Law of the Courts of Justice, 1908, 183, 184.

Tonkin
Code of Civil and Commercial Procedure, 1931, 172, 175.
Code of Criminal Procedure, 174.
Code of Indigenous Judicial Organization, 1917, 172–4.
Code of Penal Law, 1917, 172.
Code of Penal Procedure, 1917, 172.
Criminal Code, 174.

Unfederated Malay States
Civil Law (Extension) Ordinance of 1951, 141.

United Kingdom
6 Geo. IV, c. 85, 127.
Charter of Justice, 1807, 125, 127–8, 129, 132.
Charter of Justice, 1826, 125–6, 127, 128, 130, 132.
Charter of Justice, 1855, 128, 130.
Government of Burma Act, 1935, 143.
Statute of Distributions (22 & 23 Car. II, c. 10), 130–1, 134, 140.
Statute of Frauds, 1677, 233, 234.

United States
Bill of Rights, 224.
Californian Code of Civil Procedure, 232.
Homestead Acts, 238.
Philippine Autonomy Act, 1916 (Jones Law), 224.
Philippine Bill, 1902, 224.
Uniform Sales Acts, 234–5.

Vietnam
Gia-Long Code (*Hoàng Viêt*: The Annamite Code), 84–93, 95, 171, 174.
Hông-Đu'c Code (*Hông-Đu'c Thiên-nam du' ha tập*), 74–80, 91, 92.

Table of Cases

Abdullatif *v.* Mahomed Meera Lebe (1829) 4 Ky. 249, 137.
Adong *v.* Cheong Seng Chee (1922) 43 Phil. 43, 229.
Adoomeh Kakah *v.* Lebby Dain (1878) 1 Ky. 438, 132.
A.G. for Ceylon *v.* Reid [1965] A.C. 720, 149.
Alzua *v.* Johnson (1912) 21 Phil. 308, (1913) 231 U.S. 106, 227, 228.
Anchom *v.* Public Prosecutor [1940] M.L.J. 22, 139.
Arca *v.* Javier (1951) 95 Phil. 579, 230.
Atienza *v.* Castillo (1941) 72 Phil. 589, 233.

Balaqui *v.* Dongso (1929) 53 Phil. 673, 232.
Benedicto *v.* de la Rama 3 Phil. 34, 220.
Bismorte *v.* Aldecoa (1910) 17 Phil. 480, 231.
Biton *v.* Momongan (1935) 62 Phil. 7, 230.
Borres *v.* Municipality of Panay (1922) 42 Phil. 647, 231.

Caltex (Phil.) Inc. *v.* Palomar. G.R. No. 19650 of 1966, 237.
Campbell *v.* Hall (1774) 1 Cowp. 204, 125, 127, 128, 217.
Capistrano *v.* Iabine 18 Phil. 135, 220.
Caunter *v.* E.I. Co. (1830) 4 Ky. 12, 128.
Cerezo *v.* Atlantic Gulf and Pacific Co. 38 Phil. 245, 227.
Chan Pyu *v.* Saw Sin (1928) I.L.R. 6 Ran. 623 and 631, 152.
Ching Huat *v.* Co Heong (1947) 77 Phil. 988, 230.
Choa Choon Neoh *v.* Spottiswoode (1869) 1 Ky. 216, 135.
Chulas *v.* Kolson (1867) Leic. 462, (1867) Wood's Oriental Cases 30, 129, 130, 134.
Collector of Madura *v.* Moottoo Ramalinga Sathupathy (1868) 12 M.I.A. 397, 96.
Coopang Chetty *v.* Veera Padiachee & ors. (1888) 4 Ky. 364, 136.
Cuyugan *v.* Santos 34 Phil. 100, 225, 227.

Del Rosario *v.* Del Rosario C.A.-G.R. No. 1870 of 1949, 230.
Dewnes *v.* Bidwell 182 U.S. 244, 225.
Dr. Tha Mya *v.* Daw Khin Pu (1951) B.L.R. 108 (S.C.), 146.
Dr. Tha Mya *v.* Ma Khin Pu (1941) A.I.R. Ran. 81, 147.
Dorr *v.* U.S. 11 Phil. 706, 225, 228.
Duarte *v.* Dade (1915) 32 Phil. 36, 225.
Duff Development Company *v.* Kelantan Government [1924] A.C. 797, 138–9.

Estate of Haji Daing Tahira [1948] M.L.J. 62, 135.

Fatimah *v.* Armootah Pillay (1887) 4 Ky. 225, 134.
Fatimah *v.* Logan (1871) 1 Ky. 255, 124, 135.
Fidelity and Deposit Co. *v.* Wilson (1904) 8 Phil. 51, 235.

Goitia *v.* Campos Rueda (1916) 35 Phil. 252, 229.

Gorospe v. Ilayat (1924) 29 Phil. 21, 234.
Government v. Abadilla (1924) 46 Phil. 642, 234.
Hj. Abdul Rahman v. Mohamed Hassan [1917] A.C. 209, 141.
Haleemah v. Bradford (1877) Leic. 383, 133.
Harden v. Benguet Consolidated Mining Co. (1933) 58 Phil. 141, 236.
Hawah v. Daud (1865) Leic. 253, 132, 133.
Hernandez v. Andal (1947) 78 Phil. 196, 234.
Hix v. Fluemer (1931) 55 Phil. 851, 230.

In Re McCulloch Dick 38 Phil. 41, 224
In Re Shoop (1920) 41 Phil. 213, 227.
In the Estate of Choo Eng Choon decd. Choo Ang Chee v. Neo Chan Neo (1908) 12 S.S.L.R. 120, 130.
In the Goods of Abdullah (1835) 2 Ky. Ecc. Rs. 8, 125, 127–8, 129, 133.
In the Goods of Lao Leong An (1877) Leic. 418, (1893) 1 S.S.L.R. 1, 131.
In the Matter of Inche Lebedrecha (1797) 1969 Ky. 42–3, 132.
Isaac Penhas v. Tan Soo Eng [1953] A.C. 304, 131.
Ismail bin Savoosah v. Madinasah Maricar (1887) 4 Ky. 133, 129.

Jamaludin v. Hajee Abdullah (1881) 1 Ky. 503, 134.
Jemalah v. Mohamed Ali (1875) 1 Ky. 368, 129.
Jimenez v. Cañizares G.R. No 12790 of 1960, 229.

Kader Mydin v. Shatomah (1868) Leic. 260, 134.
Kamoo v. Bassett (1808) 1 Ky. 1, 125.

Kandusamy v. Suppiah (1919) 1 F.M.S.L.R. 381, 141.
Karpen Tandil v. Karpen (1895) 3 S.S.L.R. 58, 135.
Kasilag v. Rodriguez (1939) 69 Phil. 217, 232.
Kepner v. U.S. 195 U.S. 100, 11 Phil. 669, 220, 225.
Khan Bahadur Mehrban Khan v. Makna (1930) 34 C.W.N. 529 (P.C.), 151.
Kho Leng Guan v. Kho Eng Guan [1936] S.C.R. 60, 142.
Khoo Hooi Leong v. Khoo Chong Yeok [1926] A.C. 529, [1930] A.C. 346, 131–2.
Khoo Tiang Bee v. Tan Beng Gwat (1877) 1 Ky. 413, 130, 131.

Lee Joo Neo v. Lee Eng Swee (1887) 4 Ky. 325, 131.
Legarda v. Valdez (1902) 1 Phil. 148, 220.
Leonard v. Nachiappa Chettiar (1923) 4 F.M.S.L.R. 265, 141.

Ma Gyan (1897–1901) II U.B.R. 28, 145.
Ma Hnin Bwin v. U Shwe Gon (1914) 8 L.B.R. 1 (P.C.), 22.
Ma Hnin Zan v. Ma Myain 1936 A.I.R. Ran. 31, 146.
Mahomed Meera Nachair v. Inche Khatijah (1890) 4 Ky. 608, 129.
Ma Kyin Hlaing v. Maung Kyin Swi [1937] Ran. 90, 151.
Ma Kyin Mya v. Maung Sit Han (1937) R.L.R. 103, 147.
Ma Me (1892–6) II U.B.R. 45, 145.
Ma Ngwe Hnit (1921) II L.B.R. 52, 145.
Ma Pyu U (1907) 1 B.L.T. 49, 145.
Mg. Man v. Doramo (1906) 3 L.B.R. 244, 151.
Mg. Twe (1899) 1 L.B.R. 11, 145.
Mighell v. Sultan of Johore [1894] 1 Q.B. 149, 138.

Table of Cases

Mi Myin v. Nga Twe (1906) II U.B.R. 19, 145.
Miranda v. Imperial (1947) 77 Phil. 1066, 237.
Mong v. Daing Mokkah [1935] M.L.J. 147, 133.
Moraiss v. De Souza (1838) 1 Ky. 27, 128.
Motor Emporium v. Arumugam [1933] M.L.J. 276, 141.

Nagammal v. Suppiah [1940] M.L.J. 119, 135.
National Bank v. Philippine Vegetable Oil Co. (1927) 49 Phil. 857, 233.
Noordin M. M. v. Shaikh Mohd. Meah Noordin (1908) 10 S.S.L.R. 72, 133.
Nurud-din v. Siti Aminah [1929] S.S.L.R. 146, 134.

Ong Cheng Neo v. Yap Kwan Seng (1897) 1 F.M.S.L.R. Supp. 1, 140.
Ong Cheng Neo v. Yeap Cheah Neo (1872) 1 Ky. 326, 124–5.
Osorio v. Posadas (1929) 56 Phil. 748, 231.

Padilla v. Linsangan (1911) 19 Phil. 65, 235.
Pahang Consolidated Company Ltd v. State of Pahang [1933] M.L.J. 247, 139.
People v. Rosal 49 Phil. 509, 225.
Pootoo v. Vale Uta Taven & anor. (1883) 1 Ky. 622, 135.
P.P. v. White [1940] M.L.J. 214, 149.
P.P.I. v. Perfecto 43 Phil. 887, 225.

R. v. Adam Singh (1822) 2 Ky. Crim. Rs. 12, 129.
R. v. Devendra (1939) 1 M.C. 51, 136, 149.
R. v. Ojir & anor. (1886) 4 Ky. 122, 134.
R. v. Rodriguez (1887) 4 Ky. 323, 129.
R. v. Till (1809) 2 Ky. Crim. Rs. 1, 129.
R. v. Willans (1858) 3 Ky. 16, 124, 125, 128, 129, 133, 137.
Ramah v. Laton (1927) 6 F.M.S.L.R. 128, 140.
Ramirez v. Gmur (1918) 42 Phil. 855, 229.
Re Alsagoff's Trusts [1956] M.L.J. 244, 135.
Re Choo Eng Choon decd. (1911) 12 S.S.L.R. 120, 130.
Re Goodman's Trusts 50 L.J. 425, 131.
Reiss v. Memije (1910) 15 Phil. 350, 233.
Re Khoo Chow Sew (1872) 2 Ky. Ecc. Rs. 22, 129.
Re Maria Huberdina Hertogh: Mansor Adabi v. A.P. Hertogh & anor. [1950] M.L.J. 214, [1951] M.L.J. 12 & 164, 148.
Re Ma Yin Mya v. Tan Yauk Pu (1927) I.L.R. 5 Ran. 406, 151.
Repide v. Afzelius 39 Phil. 190, 227.
Re Syed Shaik Alkaff (1923) M.C. 38, 135.
Re Tan Soh Sim decd. [1951] M.L.J. 21, 140.
Re the Will of Yap Kim Seng (1924) 4 F.M.S.L.R. 313, 141.
R.M.M.S. Soobramonian Chetty (1889) P.J.L.B. 568, 144.
Robles v. Lizarraga Hermanos (1927) 50 Phil. 387, 234.
Rodyk v. Williamson (24 May 1884) [Unreported], 127.
Rokiah v. Abu Bakar (ap. E. N. Taylor, 'Aspects of Customary Inheritance in Negri Sembilan'), 133.
Rubi v. Provincial Board of Mindoro 39 Phil. 660, 221.

Sahrip v. Mitchell and Endain (1870) Leic. 466, 127, 137.
Salmah & Fatimah v. Soolong (1878) 1 Ky. 421, 132.

S. Anamalay Pillay v. Po Lan (1906) 3 L.B.R. 228, 151.
Sanchez v. U.S. 216 U.S. 167, 225.
Santos v. Aranzano G.R. No. 23828 of 1966, 231.
Santos v. Bartolome (1922) 44 Phil. 76, 231.
Shaik Abdul & ors. v. Shaik Elias Bux (1915) 1 F.M.S.L.R. 204, 140.
Shaik Madar v. Jaharrah (1874) 1 Ky. 385, 132.
Sotto v. Sotto 43 Phil. 688, 226.
Soundara Achi v. Kalyani Achi [1953] M.L.J. 147, 135.
Sultan of Johore v. Tengku Abubakar [1952] M.L.J. 115, 139.
Syed Abdullah al-Shatiri v. Shariffa Salmah [1959] M.L.J. 137, 132.
Syed Ahmad v. Fatimah (ap. E. N. Taylor, 'Aspects of Customary Inheritance in Negri Sembilan'), 133.
Syed Mohamed Yassin v. Syed Abdulrahman (1921) 15 S.S.L.R. 199, 133.

Tan Ma Shwe Zin v. Tan Ma Ngwe Zin (1932) I.L.R. 10 Ran. 97, 144, 152.
Tijah v. Mat Alli (1890) 4 Ky. 124, 134-5.

U Pe v. Maung Maung Kha (1932) I.L.R. 10 Ran. 97, 144.
U Pyinnya v. Maung Law 1929 A.I.R. Ran. 354, (1929) I.L.R. 7 Ran. 677, 146.
U.S. v. Cunha 12 Phil. 242, 226, 227.
U.S. v. Guzman 30 Phil. 416, 227.
U.S. v. Smith 39 Phil. 533, 225.
U.S. v. Tamparong (1915) 31 Phil. 321, 237.
U Teza v. Ma E. Gywe 1928 A.I.R. Ran. 3, 146.
U Tilawka v. Shwe Kan (1915) 29 I.C. 613, 146.

Valdez v. Tuason (1920) 40 Phil. 943, 230.
Villavicencio v. Dimaano (1940) G.R. No. 47087, 237.

Wassmer v. Velez (1964) G.R. No. 20089, 224.
Woon Ngee Yew v. Ng Yoon Thai [1941] M.L.J. 37, 141.

Yap Tham Thai v. Low Hup Neo (1909) 1 F.M.S.L.R. 383, 140.
Yeow Kian Kee decd: Er Gek Cheng v. Ho Ying Seng [1949] S.L.R. 78, [1949] M.L.J. 171, 131.

Introduction
A Historical Jurisprudence of South-East Asia

SOUTH-EAST Asia is a complex area from any standpoint, whether political, economic, ethnic, or religious, and its law is no exception. From Burma in the west through Thailand, Cambodia, Laos, and Vietnam to the Philippines in the north-east, and south through Malaysia and Indonesia, the number and variety of laws is bewildering. The area is marked by considerable cultural diversity[1] and so, inevitably, by a diversity of laws. The central problem is therefore to establish the means by which the material of South-East Asian laws can be classified so as to make sense of the nature of law in this area and of its historical development. To do so might be thought to pre-empt the question, what is law in the South-East Asian context? but such a result need not necessarily follow. The difficulty is that the boundaries of law are rarely defined clearly *vis-à-vis* religion, ethics, or philosophy, so that definition alone is not likely to be helpful, relying as it all too often does on ethnocentric conceptions of law.

THE FORMS OF SOUTH-EAST ASIAN LAW

We know South-East Asian laws in four distinct forms:

(i) *The Written Text*

The law texts fall into two groups, (*a*) the Oriental laws comprising the Indian-derived, the Islamic, and the Chinese-derived laws, and (*b*) the Occidental laws which are made up of the English, French, Dutch, and Spanish-American laws. In terms of the nature of law these two groups of texts have nothing in common. In the first place the language of the former group is rarely confined or specific as it is in the Occidental group of laws. There has been no development of a specialized legal vocabulary or form of presenting law such as occurred in the

[1] See Lebar *et al.* (1964), Lebar (1972).

European laws. We are not, therefore, faced with the difficulty of coping with a technical legal language but rather with the problem of uncertainty in meaning because of the looseness of language in the Oriental texts. The European-derived laws are always confined and specific as to language, and a person trained in such laws must approach the interpretation of Oriental texts with caution. Even at the level of translation one is always tempted to use terms with which one is familiar to define a foreign legal principle. The two groups of texts could not be more dissimilar in their approach to (legal) language, and this difference is reflected in the structure of the texts.

European-derived texts in South-East Asia are made up of statutes, codes of law, administrative regulations, and the like, and follow the general Western form of such documents. They are written for defined purposes, which are stated in the text itself, and generally provide for principles of interpretation and for the establishment of machinery for their enforcement. Throughout, the formal structure is highly stylized; definitional sections are common, and devices, such as schedules, which enumerate classes referred to in the main sections of the text, are also found. The pre-European texts of South-East Asia share none of these characteristics. Indeed, the lack of formal style is the single most striking characteristic, except perhaps in the Chinese-derived texts of Vietnam. However, different sorts of stylistic forms do exist in the Oriental texts, most often in the preambles or exordia. The aim of this form is to relate the content of the text to an outside source of law, not to make clear the internal arrangement of the text itself. As has often been noticed, inconsistency of content does not invalidate an Oriental text, although it may do so in the case of a European-derived text.

In the question of content the distinction between the two sorts of text is quite striking. Even the most superficial acquaintance with an Oriental text will demonstrate that large areas of (private) law are not treated at all in texts which purport to be of general application. It is clear that much was left to local customary practice. In addition, there is a good deal in the texts of a religious and ethical nature which never appears in the secular modern text.

For these reasons care must be exercised in the interpretation

Introduction

of South-East Asian texts, particularly in their use of specialized and technical terms ('right', 'duty', 'ownership') derived from European legal cultures. If one is not careful, one may attribute to the texts characteristics which they do not have, or have only to a minimal degree. For example, it used to be said that they were characteristically 'public law' documents, the implications being that private-law matters were completely unregulated and also that this terminology made sense as an analytical device. A further assumption, again drawn from the characteristics of European texts, was that the indigenous texts constituted the totality of the law. In colonial legal administration this had serious practical consequences arising from the view that because the two sorts of text were in *pari passu*, the contents of the indigenous laws could be assimilated to the European laws. Only in the Netherlands East Indies were steps taken to combat this assumption.

(ii) *Oral Law*

Much South-East Asian law existed, and continues to exist, in oral form, in marked contrast to the generality of European laws. Some of the oral forms were easily recognizable by European commentators as legal, for example, the Burmese law tales,[2] the Minangkabau *perbilangan*,[3] and so on. In addition, oral traditions in a wider sense, transmitted in forms such as the Malay/Javanese *wayang* and the Thai *nang talung*, also served and still serve to communicate moral and legal values which can be identified as such. In the largely illiterate peasant communities of South-East Asia, such forms not only serve the function of expressing generalized standards for conduct but also contain directives of varying specificity for the solution of disputes. The two functions are complementary and neither is thought of as separate from the other.

This is a form of law which, for the most part, had disappeared from European laws by the late eighteenth century. Its contrast with secular and written law codes of European origin in South-East Asia was striking. The Eastern and the European forms of law were opposed in almost every respect, and it was only in the English legal world, with its

[2] See Maung Htin Aung (1962).
[3] 'Customary sayings', see Caldecott (1918).

tradition of common law developed by the judiciary, that oral forms were at all consonant with a European-derived legal theory. Although the Dutch did attempt the preservation of oral forms of law, specifically the Netherlands East Indies *adats*, the civil law demanded the reduction of these laws to writing in the form of jurists' doctrine.

(iii) *Law in Social Institutions*

The complex ethnography of South-East Asia provides numerous examples of rules of law being identified in terms of social institutions. This is a contribution of social science to the study of indigenous law in South-East Asia: the best-known examples include van Vollenhoven's[4] 'normative systems' in Indonesian *adat*, Wilkinson's[5] 'democratic' laws in Malaya, Barton's[6] description of the Ifugao, and Guilleminet's[7] Bahnar 'code'. All attempt to describe law in terms of social institutions, and all are concerned to distinguish law from other mechanisms of social control by the use of various criteria such as sanction, the existence of 'normative' propositions, reciprocity, dispute settlement, and so on. Very often these descriptions rely upon examples taken from the field of oral law but add some extra analysis.

Such definitions of law are not those which the European systems, whether based on codes or on judicial practice, require for the general administration of law. Nor are the data which sociology produces to establish legal classes particularly attractive to the courts; for example, in English law the admissibility of anthropological evidence may well be denied because it breaches parts of the law of evidence. Such a practice is especially undesirable since the laws identified in this way are truly descriptive of legal reality.

(iv) *Indigenous Adaptations*

The final form that is of interest here is a comparatively modern phenomenon and represents an attempt by the peoples of South-East Asia to come to grips with the European-style laws. It is an attempt to make sense of the formal system in what

[4] van Vollenhoven (1918) (1931) (1933).
[5] R. J. Wilkinson (1908).
[6] Barton (1919).
[7] Guilleminet (1952).

Introduction 5

is still largely a peasant world by adapting forms derived from the formal state system. The most common example is the 'petition writer'[8] whose original function of form-filling for illiterates has been extended to the manipulation of some part of the machinery of government for the benefit of his clients. He is able to adapt administrative regulations and the formal laws for his clients' benefit. His function extends also to the adjudication of disputes in which the formal law and local custom are brought into contact as an undifferentiated mass upon the basis of which an adjustment of competing claims can be made. This mass of regulation is taken to be the law despite the lack of state enforcement. It may be that the lack of sanctions is in itself important in its gaining acceptance.

This outline of the forms of South-East Asian law serves as an introduction to the difficulties of historical jurisprudence in the area. In time, the material dates from the eighth century A.D. to the present. If one were writing a legal history (in the ordinary sense) one would be concerned with a narrative of the development of legal institutions, but the study of legal development over a period of time presents formidable problems. In some cases, there is a serious lack of continuous record, and—more important—some legal systems do not lend themselves to the narrative approach. In such cases one can only try to explain the relation between an idea of law and a variety of cultural and social *milieux*. The fact is that we are dealing with a variety of forms of law and thus with a multiplicity of legal definitions. In South-East Asia one very quickly moves away from simple narrative and into the realm of legal ideas, that is, into the realm of historical jurisprudence. At the outset it is important to emphasize that the historical study of legal ideas necessarily involves a comparative framework. The South-East Asian data alone make this essential, apart from the need to fix upon a frame of reference which is not peculiar to any existing legal order and which remains unchanging in space and time. This is not to say that one must deal with the South-East Asian material in an unduly abstract way—the body of this book demonstrates the contrary—but it does imply that legal ethnocentricity is worse than useless.

[8] See Hooker (1973a).

6 *Introduction*

There is no question of transferring the concepts of one's own legal world across cultural boundaries; foreign legal systems do not necessarily share the same view of legal reality.

THE SOUTH-EAST ASIAN LEGAL WORLD

From the point of view of literature one may regard South-East Asian legal reality as being composed of a series of interlocking legal worlds as follows:

I. Oriental Laws
   (a) The Indian Legal World (Burma, Thailand, Champā and Cambodia, and Java);
   (b) The Islamic Legal World (Island South-East Asia);
   (c) The Chinese Legal World (Vietnam);
II. Occidental Laws
   (d) The English Legal World (The Straits Settlements, Federated and Unfederated Malay States, British Borneo, and Burma);
   (e) The French Legal World (Indo-China and Siam);
   (f) The Dutch Legal World (The Netherlands East Indies);
   (g) The Spanish-American Legal World (The Philippines).

The major division in the legal worlds of South-East Asia reflects two sources of law, both identifiable from literary material which defines law in two distinct ways. The Oriental laws are founded upon conceptions of law that are absolute in nature. Thus, we have the Hindu world view, the Islamic location of law in the word of God, and the Chinese philosophies of state and family. In the various literary forms these ideas of law admit of no qualification. Public and private morality are not distinguished and the social orders that these laws regulate find their ultimate validity in extra-human or spiritual terms. In other words, the assumptions upon which the Oriental law texts are based, and which they reduce to written form, are not those of Western science. Nevertheless, they represent views of reality and of the nature of the world which have their own justification and which determine the nature of obligation. Nineteenth-century legal historians described such societies as the 'status type'.

Introduction

The Occidental laws, on the other hand, are all imports into the legal life of South-East Asia. They come from five European legal traditions, four of which (the civil laws) share a common Roman heritage. Despite substantial differences between these traditions, they all locate the source of law in the state. I say this despite substantial disagreement among Western legal philosophers as to whether this is justified or not, because, so far as South-East Asia is concerned, the colonial powers from whom the laws were derived had no qualms on the question. Laws were promulgated by government fiat and this was a sufficient validation for their implementation. The source of law was absolute, as with the Oriental laws, but it was founded upon an abstract entity which was man-made and self-justifying. The state claimed a monopoly of law promulgation and administration. Among the colonial laws of South-East Asia there were different practices as to the admission of native law but in no case was there any doubt that the right to determine a legal regime lay in the state authorities.

The division just described is based on the literary form of law, but, as explained earlier, this is by no means the only form of law in South-East Asia. In particular, one must ask, what part does the oral form play in the division just outlined? Oral law has not been a feature of European law for some centuries now, but it was and still is a basic source of law in South-East Asia, where it reflects legal reality in a way that the texts often do not. The fact that it is relevant to one set of laws and not to the other is significant. It points to a multiple source of obligation in one case and its absence in the other. The legal worlds can thus be distinguished as to the level of fragmentation of legal source. While it is difficult to reconstruct the history of oral legal tradition in detail, the fact that oral laws existed in South-East Asia cannot be denied. The omissions in the written texts of large areas of private law having immediate practical importance for the largely peasant populations of South-East Asia are warrant enough for this proposition. In addition, the colonial legal administrations found themselves faced with oral laws which they had perforce to write down and administer. There is, then, ample testimony to the existence and importance of the oral form.

The importance of this form lies not just in the multiple

source to which it points but also to its implications for legal administration. For the colonial legal administration oral laws posed a number of problems, but however serious they were it was never doubted that the laws had to be incorporated in some way into the national or state legal system. This does not seem to have been a problem in the worlds of Oriental law. The texts might make passing reference to 'custom' but beyond that little was done. The oral laws presented no problem for the administration simply, it seems, because private law was not all that closely regulated. The need for regulation depends upon the nature of law, and the Oriental laws, which in theory had to come to terms with indigenous custom, did not claim a monopoly of source sufficient to warrant regulation. The European laws, on the other hand, in claiming an absolute validity, made necessary administrative systems capable of enforcing the reality of the new legal system. The persistence of oral laws in present-day South-East Asia illustrates the failure of national legal and administrative systems to impose European-derived definitions of law.

The Oriental and Occidental laws have of course come into contact in many ways, and this has been one of the most important elements of modern South-East Asian legal history. It is in the facts of interaction and accommodation that much of the historical jurisprudence of South-East Asia has been formulated, and to a great extent the characteristics of this jurisprudence have been determined by the nature of the European laws. It is easy to see why this is so: the imported laws were those enforced by the dominant political power. But the colonial laws differed widely amongst themselves in their treatment of indigenous law. In the British colonial world, English law was the law of general application and local law was absorbed into the dominant legal system by way of precedent and implementing statute. The local laws became part of the common-law system, subject to the same rules of procedure and interpretation. Despite this, the integrated local laws were special (or 'personal') laws rather than 'common', in that they applied to persons of specified race or religion. An internal conflict between rules from disparate traditions was not entirely avoided. In the French territories local laws were subordinated to the civil law (with one or two exceptions), but

Introduction

the colonial government provided for separate indigenous tribunals operating alongside the civil-law tribunals. Conflict arose here between the two sets of tribunals as to their respective jurisdictions. French jurists were always careful to emphasize that the competence of the indigenous tribunals was derivative and dependent upon the institutions of civil law. In the Dutch territories law was applied on a racial basis; the civil law applied only to the Dutch or to persons assimilated to that status, while local laws governed the obligations of the inhabitants. The legal administration was concerned to keep separate the application and content of the law on this basis. The Dutch jurists developed a highly complex internal conflict of laws to regulate relationships between the different legal worlds. The Spanish in the Philippines merely assumed the jurisdiction of civil law, subject to the competence of canon law in some areas (e.g. family law), but local conditions often prevented the application of the civil law. Conflict of laws was not seen as an issue involving local law; conflict arose between civil and canon law. In the brief American interregnum this position continued unchanged apart from the abolition of certain canon-law principles. The conflict of laws which arose was between the institutions of the two European laws. However, conflict, in the sense of opposition of principle between the Spanish-American law and indigenous law, remains endemic in the Philippines.

The South-East Asian legal world is thus a world of conflicts of laws. This was not always so: in the pre-European period there was a coexistence of legal ideas which occasionally resulted in a blend of principle; conflict was not inevitable. Even in the case of formally exclusive systems, such as Islamic law, accommodations did take place. Serious conflict of principle is characteristic only of interactions involving European laws, all of which have an institutionalized body of 'conflicts of laws' or 'internal conflicts' in South-East Asia.

STATUS AND CONTRACT

The introduction of the element of conflict points to a radically new definition of law. For the first time in South-East Asia, laws based upon the national state claimed an exclusive and absolute sovereignty over the individual. We may thus distinguish the

Oriental and Occidental systems as being respectively *status* and *contract* systems. This terminology is taken from Sir Henry Maine's celebrated division,[9] although no opinion is offered on progressive legal development (see further below) or upon different social forms.[10] Instead, I would like to put forward the major distinctions between the two systems which appear from the South-East Asian material.

First, personal obligation is defined in status systems as a function of race, sex, caste, and religion, whereas in contract systems the individual is defined without reference to such criteria, so that obligation is a function of abstract normative propositions having absolute validity within an exclusive universe. It is of course the idea of exclusiveness of legal systems, imported via colonial law, which gives rise to the necessity for principles of conflict in contemporary South-East Asian systems.

The view which underlies these definitions is that law is essentially concerned with the distribution of personal obligation. This is not the only possible definition of law (see below), but it directs attention to the main content of the Oriental texts. They are overwhelmingly concerned with the distribution of obligation between persons of different status. Obligation is a function of status and is ascribed on the basis of status rather than on the basis of personal initiative. Prescriptively speaking, status systems limit individual initiative compared with contract systems. This is not to say that *in fact* individual initiative may not have been greater than the texts indicate; indeed, the elements of non-textual custom recorded by the colonial lawyers in the nineteenth century suggest that it was more extensive than the texts show. But whatever may have been the case in the past, there is no doubt that the definitions of the individual person in the texts were the operative definitions. They show that individual responsibility was as much a moral, ethical, or religious matter as it was a 'legal' one. Individual responsibility was highly particular and varied from status to status, from class to class, and so on. In contract systems, on the other hand, the individual is defined impersonally ('citizen', 'persons over the age of majority') and

[9] See Henry Maine (1861).
[10] For recent literature see Jackson (1972).

generally. In addition, the European-derived law texts purport to ascribe obligations completely, to the exclusion of other mechanisms of social control. The law is distinguished from other social institutions by a number of means such as its special form, language, administration, and so on. The result is that obligation is predictable and not subject to individual agreement, except where such is allowed in the general law.

The second means of distinguishing between the two systems follows from what has just been said. In both systems the particular laws are defined as absolute within the respective universes; but the legal universe is differently defined in each case. In status systems the legal universe is not thought of as a self-contained entity but is part of a wider system of thought which has moral and ethical sides to it. These are all-encompassing and provide an explanation for the total human condition. The definition of law and its validation do not therefore depend upon man's rationalizations of nature or his analysis of the natural condition, but upon a set of absolute (in some cases revealed) propositions describing the real world. The world is composed of past, present, and future generations whose relationship with nature is determined by these propositions (e.g. *dharma*, the Holy Qur'ān, the Confucian ethic). The latter depend for their validity upon epistemologies characteristic of South-East Asia and in all cases deny a distinction between legal elements and other modes of social regulation.

In contract systems, on the other hand, the definition of the legal universe is strictly confined and any connection with things not legal is by way of direct reference and not by way of necessary implication. All European laws have a body of evidence, or rules relating to such, the function of which is the relation of law to the facts of human existence. Thus, that which 'is', is not necessarily that which 'ought to be'! There is an inner logic in the definition of the legal universe which is not always reflected in the non-legal world. The two are in fact quite distinct; whether this is desirable or not is something for philosophers to argue about, but there is no doubt that the distinction exists. It means that the quality of social fact and its relevance to law are something for the law to determine on its own standards.

A third distinction between status and contract lies in the validation of law. In status systems this is not an issue, whereas in contract systems it is fundamental to the very idea of law. Law in the status system is part of a defined order, which is true because it exists. In contract systems, on the other hand, laws are either valid or invalid judged by their congruence with standards internal to a particular legal system. Such internal standards have been identified differently by legal philosophers; for example, we have rules of recognition (Hart), the grundnorm (Kelsen), chains of normatives (Ross and von Wright), not to mention sociological and natural-law theories. All these are attempts to define the authority of law, which is made necessary because law is conceived as a separate and identifiable entity within a wider social universe. Thus, issues of morality as such may be thought immaterial or, where they are considered material (e.g. Fuller's 'morality of law'), the morality concerned is not the sort of morality considered by Hinduism, Islam, or Confucianism. In its South-East Asian manifestations, law is part of a wider unity in which such problems as the 'unjust law' or the 'invalid law' do not occur because they cannot occur. This is not to deny the existence of inconsistent or competing elements within the law texts; there are many such and they are indicated in the chapters which follow. What they signify is not a debate about validity but the manifestation of law at different levels, the concept of law remaining unchanged, unchangeable, and absolute. It is exactly the same when one finds oral tradition contradicting the texts.

Finally, we distinguish between the two classes of law on the basis of administration. For status systems the administration of law is at best part of a wider political and state order. This attitude to legal administration is strikingly illustrated by the Chinese legal world (below, Chapters 3 and 4). In all status systems large areas of personal obligation were not in fact 'administered' in the usual sense. The link between law and administration was only really important where sovereignty or the prerogative of the ruler was in question. Thus, we have emphasis upon the definitions of sovereignty, upon the duties of the ruler, upon the duties owed by the people to the ruler and officers of government, and upon taxation, which was also seen

Introduction

as an expression of sovereign control. Matters of private law, on the other hand, were largely unregulated. All this is in sharp contrast to the contract laws, where the effective administration of laws is part of the definition of validity. No law that is not administered can really be law. All contract systems know the distinction between prescriptive and descriptive validity. The emphasis upon administrative validity even extends to the most mundane matters of private law, such as family law, which has little direct bearing upon sovereignty or state organization. The latter of course is regulated in minute detail because the validity of the whole corpus of law depends upon it.

These four points represent the basic differences between two views of law. For historical jurisprudence they are a watershed in legal development. It is important to realize that in modern South-East Asia both concepts of law exist, at best in an uneasy harmony and at worst in outright conflict with each other.

FROM STATUS TO CONTRACT

From the dawn of the colonial age to the present, the different origins of the laws of South-East Asia outlined in the preceding pages have had political overtones. The structure of the South-East Asian legal systems is pluralistic in nature. The municipal laws of the colonial powers, and now those of their successor states in South-East Asia, claim an absolute monopoly of source of law, legal machinery, and political support within the nation-state. Hence, only that is law which is recognized as such by state fiat. A consequence of this is that laws may be valid on two levels; if the state insists, as it must, upon its absolute right to determine what is law through the machinery of the municipal law system, then only those laws so determined are prescriptively validated. A breach of valid prescription requires the application of sanction. In municipal law this is the standard way of working and it operates perfectly well in the homelands of South-East Asia's European laws, but it does not work so well in South-East Asia itself[11] because large sections of the population do not know the contents of municipal law or, if they do, choose to regard them as not binding. They prefer the traditional status-type laws which have a descriptive validity.

[11] With the possible exception of Singapore, but even here difficulties persist. See Rajah (1974).

Whether or not one wishes to accept that informal law is 'law properly so called' is really beside the point; such laws actually do determine personal obligation, in some cases to the extent that municipal-law institutions, such as local courts, are forced to take account of them. The result is at best an internal conflict of principle or, at worst, a complete disregard by the population for the formally valid law.

The striking feature of modern South-East Asian law is a legal pluralism. The status laws have been subsumed under or absorbed into the categories and processes of the introduced municipal law so as to produce a body of hybrid rules and principles. One may see in the development of these hybrids a true example of the movement from status to contract. Like most processes of change or development it is untidy and occasionally inconsistent within itself. The dominance of the imposed laws has never been consistently exercised in any South-East Asian state and the sporadic efficiency of the administration of the imposed laws is reflected in the fragmentation of substantive and adjective law. However, the development of the personal laws, with which the second part of this book is concerned, represents the creation of a new and wholly South-East Asian body of law.

The South-East Asian states have become independent once again with the demise of colonialism following the Second World War. It is too early yet to say what forms the laws of these states will finally take. Although political ideologies have been introduced from outside the area, the traditional religions and systems of belief have continued to influence people. Similarly, the laws of status persist, despite attempts at 'modernization'. In the final analysis it is likely that the hybrid forms of law will prove the most suited to the needs of South-East Asia.

PART I
STATUS

CHAPTER 1

The Indian Legal World: The Law Texts of Burma, Thailand, Champā and Cambodia, and Java

THE PRESENCE of Indian elements in the cultures of South-East Asia is an undoubted historical fact although historians remain divided over the source, nature, and precise significance of Indian influence.[1] So far as law is concerned, there has often been an uncritical acceptance of the proposition that many South-East Asian laws are 'Hindu derived', and the 'Indian-influenced' thesis has been put forward to explain features of South-East Asian laws, sometimes with no justification. In fact the position is complex; a simple similarity of content or subject-matter between some South-East Asian texts and the law of *Manu* is rarely of itself sufficient to explain the nature and reality of the South-East Asian laws. Instead, one must look to more basic notions such as the definition of legal personality, the attribution of obligation, and the relationship between law and the natural order (including the definition of the latter), in order to understand the South-East Asian legal scene. At the same time the legal historian must be cautious because the mode of congruence of Indian law with indigenous laws has varied greatly throughout South-East Asia. In effect, while the South-East Asian data themselves inspire caution, the all-pervading brilliance of Indian legal thought tends to entice the historian into unwarranted assumptions as to the nature of law in South-East Asia.

I BURMA

The main source of Burmese law is the *Dhammathat* or law text, a

[1] See Hall (1968: 12 ff.) for an outline of the literature, and Coedès (1968) on the 'Hinduized' states of South-East Asia.

good number of which are known.² All *Dhammathats* are written in a set form and open with a formula of adoration to the Buddha—'*Namo Tassa Bhagavat Arahato Sammasambuddhassa*' (Reverence to the Blessed One, the Saint, the Most Enlightened). This is followed by the Exordium which consists of the story of Rishi Manu (or Manosara) travelling to the walls of the universe, finding the *Dhammathat*, and presenting it to King Mahasammata for promulgation. The Exordium is an important statement of the source of law and illustrates the nature of law as understood in the *Dhammathat* literature. In some texts, such as the *Dhammavilasa*, the Exordium is quite elaborate and demonstrates that the law is found or given, it is not made. The source is absolute and immutable and law is qualified as an absolute ethic. The function of the text compiler is therefore to explain and not to innovate, although some texts, such as the *Kaingza Shwemyin Dhammathat*, purport to be recensions of earlier texts (in this case of *Manosara*) whose application has been made difficult by the passage of events. In other texts, such as the *Manugye Dhammathat*, a greater emphasis than usual is placed upon the ideals of religious principle, but in all cases the absoluteness of the law is characteristic of the genera. Having said this, however, it is also true that the texts vary widely in content, and it would be an interesting exercise to relate variations in content to changing conditions in Burma at the dates during which the texts were composed.

The exposition of rules of law follows the Exordium, and the formal model is the Hindu *Dharmaśāstras* of which the text of *Manu* is the best known.³ This is not to say that the *Dhammathats* follow the form of the *śāstras* entirely; only the *Wagaru* and *Dhammavilasa* correspond in any detail and even they diverge in some respects. Among the other *Dhammathats*, *Kaingza Shwemyin*, *Manussika*, *Manosara*, *Dhammathatkungya*, *Manu Reng*, and *Kyetyo* enumerate the eighteen titles but do not rely upon them, and the later *Dhammathats*, beginning with *Manugye*, place no great emphasis upon them, while some, like *Gandi*, do not even mention the titles. The texts in fact show considerable divergence from the Indian model although the inspiration of the Indian framework is clear.

² See the lists in Forchhammer (1885: 108–9), Shwe Baw (1955).
³ See *Manu* VIII. 4–7.

The Indian Legal World 19

The divergence in content is marked: on debt, although *Wagaru* states the Hindu rule of *damdupat*,[4] it also goes on to say[5] that if the debtor pays interest equal to the principal, such must be regarded as payment toward the principal; *Manu*[6] takes a different view, and in effect makes the rule no more than that the creditor may not at any time recover by way of interest more than the principal. Again, where debts are concerned, both *Wagaru*[7] and *Dhammavilasa*[8] provide that the manner for taking an oath of guarantee for payment should vary according to the amount involved in the suit. *Manu*,[9] on the other hand, makes the nature of the oath vary with caste, and ordeals are prescribed as an alternative to the oath.

It is in marriage that perhaps the greatest differences between the *Dhammathats* and *Manu* are apparent. *Wagaru* does not mention the eight marriage rites, the prohibited degrees, or other impediments (such as caste or widowhood), and there is no suggestion that the object of marriage is to beget sons (in fulfilment of one's duty to one's ancestors). On the other hand, the eight forms of marriage set out in *Dhammavilasa* are obviously derived from *Manu*[10] although they differ considerably. For example, the rule that spouses married by any of the eight rites inherit from each other[11] is not in *Manu*, although the statement in *Dhammavilasa*[12] that 'the highest law is the law that regulates the lifelong union of husband and wife' is probably a reproduction of *Manu*,[13] 'let mutual fidelity continue until death'. In divorce, *Wagaru*[14] speaks of the five special duties which husband and wife owe each other; *Manu* deals with duties of husband and wife, but they are not and could not be called 'five special duties'. *Wagaru's* rule on divorce against a faultless spouse on surrender of all property is not in *Manu*.[15] However, *Wagaru's*[16] 'six evil practices of women' clearly has some affinity with *Manu's*[17] 'six causes of the ruin of women'. The other sections in *Wagaru* have no counterpart in *Manu*, i.e. the four kinds of pride in women, punishment of women, seven kinds of wives, division of property and children

---

[4] *Wagaru* I. 1. [5] *Ibid.* 3. [6] *Manu* VIII. 151, 154, 155.
[7] *Wagaru* I. 5. [8] *Dhammavilasa* I. 9. [9] *Manu* VIII. 109–13.
[10] *Ibid.* 24. [11] *Dhammavilasa* XIV. 81. [12] *Ibid.* XIII. 25.
[13] *Manu* IX. 101. [14] *Wagaru* III. 33. [15] *Ibid.* 34.
[16] *Ibid.* 35. [17] *Manu* IX. 13.

on divorce, the *nissaya* and *nissita* rules, and so on. In *Dhammavilasa* the striking feature is the absence of rules governing divorce by mutual consent. The text does deal with the right to divorce of the deserted wife and with the right of a husband to discard an unsatisfactory wife, e.g. for barrennesss or for producing daughters only.[18] Divorce by mutual consent requires the presence of a law-officer[19] and is conditional upon the division of the marital property. The text does not, however, deal with one of the most common occurrences in Burmese legal life, divorce by mutual consent where these two conditions are not present. On adultery, *Wagaru*[20] places its consequences in the next existence but goes on to mention the four circumstances from which it may be inferred, and these are similar to the circumstances set out in *Manu*.[21] Adultery is punished in *Wagaru*[22] by compensation which varies according to the seriousness of the offence: *Manu*,[23] on the other hand, provides that an adulterer who is not a Brahmin is punished by death or banishment. *Wagaru*[24] mentions caste in providing for compensation. The rules in the *Dhammavilasa* seem closer to those in *Manu* on adultery.[25]

On gifts, *Wagaru* does not accept the assumption implicit in *Manu*[26] that a gift to a Brahmin has special merit, although it accepts the proposition that merit to be acquired in the next existence is a valid consideration for a gift.[27] In *Wagaru*[28] mistake vitiates a gift, whereas in *Manu* it does not; similarly, *Wagaru* allows resumption when a donor becomes poor or is a relative, whilst *Manu* does not. *Wagaru* also deals at length with gifts given in consideration of sexual intercourse, a subject which is ignored in *Manu*. *Dhammavilasa*[29] has the same six kinds of gifts as in *Wagaru*, and in general its principles are the same except that it introduces the important principle that a gift is not valid unless there is delivery of possession.[30] Under

---

[18] *Dhammavilasa* XIII. 23.   [19] *Ibid.* 22.   [20] *Wagaru* IV. 47.
[21] *Manu* XIII. 356–8.   [22] *Wagaru* IV. 48.   [23] *Manu* VIII. 359.
[24] *Wagaru* IV. 57.
[25] *Dhammavilasa* XII. 6, *Manu* VII. 360, 361, *Dhammavilasa* XII. 2, *Manu* VIII. 28, 374–8, *Dhammavilasa* XII. 25, *Manu* VIII. 369–70.
[26] *Manu* III. 96, 97, 128–9.   [27] *Wagaru* V. 64.
[28] *Ibid.* 64. On the complications of resumption of gift see Kāne (1930–62: (iii) 470–75).
[29] *Dhammavilasa* IV. 1.   [30] *Ibid* 11.

inheritance there are both correspondences to and dissimilarities between *Manu* and the Burmese texts. *Wagaru*'s[31] twelve kinds of sons, of whom only six can inherit, is undoubtedly taken from *Manu*,[32] but *Wagaru*'s[33] rule of distribution between wives of different classes has no counterpart in *Manu*. *Wagaru*[34] uses the term *aurasa* (eldest child) in the Hindu-law sense as meaning the legitimate child, and the rule in *Wagaru* that joint residence is an essential condition for inheritance by adopted persons may have some connection with the Hindu rule that the unseparated son is preferred to the separated son. On the other hand, in Burmese (and other South-East Asian) customary law, the preference for unseparated children in inheritance is widespread and results from the duties which such children undertake in respect of their aged parent(s). *Wagaru*'s[35] rule regarding the division of the father's estate between the three types of son (of the lawful wife, of the concubine, and of the slave) may owe something to *Manu*.[36] In *Dhammavilasa*[37] the basic principles are that all children not defective may inherit, a wife may inherit from the husband and vice versa, and the elder children are entitled to a special share. Equal division between children is expressly rejected.[38]

Enough has now been said to demonstrate that the Burmese law texts have both marked similarities to and differences from the Indian text of *Manu*. Much of the discussion of the nature of Burmese law has revolved round its relationship to Indian legal ideas. Indeed, it is not too much to say that the descriptions of the Burmese texts have, in some cases, become distorted through the eagerness of the commentator to demonstrate an Indian derivation. The first attempt in a European language to describe the *Dhammathat* literature was made by Sir John Jardine, Judicial Commissioner, in 1882. His *Notes on Buddhist Law*[39] consisted of translations of selected rules from six *Dhammathats*, viz. *Manuvannana*,[40] *Winisayapakathani*,[41]

[31] *Wagaru* VI. 84.   [32] *Manu* IX. 158.   [33] *Wagaru* VI. 81.
[34] *Ibid.* 79.   [35] *Ibid.* 80.   [36] *Manu* IX. 151–5.
[37] *Dhammavilasa* XIV.   [38] *Ibid.* 3.
[39] Jardine (1882). They were made up as follows: Notes I, II, III on marriage; Notes IV and VIII on marriage and divorce; Notes V, VI, and VII on inheritance and partition.
[40] Notes III and V.
[41] Note III.

22   *Status*

Wagaru,[42] *Manu Reng*,[43] *Mohaviccedani*,[44] and *Dhammavilasa*.[45] Jardine's Notes had two major functions; the first was to provide guidance for the judges and magistrates who staffed the courts in British Burma and, to this end, the Notes were circulated to the courts in 1882–3. The Notes were not, and did not pretend to be, merely reproductions of the texts; they were intended to demonstrate the true nature of Burmese law for the purposes of judicial administration. This set a limit to the study of Burmese law as a system in comparative law and, not surprisingly, attention was mainly concentrated on family law, in particular upon two propositions. The first was that the mutual consent of the contracting parties was essential for a valid marriage. In this Jardine relied upon the rules of *Manugye*[46] as translated by Richardson,[47] despite the fact that there are rules in other *Dhammathats* which make necessary the consent of parent or guardian. In other words, it is probable that Jardine was citing selectively so as to find textual support for what he felt to be a desirable rule for application in the courts. The second proposition was that divorce at the instance of one party was not known in the *Dhammathats*. In this case, Jardine cited a rule from *Dhammavilasa*[48] requiring the intervention of judicial authority[49] while he ignored rules to the contrary in *Wagaru*.[50] Again, this proposition had a strictly practical import; it was raised by Jardine in response to the common judicial practice at the time of recognizing such divorces. In both cases, therefore, comparative data on Burmese law were selectively adduced for a purpose, and this must have obscured a proper judicial understanding of Burmese law.[51]

The second purpose of the Notes was to contribute toward the understanding of historical jurisprudence so far as it had a relevance for the Burmese *Dhammathats*. The initial proposition

[42] Notes IV and V. [43] Note IV. [44] Notes VI and VIII.
[45] Note VII.
[46] This *Dhammathat* obtained a pre-eminent position in Anglo-Burmese law. It was held by the Privy Council that, where its provisions were clear, reference need not be made to any other text: Ma Hnin Bwin v. U Shwe Gon (1914) 8 L.B.R. 1 (P.C.).
[47] Richardson (1896).   [48] *Dhammavilasa* XIII. 22–3.
[49] See Note II.   [50] *Wagaru* III. 33.
[51] As indeed did the title of Jardine's 'Notes'; see below, Chapter Five on 'Buddhist law'.

The Indian Legal World

was that, as a source of law, the rules in the *Dhammathats* were of more importance than custom.[52] Such a proposition betrays a profound misunderstanding of the function of the Burmese law text, and indeed of all other South-East Asian law texts. Briefly, the function of the text is only partly to provide rules of conduct; its major function is to demonstrate, explain, and justify standards for conduct within an ethic and view of man which forms an undifferentiated continuum. Such an ethic may, and does, have a number of manifestations and sources—texts and customs—but relative importance is not in question (see also below, the summary to this chapter). Source only came into question within the British colonial legal system and, in this sphere, Jardine's proposition had no validity at all.[53]

The major proposition in historical jurisprudence put forward by Jardine was that Burmese law had its origin in Hindu law. The ground for this view was the substantial similarity between the formal structure of some texts, or some provisions in the texts generally, and Indian law-books, especially the laws in the two versions of *Manu*, the *Manusmṛti* and the *Nāradasmṛti*. The explanation adopted was a historical one and is most fully developed in Forchhammer's essay[54] on the history of Burmese law published in 1885 and still the only general work on the subject. The two main features of this work are, first, the division of Burmese legal development into three periods, viz. A.D. 1100–1600, 1600–1750, and 1750–nineteenth century, a division based upon the characteristics of the *Dhammathats* as showing progressively less Indian influence. These divisions have been severely criticized[55] on the ground that such stages in development do not find support in the texts and that a reconstruction in such detail can only be speculative, given that the extant *Dhammathats* do not date from earlier than the middle of the seventeenth century. One must remember, however, that Burmese tradition preserved in the later texts dates the *Dhammathat* literature to the twelfth century and there is no reason to doubt its validity. Nevertheless, the fact remains that the texts which have been preserved date only from the seventeenth century.[56] The second main feature is the argument

---

[52] Note IV.   [53] See below, Chapter Five.   [54] See Forchhammer (1885).
[55] Furnivall (1940: 351–70). Shwe Baw (1955: 14–17).
[56] On this general question see Lingat (1949a: 286–8).

that the Burmese *Dhammathats* are ultimately derived from the Indian texts mentioned above. Forchhammer edited the *Wagaru* text, which enumerates the eighteen branches of law corresponding broadly to the eighteen *mārga* of the *Manusmṛti*, and compared the rules therein with those of the *smṛtis: Manu, Yājñavalkya, Nārada, Kātyāyana*, and even of the *Dharmasūtras*. It cannot be denied that the *Wagaru* text is related to the *Dharmaśāstra*, especially to the two versions of *Manu*, although Forchhammer is guilty of some exaggeration when he says: 'There are indeed very few passages in the Wagaru which are not clearly and distinctly Hindu law as contained in Manu and other ancient Codes.'[57] In addition, as Forchhammer rightly points out, there is hardly any trace in *Wagaru* of a religious element, but this difference from the Hindu *śāstras* is due to the fact that, of the three great divisions of the *Dharmaśāstras (ācāra, vyavahāra,* and *prāyaścitta), Wagaru*, like *Nārada*, dealt only with the second which, even in the Hindu *smṛtis*, is nearly always free of religious influence. At the same time, Buddhist elements, apart from the usual Exordium, whose importance should not be underestimated (see above), are also lacking. In other words, we have what Lingat[58] has called 'a mere civil or lay code'. The argument put forward by Forchhammer that *Wagaru* is in some way related to pre-Brahmanic Indian custom, while it has found some acceptance,[59] cannot be allowed to stand unchallenged.[60] For one thing, the rules in *Wagaru* show no similarity to the elaborate discriminations and elaborations of the *smṛtis* although as a matter of principle Hindu derivation is clear, but it is not the whole picture. Many provisions, as described earlier, show fundamental differences to *Manu*, especially in such important matters as debt, property, marriage, and re-marriage. The explanation appears to be that the authors of the *Wagaru* borrowed almost entirely from the *Vyavahāra*, that part of the Brahmanic code which deals with the disposal of lawsuits, and ignored speculations about *Dharma* in other parts of the code. So far as Buddhism is concerned, the actual rules for the disposal of lawsuits were not taken from any Buddhist ethic[61] but represented localized customary practice.

[57] Forchhammer (1885: 58).
[58] Lingat (1949a: 290).
[59] See Jolly (1928: 91–3).
[60] See Lingat (1949a: 292).
[61] Excluding of course the *Vinaya*—see Rhys Davids (1932).

The idea of the immutable nature of law and its ethical quality was linked to Buddhist principle in the Exordium and thus the genesis of law was explained in a way which comprised a self-contained epistemology. This is something noticed by all later commentators[62] who lay stress upon the 'Burmese' element in the texts.

II THAILAND

The laws of Thailand are known from the recension of 1805, the *Pramuan Kotmai Ratchakan thi Nung* (the Legal Code of RamaI), also known as the 'Law of the Three Great Seals'. This text constitutes practically all the evidence of classical Thai law[63] and, moreover, of the law as it stood in 1805. The recension of 1805 sets out the laws, not in their original form but in one amended, to an unknown extent, by successive monarchs.[64] The recension of 1805 was made necessary by the destruction in 1767 of Ayut'ia by the Burmese in which something like 90 per cent of the legal materials available at the time were lost.[65] A new codification thus became necessary, although the work did not begin until 1804. The occasion was provided by a case in which the husband appealed against the decision of the court in granting a divorce which was not quite in defiance of the rules then existing[66] but manifestly unjust. The rules themselves were found on investigation by Rama I to be unsatisfactory, and a committee was established by the King to examine the whole of the law texts then available.[67]

The committee was instructed to examine the laws with regard to their congruence with the Pali canon; where the laws did not agree, they were to be altered accordingly in order to restore their purity. Provisions which were manifestly unjust or

---

[62] See, for example, E Maung (1951), Hla Aung (1969), Maung Kyin Swi (1966).
[63] With the exception of legislation promulgated in Sukhodaya in A.D. 1397. See A. B. Griswold & Prasert Ṇa Nagara (1969).
[64] There is no complete translation of the whole text in any European language. However, translations of substantial portions exist in Lingat (1952–5: (i) 149–64), Lingat (1943) (1936), Duplatre (1922), Varasiri (1929), Gerini (1895), Low (1839) (1847)—caution must be exercised in the last two sources. Further references are cited below.
[65] See Wenk (1968: 35) citing a decree of Rama I, 1794, in which it is said that nine-tenths of the legal manuscripts were lost.
[66] Now no longer in existence—the earlier texts were destroyed after the revision of 1804–5.
[67] See Wenk (1968: 36) for its composition.

in contradiction to the Pali canon were attributed to the acts of dishonest officials, for it was deemed impossible that the former kings of Thailand had purposely made unjust rulings.[68] The intention was not to introduce a new system of law or to subject the laws to textual criticism but to eliminate the falsifications and restore the original laws. The extent to which such an objective was actually achieved cannot definitely be ascertained because the pre-1804 texts have not been preserved.[69] However, the work of the committee was completed in eleven months, and it is difficult to suppose that in so short a space of time all the laws were reclassified. It is far more likely that the old divisions were taken over. The law promulgated by King Rāmarāja of Ayut'ia in A.D. 1397 certainly shows that some specific institutions, such as the law on abduction, the *sakti-nā*,[70] and the organization of the population into territorial groups, were already in existence at the end of the fourteenth century.[71] After the revision had been completed, the text was sealed with three seals and copies were deposited in the Law Court, the Royal Apartment, and the Assembly Hall of the Ministers.

The most interesting feature about the process of revision is its stated motive—to restore the laws to their original purity for the better administration of justice. There was no question of the introduction of new law; the concept of law itself, as a set of ethical propositions in the social order, remained unaffected. New laws, in the form of freshly promulgated decrees, were of course issued, but their function was the maintenance of the existing legal order. The *Phra Thammasat*,[72] as the *Grundnorm*, occupied pride of place.

The titles or heads of the 1805 recension as given in the three-volume edition by Lingat published in 1938[73] are as follows:

Vol. I. The *Thammasat*
Palace Law
Law of Procedure
Fines and Compensation

[68] See Lingat (1929–30: 21).
[69] See Wenk (1968: 37) and the sources there cited.
[70] See further below.
[71] Griswold & Prasert Ṇa Nagara (1969: 111 ff.).
[72] The Thai version of the *Dharmaśāstra*.
[73] By Thammasat University, Bangkok.

The Indian Legal World 27

    Law of the Civil Hierarchy
    Laws of the Military and Provincial Hierarchies
    Laws on the Division of People
    Litigation
    Witnesses
    Trials by Ordeal
    Judges
    The Carrying of Appeals
Vol. II. Husband and Wife
    Slavery
    Kidnapping
    Inheritance
    Debt
    Miscellaneous Laws
    Quarrels
    Theft
    Crimes against the Government
    Treason
Vol. III. The Laws regulating the Affairs of the Clergy[74]
    The Thirty-six Rules
    Royal Decrees of Ayut'ia period
    A Royal Decree of Thonburi period
    Royal Decrees of Rama I.

The last volume contains decrees in their original forms. Such were issued by all Thai kings (see below). The rules in the first two volumes are stated in abstract and general terms in sections (*mātrā*). The titles or types of lawsuits traditionally characteristic of the Hindu (*Manu*) texts, and partially adhered to in Burma, increase in the Thai text from eighteen to thirty-nine. This greater elaboration reflects an attitude to legal thought which demonstrates both a peculiarly Thai view as to the sources of law and an increasing technical sophistication. To take, first, the question of source, the *Thammasat* remains primary. As Prince Dhani Nivat says:

According, then, to the *Thammasat*, the ideal monarch abides steadfastly in the ten kingly virtues, constantly upholding the five common precepts ... He takes pain to study the *Thammasat* and to keep the four principles of justice, namely: to assess the right or wrong of all service or disservice rendered unto him, to uphold the righteous and truthful, to acquire riches through none but just means and to maintain the prosperity of his state through none but just means.[74] This is a peculiar and essentially Thai point of view of the *Dharmaśāstra*, and I use the Hindu term rather than the Thai as emphasizing its unique nature. From the time of Rāmādhipati, who founded the Kingdom of Ayut'ia in the mid-fourteenth century, the *Dhammasattaham*[76] are known to have been in use and this seems to be the key to the Thai view of law. It is a strictly practical one, and it expressed itself in multiple and detailed subdivisions of the *śāstra* titles, to the extent that the Thai *Thammasat* became the expression *of* the law and not just the standard *for* law. The bureaucracy was already highly specialized even in the fifteenth century, and large parts of the recension of 1805 deal, under the administrative heads (*lakṣaṇa*) of the *śāstras*, with the administration of the kingdom. Not surprisingly it is in the administrative areas of the law that change was more or less constant. For example, in the Laws relating to the Civil, Military, and Provincial Hierarchies which set out the ranks and titles of officials and the grades of officialdom, change was frequent. Thus, if the rank of a certain grade of official was changed then the laws as to function, duty, type of emolument, and so on in relation to that office were also changed.[77] But such change did not affect the immutability of legal principle stemming from the *Thammasat*.

This fact should not, however, be allowed to obscure the change in conception as between the *Thammasat*[78] and the *Dharmaśāstra*. The essential change is in the division of law into substantial and fundamental, and derivative and procedural. These two sets of terms indicate an important shift in the conscious appreciation of the Indian heritage. The Thai text combines laws of many different dates,[79] but in its final version the laws of Rama I became authoritative by fiat of the King. It is this which provides the key to understanding the Thai laws: the practice of connecting royal decisions (*Rājasattham*) with the

[74] See Wenk (1968: 37–41) on the revision of the Buddhist Canon under the order of Rama I in 1788.
[75] Dhani Nivat (1947: 163).
[76] The Pali equivalent of Sanskrit *Dharmaśāstra*.
[77] See Rabibhadana (1969: 189 f.).
[78] More properly, in its hybrid form—*Dhammasattha*.
[79] See Rabibhadana (1969: 188–9).

rules of the *Thammasat*. It seems that the Siamese kings very early made a habit of collecting the ordinances of their predecessors and this practice evolved into the *Rājasattham* literature. Such were records of real decisions; in no case were they fabrications or stories. The authority of the record depended mainly upon the reputation of the ruler and the generality and purpose of the particular decrees. At some point in time, which Lingat[80] puts at the end of the sixteenth century, but which is unlikely to be known with certainty, the *Rājasattham* became amalgamated into the forms of the *Dhammasattham*. The latter are the fundamental categories (*mūla-attha*), the categories of *Manu* (or *Manosāra*). They are limited in number, having been enunciated once and for all by *Manu*. The derivative categories are the *sākha-attha*, the rules and precepts issued by the rulers which have a reference to and are an application of the first. They are many and various and become absorbed into the *Dhammasattham* when reduced to an abstract statement under one of the titles. Decisions of the King thus became permanent rules, not because they emanated from kings but because they became a part of the Eternal Law and so took on its authority.

The technical process by which this was done is known to us both from the account of the revision of the 1805 text and from another text preserved in the law of 1805, the Law in Thirty-six Articles. Here, one of the last kings of Ayut'ia, probably Boromakot, ordered his judicial functionaries, most of whom were Brahmins, to examine edicts issued by his predecessor and write them into *mātras* so that they might be added to the body of the law.[81] Siamese laws were thus subject to periodical revisions. The edicts of the King were not 'law' in the proper sense unless promoted to that status by the process just outlined. This is the most distinct characteristic of Siamese laws and has led commentators such as Lingat[81] to describe the laws as 'a real code' apparently because, within fairly elastic limits, the King was very near to becoming a legislator. He was not of course entirely such; even Rama I ordered a revision for the sole purpose of purifying the laws. Indeed, at the beginning of his reign he had ordered a revision of the Buddhist scriptures for the

---
[80] Lingat (1950: 27).
[81] *Ibid.* 28.

same purpose and he specifically referred to it in discussing the legal revision of 1805.

Perhaps the second most interesting single feature of Thai law for the legal historian is the nature of the legal personality that it reveals. This was the division of persons into four main categories: the princely group (*chao*), the nobles (*khunnang*), the common people (*phrai*), and the bondsmen (*that*).[83] The legal rights and duties of each class were provided for in the law and throughout each title of the laws, the rules for the definition and distribution of obligation varied depending upon the rank being described. The most formal expression of this was found in the *śakti-nā* (dignity marks) system; under this system the amount of *śakti-nā* was expressed as an entitlement to a certain area of land depending upon rank. The King's *śakti-nā* was unlimited and so on downwards, depending upon one's rank within each of the four categories of persons. The laws of the Civil, Military, and Provincial Hierarchies were mainly concerned with describing and setting out *śakti-nā*.[84] In the circumstances of the Thai economic system where land was plentiful and the population relatively small, *śakti-nā* meant the control over manpower to exploit the wealth of the soil. Legal classification, therefore, had an essentially economic and political function. Nowhere was this more clearly demonstrated than in the class *that* or bondsman. It was divided into several categories, 'redeemable'[85] or 'temporary'[86] bondsmen, those who had been redeemed for full value ('absolute' bondsmen), and finally those who had been redeemed but not used (an 'interest-bearing' bondsman). This last is the most interesting class; such persons were pledged as security for debt, they did not actually work for and reside with the buyer. The only obligation was to pay interest on the money advanced. In fact, by Royal Decree of 1794, a buyer was forbidden to take possession, he could only enforce the payment of interest. This is more properly a case of personal security for debt, although it is treated in section 3 of the Law on Slavery. The explanation for this classification would appear to be that the idea of a personal bond between two individuals in a relation of superiority and

[82] *Ibid.*
[84] *Ibid.* 113–14.
[86] S. J. Smith (1880: 1).
[83] For details see Rabibhadana (1969: 98 ff.).
[85] Quaritch Wales (1934: 61).

inferiority, rather than the idea of debt as an abstract, is the determinant form of classification. The earlier discussion of categories of person in Thai law demonstrates this obvious point. The Law on Debt provides a further illustration of this,[87] and, indeed, the use of concrete categories rather than schemes of abstract principles was a consistent feature of the organization of Thai society as a whole.

The King was the ruler of people and not primarily a *territorial* sovereign.[88] To a certain extent this was true of other South-East Asian systems of kingship, as indeed it was in medieval Europe,[89] but the Thai case, as stated in the *Dhammasattham*, presents a view in which the position of the King fundamentally determines the idea of legal personality. Historically, there were at least three principles upon which the Thai monarchy rested. First, at the time of Sukhothai the dominant view was that the King was a patriarchal figure. Second, there was the theory of divine kingship, under Brahmin influence, in which the person of the King was assimilated with God. The Brahminic elements placed kingship in the cosmic order.[90] The third principle, and eventually the most important, was that derived from the *Dharmaśāstra*, where the ideal monarch was a King of Righteousness abiding in the Ten Kingly Virtues and pursuing the Four Proper Modes of Conduct. The rules of conduct were associated with the concept of *Ĉakravārtin*—the sovereign of the universe. It was this last view which was the most influential at the time of Rama I. The consequence of all three views was of course the absolute monarchy, but, in the latter, kingship was a symbol of *Dharma* itself whose function was not legislation but the preservation of the sacred laws. This returns us to the earlier discussion of the *Dhammasattham* in the laws of 1805. It implies the attribution of obligation in terms which, although recognizing individual responsibility, were founded upon relationships of superiority and inferiority expressed in an order of rank.

The legal complex constituting these laws has given rise to the same sorts of misapprehension as arose over the Burmese texts.

[87] See Archer (1885). Some caution should be exercised in using this source as there are many inaccuracies.
[88] Rabibhadana (1969: 40 ff.).
[89] See Maine (1861: 60).
[90] See Dhani Nivat (1947).

It was common, for example, to see an equation made between the Thai laws and Hindu law because the heads of *Manu* appear in the Thai texts.[91] As we have seen, such a correspondence is, at best, misleading; rather more interesting are modern comments on Thai law. Because Thailand was never a colony, its laws have, except for the specialist (or missionary), remained something of a *terra incognita*. Owing, however, to the post-war interest in South-East Asia, more commentators have mentioned Thai law and, almost without exception, have described it in terms more suitable for a manual of a rather ethnocentric political science than for comparative law. One finds the *Thammasat*, for example, described as a 'Constitution' or a 'Bill of Rights'.[92] Nothing more unsuitable could be imagined! The assumption underlying the use of such terms illustrates a historical fallacy: that Western principles of sovereignty are valid for all cases, whatever their cultural background. In essence, this is the same criticism that is levelled above against the early English commentators on the Burmese texts and it is somewhat surprising to see it repeated at the present time. Historical jurisprudence is of course riddled with assumptions of this sort, but, as Sir Paul Vinogradoff[93] pointed out half a century ago and as F. S. C. Northrop[94] has emphasized in regard to comparative law, an apparent similarity in function does not imply an equivalent set of jurisprudential propositions. The Thai kings may have been legislators, but this did not mean the existence of a consistent body of legislation. Similarly, obligation was attributed to the individual—group or communal obligation being unknown—but the individual was defined in terms of a set of preordained characteristics external to him, such as *śakti-nā*. Thus, for example, in crime wounds were classified in accordance with their nature and in accordance with the weapon or instrument used. Penalties were assessed on the basis of rank, and intent as such was overridden by the nature of the act itself.

III CHAMPĀ AND CAMBODIA

The *Dharmaśāstras* and other *śāstras* were studied in the royal

---

[91] See Masao (1905). [92] Darling (1970: 200–2). See also Chomchai (1965).
[93] Vinogradoff (1920 (i)): 147 ff.).
[94] Northrop (1960).

courts of Champā and Cambodia. King Bhavavarman I[95] was known to have had two councillors versed in the *Dharmaśāstra* and *Arthaśāstra*.[96] At the beginning of the eleventh century King Sūryavavarman I boasted of 'having for his feet the *Bhāṣya*, for his hands the *Kāvyas*, for his organs the six *Darśanas*, and for his head the *Dharmaśāstras*'.[97] His successor, Udayādityavarman II (1049–66), claimed to have learned the sciences of *Siddhānta*, *Vyākarṇa*, the *Dharmaśāstras*, and the other *śāstras*. There is, therefore, ample evidence of Hindu *smṛti* learning, and *Manu* in its original text was known by the end of the ninth century at least; an inscription of Yaśovarman I (889–900), the fourth in line of the Kings of Angkor, reproduces textually a *śloka* of Book II of the *Manusmṛti*.[98] Inscriptions of the end of the eighth century also refer to a passage from Book VII of *Manu*, and the three steles of Mi-so'n show that the 'science of the *dharma*' was studied from an Indian text. The first stele, dated A.D. 1081, relates that King Harivarman IV has 'maintained the eighteen heads of litigation' (*aṣṭādaśa margavyavahāra*) established in *Manu* as a method of legal classification.[99] The second stele, dated 1088, also declares that King Jaya Indravarman II follows the eighteen *mārgas* of *Manu*. The third, dated 1172, boasts that King Jaya Indravarman IV is well versed in the *tanatap* or rules in the sense referred to in the *dharma*:[1] he follows '*Nāradīya* and the *Bhārgavīya*', that is, recensions of *Manu*.

As might be expected from inscriptions erected by rulers, the Cham inscriptions glorify the ruler, but in the Yang Tikuh inscription, written at the end of the eighth century, King Indravarman I refers to the celebrated passage at the beginning of Book VII of *Manu* when he boasts of having united in his own person the powers of Caṇḍa, Indra, Agni, Yama, and Kuvera, and, by his prowess, to have equalled the exploits of these kings. The kings of Champā also claimed descent from Śiva, who was believed to have sent the mythical ancestor, Uroja, to earth with a *liṅga* which the god himself had given him.[2]

[95] His date of accession is put at A.D. 550.
[96] Cf. Bergaigne (1893: 69).
[97] Cited in Lingat (1949: 273).
[98] *Ibid.* 274.
[99] See B.É.F.E.O. IV 938, Majumdar (1930: 165).
[1] See B.ÉF.E.O. V 173.
[2] Inscribed on the Dông-du'o'ng stele, A.D. 875. See B.É.F.E.O. IV 91. See also Coedès (1968: 101 f.) on the cult of the *liṅga* and its significance for royal sovereignty.

The evidence so far adduced is all from epigraphic sources which, by their nature, prevent us from attaining a full understanding of the more detailed rules of law and their administration in medieval Champā and Cambodia. However, all the evidence available has been collected by Sahai[3] in his description of the administrative organization of Cambodia from the sixth to the thirteenth centuries. From this several important points emerge. First, the gravest crimes (*mahāpātaka*) and the three sorts of offenders are as cited in *Manu*.[4] The classification of the heads of litigation is also followed,[5] and the heads are set out on the Prè Rup stele.[6] In the case of punishments, the *varṇa* of the individual concerned was important and the penalty was aggravated by the rank of the culpable person. Brahmins, however, were not subject to physical punishment, expulsion being the gravest penalty they could suffer.[7] A fines list is known[8] in which the highest penalties are exacted for those of higher rank, an idea quite familiar in the Indian *śāstras*.[9] Only the common people (*sāmānyajana*), however, were subjected to corporal punishment. The different forms of punishment prescribed for detailed offences were modelled upon the Indian system as set out in *Manu* and *Nārada*. A number of inscriptions from the tenth and eleventh centuries describe the exactions of such penalties.[10]

In the system of judicial functionaries, indigenous elements appear. While the King was the fountain of justice who could absolve penalties already imposed and to whom subjects had a right of petition, many texts[11] also mention a central (*vraḥ sabhā nagara*) and a local or territorial tribunal (*vraḥ sabhā viṣaya* or *vraḥ sabhā sruk*). The respective jurisdictions of these bodies is not known. The actual seat of the tribunal is also described as *vraḥ dharmādhikaraṇa*. The process of litigation was composed of

---

[3] Sahai (1970: 87 ff.) summarizing earlier work. Attention is here directed to his excellent bibliography. See also Puri (1956), Chatterjee (1964).
[4] *Manu* XI.
[5] *Manu* VIII. 4–7, *Nārada* I. 16–19.
[6] Sahai (1970: 88) and the sources there cited.
[7] See also Leclère (1894: 299), and Mabbett (1977) on *varṇa*.
[8] Sahai (1970: 95).
[9] See Kāne (1930–62: (iii) 395).
[10] Sahai (1970: 97 ff.).
[11] *Ibid.* 99 ff.

a plaint, a response, an examination by the tribunal, and a decision, and *śāstric* terms were employed for the process; in the description of material fact, however, Khmer terms were used. The formal style of the proceeding thus closely resembled the Indian *vyavahāra-mātṛkā*.[12] The system of witnesses (*sākṣin*) and of evidence in general was modelled on Indian practice. Ordeals were used. Finally, it is worth noting that individual title to property was apparently guaranteed by the judicial officers, and a number of texts set out the process of proof of title.[13]

From the limited evidence of the documents at our disposal it may be said that the concept of law in Champā and Cambodia attempted to conform to an Indian-based ideal. The *śāstras* were well known, at least in the upper levels of society, and, whether followed in detail or not, they must have imposed their own view of law.[14] Local practice did, however, exist, as is evident from the rules about property in land alluded to above, but the extent to which the *śāstras* were modified or replaced among the masses is unknown.[15]

IV JAVA

The laws of Java are known to us through three types of document. (*a*) inscriptions of *jayapattra*, (*b*) taxation and land charters, and (*c*) the law-books of Java and Bali.

(*a*) *The jayapattra or 'note of victory'*. This was a document issued to the winner of a lawsuit; it was part of the classical law of India and, so far as is known, was issued in respect of claims of a civil nature.[16] Its aim was to demonstrate conclusively that an action had been settled, and ideally it should have contained a statement by both parties, the evidence considered, the law text (*smṛti*) applied, and the decision of the judge authenticated by seal.[17] A considerable number of Javanese *jayapattra* are known,[18] the earliest of which were found on inscriptions dating

---

[12] See Kāne (1930–62: (iii) 245–47).
[13] Sahai 1970: 110–11, Rickleffs (1967).
[14] Lingat (1949: 289) is strongly of this view.
[15] But see the short note by Youran (1967).
[16] Kāne (1930–62: (iii) 380–1).
[17] See Kāne (1930–62: (iii) 380–2).
[18] See Pigeaud (1960–2: (iii) 143–50, 151–5, 175–7, 166–8). See also de Casparis (1956: 330–7).

from A.D. 907 and 922, both the result of civil suits.[19] They are clearly modelled upon an Indian original, which is not surprising since Indian legal theory was known in Java as early as the eighth century: the evidence of inscriptions dated A.D. 732 and 794 refers to *Manu* and demonstrates the use of Sanskrit models in Javanese legal transactions.[20] However, the *jayapattra* of this period are not strictly comparable with those of India; in that of A.D. 922 no reference is made to the *smṛti*, and what was clearly a local law of some sophistication was applied. Further, in India, the conduct of proceedings was in the hands of a judge (*prāḍivāka*), whereas in Java the trial was conducted by a *samget*[21] (a judge-arbitrator) assisted by a council of notables whose decision was thus of a collegiate nature.[22] In addition, the proceedings seem to have been in the nature of searching for a compromise, thus negating the need for the citation of *smṛti*, a reference to which need not necessarily be basic to a decision. It seems, then, that the Javanese *jayapattra* was a *form* for recording a decision based upon an Indian model but did not require the application of principles of Indian law.[23]

The Javanese nature of the *jayapattra* had become even more pronounced by the fourteenth century, by which time they were known as *jayasong*. The style had also become more elaborate, and the *jayasong* of the period now referred to 'lawbooks' and to sources of law distinctly Javanese. The Decree Jaya Song[24] of A.D. 1350 was an action to recover land which had been in the defendant's possession for three generations, i.e. about one hundred years before the action. The defendant's case was that the passage of time (*kadalu-warsa*) had converted what had originally been a pledge of land into an outright transfer. This was not accepted by the tribunal, but the interesting point is that this is a principle of Javanese *adat* still very much alive today.[25] The Decree thus bears out the long-held opinion that the *kadalu-warsa* rule is of considerable antiquity.

This decree and later *jayasong* were written in an elaborate

[19] See Hoadley (1971: 100) for references to the Dutch sources.
[20] See de Casparis (1956: 335–7).
[21] Van Naerssen (1933: 241–4) on the *samget*.
[22] See Jayaswal (1920), Jolly (1921).
[23] See further Hoadley (1971: 101).
[24] Pigeaud (1960–2: (iii) Decree Jaya Song).
[25] See Subekti & Tamara (1965: 158–60).

The Indian Legal World 37

style; and the use of rigid forms, as is well known in legal history, tends both to encourage the growth of a technical procedure and to emphasize the importance of the source of law. As to technical procedure, the Decree mentions an executive council, and a college of legal specialists (*upapatti*) whose function was to dispense justice. These groups replaced the earlier *samget*. As to sources, the Decree specified the following:

... The opinions of the law-books [were] sought, [as well as] the opinion of the country [and information on] matters of yore.... Reliant on the essential learning found in the honoured holy Kutāra Mānawa, the law-books ... [following] the character and customs of the honoured scholars, [and] the judges of lawsuits.... Inquiries [were made] in the locality ... in order to get information on right and wrong.[26]

This passage classifies the sources of law as written and unwritten, that is, as law-books and local practice, an early example of the typically Javanese dual source of law. These sources were, however, united in the *jayasong*.

(*b*) *The Tax and Land Charters*. The group of such charters originating from the middle of the fourteenth century provides valuable information on the legal thought of the period. The earliest, the *Sarwadharma* Charter[27] issued in A.D. 1269 in the reign of Kĕrtanegara of Singosari (1268–92), defines religious domain land (*dharma*) and exempts it from the taxes and levies ordinarily due to the ruler.[28] Local payments, such as those for irrigation services, were also made exempt. Privileges granted in the Charter included the rights to wear specified personal ornaments and clothing, to treat bondsmen in a certain way, and, generally, to act in a manner consistent with the status conferred by the Charter. The Charter refers to corvée labour and to an annual tax[29] in kind due at the time of the rice harvest which was the principal source of royal revenue.[30] The legal relationship between the religious domain and neighbouring

[26] Pigeaud (1960–2: (iii) 154). Decree Jaya Song, 5, verse 5 to 6, recto 1–2.
[27] Ibid. (iii) 143–50, (iv) 381–90).
[28] 4, verso 3–7.
[29] It is noticeable that in the terms of the charter the right to tax is strictly personal in nature as deriving from the king. It is part of the royal prerogative or, more exactly, taxation is an expression of royal power over the individual. The nature of royal power is thus personal, and is expressed in concrete terms in relation to specified individuals; the nature of sovereignty is thus personal and not territorial.
[30] See the *Nagarakṛtāgama*, 83–5.

38 *Status*

secular lands is indicated in the term *pangāshrayan*—'place where to ask for support', i.e. the religious domain was dependent upon the secular for labour service because, at the time, religious personnel (*wiku*) were not allowed to perform manual labour in agriculture.

The Ferry Charter[31] of 1358, although incomplete, provides more information on the sources and characteristics of mid-fourteenth-century Javanese law. As to source, the provisions of the Charter are said to be 'without [prejudice to] the honoured proclaimers of the law, the judges of lawsuits...[32] absorbed in the explanation of books of learning, *Kuṭāra Mānawa*... [who] are devoted to the discussion of the books... *Kuṭāra Mānawa* with a view to acquiring firm knowledge'.[33] In other words, it is a document granting rights which can in no way exclude the general law. Rather, the effect of the Charter in its terms was to subject the recipient ferrymen to the King's justice, to the exclusion of local custom. In return, the ferrymen were permitted to worship in various specified ways, to organize gambling, to fix fees, and their liability in respect of lost and stolen goods was established. Similar grants of privileges are known from other charters,[34] one of the most interesting of which is the *Rĕnĕk* Charter,[35] which, in describing a dispute as to occupation of land, itemizes the estates in land known in fourteenth-century Java. These are: religious domains (*dharma*), private estates (*sīma*), family lands (*wangsha*), lands sacred to the servants of the spirits (*hila-hila hulun hyang*), halls (*kuṭi*), and artisans' dwellings (*kalagyan*).[36] In addition it describes the dispute process, and here, as in the early *jayapattra* mentioned above, the process was characteristically mediation rather than adjudication. It is also worth noting that the legal evidence (*pramāṇa*) of title was normally a royal charter, but where, as in most cases, such did not exist, immemorial tradition was taken to be sufficient.

(*c*) *The law-books of the fourteenth century.* Medieval Javanese law-books have come down to us in the form of manuscripts preserved only in the island of Bali. Many such are known:

[31] Pigeaud (1960–2: (iii) 156–62, (iv) 399–411).   [32] 3, recto 1.
[33] 3, recto 6.
[34] The Biluluk Charters of A.D. 1366, 1391, and 1395 in Pigeaud 1960–2: (iii) 166–8, (iv) 416–32.
[35] *Ibid.* (iii) 169–70, (iv) 433–42.   [36] *Ibid.* (iv) 251 ff.

Friederich lists the following named texts:[37] *Âgama, Adhigama, Dewâgama, Sarasamuscaya (Sârasamuccaya), Duṣṭakâlabhaya, Swarajambu Swayambhu, Dewadaṇḍa,* and *Yajñasadna*. Other texts have also been described by van Eck[38] (*Darma upapati— Dharmopapatti*) and Raffles[39] (*Çastra Menava*). Much of the discussion of these texts has been concentrated upon the extent to which they are copies of Indian texts, especially of the laws of *Manu*. As we shall see, the (perhaps excessive) attention paid to Indian attributes has tended to distort the descriptions of the texts themselves.

The texts of the laws usually attributed to fourteenth-century Madjapahit are the well-known *Âgama* described by Jonker[40] and, in a more recent Indonesian version, by Slametmuljana.[41] The texts are Leiden MS. No. 38, which is untitled although it has *Âgama* written on the outside, and British Library MS 12277,[42] which is also untitled although it is described on its cover as the *Cuntara Manava Sastra* ('Institute of Manu'). It was obtained by John Crawfurd from the Rajah of Bliling in 1814. Both texts correspond closely, although the B.L. MS lists the dominions of Madjapahit but omits Art. 79 and ends at Art. 183 of the Leiden MS. The attribution of the texts to Madjapahit is made on the grounds that their language and grammar are Javanese rather than Balinese; but the manuscripts themselves must be of comparatively recent date since the language is not archaic even compared with present-day Balinese law-books. There is no historical evidence for the descent of such texts from Madjapahit, but for a number of reasons we are almost certainly justified in describing the known texts as copies of texts extant in Madjapahit. First, the *Nagarakṛtāgama* provides evidence of a type of social order and culture which is not only reflected in but is essential to the *Âgama* manuscripts (see further below). Second, in paragraph 73/1 of the *Nagarakṛtāgama* a lawbook called *Âgama* (i.e. 'that which is handed down', 'knowledge', 'learning') is specifically mentioned as being in existence. Third, the *Âgama* refers to itself as the *Kuṭara Mânawaçâstra* (ss. 23, 65) and the term *Kuṭara* is again found in the

---

[37] See Jonker (1885: 3).
[38] Jonker (1885: 3) for references.　　[39] Raffles (1817: Appendix c).
[40] Jonker (1885).　　[41] Slametmuljana (1967).
[42] B.L. MS. 12336 is a copy of the same text made by Crawfurd.

Nagarakṛtāgama. This word has provided some difficulty; it appears in Javanese sources, such as the *Nagarakṛtāgama*, and has been interpreted as a bastardization of the Indian *Kottama*, 'one who follows'.[43] The implication is that there were two law-books, *Kuṭara* and *Manu*. It is well established that the text which we are describing is itself a compilation from a number of earlier texts, but the implication that there are two major sources is suggestive. It has led one authority[44] to say that during the fourteenth century a law-book based upon the laws of *Manu* was replaced by a more indigenous Javanese book. In so far as this recognizes the eclecticism of sources it is unexceptionable, but it can mean no more than that: the idea of an abrupt change from one *concept* of law to another is not typical of the Javanese. Having said this, there is no doubt that the *Âgama* does exhibit important distinctions within itself as to particular rules. Indeed, section 121 refers the source of the text to both a *Kuṭara Mânawa-çâstra* and a *Mânawa-Dharma-çâstra* and states two different regulations on the forfeiture of pledge, while expressly forbidding any preference between the laws. But as Jonker demonstrates,[45] these diverse sources represent a Javanese attempt to formulate a text in which elements from a number of Indian sources, including *Manu* and also some unknown sources are combined. For example, section 23 has the term *Kuṭara Mânawa-Dharma-çâstra* as a composite description of the sources, although in fact the first part of the text is much more closely related to *Manu* than is the latter. At the same time indigenous features appear in all parts of the text.

In common with all South-East Asian texts (except the Vietnamese) the arrangement of subject-matter is haphazard and repetitive; in the arrangement adopted by Jonker and continued by Slametmuljana the text is divided into 275 sections arranged in nineteen chapters. As we can see, this represents a slight elaboration on the eighteen titles of law set out in *Manu* VIII. 4-7.

1. Fines
2. Homicide
3. Slaves
4. The eight varieties of Theft
5. Crimes of Violence

[43] Jonker (1885: 11 and the sources there cited). In the laws of classical India it refers to a commentary on the main texts.
[44] D. G. E. Hall (1968: 90).   [45] Jonker (1885: 17–20).

6. Sale
7. Mortgage
8. Debt
9. Pledge and Security
10. Dower
11. Marriage
12. Unlawful sexual intercourse (lit. 'Pollution')
13. Inheritance
14. Insults
15. Assault
16. Negligence and Reckless Behaviour
17. Quarrelling
18. Land
19. Slander

Throughout the text Sanskrit terms are used as the main classifiers, although usually the reference has been extended to take account of local Javanese conditions. For example, in Chapter 4 the *astacorah* (Skt. *aṣṭacora*—eight varieties of theft) include the man who has committed theft, the man who incited another to theft, the man who gives food to a thief, the man who lodges a thief, the man who is on friendly terms with a thief, the man who gives information to a thief, the man who helps a thief, and the man who hides a thief. These classes are comparable to those in *Manu* IX. 278 and *Yājñavalkya* II. 276. Again, the *Āgama* describes the six or eight varieties of felony (ch. 5) by reference to *sadtatayi* (Skt. *ṣaḍātatāyin*—a person who threatens or endeavours to kill or commit a serious crime of violence). In the *Āgama* the term refers to the following; the incendiary, the prisoner, the amuck-runner, the man who slanders the king, the witch or sorcerer, and the man who violates a married woman. The technical terms for these criminals are given in a corrupted Sanskrit verse with a Javanese paraphrase.

Another interesting example is the provision (ch. 5) on crimes of violence—*sāhasa* from the Sanskrit *sāhasa*. The *Āgama* gives a definition which is a cross between accounts of its nature and its limits as described in *Manu*. The term is derived from *sāhas* (force) and, in the *Āgama*, it is used interchangeably with *walat* (Skt. *balātkāra*—employment of violence) or with compounds such as *sāhasa a-malat*—to appropriate in a violent or wrongful way. It has a wide range of reference in the *Āgama*, such as stealing, robbing, raping, calamities sent by a divine power in return for offences, and punishment for disrespectful treatment toward persons or objects worthy of veneration. On the other hand, the Javanese *děṇḍaparuṣya*—striking another, wounding, spitting—is directly derived from the Sanskrit *daṇḍapāruṣya* meaning assault.

Chapter 12 of the Âgama deals with unlawful sexual intercourse; the chapter is headed *paradara* (adultery), a direct use of the Sanskrit term. In the *Âgama*, however, the term refers also to taking hold of a woman of blameless conduct, making unchaste proposals to such a woman, entering her residence without permission, or suing a woman for divorce without valid reason.

The classification of slaves in the *Âgama* (ss. 15, 169, 270) is taken directly from *Manu* VIII. 415–16, i.e. those captured in battle (Jav. *dhwajahṛta*, Skt. *dhvajahṛta*), born in the house (*gṛhaja*), taken for the non-payment of a fine (*daṇḍadāsa*), or who serve for their food (*bhaktadāsa*).

Indian influence is again apparent in chapter 1 of the *Âgama*, on fines. These were classified on the following principles:

(a) By looking at the caste to which the wrongdoer and the offended person belonged. For example, section 221 provides that if a *sudra* abuses a *satria* he is to be fined five *tali*, but only one for abusing a farmer (*petani*). On the other hand, if a *satria* abuses a farmer the fine is 1,000 *tali*, but 2,000 if the position is reversed (s. 220).

(b) By considering the limbs that were damaged and the extent of damage; section 231 provides for penalties assessed according to the part of the body injured, thus one lakh (100,000) for an injury in the centre of the body and two lakhs for injury to the head or neck, the fines to be paid to the king.

(c) By looking at the result of the crime; this is a continuation of (b), and section 230 deals with the use of arms or instruments in assault and lists fines depending upon the nature of the weapon.

(d) By considering the time at which the event took place. Section 66 provides for individual and communal fines for ordinary theft, fines to the king and double the value of the goods to the owner, but death if the theft took place at night. The last provision is peculiarly Javanese.

(e) Knowledge; section 248 assesses the action of an employee resulting in loss to the employer according to whether or not he had knowledge and understanding of his breach of duty.

(f) The value of the object in question; thus theft was punished by reference to the value of the thing stolen. However,

The Indian Legal World

section 62 is interesting for it provides that different penalties may be imposed depending upon whether the injured person is a *sudra* or a farmer. Failure to pay a fine made an offender into the king's slave (*kawula*) as provided in section 24, but under section 31 daily work of the slave counts towards the payment of the fine. The work of the man counted twice that of a woman!

The two major features of the fines system which appear throughout all sections of the text are, first, that fines were based upon some sort of ranking system which resembled the Hindu *varṇa* system. There can be little doubt about the importance and effectiveness of such a fines system in view of the passages in the *Nagarakṛtāgama* dealing with lands granted to Shivite and Vishnu-ite priests and the difficult relations which sometimes existed between them and the neighbouring peasants and landed aristocracy. The charters mentioned above (pp. 37–8) bear witness to the importance of this aspect of Indian legal thought. It is worth noting also that *Manu* is stated to be the incarnation of Vishnu in the *Âgama*. The second feature is that a native Javanese element is grafted on to this scheme. The principle is that compensation must be paid to the injured person. Although fines are paid to the ruler, the injured person gets double or treble the value in compensation. Intention was thus strictly irrelevant; whether it was present or not in, say, manslaughter, compensation ('blood money') still had to be paid (ss. 7, 190, 232). Such payment was called by different names (*pangliçawa, patukuçawa*), but in all cases the import of the payment was to cleanse of guilt. In other words, the public law aspect—the involvement of the 'state'—typical of Hindu law of the medieval period was supplemented by compensation to the individual. It was possible to buy off punishment (s. 25), and the right of self-defence was highly developed (ss. 255–7). Another factor is that the public law aspect of punishment, e.g. mutilation, is not found in those provisions of the text which are clearly of Javanese origin. Thus the text itself contains discrepancies: for example, adultery might be punished by a fine payable to the husband (s. 134) but it was also punishable by death (s. 179). This reflects not just a conflict of source but also a conflict of concept—it is difficult to relate punishment assessed according to rank to mere compensation whatever the circumstance.[46] The Javanese law thus presents an example of inner tension in legal thought. We can illustrate this by looking a little more closely at the sections which deal with damages. Sections 241 and 242 both provide for the payment of damages in multiples of twice or four times the objects damaged and both make clear that intent is irrelevant. Section 19 even provides that when a woman is killed for no cause—as in a mistaken belief that she has committed adultery—then not only are her debts to be paid twice over but a cleansing fee (*patukuçawa*) of four times the amount is also necessary. In all such cases, the Indian original is silent. It was also possible for a person condemned to death to buy himself off (ss. 21, 56), except in the case of sorcery (s. 20); and the sorcerer's relatives in both the descending and the ascending generation could also be put to death (s. 13) by order of the ruler. The king himself was justified in imposing such penalties for the purpose of state order and for the protection of the individual (s. 6). No retribution followed the king in giving such orders because they were part of the ruler's duty (s. 11). Section 2 states: 'The duty which must be performed by the ruler if he wishes tranquillity in his realm is to enforce the proper punishment and to levy the appropriate fine.' The various forms of punishment and fine are described in almost all sections and are evidence of the fact that the *Âgama*, like all South-East Asian texts, is basically a list of penalties.

In the case of (contractual) transactions between individuals, the same view is evident; the emphasis is not on defining obligation but on setting limits to the power to invoke rules that determine obligation. Thus, in the case of pledge, the sole emphasis is on setting limits of time from which the contract of pledge is ended (ss. 110–15). There is no effort to state the basis of obligation apart from the time limit; it is interesting to note that this is a feature of modern *adat* law in Indonesia.[47] Effluxion of time sufficient to change the ownership of land was also known in the *Âgama* (ss. 84–5), and this again is a principle known to modern *adat*. However, the law of debt in the *Âgama* remains that of *Manu*, although in the light of the preceding comments it is difficult to see how it could have been applied.

The simplistic nature of individual transactions is paralleled

[46] On crimes of violence see Van Naerssen (1956).
[47] See Ter Haar (1948: 124).

The Indian Legal World 45

in the *Āgama* by the somewhat limited treatment accorded to the concept of ownership in general. Apart from a statement in section 100 that the ruler is the 'owner of the soil', which even in strictly Indian terms can hardly be correct, the main point about ownership is that basic rights are subsumed into a discussion of land pledge. The acquistion of land is taken for granted and the only point at issue as requiring regulation is not the sovereign's right *vis-à-vis* the subject but the equation of occupation with ownership, which is a matter involving the individual. The phrase *maler ring ananda*, which appears in the important section 268, may be translated as '[the land] remains with the person who pledged it'. The question of course is whether this person still retained the ownership. It seems probable that he did, given the general right of redemption (ss. 84–5) in the *Āgama* designated by the common use of the term *ngagaḍe*, which means redemption. It is also worth pointing out that such an institution is still current in the Malay/Indonesian world. Further, sections 132–3 lay stress on the primacy of the family, however widely defined, as the land-holding unit, to the extent that one who did not allow his blood relatives to have land was punished, and one who falsely claimed land as his own was described as one who falsely pretended to a blood relationship. The development of land matters is thus quite localized in Javanese terms.

The same is true of inheritance. The master's right to succeed to the property of a slave is established (ss. 10, 153, 164), and the law provides for succession to the property acquired on the marriage of a slave with a free woman (s. 12). In the case of death of the spouses without children, the property brought to the marriage is returned to the respective parents (or, presumably, to their successors). Spouses inherit from each other, and children inherit primarily from the father (s. 97). The text is not clear as to whether only sons or both sons and daughters can inherit. These sections describe inheritance as a nuclear family or at least a kindred affair, but section 197 provides that the eldest son can take four-fifths of the inheritance in advance; this is an Indian law provision known as *uddhāra*, and it clearly contradicts the provisions of the later sections just mentioned.

In regard to marriage, the text is quite clear that a brideprice (*tukon*) was demanded, and the relationship between the giver of the price and the father of the girl was likened to that between a buyer and a seller (ss. 96, 112), but this should not be taken too seriously because the wife always inherited from her husband. It is interesting, however, that while in *Manu* IX. 98 'not even a *Sudra* may receive the marriage price (*çulka*)', in *Manu* VIII. 366, IX. 93, 97, such a price is mentioned as the usual one in marriage transactions. The *Âgama*, on the other hand, treats of the purchase price (*pasěsěmbah* or *patuku susu*) in detail (ss. 256–7). Community of goods within the marriage was recognized (ss. 123, 196), and the sections themselves seem to parallel closely the well-known rules on (*sa*)*pencharian* property. Divorce was the prerogative of the male (s. 192), although under certain circumstances, such as insanity or absence, a woman might marry again (ss. 193–4). This is a right both denied (*Manu* V.162, IX.65) and permitted (*Wasiṣṭha* XVII.76) in the Hindu law-books.

This sketch of the *Âgama* demonstrates that, as with other South-East Asian law texts, the connection between religion, law, and man's view of himself in relation to the natural world was the basic concern of the text. Indian influence on the text was both direct and immediate in that many sections were either copies or adaptations of Indian material, usually, though not always, from *Manu*. The *Âgama* was made known 'for the well-being of humanity'. More important, the spirit and tone of the text owe much to Indian legal thought; the philosophical basis of order and its connection with religious philosophy is unmistakably Indian. At the same time the text demonstrates a number of adaptations to local conditions, for example, the emphasis on compensation and the avoidance of *varṇa* rules (which are also mentioned in the *Nagarakṛtāgama*).

With the coming of Islam to Indonesia a new class of law text appeared which attempted a reconciliation of Javanese ideas with a new legal and ethical system.[48] The original texts continued, however, to exert influence in two ways. First, they provided a model for later legal compilations and, second, they continued to influence the content of substantive law in so far as they expressed indigenous principles. (The persistence of the *jayasong* form is one example).[49] The texts have even had

[48] See Vreede (1941) and Pigeaud (1967: (i) 304–14) for a description of the *mss*.
[49] See Hoadley (1971). See also Kern (1927).

The Indian Legal World

something of an emotional appeal in the early years of Indonesian independence.[50] In Bali of course they continue to form the basis of Balinese law.[51]

In this outline of the Indian-derived South-East Asian law texts we have seen something of the development of the classical Hindu law in new environments. Although the texts provided a number of solutions to the problem of cultural adaptation, they have a unity which is deeper than the mere structural framework. The idea of law is not limited to definitions of 'coercive' elements or 'rules'; it transcends these definitions. Law rests upon concepts of religion that give rise to rules of conduct which ought to be observed by reason of social condition. It is among these rules that rules of law are to be found; they are expressions of the natural order in terms of duty (*dharma*). The definition of the latter varies from one set of texts to another,[52] but the basic impact of all texts is with the idea of obligation in relation to local conditions. It is the concentration upon the link between obligation (stated in immutable and absolute principles) and the local conditions of life and society that gives a unity to the Indian-derived texts. This question is considered further in Chapter 4.

[50] See Slametmuljana (1967: 17–18).
[51] See Korn (1960) and, more specifically, Hunger (1935) on inheritance.
[52] See, for example, Mulder (1970) and Singaravelu (1968).

CHAPTER 2

The Islamic Legal World: The Law Texts of Island South-East Asia

THE MUSLIM lands of South-East Asia stretch from southern Thailand,[1] through Malaysia (including Malaysian Borneo) and the islands of Indonesia to the southern Philippines.[2] Islam is an exclusive religion which not only regulates man's relations with God but also with other men—both Muslim and unbeliever. The religion of Islam contains within itself a legal system with its own well-defined body of principle, doctrine, and process.[3] However, the strict principles of Islamic jurisprudence have by no means been fully adhered to in South-East Asia. The law texts inspired by Islam in island South-East Asia amply demonstrate this point in their observance of local traditions and customs. Indeed, custom ('urf) itself has a well-defined place in Islamic legal history (see below, Chapter 4). In addition, Islam came to South-East Asia via the Indian subcontinent[4] and was thus in a form which tolerated metaphysical speculation of the type made popular by Sūfī mystics. The teachings of the latter became an important intellectual element in local societies throughout the whole of the Malay/Muslim world.[5] Their influence was due to their toleration of popular usage and beliefs[6] which might not always be in strict accord with Muslim orthodoxy.

The main centres for the diffusion of Islam were the trading

---

[1] In the *Changwats* (districts) of Pattani, Narathiwat, Yala, and Satun. See section 6 of the Act Promulgating Bk. V of the Civil and Commercial Code B.E. 2477, B.E. 2489 of Thailand.
[2] Magindanao, Mindanao and Sulu and adjacent small island clusters.
[3] See Schacht (1964) for an introduction.
[4] See Marrison (1951).
[5] See Winstedt (1947a: 33–44).
[6] See Gibb (1945: 25). On the local element in Malaya see Syed Muhammad Naguib Al-Attas (1972).

The Islamic Legal World

stations of the western side of the Indonesian archipelago and the Malayan peninsula, especially Malacca in the late fourteenth and early fifteenth centuries. The days of Malacca's glory saw Islam advance from being the faith of foreign traders to becoming the faith of kings and courts. The penetration of Islam was peaceful despite claims of Muslim conquest in pseudo-historical texts such as the *Babab Tanah Djawi*, although it is true that the advance of Islam was occasionally a response to an aggressive Christian imperialism.[7] It was also, in some cases, part of a policy of local political aggrandizement.[8]

The impact of Islam in island South-East Asia can best be summed up not as conversion proper but as the absorbing of Islamic elements by native cultures. There was little change in mass intellectual attitudes, which is what conversion implies, but there was an accommodation between Islamic principle and indigenous metaphysics. Naturally, the extent and nature of the accommodation varied from place to place, but even in the remoter parts of the island archipelago Islamic law never became the only source of law. In areas such as Java, Islamic principles never replaced the *adats*. In most other areas a composite system emerged in which Islamic elements coexisted or, sometimes, blended with local elements. It is this composite which constitutes the Islamic legal text in South-East Asia.

I THE SOUTH-EAST ASIAN TEXTS

There are a great number of texts, and for the purposes of description one may divide them into three geographical groups: Malacca and Malacca-derived texts in Malaya;[9] the Moro and Sulu texts (see below); and the texts of Sumatra and the islands of the Indonesian archipelago.[10] Despite considerable local variation, the texts have in common an Islamic element which essentially consists of the following. First, the texts locate the origin of law in the Islamic ethic as understood by the authority responsible for promulgating the law. In all cases the emphasis is on the nature of sovereignty; indeed, it is

[7] Especially in the south Philippines. See Majul (1973).
[8] As in the Celebes. See Noorduyn (1956: 250).
[9] Including the texts of Brunei. See Winstedt (1923).
[10] See de Hollander (1893), Caron (1937). For a 'structural' analysis of South Sumatran (Bengkulu) texts see Moyer (1975). For Java see Pigeaud (1967: (i) 304–14).

not too much to say that in many cases the aim of the Islamic text is to legitimize the position of the ruler. The nature of law was thus determined by means of the ruler's prerogative as *Berkhalifah* (the vice-regent of God on earth). The sultan was the source of God's order on earth and intermediate between God and man. Law defined in premisses such as these was quite distinct from the local laws (*adats*) administered at village level. The latter were limited in scope, oral in form, and so fact-dependent that at times they reached the point of incoherence. The texts, on the other hand, state a law which is absolute in quality, certain as to source, and universal in scope.

Second, the texts, which date from the seventeenth to the nineteenth centuries, attempt to state the basic rules of Islam, including the notions of the sovereignty of God and the community of the faithful, in a form which is compatible with local cultural patterns. The result is a mixture of legal rules representing a number of ideas of law which are often so diversified as to be conflicting. This was true for the whole of the Islamized area and it gave rise to a good deal of discussion amongst nineteenth-century legal historians. For those who were interested in the historical development of the law and in establishing different classes of legal development in terms of the theories of Sir Henry Maine, the Islamic texts provided an interesting problem. On the one hand, the texts, while containing a good number of Islamic provisions, were not enforced, in any sense, as Islamic law. On the other, the non-Islamic parts of the texts contain local rules, *some* but not all of which have a relation to indigenous practice. Further, there were, in all the Islamized areas, local *adat* (customary) laws, most of them in oral form, dealing with both private law (mainly land holding and distribution) and public law. In trying to make sense of this situation, writers such as Wilkinson and Winstedt posited hypothetical laws of legal development to explain what they saw as discrepancies and difficulties in the texts. 'Hindu influence' was a favourite catchphrase to 'explain' the otherwise inexplicable,[11] although it is wholly inappropriate. The problem lies in the source of law, the distinction between secular and sacred sources, and, what is more difficult,

---

[11] See Hooker (1973: 497–8) for an account of the reasoning adopted.

The Islamic Legal World 51

the tension between a theory of absolute sovereignty and the reality of law in day-to-day administration.

Enough has been said to illustrate something of the complexity in the Islamic texts. In the space available it is impossible to deal with all known texts; this defect is offset to a large extent, however, by the fact that in general the texts owe a good deal one to another because of the practice of copying and re-copying manuscripts. The problem of the existence of an original manuscript, or group of manuscripts is outside the scope of this book, but we may be reasonably certain that the characteristic legal ideas already mentioned truly reflect the historical reality of the Islamic legal word in South-East Asia.[12] To illustrate the characteristics of this world we shall take two examples: the (Malay) Malacca and Malacca-derived texts[13] and the *Luwaran* of Magindanao and the Sulu Codes of the southern Philippines.

II THE (MALAY) MALACCA AND MALACCA-DERIVED TEXTS

The Malacca or 'Malayan' group of texts is amongst the best-known of the Islamic legal literature of South-East Asia. There are three further reasons for choosing this group of texts. First, Malacca was one of the earliest centres for the diffusion of Islam in the South-East Asian archipelago and it is in this area that one might reasonably expect to identify the structure of Islamic legal thought as it was understood in the sultanates of medieval South-East Asia. As it is, we have documentary evidence from the *Sejarah Melayu*[14] which throws light on the nature of Islam as this was understood by the intellectual elements in the court circles of the time. Second, the Malayan manuscripts form a group because of the copying and re-copying which took place among them and, although from this point of view they are mainly of interest to philologists, they demonstrate in an extraordinarily vivid way the peculiar status that written laws attained in the Malay world. One finds fidelity to the written

[12] For further references see van Ronkel (1919) (1921).
[13] Excluding the so-called 'Brunei Code' which is merely a corrupt version of a Malacca manuscript. See Winstedt (1923); see also Dulaurier (1845) on a Bugis maritime text.
[14] See, e.g., the preamble to c. I, and the account of the conversion of Raja Tengah in c. vi.83–4.

text but, at the same time, the texts were used as a means of integrating legal rules into a political system so that expedient changes were given an Islamic (legal) colouring. Finally, the manuscript sources of the Malayan texts are known in detail and, although arguments still occur over the provenance of some manuscripts, the connection between manuscripts is pretty well established.

The main texts are as follows:

(a) *The* Undang2 Kerajaan (*The Laws of the King*). This is not a particularly old text, Kempe and Winstedt[15] describe the nineteenth-century manuscripts as copies of an original, or possibly originals, compiled in the reign of Sultan Abd. al-Ghafur[16] (A.D. 1592–1614). The laws purport to relate to Perak, Pahang, and Johore;[17] their interest for the legal historian lies in the fact that the contents fall into two sections, one Islamic and the other non-Islamic. The latter comprises the first twenty-three sections. The preamble sets out a detailed description of high offices of state, including matters of finance and trade, the police, and so on. In addition, it includes a passage, almost certainly taken from some Islamic text, enjoining perfect obedience upon the ruler's subjects because '[unlike] infidels ye are like men that dive into the sea for pearls, who have been given nose and mouth that they may breathe.... Be not heedless of this world and the hereafter.' In other words, the duty of obedience is dictated by reference to religion; this attests not only to the importance of belief but also indicates a duty to the ruler whose place in the Islamic world is thus reinforced.

The first section begins with the well-known prohibition upon the wearing of yellow and of certain clothes and decorations. This is the same provision which appears in the '*Qanun*' [*Kanun*] 'Law of the Dato' Kota Star[18] and is common in the regalia regulations of the Malay, Sumatran, and Celebes sultanates. The reference is often ascribed to 'Hindu influence',

---

[15] Kempe & Winstedt (1948: 1–2) based on Maxwell MSS. 17 and 20.
[16] Sultan of Pahang. See Linehan 1936: 29–34 for what is known of his life.
[17] See also Logan (1855: 71–95), who translates the 'Laws of Johore', almost certainly taken from Raffles MS. 33 and thus a part of the Malacca texts—see below.
[18] Section 5. See Winstedt (1928: 10).

apparently because of supposed parallels in *Manu*[19] and the correspondence frequently observed between the ceremonies of installation in the Malay states and those in Buddhist Siam and Burma to the north.[20] However, it is doubtful whether the sumptuary regulations indicate more than a system of ranks, although the installation ceremonies do of course have a well-attested and rather wider cosmological significance.[21]

The first twenty-three sections set out rules on slavery and the finding of goods and punishments for various offences of both a public law and a private law nature. By far the majority of these sections are concerned with slavery, and include penalties for some rather improbable sexual offences committed by slaves. These sections do, however, indicate the importance of slavery—to the text patron at least. By contrast, the more important practical matters of cultivation are given only two sections, sections 2 and 3, which deal with the duty of cultivators to fence crops and refer rather obscurely to the rights of cultivation on abandoned rice-fields.

The Islamic portion of the text (ss. 24–66) contains rules, some of the Shāfi'ī derivation, which are Islamic in tone and occasionally in substance (esp. ss. 45, 63). It is not, however, true to say that these sections 'are Islamic': they represent an adaptation of Islamic principle to the facts of life at the period. For example, section 29 states that guarantees can only be given in accordance with Muslim law but the text goes on to state in later passages rules which are clearly local in origin. Similarly, slavery is dealt with in section 26 under the heading of 'flawed goods' and is in some conflict with the earlier part of the text laws. Attempts are also made to prohibit traditional practices, as in section 38, which prohibits the letting of land in return for part of the crop in payment. Occasionally there are restrictive provisions, such as section 41, which provides that the feller of a forest must be a Muslim. On the other hand, the Islamic law of gifts is repeated in simplified form (s. 42), and a rather inpractical fines list based upon camels and distinguishing

---

[19] The reference is really to the divine nature of kingship. See Lingat (1973: 207 f.). and *Manu* v.93, vii.8, 14. For the South-East Asian parallels see Heine-Geldern (1942–3).
[20] See Winstedt (1947).
[21] See Heine-Geldern (1942–3).

between Muslims, Christians, and Jews (s. 48) also has clear links with Middle Eastern concepts of fines. The Islamic penalties of mutilation for theft are repeated (s. 53), but there is no evidence that they were ever enforced generally in the Malay states. Apostasy is to be punished by death (s. 59) and oaths are given in Islamic forms (s. 65). Section 67, however, is a copy of sections 25–7 of the Malacca laws and provides, in short form, for trespass of cattle, debts, punishments, and so on in terms which contradict those immediately preceding and following the section. It is a striking example of the inner conflict within the text as a whole.

(b) *The Kedah Laws*. The manuscript of these laws was obtained from the *Dato' Luar* of Kelantan and was thought at first to be the ancient laws of that state. However, as Winstedt[22] made clear, the manuscript was written under the auspices of a number of Kedah sultans. It contains four distinct sets of laws written between A.D. 1650 and 1784:

(i) *Port Laws* dated 1650;
(ii) *Tembĕra Dato' Sri Paduka Tuan* dated 1078 A.H. (A.D. 1667);
(iii) *Hukum Qanun* [*Kanun*] *Dato' Star*—no date;
(iv) *Undang2* dated 1199 A.H. (A.D. 1784).

In addition, there is a chapter on the *bunga mas* ('golden flowers'), a symbolic acknowledgement of suzerainty sent triennially to the kings of Siam.[23]

The manuscript as a whole covers a period of little less than 150 years, straddling the seventeenth and eighteenth centuries. Consistency of treatment can hardly be expected within such a period, and in fact the sources of the manuscript are known to be quite disparate. The *Undang2* of 1784 purports to have been concluded in the reign of Sultan Jamal al-'Alam Badr who ruled Acheh from A.D. 1703 to 1726, and an Achinese copy of the same year is listed in van Ronkel's catalogue.[24] Except for some inaccuracies, the *Undang2* copy of sections 1–23 of the Malacca laws is as edited by van Ronkel.[25]

[22] Winstedt (1928: 1).
[23] See further Mustaffa Tam (1960).
[24] van Ronkel (1921: 48, 307). Another text is referred to in de Hollander (1893: 253–7). See also the translation in Dulaurier (1845).
[25] van Ronkel (1919). Another edition is also listed in van Ronkel (1921: 299).

The Islamic Legal World

The text of the *Dato' Sri Paduka Tuan* of 1667[26] is interesting because the first three sections require the observance of Islamic precepts. Section 1 forbids sinning against the commands of Allah; section 2 orders observance of the daily prayers—the recalcitrant to be punished by being yoked at the neck; and section 3 says that 'land owners should pay religious tithes'. These laws are severely practical in nature and are obviously designed to remedy common abuses of the time. It is interesting to note that two of the main "pillars of Islam'—the prayers and the *zakat* and *fitrah*—should have had to be specifically legislated for in the middle of the seventeenth century.

The undated Qanun Law of the Dato' Kota Star presents quite a different picture. Its provisions relate almost solely to rules which could have had meaning for only a small section of the population. They are concerned mainly with defining the nature of sovereignty in the Malay states of the seventeenth century. It sets out (s.2) 'four immutable rules for Rulers', viz. to pardon the sins of their bondmen, to be generous, to inquire into offences, and to carry out the law. The Ruler has courteous manners, he does good works and puts down evil, and he issues orders and does not revoke them (s. 3). There are five words which are appropriate to rulers only: *kami*,[27] *kita*,[28] *patek*,[29] *derma*,[30] and *kurnia*.[31] Sections 5–7 lay down regulations on the use of various coloured clothing, flags, banners and also set out orders of ceremonial precedence. The portion of the text[32] which describes the *bunga mas* also lists similar regulations.

Finally, there are the Port Laws dated A.D. 1650. They are in thirty-seven sections, section 3 of which names the officers under whose direction the laws were compiled. The purpose of the laws was to determine the customs of the port and the duties of the harbour officials. The bulk of the sections (ss. 7–9, 15–26) list taxes on goods and provide for methods of payment. These sections are elaborate and minute in detail. Taxes were paid in kind and in gold, but section 23 forbade the use of tin as currency. Taxes were levied both upon the tonnage of the ship

---

[26] Winstedt (1928: 8–9). [27] 'We'. Also a ceremonious first person singular.
[28] Ditto.
[29] 'Your humble slave'—used by subjects when addressing their sovereign.
[30] 'Condescending kindness', 'benevolence'.
[31] Bounty or grace from a superior. [32] Winstedt (1928: 12–13).

(measured in a unit called *koyan*—ss. 18–20) and upon the type of cargo carried. There were special provisions for ships carrying tin (s. 22). The rest of the laws are taken up with two further matters: first, sections 27–9 provide for the maintenance of peace and good order. Various forms of gambling, unlawful sales, and drinking alcohol are prohibited. Wrongdoers were to be arrested by the harbour officials and punished by order of the Raja. Section 27 also provides that whoever breaks the Fast in the Fasting Month is to be punished by beating. Section 28 further provides that 'all measures and weights shall be uniform, according to the word of God in the Holy Qur'ān', but what these are is not specified. In fact, the weights and measures used were those common throughout island South-East Asia. Section 29 provides interesting information on disputes and shows some grasp of the problems of conflicts of laws. If a stranger sued a native of the state, the inquiry was held in accordance with the law of the state. The inquiry was conducted by the harbour officials *or* in the mosque, where, presumably, Islamic law was applied. If for some reason the inquiry could not be concluded in either of these forums, it went to the Ruler's adjudication 'in whose court there are many authorities on Islamic law'.

The last notable matter in the laws were the conventions set out in section 35 for the receipt of letters from local rulers and also from the European trading companies. They give some idea of the relative status of local rulers and include the revealing statement that in the case of the Governor of Malacca '[his] letters are received differently from those between Rajas, because salutes are a higher honour for an infidel of that kind'. In fact letters from the (Dutch) Governor of Malacca were received with the highest honours of all.

To sum up: the Kedah port laws regulated the collection of port dues and taxes, provided some minimal instructions for the administration of justice, and dealt with relations with foreign powers. They thus constitute an administrative code and provide an outline for foreign relations. When taken with the other sections of the Kedah manuscript, they give a picture of an efficiently organized port kingdom whose public law was of no little sophistication.

(*c*) *The Perak Laws.* The law texts of Perak present serious difficulties to the legal historian. The diversity of their origins and contents mirrors that of the components of Perak culture. As well as the *Undang2 Kerajaan* (see above, (*a*)), which professes to be the 'laws of Perak, Pahang, and Johor', a second code called the *Undang2 Minangkabau* or the *Undang2 Dua-Belas* is also known.[33] In addition, there are the Ninety-Nine Laws of Perak,[34] the manuscript of which is in the possession of descendants of their Sayid compiler.

(i) *The* Undang2 Minangkabau (*The Minangkabau Laws*)
This law is contained in Maxwell MS 44 deposited in the library of the Royal Asiatic Society; an outline translation and commentary has been published by Winstedt.[35] The text is dated 1292 A.H. (A.D. 1875) and was copied in Penang. It contains a list of Perak Sultans and Chiefs, a list of Istanbul Sultans, and a list of Perak place-names. These lists had a significance every bit as important as the rules themselves: they were intended to legitimize the text by relating it to past occupants of power. The point was, not to trace with historical accuracy a line of rulers but, by the association of their names, to give an authenticity to the laws. The text includes the apocryphal history of Perak's early rulers, although with some omissions.[36] The history begins with a rather cryptic comment that the line of Marong Mahawangsa had died out in Perak. It may well be that this is a reference to the Sailendras of Sri Vijaya, the memory of whose rule, at least in its legal aspects, long persisted in island South-East Asia. The text then relates how in 1091 A.H. (A.D. 1680) two 'white' Semang[37] living in the region of the (Sungei) Plus river found first a male infant in a bamboo, whom they named *Dato' Changkat Pelandok*,[38] and later a girl child in the river foam, whom they named *Dato' Temong*. The two foundlings later married, but, having no children, adopted one 'Tun Saban, a descendant of former chiefs'. The daughter of the latter married a Minangkabau prince who

[33] Winstedt (1953).
[34] Rigby (1908) reprinted in Hooker (1970: 57–82).
[35] Winstedt (1953).
[36] See Winstedt & Wilkinson (1934: 122–4).
[37] An aboriginal negrito group inhabiting north Perak.
[38] 'The Lord Trickster of the Hills'. This title probably has some connection with the well-known *pelandok* stories of Malaya. The 'princess of the foam' is a well-known Malay myth. See Ras (1968: 81 ff.) and the 'Hikayat Raja-Raja Pasai' in *Journal of the Royal Asiatic Society—Malayan Branch* 33 (2): 167–8.

became Sultan Ahmad Taju'd-din Shah of Perak. His nephew, *from Johore*, usurped the throne, whereupon Tun Saban, still alive, took up arms but was killed by a Minangkabau warrior, Megat Terawis, who married his daughter and succeeded him as *Bendahara* (Chief Minister). This story introduces yet another foreign element into the Malayan law texts; the Minangkabau were from west Sumatra, and their immigration into the Malay peninsula began in the middle of the seventeenth century. The linking of the royal line of descent with the non-Malay indigenous inhabitants (*orang asli*) is a typical Minangkabau device to legitimate the status of the immigrants.[39] We have already had a possible reference to the Sailendra of Sri Vijaya and the text also mentions a usurper from Johore. The latter reference is significant because by the early years of the eighteenth century the influence and power of once-proud Johore were on the wane. In both Perak and Johore the immigrant and aggressive Bugis from the Celebes were taking control of royal dynasties, a development that coincided with an increasing Minangkabau immigration. It is probable that the text reflects this political change by equating the Bugis with Johore and by attempting to reconcile their assumption of power in Perak with the arrival of the Minangkabau. The text thus represents an effort, typical of the Malay intellectual world, to reconcile opposing factions. One historical inaccuracy is worth noting: Sultan Ahmad Taju'd-din Shah was not a ruler of Perak but the Sultan of *Kedah* who conquered the northern part of Perak in A.D. 1816–18.

In the text of the laws the immigrant Minangkabau style is clearly distinguishable. Many of the well-known *perbilangan* (customary sayings) are included,[40] but even without this evidence, the Minangkabau influence is obvious. It expresses itself in two ways, the first of which is its emphasis on agricultural regulation. The more interesting portions of the text are those dealing with the definition of law. As is usual in Malay texts, the definitions occur throughout the text, but the peculiarly Minangkabau feature is their philosophical aspect. Section 33 details eight *kinds* of law: of God, of the Holy Qur'ān,

---

[39] Hence the Biduanda of Negri Sembilan.
[40] For *perbilangan* see the following: Caldecott (1918), Hale (1898). See also below on the *Undang2 Sungei Ujong*.

customary, of the king, of intelligence, of administration (*hukum pĕrentah*), and two unidentified kinds, (*hukum sakir*) and (*hukum manjapĕri*). Section 34 goes on to establish three systems (as opposed to kinds) of law, viz. of intelligence, of custom, and of the Qur'ān. If the first is conflicting, then one resorts to the second; if the second is conflicting (*bĕrsalahan*) then to the Qur'ān. Apart from being a splendid example of Minangkabau juridicial free-thinking of the infinite-regress type, these propositions clearly distinguish between Islamic and other forms of law. Thus, section 5 says, 'for offences against custom one applies its rules and examples (*adat yang bĕrtuladan yang bĕrlukis bĕrlĕmbaga*); for offences against religion Islamic law.' Section 6 discusses the 'law of reason' (*hukum 'akal*), which is defined in Islamic terms as the process of distinguishing between the conclusive (*wajib*), the impossible (*mustahil*), and the possible (*ja'iz*): this is elaborated in sections 79 and 80, the last of which distinguishes between the sources of the respective laws, i.e. practice and authoritative documents. True justice, however, is described as 'Islamic' because it is based upon *dalil, hadith, ijma'*, and *kias* (s. 89), and section 74 reserves for Islamic law questions of marriage, divorce, inheritance, debt, and slavery.

(ii) *The Ninety-nine Laws of Perak*[41]

With these laws we come to one of the most remarkably developed texts in Islamized South-East Asia. One should perhaps expect this because its author was a member of the Saiyid family and, according to Rigby's translation of the preamble, the laws were brought to the East by one Saiyid Hasan during the reign of Ahmad Taju'd-din, who, as mentioned above, was ruler of Kedah in the early years of the nineteenth century. The text locates the origin of law in Islam; the immediate source for the text is attributed to Nushirwan the Just who was overlord of 'Medayan',[42] 'Damsek',[43] 'Zabin Seradin',[44] 'Sabi',[45] 'Turan',[46] 'Udaya',[47] and 'Satin Dulin'.[48] Such a pedigree is entirely fanciful but it serves to place the rules in an ancient line originating in the Middle East, specifically in

[41] See above, n. 34 for references.
[42] Ctesiphon.
[43] Damascus.
[44] Unidentified.
[45] Sheba.
[46] Turkestan.
[47] Siam, i.e. Kedah? See Gerini (1909: 182, 184 nn., 190).
[48] Kastan Dzurian—the ancient name of Perak.

Persia, as the reference to Nushirwan of Ctesiphon attests. The author had a fair knowledge of geography and also of Islamic law; the text contains large portions of Islamic law which have been integrated with local Malay custom. The opposition of Islam and local custom characteristic of the Minangkabau texts is absent. Furthermore, there are no references to Islam and custom as separate entities or as alternatives, which are a feature of the Malacca text (see below). Instead, there is an almost bland statement of rules which, though not necessarily Islamic, assume the primacy of Islamic principle. It is assumed that the individual is a Muslim who fully carries out his religious duties; he is also an agriculturist with his own special needs[49] and a subject of the ruler, his relationship with whom the text is at pains to establish.[50] It may justly be said that these laws represent an elaborate final stage in the development of the Malay text in their sophistication and in the extent to which Islamic principle is absorbed. However, certain features of indigenous South-East Asian tradition persist. The Ninety-Nine Laws devote a considerable number of sections[51] to the regulation of witchcraft and sorcery, activities that are forbidden in the Holy Qur'ān. Section 29 illustrates the way in which the Ninety-Nine Laws manage to absorb these practices: it sets out, in simple form, a scale of payment for the *pawang* (magical practitioner), and sections 29 and 95 also specify fees.

One final point should be mentioned: the laws are set out in the form of *responsa*, i.e. question and answer. It argues for Persian influence and, in keeping with the preamble and contents, demonstrates a considerable degree of juristic sophistication.

(*d*) *The* Undang2 Sungei Ujong (*The Sungei Ujong Laws*). With these laws[52] we return to the Minangkabau texts described earlier (see above (*c*) (i)). The Sungei Ujong[53] text is known from Maxwell MSS 118 and 118(a), the former in Jawi, the latter Romanized. Both texts date from about 1904. The language of the texts is Minangkabau, but the texts lack the

[49] See ss. 13, 17, 19, 43, 46, 47, 33, 35, 69, 44, 42, 15, 66, 85, 83, 61, 9, 84, 37, 5, 38, 67, 86, 68, 6, 30, 41, 7, 54, 82, 39, 75, 31, 53, 50, 81, 57.
[50] See ss. 11, 99, 93, 78, 12, 24, 77.
[51] ss. 59, 80, 29, 60, 28, 96.
[52] Winstedt and de Josselin de Jong (1954).
[53] A district in Negri Sembilan. For its *adat* constitution see Hooker (1972: 147–58).

typical *Tambo Minangkabau*[54] and merely state rules of law—mostly on land and property matters—which assume a matrilineal form of social organization. They do, however, have the usual Minangkabau discussion on the sources of law; section 6 lists them as follows: ancient custom, created custom, inherited law, decisions of common accord, ancient lore that awaits ratification, and decisions to be reached by later deliberation. Sections 8–13 elaborate upon these divisions.[55] The systems of law recognized are set out in section 17; the first division of the law, called by Winstedt and de Josselin de Jong[56] 'constitutional law', merely says that clans consist of lineages and makes a reference to village elders. The complete details of clan and village structure are known from the *perbilangan* collected at the end of the nineteenth century.[57] Section 17 goes on to describe in detail the principle of retribution for an offence. In the many examples given, the common feature is that restitution and compensation are the operative principles. Finally, there are the so-called 'Twenty Laws', divided into the 'Twelve' and the 'Eight' (ss. 21–31). Between them they describe a number of offences of violence and the evidence which indicates that such an offence has occurred. The significance of the division is not immediately apparent, although 'Twelve' is always a suggestive number in Negri Sembilan, referring to the traditional Twelve Clans. The reference to 'Eight' is not clear, and there is certainly no functional significance in the two divisions; it might well be that the significance is to be found in Minangkabau (West Sumatra) proper.

The most striking feature of the text is the provision made for some accommodation with Islam. As is well known, the *adat Minangkabau* differs fundamentally from the provisions of Islamic law in certain important respects, notably in the regulations for inheritance and marriage. Consequently a good deal of attention is given to the problems of conflict and congruence of these laws by Minangkabau writers.[58] The

[54] The story of the origin and history of Minangkabau. For further sources see van Ronkel (1921: 47–60), Overbeck (1926: 233–59).
[55] See Winstedt & de Josselin de Jong (1954: 10–11).
[56] *Ibid.* 13.
[57] Caldecott (1918), Hale (1898). For analysis see Hooker (1972: 34–49).
[58] See, for example, the contributions in Mochtar Naim (1968).

Sungei Ujong text is no exception: section 8 says that *adat* may agree with *hukum shara* or contravene it, and in section 13 the phrase *kullu baladi qiyâmuhu bi 'âdatihi* 'each state is founded upon wonted custom [and Islamic law]' appears. Again, in section 32 law is defined in terms of custom, but in section 66 Islamic law is said to be enforced whereas *adat* is said to be that with which one acts in conformity. Questions of custom are decided by unanimity, but Islamic law demands an inquiry into the strengths and weaknesses of the opposing arguments. In the same section, however, custom is said to be based upon law and law to be based upon the Holy Qur'ān. 'Law is founded upon diamonds, custom on stone, religious law on proofs, customary procedure on agreement.' The mythical originators of the *adat*, the *Dato' Katumanggungan*, and the *Dato' Parapateh Sabatang* are also said in section 87 to follow the teachings of the Holy Qur'ān, for as Allah Most High said, *Innî jâ' ilun fî 'l- ordi khalîfatan* 'verily I made man King upon earth to be My deputy'.

(*e*) *The Malacca Laws.* Finally we come to the Malacca laws, the original of all the island South-East Asia texts and the most important because upon their form were based the ideas which later flowered in the texts just described.

The Malacca laws fall into two parts: the Maritime Code[59] and the general Malacca Code.[60] They may be dated respectively A.D. 1488 and 1446–56,[61] i.e. the height of Malacca's glory. The origin or the inspiration of texts such as these is always difficult to identify, but we may hazard three guesses: first, remembered memories of the great Javanese texts. One must not forget that *Paramesvara* (Megat Iskander Shah), the founder of the Malacca dynasty, was traditionally said to be a refugee from Java. Further, if the dating of the texts is accurate, the fourth ruler of Malacca, Raja Kasim (Sultan Muzaffar Shah), A.D. 1446–59, was himself a Tamil Muslim to whom, and to whose court, the idea of a written set of laws would be not only natural but necessary. Second, the same Sultan Muzaffar saw the flowering of Malacca as a commercial power in the Straits, which made it necessary to organize trade matters and to state the nature of his sovereignty for political purposes. The

---

[59] Winstedt & de Josselin de Jong (1956).
[60] Kempe & Winstedt (1952).
[61] Winstedt (1953a). Breda MS. 6619 gives A.D. 1656 as the date of the Maritime laws.

Sejarah Melayu itself provides abundant evidence of the Malacca rulers' attempts to do just this. Finally, the time of the text was also the time in which Islam's grip on island South-East Asia began to obtain its firmest hold. In brief, the motivating forces were past example (probably from Java and possibly Sri Vijaya), commercial and political expediency, and, finally, the impulse of the Islamic ethic. In fact, the Maritime laws are attributed to the Sultan Mahmud Shah himself (A.D. 1488–1511).

The Martitime laws bear out the commercial motive to a considerable extent. The manuscripts collated for Winstedt and de Josselin de Jong's translation have been described elsewhere,[62] and, if nothing else, they attest to the multiplicity of versions and the wide circulation which the text had in island South-East Asia. Manuscripts refer to Makassar, Patani, Pagar Ruyong, Riau, as well as to all the Malay States. The text opens with the statement that the laws were given by Sultan Mahmud Shah as a result of a request by sea-captains who desired a code of regulations.[63] The twenty-four sections of the code proper are mainly concerned with discipline at sea and ordering the practical affairs of interest to the shipping trade. Section 1 describes the officers of a ship and details their duties and functions. The text deals with the following matters:

(i) Discipline aboard ship: rules for discipline are set out in sections 1, 6, 7, 14, 19. The first provides for the flogging of sailors who resist lawful commands. Section 6 provides for the punishment of those persons who use disrespectful language to the captain. Section 7 details the four crimes punishable by death on board ship. These are: disloyalty to the captain; conspiracy to kill the captain, officers, or supercargo; wearing a weapon while all other members of the crew are unarmed; and 'bad conduct'. Section 14 prohibits the movement of sailors to certain parts of the ship (e.g. the cabins) and provides for flogging. Finally, section 19, while not prohibiting fighting on board, makes it punishable if it results in damage to the ship or if it occurs in the stern or near the officers' quarters.

(ii) Fornication aboard ship. The punishment for adultery is death, but if the offenders are unmarried the punishment is

[62] Winstedt & de Josselin de Jong (1956: 22–4).
[63] Section 22 gives their names and the titles subsequently awarded to them.

flogging (100 lashes) and the offenders are obliged to marry (presumably if they were still able!).

(iii) Trading. The captain had the major trading rights. Under section 20 he alone was permitted to trade on his own account for the first four days in a foreign port, and only after that could the officers, supercargo, and then the crew, trade. No member of the crew might offer a higher price for goods than the price established by the captain. In the case of found goods the captain took a share (s. 3), and he was also entitled to a captured runaway slave or to a share in the slave's price (s. 4).

(iv) The conduct of the ship. The rights and duties of the navigator are set out in detail in section 9. Sections 11 and 12 deal respectively with the loss of cargo owing to storm and to collision, the latter providing for a two-thirds indemnity. The duty of the watchmen is set out in section 15. If the ship is late in sailing through the fault of the captain he is responsible for financial loss.

(v) Supercargo. A supercargo travelled on condition that he purchased a division of the hold, or loaned the captain money, or contracted to pay the captain up to 2–30 per cent of his takings (s. 10). If he wished to go ashore, he forfeited the sum laid out, although if he left for a good reason, a proportion or the whole of the sum might be returned to him.

These are the main provisions of the Maritime laws; they reflect the needs of a fairly sophisticated trading community. There were even provisions for borrowing and for interest rates (10 per cent) which, though rudimentary, were developed much further in the later Kedah laws. References to Islam are slight; the captain is described as being 'as it were, a Caliph' on board his own ship, and the navigator is enjoined 'to pray to Allah and His Prophet, for he is as an *Imam* on board a ship'. The paucity of Islamic reference is understandable in the light of the purpose of the text[64]—to regulate the conduct of trading at sea.

These comments do not apply to the general Malacca laws. The general laws are known from a large number of texts which have been collated by Dutch and English scholars. We have not

---

[64] There is also a small appendix which, apart from repeating provisions already made, sets out (s. 4) bonus shares for successful trips.

The Islamic Legal World 65

only van Ronkel's edition[65] of the Malacca laws but also Kempe and Winstedt's edition of both the Pahang law[66] and Raffles MS 33:[67] it is this complex which we take as our text for present purposes. The texts in question do not confine themselves to Malacca alone. Folio 59 of Raffles MS 33 professes to contain the laws of Johore[68] and folios 62–64 give the laws of slavery applicable to Selangor.[69] The latter are very close to the provisions of section 15 of the *Undang2 Kerajaan* (see above). Further, folio 59 of Raffles MS 33 contains much the same material as sections 22, 68–70, and 76 of the *Undang2 Kerajaan*. A full description of the Malacca manuscripts, with translation and commentary has recently been published and the reader is referred to that volume for a full account.[70]

The texts deal with the by now familiar wide range of subject-matter which we may summarize as follows:

(i) Debts and Bondsmen: The contracting of a debt by a man who later dies leaves his widow liable for a third only. A debt contracted without the knowledge of wife and children absolves them from liability (Raffles s. 6; van Ronkel, s. 26). Bondsmen and bondswomen are under the 'same customary law as slaves' (*adat-nya sĕpĕrti hamba*), except that striking or offending against a debtor's wife or children cancels the debt (Raffles, s. 12). If a slave or bondsman offends against a free man, his master is responsible to the extent of the slave's value (Raffles, s. 13). If a slave or bondsman died while under the order of another, that person had to pay the owner his value. The killing of a slave was an offence against the *Raja* and the drawing of blood from a slave offended against officialdom (*orang bĕkĕrja*) (Raffles, s. 15). Debts were a first charge on a deceased estate, only after their settlement was the residue divided, with male and female descendants taking equal shares (*sama bagi laki-laki ada ia atau pĕrĕmpuan*). Debts were similarly divided (Raffles, ss. 22, 28). So far as borrowing was concerned, one might not borrow that which was useless or impermanent. The borrower was liable for damage. (This part of Raffles s. 28 is the same as section 32 of

[65] van Ronkel (1919).   [66] Kempe & Winstedt (1948).
[67] Kempe & Winstedt (1952). See also W. E. Maxwell (1884: 175 ff.) and Newbold (1839: (ii) 231 ff.).
[68] See also Logan (1855).   [69] See Kempe & Winstedt (1952: 18–19).
[70] See Liaw (1976).

the *Undang2 Kerajaan*). Borrowing of capital was governed by customary law, and if the sum borrowed was to be used for trading for profit then there could be no agreement to repay in a term of months and years (Raffles, s. 10).[71] The same section 10 also deals with credit transactions. Purchasers might pay deposits but if a purchaser broke his agreement he forfeited double his deposit. In the case of credit sales the creditor had to allow full time for payment. Traders had to be sane and adult (Raffles, s. 45; see also ss. 47–8).

(ii) Crimes: Adultery was defined as a crime, and where it occurred between two free persons the penalty was death (Raffles, s. 18). Section 19 provides that the killing of a bondsman results in the killer himself becoming a bondsman of the *Raja*. Killing a rival in love (*madu*) was punishable by death, but the accused could redeem his life by payment. Ordeals were prescribed; section 25 describes an ordeal by diving. It also describes an interesting ordeal called 'dicing'. Two letters are written and folded to look identical but one invoked the Prophet and the other Iblis. The man who took the former won. This passage may be compared with section 14 of van Ronkel and section 91 of the *Undang2 Kerajaan*.

(iii) Marriage and Divorce: These sections contain some of the most interesting in the whole laws. Section 20 lays it down that when a marriage takes place the guardians (*wali*) should inquire as to the separate property of the man and woman so that on divorce it may be returned to the owner, while property acquired during coverture is divided equally. This is the well-known *pencharian* rule that is still a feature of Malay *adat*. Sections 40–3 of folio 43 of Raffles MS. 33 deal respectively with the qualifications and appointment of a *wali*, with witnesses,[72] with the physical disabilities that render a marriage void, with divorce, and with the religious qualifications of a Muslim bride. All these sections are based fairly closely on the *Shāfiʿī* law. However, section 21 lays it down that if a husband guiltless of an offence under religious *and* customary law (*adat*) refuses his wife a divorce, she can leave him in the clothes she wears but must return the marriage payment (*isi kahwin*) or otherwise pay for

---

[71] See *contra* s. 8 of the Maritime Laws.
[72] Sections 23–4 of Raffles MS. 33, folio 9 also detail Muslim qualifications and are similar in terms to s. 63 of the *Undang2 Kerajaan*.

the divorce (*měněbus talak sa-tahil sa-paha*). If she desires a divorce because she cannot endure her husband's behaviour, but not because of an offence under Islamic law (*tě tapi bělum lagi harus bercherai kapada hukum shara*), then she may get a divorce in accordance with custom by returning half the marriage payment. On the distribution of property in these cases, the man takes that acquired during coverture, but if the man wishes to divorce his wife without fault then he takes a one-third share only of the property jointly acquired.[73] Marriage payments not paid at the time of marriage must be paid at divorce, but if there is issue the child or children may be surrendered instead (*anak itu-lah akan isi kahwin-nya*).

(iv) Property: Until recently the clearest and most generally available exposition of the proprietary rights contained in the Malacca laws was Newbold's account first published in 1839.[74] Sections 17–21 deal with the ownership of fruit-trees, mortgages, the classification of land (i.e. occupied (*tanah hidup*) and unoccupied (*tanah mati*)), and the rent of land. Special provisions exist for damage to land (s. 23) and for the giving of land under pledge (s. 25) so that the donee might bring it under cultivation; this transaction was known as *tanah kuwasan* and the donor's share was limited to one-tenth of the produce. Specific regulations for the methods of land use were further set out in ss. 58, 63–5, 71, 78.

(v) Classification of law: This is dealt with in section 41, which distinguishes three types of law, (1) the *Sharī'a*, (2) *Akal* or 'reason',[75] and (3) *Adat* or local custom. As sources to which one may apply they are ranked in the order (1) to (3), and the opening verse of section 41 says, 'Whenever possible the *Sharī'a* must be adhered to in preference to the other two.'

The Islamic element is clear in the Malacca laws, but equally clear is the retention of indigenous features in all portions of the law. Religion and custom are often mentioned together in the same section. Folios 61–62 of Raffles MS. 33 consist of a short

[73] It is interesting to note that the term *chakara* is used for *harta sapencharian*. The former is in fact a Bugis term.
[74] Newbold (1839: (ii) 231 ff.). See also W. E. Maxwell (1884: 175 ff.) for a comparative survey of Malacca, Perak, and Minangkabau laws on property. But see now Liaw (1976: 111 ff.).
[75] Probably equivalent to the Arabic *qiyās*.

chapter addressed to Allah and His Prophet asking pardon because many of the laws violate Islamic law. The folio pleads, however, that it makes for peace to record custom, traditional from the time of Sultan Mahmud. In other words, the opposition is recognized but is justified on practical grounds; the Malacca law does not, as do later laws (especially Minangkabau), attempt a reconciliation. Islam was accepted for what it was—an ethical system which conflicted in some respects with established tradition. This is a reflection of the relatively non-legalistic character of Islam in the sixteenth and seventeenth centuries. It is only with the later texts, and with eighteenth- and nineteenth-century interpolations, that increasing Islamic legalism forced on the text-writers the various responses that have been described.

III   *THE* LUWARAN *AND THE SULU CODES*

These two codes of law originated in the Magindanao and Sulu areas of the southern Philippines. They were both inspired by Islam and, perhaps uniquely in South-East Asia, attempted to breathe life into a form of government planned on the same lines as that of the Arabian Caliphates of the seventeenth and eighteenth centuries. The extent to which they were successful can be judged from what follows.

(a) *The* Luwaran *of Magindanao.* The term *Luwaran* means 'selection', and the code referred to by this name is a selection of laws taken from a number of Arabic books[76] and combined with local practice. In common with other South-East Asian texts the *Luwaran* is eclectic as to sources and composite in its nature. The original manuscript (probably early eighteenth century), described by Saleeby,[77] is written (in Arabic script) in the language of Mindanao with Arabic marginal quotations. The latter are copied separately and are also translated. A table indicating the Arabic quotation which corresponds to each article of the *Luwaran* is attached to the introduction to the translation.[78]

The *Luwaran* begins with an invocation to Allah; eighty-five

[76] Chiefly from the *Minhaj-l-Arifeen.*
[77] Saleeby (1905: 64 ff.).
[78] See ibid. 81 ff.

The Islamic Legal World 69

articles follow, plus an appendix specifying the compensation payable for various types of wound.[79] The articles deal with a wide variety of subjects, including property, relations between the sexes (both illicit and legitimate), gifts, oaths, slavery, debt, salvage, partnership, and injury caused by accident. None of these provisions discloses any obvious Islamic influence; the latter is apparent only in sections 80–5 on inheritance, where some attempt is made to follow the Islamic system although local modifications are still apparent. The Islamic element is entirely confined to the marginal quotations[80] which appear alongside the sections of the *Luwaran*. The function of the quotations is to validate the *Luwaran* provisions. In many cases the link between the Arabic quotation and *Luwaran* provision is clear; e.g. section 8 of the *Luwaran* providing for the payment of a fine for entering the house of another without consent is backed up by quotation no. 12 which reads, 'God said, "To you believers I say, you shall not enter the houses of others without their permission."' Again, quotations nos. 100–8, corresponding to sections 80–5, refer to the rules of the Qur'ān on inheritance. On the other hand, the source of many of the quotations is difficult to ascertain and in some cases their relevance to sections of the *Luwaran* is not clear.

The *Luwaran* is almost certainly unique in the Islamized South-East Asian texts in setting out indigenous and (supposedly) Arabic provisions in parallel. It illustrates a clear separation of the local from the imported element. Further, Islam as such is only occasionally represented in the Arabic quotations. It seems that although the function of the quotation was to validate the local law, the validation was *culture* orientated rather than strictly religious in origin. The homeland of Islam was Arabia, and this fact seems to have reinforced the prestige of things Arabic rather than making Islamic provisions more obvious in the *Luwaran*.

(*b*) *The Sulu Codes*. A number of Sulu codes are known to have been written and promulgated. Perhaps the two most readily available and quite typical texts are those of 1877 and 1902[81]

---

[79] The incidence of physical violence seems to have been high amongst the Muslims of Mindanao and Sulu, and recent ethnography suggests that it remains so. See Kiefer (1972).
[80] Translated and listed in Saleeby (1905: 82 ff.).   [81] Ibid. 89 and 94.

which have two characteristics more or less peculiar to Islamized South-East Asia. First, there is no attempt at defining the nature of law or of laying down substantive principles except in terms of a fines list. The codes of 1877 and 1902 are little more than fines lists (for theft, sexual offences, assault, etc.) and differ only in the severity of penalty imposed. In fact, they bear a striking resemblance to the Dayak fines lists drawn up in the latter part of the nineteenth century by British colonial officers in Sarawak.[82] Second, the purpose of the codes, as expressed in penalties, is clearly to channel resources to the Sultan and high officers (*Datu*). The codes are thus overtly political documents and have a fiscal function. Their acceptance or rejection was thus largely a matter of the support a code could muster from persons paying and collecting the fines. Apart from a preamble asking the blessing of God, neither code has any overt connection with Islam.

The problem which the Sulu codes raise is the extent to which island South-East Asian law texts regard penalty as the basis of law. An important corollary is the extent to which Islam reinforced this attitude. All the texts contain detailed provisions for fine and punishment relating to offences considered serious in Sulu society. There is a notable lack of rules relating to a full description of land matters, inheritance, and so on. Rules on these matters were known in other ways, for example, through local *adats*, but the important thing is that these codes, unlike most other texts produced by a Muslim people, ignore them completely. The definition of *written* law is limited to actions which constitute severe disturbances (which we should call criminal) of the social order. There is also a conspicuous absence of Islamic principle, although the peoples of Sulu were and are Muslim. We thus have a separation of spheres—the legal and the religious—to a degree that is quite remarkable in the Muslim lands. Even in the *Luwaran* the presence of a validating link is specifically indicated. The legal *raison d'être* of the Sulu codes, then, is as different from that of, say, the Malacca laws, as it could possibly be. The definition of law in the Sulu codes was such that a recourse to Islamic principle was neither necessary nor desirable.

---

[82] See Richards (1963) (1964).

IV SUMMARY

Any attempt to summarize the characteristic features of the texts just described is probably a hazardous and speculative exercise, but such an attempt is necessary, if only to show the complexity of the material. To this end we may look at the texts in terms of two oppositions.

(a) *The reality and the theory of law.* In the texts in general there is a consistent opposition between the practical and the theoretical; at its most simple one can divide the contents of the text into those which deal with practical matters and those which are speculative in nature. It is tempting to call this division a distinction between 'rules' and 'principles' except that the balance between the two in many texts is either absent or distorted. For example, while the Sulu code is heavily rule-oriented the Minangkabau texts carry speculative principle-building to quite extreme lengths. But even in a text such as the Malacca text, in which there is a reasonably even division of content, the two parts bear no relation to each other. 'Rules' are not necessarily derived from 'principle', and it makes little sense to talk in such terms. One is forced to accept that texts are internally inconsistent, but, by opposing rule and principle, one can see how the inconsistency arises.

(b) *The definition of the individual.* All texts define the individual in absolute terms ('sovereign', 'officers of the sovereign', 'free men', 'slaves') which prescribe relevant rights and obligations. A person's freedom of action is thus limited by an ascribed status. Although all texts proceed on this principle, the definition of status is, however, by no means the same throughout the texts. In some the Islamic definition is said to be preferable to the local definition. More commonly, both sorts of definition appear in the same text, thus demonstrating yet another type of internal inconsistency. A definition in terms of status is nothing if not exclusive, as Sir Henry Maine long ago pointed out, so that the later texts pay increasing attention to conflicts between Islam and local tradition. This was due in part to an increasing legalism in the practice of Islam, and in part to a search for an absolute source of law. The result was an Islamized written text which was not Islamic in its provisions but which, in its ethic and purpose, was intended to promote the well-being of the world of Islam (see further Chapter 4).

In island South-East Asia, the exception to all these comments has been Java and the Javanese world. As we saw in discussing the laws of Java in the last chapter, the maintenance of a certain conception of status was essential to the legal thought of the medieval period. The idea of conciliation or compromise was essential, and the conciliatory procedures embodied in the later *jayasong*[83] illustrate a process of dispute settlement in which the state was involved only minimally. The attempt to find a peaceful solution was one of the most important of the Javanese official's tasks, a function which is both pre- and post-Islamic. The introduction of Islam did not upset the highly organized structure of the Javanese state. In the realm of legal ideas, Islamic teaching placed the king in a less august position than formerly—as God's representative (*kalipatullah*) rather than, as in the Hindu-Javanese view, a manifestation of God (generally *Wisnu*). Even this title was not assumed until relatively late in the history of Mataram, being borne by Amangkurat IV (1719-24) of Jogjakarta.[84] In the traditional histories of Java, the *Babab Tanah Djawi* (*c.* 1613-45) and the *Babab Mataram* (*c.* 1822-55), the place of the Muslim sages in the fall of Madjapahit and the rise of Muslim Mataram is emphasized.[85] But none of this made any essential change in the practice or theory of rule or of law in Muslim Java. The strength, complexity, and brilliance of Javanese legal ideas persisted, and the most that Islam achieved was the sporadic observance of its laws at local level.

[83] See Hoadley (1971).
[84] See Lekkerkerker (1938: 339).
[85] Moertono (1963: 30 ff.).

CHAPTER 3

The Chinese Legal World: The Vietnamese Texts

THIS CHAPTER is concerned with the legacy of classical Chinese legal thought in South-East Asia; we exclude from consideration the substantive body of 'Chinese law and custom' which grew up under colonial aegis in the nineteenth century. The latter really represents an adaptation of local Chinese custom, or what was taken to be be such, to European laws (see below Chapters 5 and 6) and bears little or no resemblance to the written laws of China. In South-East Asia the impact of classical Chinese law was almost wholly confined to what is now Vietnam, and the law itself was but one aspect of the cultural influence exerted by China from the Han period onwards. This influence was apparent from the foundation of the first recognizably 'Vietnamese' state in A.D. 939, which, after a short Chinese interregnum, developed over the succeeding three hundred years or so into a state modelled upon the Chinese example. The sinicization of Vietnamese institutions is a fact of history, admired on all sides, although the precise significance of individual examples is still open to dispute.[1] So far as law is concerned, it is obvious that the Vietnamese texts are Chinese in origin, conception, and elaboration. Having said this, it must also be said that the *general* Vietnamese law cannot have 'been Chinese' simply because the texts do not deal with large areas of private law (e.g. land and property matters).[2] The texts, therefore, represent only one aspect of law, but in this field (i.e. primarily in definition and legal theory) the Chinese connection is plain. Even in the more mundane fields of land distribution, local administration, and financial reform, the Chinese derivation of regulations is apparent.[3] This should not, however, be overstressed; in the reign of Lê Thánh-tông (1460–

[1] See, for example, the contributions in Wickberg (1969).
[2] See Chapter 4 for the significance of this fact in relation to cultural borrowing.
[3] See, for example, Schreiner (1900: (i) 94 ff.). For a full description see Young (1976).

97), a good number of local regulations were promulgated relating to public order, religious reform, agricultural development, and land taxation. It was in this period also that the principle that rights of occupation were dependent upon cultivation were first embodied in a written decree.[4] The greatest achievement of the period, however, was the promulgation of the first Vietnamese law texts, the *Hông Đứ'c* Code, in A.D. 1483.

I THE HÔNG ĐÚ'C CODE

The promulgation of a complex code such as this did not of itself establish a completely new legal system. The Code relied upon a system of legal administration that had been formulated by the earlier Lê rulers. It presupposed a fairly sophisticated bureaucratic system administered by a skilled cadre of officials. An important element of the bureaucracy was the 'Sovereign Council' which had both administrative and judicial functions; subject to the royal prerogative, it controlled provincial administration.[5]

The Code began with a set of general provisions and definitions, as did the Chinese codes of this and later eras. It commenced with a fivefold division of punishment—the so-called 'Five Penalties'. These are described in Art. 1 as whippings of varying degrees of severity; involuntary servitude such as forced labour; exile, often combined with beating or chaining; death by decapitation; and finally, strangulation or 'slow death' (literally cutting apart the person being punished).[6] The influence of the *T'ang* Code is clear in this arrangement.[7]

Article 2 of the Code ranked crime in ten classes in a descending order. The first, rebellion or conspiracy to rebellion, was specifically described as an offence against the ruler and thus against the ethic of the state itself. The position of the Emperor, who was regarded as combining in himself a representation of the people with his links to imperial ancestors,

---
[4] Ibid. 98 ff. For an outline of the political history of the period see Buttinger (1958: 129–97, especially at n. 24), Coedès (1962: 204–8).
[5] See Taboulet (1955: 55), Schreiner (1900: (i) 100 ff.), Vu Van Hien (1940).
[6] See Deloustal (1909: 91–6).
[7] It is probable that the *T'ang* principles were not known in their original form but in either the *Ta Ming Lü* or *Ming* Code of A.D. 1373–4 or the definitive Ming versions of 1389 and later.

The Chinese Legal World 75

made this a personal crime and an offence against the state. The definition of the state in terms of the Emperor's person had a close parallel with Chinese thought of the time. The second crime, grand rebellion or disloyalty, involved the destruction or attempted destruction of the royal tombs of the sovereign's ancestors. The penalty was the death of the offender and of his wife or children. The penalties under the Chinese codes, from which this is clearly copied, were rather more severe in that they extended to a wider range of relatives. The third crime was treason, which is defined as turning against one's country and aiding rebellion. The fourth was rebellion against one's family, and a scale of penalties was laid down for striking or plotting the death of patrilineal and agnatic relatives. This crime was linked to the fifth, the killing of members of one's own family and the mutilation of females. The penalty was death, as it was also in the Chinese codes. The crime was known as 'absence of reason', which was not a defence to criminal liability but a definition of depravity. The sixth class was a continuation of the first two, and stated penalties for failing to show a proper degree of respect to the Ruler; it included such things as using incorrect language, failing to respond respectfully to a royal envoy, and theft from royal property. In addition, the offences listed under this crime included failure in one's official duties.[8] The seventh class, offences against filial piety, was more or less a continuation of the fourth and fifth crimes, and the Code provided penalties for accusations against or injury to senior relatives including the parents and grandparents of one's spouse. It laid down the degrees of mourning which had to be observed on the death of relatives of a senior generation and forbade remarriage during that period. The eighth crime, conspiring to sell or murder one's parents and falsely accusing one's spouse, continued the protection of the family on Confucian lines, as did a part of the ninth class which prohibited rejoicing on learning of a spouse's death and re-marriage within the mourning period. The ninth class also prohibited the killing or wounding of one's superior such as a public officer, army officer or teacher. Finally, incest within a series of stated degrees was forbidden on pain of death.

Articles 3 and 4 of the Code established certain categories of

[8] Further elaborated in Arts. 110–11 and 115.

persons as privileged. They included relatives of the sovereign and those in his immediate service, certain officers of the state, and persons whose virtue and wisdom had been officially recognized. These persons could be punished only by the sovereign and complaints against them had to be made in special form to the sovereign. The imposition of sanctions was at the sovereign's discretion. This scheme was also characteristic of the Chinese codes, although a greater discretion was allowed as far as punishment was concerned in the *Hông Đú'c* than in the later *Ming* and *Ch'ing* codes.

Matters of crime or offences against public order were dealt with in more detail in Book IV of the Code. The emphasis in Book IV was not on the structure and ethics of the state system so much as on punishment for crime (in the Western sense) *simpliciter*, although the later sections (arts. 410–37) repeated the earlier summary in some detail. In addition it was provided that the property of a culprit and his accessories over and above that necessary to make restitution was forfeit (art. 425). Recidivism was punished by death (art. 428). Theft of the property of a foreign ambassador was specifically punished in art. 437 and matters of a general criminal character were also dealt with in detail. They included punishment for extortion, for which the penalty was the same as theft (art. 435), and unlawful entry (art. 449). It is notable that in the latter case a householder might kill an intruder immediately although killing after subduing the intruder was an offence (art. 449); this was a feature of many other South-East Asian texts as well as of the Chinese codes. Disorderly conduct, which was widely defined, was punished in a variety of ways (arts. 464–98). It is interesting that punishment could be administered at village level by the authority of the village elders (*lý tru'ở'ng*).

The other books of the Code dealt with administration, ritual, and war. In each case the Chinese model was followed closely. It is in matters of family law, defined as marriage, divorce, inheritance, succession, and so on, that markedly unique features appear in the Vietnamese text. The general principles of family law were laid down in Arts. 313–73 of the Code. In addition to the Code there was the *Hông Đú'c Thiênnam du' ha tập*, a miscellaneous collection, in 100 volumes,[9]

[9] Of which only six survive.

The Chinese Legal World 77

containing matter on the mandarinate and on literature, with a small section of about fifty leaves on law.

The latter provided detailed regulations on marriage for all classes of society. The Code did not define the elements of marriage apart from attributing a religious significance to it (art. 313);[10] the *Thiên-nam du' ha tập* set out the details of marriage payments, receipts for such payments, the ritual ceremonies necessary, the payments due to the intermediary or go-between, the marriage contract, and so on. The specific rules were local and owed little if anything to Chinese concepts. Similarly, divorce and repudiation were regulated outside the Code; divorce was recognized on a number of grounds, including jealousy, failure to produce children, contagious sickness (e.g. leprosy), wife's adultery, lack of respect for the parents of either spouse, quarrelling, and theft. Divorce was not permitted where a wife had undertaken three years' mourning for the deceased parents of her husband, or where a couple had been poor when they had married and then become wealthy. It was also forbidden to divorce a wife who would not have a paternal home to go to because her parents were dead. The rules on divorce were contained in a codification promulgated in 1485 during Lê Thánh-tông's reign. The main effect of this codification, in addition to stating grounds, was to formalize the process. Divorces had to be in writing (art. 62), and each party kept a copy of the letter, signed or marked by both parties, stating the fact of divorce. Divorces carried out by any other means after 1485 were not recognized.[11]

The Code, whilst leaving a large part of family law to be regulated by other means, did contain a number of articles (373–8) on inheritance and distribution. The peculiarly Vietnamese provision in this area was that daughters as well as sons could inherit and act as trustees of ancestral cult moneys. Further, a child who had been discriminated against in inheritance could apply to the local mandarinate in a formal process to request redistribution.

This brief description of the *Hông Đú'c* Code and the fact that additional texts were used alongside the Code gives a picture of a legal culture that is in some ways a reflection of the Chinese

[10] See Deloustal (1909: 364 ff., 480 ff.).
[11] Ibid. 478–9.

model and in others a quite distinct creation. In the view of the nature and function of law to which it gave rise it is Chinese, but in the descriptive reality of important sections of the civil law the Code is wholly indigenous. If we examine the assimilation of the Chinese and Vietnamese legal models some interesting points arise. The use of the Chinese formal structure by the Lê rulers is in a pattern of borrowing typical of South-East Asian texts. But the borrowing is no slavish adherence; the *Hông Đú'c* Code is a simpler and less complete version of the Chinese model. Its closest parallels are in the general provisions which define law in terms of sovereignty and equate the ruler, the state, and ethical principle. This amounts to something more than the borrowing of institutional forms; it was a definition of sovereignty in terms of Confucian principle—notably in the idea of Righteousness. It supplied an ideal *form* for Vietnamese legal structure.[12] If we turn to the peculiarly Vietnamese provisions of the Code, we find strong contrasts with the *T'ang* codes. Daughters could inherit and serve as trustees of ancestral cult funds. Secondary wives, even those who had borne no children, could claim from their deceased husbands' estate; husbands who deserted their wives for five months (or one year if there were children) lost all conjugal rights. These features of the Code are unique in the East Asian laws. Much ink has been spilled in attempting to account for these features of the *Hông Đú'c*; views range from theories about matriarchal influence, to theories of politically motivated concessions to the female sex for the contribution it made in the wars against China of A.D. 1406–27.[13] Without going into the merits or demerits of these theories, it is as well to point out that there may be a rather more mundane explanation. The facts of agricultural life in South-East Asia were and are such that women's rights to property and to control over marital property are an essential part of any general marriage law. The outstanding example, well known to the colonial French administration, is the widow's right to control family property,[14] which was a part of general Vietnamese law. Similarly, the distribution of property jointly

---

[12] See Whitmore (1969: 5–6) for a similar argument on the adaptation of Chinese government structure in fifteenth-century Vietnam.
[13] See Woodside (1971: 45–6). See also Lam (1969) for the later fifteenth century.
[14] See Hooker (1975: 235–39).

acquired during coverture was based upon recognized female shares, a feature common to all South-East Asian laws. It is in this sphere that one must look for explanations of the Code provisions.

Much of the difficulty in interpreting the Hông Đứ'c arises from two factors: the undoubtedly Chinese *form* of the text and the obvious adoption of the Confucian ethic, if only for a limited purpose.[15] Even if taken at face value, these two factors do not provide a sufficient explanation for all the provisions of the Code. The search for 'Chinese', 'Vietnamese', or 'Sino-Vietnamese' features is unhelpful because the issue is being put the wrong way. The mistake lies in expecting consistency throughout the Hông Đứ'c despite the fact that consistency is notably absent. Further, it is too often forgotten that the provisions of the Code were constantly supplemented by other regulations and by the issue of royal decrees. Instead of looking for similarities of source, we should look at the function of the Hông Đứ'c; the Chinese example is a model, but its function is to define law in terms of sovereignty. This means that the source of law is absolute, i.e. in the state; however, the regulation of activities which do not affect a definition in these terms can remain a matter for local administration. In China itself the activities of local or specialized administrations in this sense are well known[16] but none of them derogated from the basic function of the written text. In Vietnam, however, if only because of the small size of the population involved and its relative homogeneity from a legal point of view, the Hông Đứ'c had perforce to demonstrate some descriptive validity, i.e. to reflect the living legal practice of the mass of the population. Although local machinery existed, it was by no means sophisticated enough both to describe (and uphold) a national sovereignty and, at the same time, to carry out local administration. The mandarinate was directed to apply the Code,[17] but even the most minimal application required some relation with reality, and its function, so far as was possible in the Chinese form, was to apply real elements of indigenous law. That indigenous law is only partially described in the Code, and is

[15] See McAleavy (1958) on điền and (1958a) on hu'o'ng-hòa.
[16] See S. van der Sprenkel (1966).
[17] See Pompei (1940), Tran-Chanh-Thanh (1943).

80   Status

mostly contained in extra-Code forms, is a reflection on the Chinese model rather than on the internal consistency of the *Hông Đú'c* itself. An over-emphasis upon internal consistency is almost certainly fatal to an assessment of the Code, one should pursue an inquiry in the terms outlined above, and it should be borne in mind that the text had to reflect Vietnamese legal reality.

II THE *GIA-LONG* OR *THE HOÀNG VIET* (IMPERIAL VIETNAMESE) CODE

After the bloody dynastic struggles of the seventeenth and eighteenth centuries, Vietnam emerged as a unified state under the Nguyễn dynasty, the founder of which, Nguyễn Phúc Ánh, adopted the name of Gia-Long on his accession in June 1802. The code which bears this name was promulgated in 1812; its purpose, clearly stated in the preface, was to regulate the affairs of a people grown 'corrupt and malicious' for whom the laws of the Lê, in particular the *Hông Đú'c*, had become insufficient. The new law was to be received by administrative functionaries as a clear and precise rule. The Code was to be consonant with the *Hông Đú'c* only in so far as the latter was a faithful reflection of the laws of the *T'ang* and the later *Ch'ing* (i.e. the *Ta Ch'ing Lü Li*).[18] In other words, there was a clearly-expressed conscious recourse to the Chinese codes, and this is borne out by the arrangement of the *Hoàng Việt*.

The Code consists of twenty-two books organized in nine major divisions: Tables of Laws, Laws Concerning Definition, Administration, Civil Law, Rites, Military, Crime, Public Works, and Rules for the Disposition of Cases by Analogy. This arrangement follows closely though not exactly the divisions of the *Ch'ing* laws,[19] and the *Gia-Long* Code was, as stated above, a conscious effort at imitation. Not surprisingly, the central position of the sovereign is described in almost identical terms in the codes of *Gia-Long* and the *Ch'ing*. The second article in both codes is concerned with defining offences against the ruler whose position, as in the *Hông Đú'c*, both defines a state sovereignty and validates the propriety of the social order. The penalties set out in Art. 1 of each code are identical, as is the definition of privileged classes in Art. 3. In the major divisions

[18] See Philastre (1876: (i) 8–11).   [19] See Bodde & Morris (1968: 52–75).

The Chinese Legal World

of Rites, Military, and Public Works there was little or no change—in keeping with the aim of Gia-Long to legitimize the state organization on the Chinese model. The same applied in respect of the 'great crimes', rebellion and treason.

There are, however, some surprising provisions. In marriage and divorce the provisions of the *Gia-Long* Code parallel very closely those of the *Ta Ch'ing Lü Li*. Thus Art. 94 of the *Gia-Long* Code made detailed regulations for contracts of marriage, specifying the names, ages, and physical condition of the parties. This is a direct translation of Arts. 101-5 of the *Ta Ch'ing Lü Li*.[20] Article 94 also provided that a prior promise to marry or pre-marital sexual intercourse nullified any contract to marriage, a provision which appears in the *Ch'ing* Code (art. ci). Breach of contract resulted in criminal sanctions in both the Vietnamese and the Chinese codes. Grounds for divorce remained substantially similar to these in the *Hông Đú'c* although they were elaborated more fully in memorials attached to the *Gia-Long* Code and modelled directly on the *Ta Ch'ing Lü Li* (arts. 94-109). Divorce by mutual consent remained.

As already mentioned, the first forty-six articles provide a set of definitions and classifications of crime and punishment copied directly from the *Ch'ing* Code. These include the five penalties, the ten crimes, the privileged classes, and the relationship between class, offence, and punishment. Further sections deal with the rights and duties of officers of government and describe the ways in which offences by such officers were to be investigated and punished. This part of the Code also deals with mitigation of punishment for reasons of age or infirmity. Article 24 (art. 25 in the *Ch'ing* Code) is interesting: it provides that an offender who surrenders to the magistrate and confesses before his offence is discovered shall be pardoned although any claim on his property by government or an individual shall still be satisfied. This is the well-known principle of 'voluntary surrender' (*tzu-shou*) of Chinese law.[21] However, specifically Vietnamese provisions also appeared, as in Arts. 37 and 41 dealing respectively with the duties of parents and with religious organization.

Administrative law comprised twenty-seven articles divided

[20] See Philastre (1876: (i) 496 ff.).   [21] See Rickett (1971: 798-9).

into two books. Book 1 (13 arts.) is concerned with the system of government administration. Its articles provide for succession to rank and title by the male successor to an officer (art. 49) but also set limits on the powers of officers of state to solicit hereditary honours (art. 50). The rest of Book 1 is concerned with miscellaneous matters such as the qualification by examination for office, attendance of officers at court, collusion between officers, misconduct of officers, and the irregular interference by a superior in the functions of a subordinate. Book 1 was itself substantially amended in the reigns of Gia-Long and his successors who periodically published edicts aimed at preventing the abuses indicated. From the number of such edicts[22] it would appear that administration was a constant problem.

Book 2 (arts. 59-72) regulates the conduct of the magistracy.[23] Article 59 is interesting in that it specifically imposed a duty on the magistrate fully to know the laws and to administer them in the proper spirit. Penalties, including fines and caning, were imposed where a magistrate failed to satisfy his superiors that he had the required degree of knowledge of the laws. Further penalties were imposed for the non-execution of the sovereign's edict, for destroying or discrediting the seals of office, for errors in public documents, for neglecting to make the proper reports, for altering the contents of a sovereign's dispatch, and for using an official seal imperfectly.

The third section of the *Gia-Long* Code, the civil laws, is one of the largest, comprising sixty-six articles divided into seven books. Book 1 (11 arts.) regulates the enrolment of the people on the official registers both by family and by individual name (arts. 73-4). Special provision is made for monasteries or religious foundations (art. 75), as in the *Ch'ing* Code (art. 77). The remainder of the book sets out basic rules for the distribution of personal services required by the state (art. 79), penalties for evasion, and prohibitions on individuals prematurely separating from their families or partitioning family property (arts. 82-3). In these cases the prosecution was

[22] See Philastre (1876: (i) 284-319); Woodside (1971: 83 ff.) on communications between the provinces and the throne and the attempts by the rulers to regulate the powers of the secretariat.
[23] Translated by Philastre, perhaps a little misleadingly, as *règles d'administration publique*.

brought on the initiative of the elder generation. The effect of this book is thus to define the individual as a member of the family, which was the basic unit for state service. The same provisions existed in Book 1 of the Third Division of the *Ch'ing* Code—the so-called 'Fiscal Laws'.

Book 2 (arts. 84–93) of the section on civil law is concerned with cultivation, tenements, and habitations. It provides for taxes on rice land (art. 84) and for a reduction in tax when damage caused by natural calamity occurs. In the latter case, officials were required personally to inspect the lands affected (art. 85). Article 86 deals with the status of lands of the nobility and officers of government, and Art. 87 provides penalties for fraudulent sale of lands and tenements. Penalties were also provided for the unjustified occupation and cultivation of land belonging to others, for the damaging of harvests, for the theft of produce, and for leaving land uncultivated or neglected. The provisions of this book parallel closely Book 2 of the *Ch'ing* Fiscal Laws.

Book 3 (arts. 94–109) concerns marriage. Article 94 states the conditions of marriage, a breach of which invalidated any union. It had to be stated in the contract that the parties were not diseased, infirm, or under age, that they were not within the prohibited degrees, and that the contracting families approved of the match. Marriage articles had to be drawn up and they had the status of a contract, breach of which involved penalties. Article 94 also regulated the rights of senior male members of a family to contract marriages on behalf of junior members. Marriages between persons having the same family name were forbidden (art. 100).[24] Lending wives or daughters on hire, and marriage during the mourning periods were also forbidden on pain of caning (art. 98). Marriage during the imprisonment of parents was punishable by caning (art. 99), but if the marriage was contracted at the parents' request, no punishment was then imposed. Marriages with female musicians or comedians were forbidden to government officers, and such a union was void and the marriage gift was forfeited to government. Marriages to concubines, absconded females, and slaves were also forbidden (arts. 102, 107). Article 96 provided for the ordering of ranks between wives. Priests were forbidden to marry under pain of

[24] See Woodside (1971: 44).

beating and expulsion from the Buddhist clergy (art. 106). Where an unlawful marriage was arranged the parties to such were not punished; penalties fell upon the persons responsible for the arrangements; however, if the persons arranging the marriage fell outside the categories of immediate paternal senior relatives, then the husband and wife might be punished as accessories. Divorce was provided for in Art. 108, and a wife might be divorced for barrenness, talkativeness, infidelity, disregard of husband's parents, theft, bad temper, and infirmity. She could not be divorced if she had mourned her husband's parents for three years, if the family had become rich after having been poor before the marriage, or if she had no parents living to receive her back again. A husband who divorced his wife despite such conditions was subject to punishment. An absconding wife was punished by caning and might be sold into 'marriage' by her husband. The article also provides penalties for the harbouring of fugitive wives; they applied to secondary wives except that the penalties were somewhat reduced. This book follows very closely Book 3 of the *Ch'ing* Fiscal Laws.

Book 4 (arts. 110–31) deals with public property in revenue and goods. It set out the periods for collecting revenues in kind (art. 111), the rules for allocating the revenues due (art. 112), penalties for concealing or wasting the revenues set apart for government (art. 114), or for privately lending public revenue or public property (arts. 116–17). The receipt, transfer, and expenditure of the revenue were also regulated (art. 118), as were the fraudulent appropriation of public property (art. 119) and the answerability of public officers for each other's acts (art. 119). There were detailed regulations for the conduct of government officers (arts. 122–4), including damages for the loss of public goods (art. 127) and rules for the transmission of goods from the provinces to the centre (art. 128). These rules were enforced by regulations for forfeiture and restitution of both individual and, more important, family property (art. 131). This book followed very closely Book 4 of the *Ch'ing* Fiscal Laws.

Book 5 (arts. 132–3) deals very briefly with duties and customs, concentrating on contraband and maritime contraband. It is an exact copy of Book 5 of the *Ch'ing* Fiscal Laws, although much less detailed, as befits a state in which the market economy was less important than in China.

Book 6 (arts. 134–6) deals with usury, wastage of property held on some form of trust, and lost property. The provisions are the same as those of Book 6 of the *Ch'ing* Fiscal Laws.

Finally, Book 7 (arts. 137–8) deals with sales and markets and is concerned mainly with licences for commercial agents and with penalties for using false weights, measures, or scales. It is a brief summary of Book 7 of the *Ch'ing* Fiscal Laws.

The next section of the *Gia-Long* Code is concerned with Rites, the rules relating to which are contained in two books (arts. 139–64).

Book 1 (arts. 139–44) on the sacred rites is mainly penal in nature in that it punishes such offences as destroying altars and sacred terraces, provides for the care of tombs of distinguished personages, punishes the dishonouring of the spirits by unlicensed forms of worship,[25] and punishes the activities of magicians and teachers of 'false and pernicious doctrine'. The book is an abridged version of Book 1 of the *Ch'ing* Ritual Laws.

Book 2 (arts. 145–64) contains miscellaneous provisions, modelled largely on Book 2 of the *Ch'ing* Ritual Laws, which fall into four classes. First, there are the regulations on the preparation of medicines and provisions for the sovereign (art. 145) and for the care of the sovereign's goods (art. 145). Second, there are a number of articles which establish the proper forms of address to be used by officers of government to the sovereign (art. 150–1) and which also regulate the relations between the officers themselves (arts. 153–5) and include a prohibition on official messengers from treating officers of the districts in a contemptuous manner (art. 155). Third, there are a number of sumptuary laws regulating the dress and conduct of priests and other persons (art. 158). Finally, there are rules governing funerals (art. 162) and mourning (art. 163), including concealing the occasion of mourning. Country festivals are also dealt with (art. 163), and magicians and fortune-tellers are forbidden to foretell public events (art. 157).

The next section of the *Gia-Long* Code, the fifth, deals with military law in Arts. 165–222, divided into five books. These are

[25] This gave rise to problems with Roman Catholics in the reigns of Minh-mạng (1820–41) and Thiệu-trị (1841–7).

an exact copy of the five books of the fifth division of the *Ch'ing* Code. They deal with the protection of the sovereign's residence, the government of the armed forces, the protection of the frontier, the supply of horses and cattle, and expresses and public posts. The last was a public institution, but on occasion private property might be transmitted by public post.

The penultimate section of the *Gia-Long* Code was concerned with criminal law (arts. 223-388) in eleven books. Book 1 is entitled 'Robbery and Theft' and, apart from repeating the crimes of treason and renunciation of allegiance (arts. 223-4) already stated in the first definitional section of the Code, it deals with a miscellany of crimes of theft, with and without violence, concerning public and private property. The definition of crime is quite sophisticated and a distinction is drawn between theft and robbery: crime is distinguished from an attempt to commit crime (art. 249). Sorcery and magic are crimes (art. 225) and so are sacrilege (art. 226) and disturbing graves (art. 245). This book is a copy of Book 1 of the sixth division (criminal laws) of the *Ch'ing* Code.

Book 2 (arts. 251-70) is concerned with homicide. The striking feature of this book for the comparative lawyer is the existence of special classes of murder involving family members. This was a crime especially abhorrent, and there are sections on parricide (art. 253), on widows killing their deceased husbands' relations (art. 255), on killing a son or grandson and attributing the crime to an innocent person (art. 263), and compromising or concealing the crime of killing an elder relation (art. 269). Special penalties were also provided for the killing of an officer of government (art. 252). This book is a copy of Book 2 of the sixth division (criminal laws) of the *Ch'ing* Code.

Book 3 (arts. 271-92) deals with quarrelling and fighting. The most notable feature is that the penalty for the same act varies according to where the act took place and the status of the persons involved. Thus quarrelling in the sovereign's palace (art. 273) and striking an individual of the royal blood (art. 274) or an officer of government (art. 275) were punished far more severely than an ordinary affray between equals in a public place (art. 271). There were specific classes of the crime involving superior and inferior officers of government (arts. 276-8), slaves and free persons assaulting each other (arts. 282-3), and masters and apprentices striking each other (art. 280). Especially heinous were a wife striking her husband (art. 284) and assaults within stated degrees of relationships (arts. 285–92). This book is a copy of Book 3 of the sixth division (criminal law) of the *Ch'ing* Code.

Book 4 (arts. 293–300) is concerned with abusive language, and penalties are distinguished in severity depending upon the status of the persons involved as in the previous book. This book is a copy of Book 4 of the sixth division (criminal law) of the *Ch'ing* Code.

Book 5 (arts. 301–11) concerns indictments and informations relating to criminal matters. It contains matters both of process and of principle. Rules are laid down preventing irregularities in the presentation of information (art. 301), penalties are stated for declining to receive information (art. 303), and the offering of evidence by criminals in confinement is also regulated (art. 308). On matters of principle, anonymous information is regulated (art. 302), false and malicious information (art. 305) and promoting litigation (art. 309) are both punished (art. 311). This book is a copy of Book 5 of the sixth division (criminal laws) of the *Ch'ing* Code.

Book 6 (arts. 312–20) deals with bribery and corruption. The general principle, stated in Art. 312, is that officials who accept bribes are to be punished in proportion to the amount accepted. A scale of punishments was set up[26] regulating in minute detail the amount of fines and providing for the acceptance of goods which were valued at so many ounces of silver. The other articles of this book provided for specific instances of corruption. It is a rather less elaborate version of Book 6 of the sixth division (criminal law) of the *Ch'ing* Code.

Book 7 (arts. 321–31) is on forging and frauds, and, as might be expected, the offences described relate almost entirely to the falsification of official documents (art. 321–2), counterfeiting of seals (art. 324) and currency (art. 325), and impersonating an officer of state (art. 326). It was also an offence to pretend sickness or death for one's own purposes (art. 330) or to seduce other persons to transgress the laws (art. 331). This book is based upon Book 7 of the sixth division (criminal laws) of the *Ch'ing* Code with some adaptations to suit local conditions.

[26] See Philastre (1876: (ii) 455–65).

Thus, Art. 235 on counterfeiting coin dealt in terms of copper rather than silver as in the *Ch'ing* Code.

Book 8 (arts. 332–40) dealt with incest and adultery. Criminal intercourse was defined as adultery or as rape. The penalty for the former was beating and for the latter death by strangulation (art. 332). Conniving at, or consenting to, criminal intercourse was also a crime (art. 333). The crime of incest was defined in Art. 334 as including relations to the fourth degree, and, where applicable, inferior wives. The penalty for incest was death by strangulation. A false accusation of incest by a woman against her husband's father was punished by strangulation (art. 335). Intercourse between free persons and slaves or between a servant and the master's wife was punishable (art. 336). Officers of government were forbidden to frequent the company of prostitutes or actresses (art. 340). The Buddhist clergy were likewise forbidden (art. 338). In general, this book is a reproduction of Book 8 of the sixth division (criminal law) of the *Ch'ing* Code.

Book 9 (arts. 341–51) deals with a number of miscellaneous offences, including defacing public monuments (art. 341), gaming (art. 343), castration (art. 344), compromising offences and withholding them from the cognizance of the magistrate (art. 346), and putting on theatrical representations without licence (art. 349). The most notable article in this book is Art. 351, which punishes by beating improper conduct contrary to the spirit of the laws although not in breach of any specific article. It is a direct copy of Art. 386 of Book 9 of the sixth division (criminal laws) of the *Ch'ing* Code.

Book 10 (arts. 352–9) regulates arrests and imprisonment. Penalties are provided for allowing prisoners to escape (art. 357) and for assisting and concealing criminals (art. 358). This book is a copy of Book 10 of the sixth division (criminal law) of the *Ch'ing* Code.

Book 11 (arts. 360–88) is the last book on crime and deals with imprisonment, judgment, and execution. Articles 360–8 set out the rules for the keeping of prisoners and the conditions of imprisonment and provide penalties for encouraging prisoners to make groundless appeals. Article 369 provides that torture is not to be used in the judicial examination of the aged or children although it may be used for other persons. The

The Chinese Legal World 89

remaining articles of this book governed sentencing, the infliction of punishment, including special punishment for female offenders (art. 385), and execution. This book is a copy of Book 11 of the sixth division of the *Ch'ing* Code.

Finally, the *Gia-Long* Code dealt with Public Works in two books. Book 1 (arts. 389–94) provided for the erection and maintenance of public buildings and included penalties for unauthorized expenditure. Book 2 (arts. 395–8) dealt with public ways, including provision for building river embankments, roads, and bridges. Penalties were provided for damaging such or neglecting repairs. These books are rather less elaborate versions of Books 1 and 2 of the seventh division (laws relating to public works) of the *Ch'ing* Code.

The view of law that the Code of *Gia-Long*[27] presents to the legal historian is one that reproduces Chinese concepts of the nature of law. The text is punitive in nature, operating in a vertical direction from the state to the individual. Many matters of a civil nature were entirely ignored (e.g. contracts) or were given only limited treatment within the penal format (e.g. property rights, inheritance). The Code was really concerned with acts of moral impropriety or criminal violence which appeared to its framers to be a disruption of the social order. The individual did not bring an action against another person but made a complaint to an officer of government, who then decided whether or not to prosecute in the strictest meaning of that term. The primacy of bureaucracy[28] in the legal administration explains the detailed appeals procedure which results in the carrying of an appeal to the very highest levels.

There seem to be four major characteristics in the Vietnamese texts, both *Hông Đú'c* and *Gia-Long*, which owe their origin to this view of law. First, the Codes attempt to make punishment fit the crime. There is an attempt to foresee variations in offences and to provide specific penalties for each. Thus, homicide is differentiated into types and the appropriate penalty is specified for each. Such differentiations are not based on motive; intent as such is relevant but not decisive in assessing

---

[27] See McAleavy (1958) on the interpretation of Art. 95 offered by Philastre concerning *điền*.
[28] See, for comparison, Weber (1966: 264) on the Chinese bureaucracy. See also O. van der Sprenkel (1964).

penalty. More important is the status, social or familial, of the offender and his victim. This is not a feature of Western legal thought but it is basic to a code springing from Confucian legal thought. We thus have parricide, homicide of an official, of a senior by a junior, of slave by master and vice versa, of a child by a father, and so on. Even a false accusation of homicide is punishable. In addition the means by which a homicide is committed is important. In the Codes different means, such as homicide by poison, by improper administration of medicine, by deprivation of food, and so on, are quite distinct. These are examples of the 'principle of differentiation' which are Confucian in origin[29] and are aimed at maximizing justice by enabling the law to fit all foreseeable circumstances as closely as possible. The difficulties in the application of such a principle are obvious and must have led to a somewhat disturbing use of judgment by analogy. Hence the strict injunction on the magistrate to know and apply the laws, and the issue of the sovereign's edicts to support this injunction.

Second, differentiation by social status was an important element in the Vietnamese codes, which provide penalties differing sharply according to the relative class of the offender and his victim. The punishment of beating is an example in which the variations were particularly marked. Third, the codes recognized certain categories of persons as deserving of special judicial procedure and so elevated them as a whole from the mass of the common people. In Vietnam this class included the sovereign and his relatives and servants, as well as 'persons of great merit' and the mandarinate. The last is the most significant group, and its members could not be investigated or arrested without permission of the sovereign; even when found guilty they, and their immediate families, could have their sentences reviewed by the sovereign with a view to reduction. Heavy caning, for example, was often commuted to a monetary fine. On the other hand certain offences, usually relating to the unjustified assumption of sovereign powers (mostly expressed in sumptuary laws), exposed the mandarinate to correspondingly heavier penalties than were prescribed for the ordinary man. Finally, the laws recognized intra-family distinctions based upon sex, seniority, and degree of kinship. The mourning

[29] See Bodde & Morris (1967: 31 ff.) on the *Ch'ing* Code.

relationships are of key importance for determining important legal distinctions. The first degree was in effect the most important; it included the son(s) and unmarried daughter(s) who mourned their parents, a wife who mourned her husband or husband's parents, and a concubine who mourned her master. The mourning system was based on the superiority of senior generation over junior generation and of male over female. This meant that the duties owed by the senior or superior in any relationship were less than those owed by their reciprocals. The central value that these rules protect is filial piety and the family unit in general, the importance of which even overrode the subject–state relationship. Thus, where an individual was punished by law, an important element in assessing punishment was his relationship to members of his family. Closer relatives might suffer and their punishment was always proportionately greater than that of more remote relatives. This is the explanation for the accompanying law, that relatives were forbidden to conceal the crime of one of their members. Unfilial accusations were harshly punished for the same reason, and a family was responsible in the case of treason by one of its members.

To what extent did the *Gia-Long* Code represent legal reality in Vietnam? The sinicized nature of the Code gives the clue to the answer. Unlike the earlier *Hông Đú'c*, there is little on the face of the *Gia-Long* text expressing indigenous Vietnamese features.[30] Like its Chinese progenitor, the Code left large areas of legal life unregulated or only imperfectly regulated (e.g. property, inheritance, marriage). Its function was to preserve the sovereignty of a certain type of state order and to regulate the actions of individuals only in relation to this function. Much was left to local customary law, applied and controlled on a village basis, although the Code did provide a sinicizing framework here as well. In this sense, the Code existed on two levels whose mutual incompatibility made necessary extra regulation. For example, in 1803–4 the Emperor Gia-Long promulgated a set of regulations to control the activities of village communities. These regulations, the *Hu'o'ng Dòng Điêu Lệ*, attempted to enforce the Confucian 'six rites' in marriage and to forbid traditional practices such as the mortgage of land

[30] See above, n. 27.

as part of the marriage settlement. The failure of the regulations is amply attested by the continuing difficulty that the French had in dealing with the same practices. The local legal institutions were thus not left undisturbed as they mostly were in China, but were continually under attack by edicts attempting to reinforce the Code. At the same time, however, theoretical propositions, for example, those which describe the nature of the proper family system, were to some degree reflected in reality. The sections of the Code which dealt with this enforced a system of relationships which came to form an important sub-structure of provincial administration. The family was the unit of social and political control, it was localized in a particular village, and by means of the government registers it was subjected to taxation, corvée, and so on. Individual duties were defined in familial terms as were the state duties owed by the individual; for example, desertion from the army or serious crime resulted respectively in family liability to replace the deserter or suffer various grades of punishment. This is not to deny that the desired family organization was something of a stereotype; it properly applied only to the upper classes, but the basic relationship of superiority–inferiority was to some extent characteristic of all strata of Vietnamese society. Such religious observances as family worship were at least as important in Vietnam as in China. On the other hand, the Chinese ideal of lineage surname exogamy just could not be attained, almost certainly because of the (unexplained) paucity of Vietnamese surnames.

Important principles of law were contained in extra-Code rules. Such were the rights of women to property, a right enshrined in the *Hông Đức* but ignored in the *Gia-Long*. The rights of the widow to usufruct of and control over family property were extensive and were enforced in the later French colonies.[31] Again, in the matter of most concern to a peasant community—land distribution and ownership—detailed and complex rules relating to classes of land and a variety of occupations existed.[32] These had a direct link with the Chinese-style bureaucracy of Vietnam through resource surveys and tax collection. The central administration attempted always to

[31] See below, Chapter 6.
[32] See Adams & Hancock (1970) for a brief summary.

control village lands. A law of 1803 forbade the sale of communal land (*cong điên*); it was reissued in 1844, but the control of the centre over land was successful only to a limited degree. The actual laws applied in land matters were very much a local matter and, as in all peasant communities, were tied to marriage and succession.

The basic unit of settlement in the countryside was the *xã*—or village—usually referred to by the French as 'commune', a term which tends to imply a position in the state system somewhat at variance with the facts. *Xã* were recognized local units under the control of a council of notables who interposed themselves between the village members and the bureaucratic system. They attempted to cultivate an attitude of independence towards the bureaucratic hierarchy[33] and, to the legal historian, this shows itself most clearly in the application of local laws on the matters indicated above. But the competence of the village notables was probably limited to those areas where the Code itself did not provide regulations; the ordinary duties in administrative matters such as corvée, reporting the number of taxable males, apprehending absconding peasants, and so on were enforced by the local bureaucracy on pain of flogging and fining. Edicts of the sovereign also applied in matters not dealt with by the Code; thus a law of 1830 controlled village land transactions by ordering that all sales be recorded and forbidding mortgages to extend for a period longer than thirty years.[34]

SUMMARY: VIETNAM AND CHINA

One must accept that, in essence, the basic world and legal order of Vietnam was Chinese, although specifically local elements were incorporated into the laws. In this, the Codes of the Vietnamese do not differ from the local codes of the Indian and Islamic legal worlds of South-East Asia. However, there is one unique aspect of the Chinese–Vietnamese situation that is of interest to the legal historian; this is the so-called 'tributary relationship' between China and Vietnam that was characterized by Chinese dominance, suzerainty, or hegemony. The tributary state was regarded as a buffer between China and the

[33] See Woodside (1971: 153 ff.).
[34] Cited ibid. 158.

outside world, while for its part the tributary benefited by its contact with a 'higher civilization' and could also petition for material help in certain circumstances.[35] The ruler of the tribute state was invested by the Emperor of China and received a seal from him, thus fully validating his position. Tribute missions were sent (in the case of Annam every four years), and the Chinese calendar and method of writing were adopted. The relationship mingled elements both of practical politics and of ethical and cultural principle[36] and is not strictly comparable to inter-state relations on the Western model,[37] a fact which the French chose to ignore.[38] The Vietnamese law texts existed within this system and so formed part of a political continuum emanating from a Chinese centre. They are thus "Chinese derived" but at the same time by no means do they completely reflect the Vietnamese legal world.

[35] See Laffey (1969).
[36] See Langlet (1970). The Vietnamese in their turn attempted a similar relationship with neighbouring subordinate territories. See Nguyen (1975).
[37] See Alexandrowicz (1967) on the law of nations in the East Indies for examples.
[38] See Mäding (1967).

CHAPTER 4

The South-East Asian Law Texts: Cultural Borrowing and the Concept of Law

THE PRECEDING outlines of the South-East Asian law texts indicate that they are derivative and form part of a general pattern of cultural borrowing. The older generation of legal historians would even go further and maintain that the use of 'Indian', 'Islamic', and 'Chinese' is not only essential to the understanding of the South-East Asian texts (which is perfectly right) but that the texts are little more than copies of the originals. This can be a dangerous oversimplification, and the purpose of this chapter is to examine the cultural borrowing in order to show the relevance of the Indian, Islamic, and Chinese traditions for the legal historian of South-East Asia.

The South-East Asian texts, and indeed Oriental law texts in general, as well as ancient Middle Eastern and European codes,[1] raise a number of important issues. In general legal history, such texts have been regarded as illustrating stages in the development of law[2] rather than as documents to be studied for their own sake. Moreover, although the Oriental texts generally are assumed to be 'law' in some recognizable sense, it is often denied that they rest upon traditions of legal or jurisprudential analysis.[3] The *Ta Ch'ing Lü Li*, for example, is sometimes classed as a manual for magistrates, instructing them in their duties,[4] as is its Vietnamese 'imitation', the *Gia-Long* Code.[5] Other texts have been interpreted as documents that

---

[1] There are also the ancient Codes of Hammurabi, the Hittites, and so on (see Driver & Miles (1955–6)). In addition the early European codes of the Visigoths, Burgundians, Saxons and others present important points of departure from modern municipal laws.

[2] See, for example, Diamond (1935), (1951), (1971), and Jackson (1972). The most famous example is the work of Sir Henry Maine; cf. Maine (1861), (1875), (1883), and (1895).

[3] This is not true of the Islamic and Hindu laws.

[4] Cf. Jones (1974: 331).   [5] Cf. Philastre (1876).

merely attempt to legitimize an indigenous form of sovereignty.[6] In any study of the South-East Asian texts, therefore, one has to contend not only with the question of cultural borrowing but also with the interpretation of the texts themselves.[7] Even here fundamental difficulties persist, most often in the definition of law. The texts do not always state actual rules for the conduct of day-to-day affairs: they contain material which is both dynastic and historical, religious and secular; the concept of law is undifferentiated and must therefore be sought in historical fact. Even a historical chronology of law (however such be defined) is not always possible because much manuscript copying has occurred.

The existence of cultural borrowing also involves an assessment of the relationship between law and religion. In the case of Islamic law it is a fact that in many states the dictates of Islam were not followed to the exclusion of other rules in matters as important as family law and property law.[8] Islam has a prescriptive validity for all Muslims but not necessarily a descriptive validity. In the case of the Hindu law texts, Lingat's discussion of *dharma* and custom[9] has demonstrated that the law promulgated in the *śāstras* differs from custom both by origin and by intent. This was a problem that exercised both the earliest commentators on the *śāstras* and the courts of colonial India. The latter decided that custom, when proved, could override the texts.[10] But even before the advent of the colonial power, Hindu commentators noted the conflicts between *dharma* and custom and attempted to reconcile them in a number of different ways.[11] The interpretation and application of the *śāstras* still provide difficulties for the courts in India today.[12]

The Burmese texts, on the other hand, raise yet another difficulty. The Buddhist ethic does not distinguish between law, morality, or custom, and although the British colonial courts

[6] Cf. Hooker (1968: 170). See also Moertono (1963) on Java.
[7] Including the often difficult question of sources, since most, though not all, of the extant texts are known only in later recensions dating from the seventeenth–nineteenth centuries
[8] Cf. J. N. D. Anderson (1959), (1965), (1970), Prins (1954), Hooker (1972).
[9] Cf. Lingat (1973: 176–206).
[10] *Collector of Madura* v. *Moottoo Ramalinga Sathupathy* (1868) 12 M.I.A. 397.
[11] Lingat (1973: 203 ff.). [12] See the cases cited in Derrett (1968: 299 ff.).

developed a bastard 'Burmese Buddhist law',[13] an assessment of the texts still gives rise to considerable difficulty.[14] The same difficulty arises with the texts of Thai law, especially with the *Thammasat*, a set of basic moral principles to which the ideal monarch was expected to conform.[15] They could not be altered by the king, and the orders and proclamations made by the ruler in the course of his reign were valid only during that reign. This led Robert Lingat to say that 'there was apparently no place for what we call law'.[16]

The issues raised by the texts are twofold: first, the relationship between the texts and actual behaviour, i.e. law and custom; and second, whether the texts can properly be called 'law'. Attempts have been made to interpret some texts, both European and Oriental, on the basis of sociological data; for example, the Roman XII Tables.[17] The relation between codes and indigenous collections of cases has also been examined for the purpose of demonstrating how a code worked in practice.[18] So far as definition is concerned, the 'properly legal' nature of texts owes much to the formulations of the nineteenth-century legal historians. For example, law was equated with the particular faculties and tendencies of a people by Savigny;[19] with the definition of a movement from status to contract by Sir Henry Maine[20]—this was, moreover, demonstrated to be a partly valid progression on data from the courts of British India.[21] The religious elements in the texts caused difficulties in the definition of law, and views on this question still vary widely.[22] Similarly, the nature of the texts themselves raises problems in terms of legal categories; these have been variously described as 'legislation'[23] and as 'Bills of Rights'.[24] The idea of an evolutionary progression is encountered in Sir Paul Vinogradoff's theory of juridicial evolution[25] and in the study of medieval European texts. English scholars, for example, distinguished law as written and

[13] Cf. Mootham (1939).
[15] *Prince* Dhani Nivat (1954: 163).
[17] MacCormack (1971).
[19] Friedrich Karl von Savigny (1814).
[21] Mayne (1885), (1887).
[23] Ibid. See *contra* Bartholomew (1960).
[25] Vinogradoff (1920), (1925).
[14] Lingat (1950).
[16] Lingat (1950: 26).
[18] Harrison (1964).
[20] Maine (1861).
[22] Diamond (1935), (1951), (1971).
[24] Darling (1970).

custom as not written[26] and discussed the law–custom dichotomy in terms of the nineteenth-century distinction between laws of general and laws of special application. Again, German scholars in their histories of German private law[27] attempted to show the similarity of historical entities to nineteenth-century German legal conceptions; in doing so they made use of the modern distinction between the physical person and the legal *persona*.

Law texts thus present a series of problems: in definition, in deciding upon a proper method of description, and so on. There are areas of what one would understand to be law that are not treated in the texts and vice versa. Often it is difficult to decide whether the texts were ever central to the legal life of a people. The South-East Asian texts share these problems and are thus a part of general jurisprudence.

There are perhaps two main issues which occur in all the texts: the indeterminancy of law and ethics, and the definition of the individual and whether the texts are descriptive of legal reality.

I LAW AS AN EXPRESSION OF A NATURAL AND MORAL ORDER

That the texts are assumed without question to be law is probably due to two factors: first, they are written and, second, they deal with the relationship between ruler and ruled and, in so doing, they imply or state forms of political organization. The difficulty, however, is that the idea of law is undifferentiated from religion, dynastic history, the organization of a bureaucracy, and so on. The fact that a text is in writing in itself predisposes Western commentators to regard it as law in some sense. This is understandable, if ethnocentric; however, it does not dispose of the main issue, the legal significance of the texts. Naturally, the precise nature of this will vary from one culture to another, but are there basic features in common which in some way identify law?

The overwhelming impression one gets from even a cursory reading of the texts is that they are descriptive of a natural and social order. The concept of law that the texts present is a regulation of human behaviour that is a part of the nature of things. Law is not just concerned with an individual system of

[26] Pollock (1883).   [27] Huebner (1908).

The South-East Asian Law Texts

obligation, though all texts contain prescriptions, it is also an irreducible datum of the moral and social world. No individual can escape from law in this sense; it is authoritative by the force of its being.

The Hindu *dharma* is essentially a 'rule of interdependence',[28] founded on a hierarchy corresponding to the nature of things and necessary for the maintenance of the social order. The concept envelops both the moral and the physical world, and in the Indian law texts it refers to the totality of obligations ascribed to an individual in accord with his status (*varṇa*) and place in life. It is a morality addressed to the individual in society, but it is also natural as being in accord with the physical and non-physical worlds. The sources of *dharma* are the Veda, Tradition, and Good Custom. In the form of the *dharma-śāstra*, the Hindu conception of the social and natural orders is given its juridical character. The *śāstra* do not neglect the observance and practice of religion and ritual but they give in detail the rules which should guide the king in the exercise of his duties. The most celebrated is the *Manu-smṛti* or *Manava-dharma-śāstra*, known in English as the Code of Manu, which was not only the major *smṛti* in India[29] but was also one of the most important, perhaps the most important element of Indian civilization translated to the states of South-East Asia.

The *Manu-smṛti* is divided into twelve books. The first relates how the Great Sages approached Manu and asked him to tell them the *dharma* of all the castes. In his reply Manu describes the creation of the world by Brahmā, his own birth as issue of Brahmā, his creation of the Great Sages who had as issue seven other Manus whose task it is to create and re-create the world during the alternate creation and destruction of the cosmos. Book II explains the sources of *dharma*, lists the sacrifices and purificatory ceremonies (*saṃskāra*), and sets out in detail the conduct proper to a Brahminical student. Books III–V are devoted to the second stage of the life of the *dvija* (twice born) in which he takes a wife and becomes a householder. Book III deals with marriage, the duties of spouses, the performance of daily ritual, and the rules relating to hospitality. Book IV is concerned with the way of life permitted to a Brahmin and

[28] Lingat (1973: 211).
[29] For a description of the others see Lingat (1973: 97–106).

concentrates especially on diet, as does the first part of Book V. The latter part of Book V is concerned with pollution and purification, and the last verses speak of the duties of women. Book VI deals with the last two phases of life, that of hermit and that of mendicant monk. These books do not contain anything new by comparison with the earlier *dharma-sūtras*, although the arrangement and development of the rules is often different.

In Books VII–IX lies the great originality of the *Manu-smṛti*. Book VII deals with the ruler and subject, with punishment, war, the organization of government, taxes, and the policies to be followed toward neighbouring states.[30] It is concerned largely with the politics of power. Books VIII and IX deal with the regulation of disputes in private law in so far as they relate to the justice dispensed by the king. They attempt to enumerate the different types of dispute and to describe the types of litigation that could possibly arise. Book VII reduces all disputes that could be brought to the royal court to eighteen heads,[31] and in Book VIII an attempt is made to set out the rules that the court should apply in deciding on the issues. There are rules as to the composition of the tribunal, as to proof and witnesses, as to debts, weights and measures, and so on. Book IX sets out the duties of husband and wife, rules of inheritance, and a further exposition of the royal administration of justice. The function of the king is compared to that of the gods and the elements (IX.303–12). Book X deals with the mixing of *varṇas*, and Book XI is concerned with gifts to be made to persons in need and with penance and expiation. Book XII, the last, resembles the first book in its philosophical and religious nature.

This summary indicates something of the complexity and richness of the Code. It is not sufficient merely to dismiss it as a 'stage' in the evolution of law;[32] rather, it should be considered as an attempt to explain a normative system based on the facts of moral life within the terms of a cosmological order. The office of the King is regarded as an institution necessary to the maintenance of the social order 'established by the Creator for the good of creatures'.[33] The royal function was instituted by

[30] For a Thai version of this see Wolters (1969).
[31] The classification adopted is not haphazard but is in an order corresponding to the economic conditions of the period. See Jolly (1928: 35).
[32] Diamond (1971: 113). See also Jackson (1975).
[33] Lingat (1973: 207).

The South-East Asian Law Texts

the gods, and *kṣatra*, the foundation of all royalty, is associated with *Rāja-dharma*, the totality of duties which constitute the King's function. The latter is founded on the nature of things, and to violate it is to violate one's destiny. The *dharma* of the King is the protection of his subjects and the Code of Manu goes so far as to calculate the portions of merits and sins passing to the King (Bk. VIII.304). The relationship between King and subject is one of mutual interdependence because the spiritual merit of each depends upon the other. The King is subject to *dharma*, and yet particular rules of the *dharma* get their stability only through an exercise of the King's will. The King may intervene to make his subjects respect the rules of conduct prescribed in the *śāstras*; he must see to it that penances enjoined upon men to expiate their sins are carried out; and he acts as supreme arbitrator in disputes under the *śāstras*. In these senses the *Rājadharma* presides over all *dharmas*.

The codes in which these ideas are contained might well seem imperfect to the European lawyer in that much is missing from them. They are not uncommonly thought of as having no relation to day-to-day reality and, because of this, as not being 'really law'.[34] But to take this view is to miss the point of the texts; as Robert Lingat says: 'The Hindu system sustained the unity of the Indian world, thanks to the undisputed authority of the law. That unity was unrealisable at a lower level, but was realised on the higher level in an ideal participation amongst all Hindus. The ideal received the dynamic imparted to it by faith, by Hinduism itself....'[35]

This view of law is not confined to India; it is characteristic also of the Indianized states[36] of South-East Asia. In Cambodia and Champā, the lands of Sanskrit culture, the Hindu doctrines of law were followed in their original purity, although, as the epigraphy shows, some modifications were made.[37] The same is true, to a lesser extent, of Burma. The Burmese *dhammathat* was an attempt to use the Hindu system as a model in an environment entirely given over to the Buddhist faith. The Code of *Wagaru*, for example, retains the *śāstric* classification of

---

[34] On the issue of custom *vis-à-vis* the texts see below, pp. 109–118.
[35] Lingat (1973: 259).
[36] Cf. Coedès (1968).
[37] Lingat (1949), Sahai (1970).

contentious matters into eighteen heads but the content of the texts is very much a matter of local Burmese rules. The Hindu system was not, as was maintained in the nineteenth century,[38] introduced as such but was used as a guide to form. Although the Buddhist religion did not contain any revelation on the social order, the *dhammathats* were held to originate on the *cakkavāla*, the wall which surrounds the universe, and were given to man by the hermit Manu. This personage has nothing in common with the Manu of the *smṛti* except his name, but the choice of this name emphasizes the separation of the texts from the world of Buddha. The laws of Buddha reveal the conditions of salvation, whilst those of Manu, the bringer of the law from the walls of the world, determine the conditions of social life.[39] However, the law of the *dhammathats*, like that of the *śāstras*, transcends the world which it rules. It is bound to the cosmic order and is free from the will of men. It was a universal law in the Hinayana Buddhist world.

In pre-twentieth-century Thailand we also have a *dhammasattha* dating from the fourteenth century.[40] In many respects it is very close to the Code of *Wagaru* but it does introduce an important new distinction. Contentious matters are no longer reduced to the classical eighteen titles of law but are classified into ten rules of procedure and twenty-nine rules of 'substantive law'. The most important innovation is a new source of law, the rules derived through litigation (*sākha-attha*) from the primary rules which Manu (Manosara) read on the walls of the universe. These secondary rules come from the ruler[41] in the form of decrees arising out of disputes (*Rājasattham*); they were incorporated into the texts and formed part of the whole law. However, they are not, strictly speaking, innovations; the law laid down had authority only when it conformed to *dhammasattha* precepts, i.e. only when it expressed the royal will[42] in accordance with the view of nature expressed in the texts of the law. But it did have the effect of putting the King in the centre of the legal world, and the texts became more immediately a

[38] Cf. Forchhammer (1885). See also Khetarpal (1968).
[39] Lingat (1951).
[40] These are now known mainly in the text, the 'Three Great Seals', of 1805. Cf. Lingat (1929–30). See also Griswold & Prasert Na Nagara (1969).
[41] See Quaritch Wales (1934).
[42] For conflicting theories about the nature of royal power see Chomchai (1965).

foundation for and justification of kingly power than was the case in India proper.[43] This is characteristic also of the Javanese and Malay texts of the Indonesian archipelago. Indeed, the overwhelming impression one gets from such texts is that although they contain rules for the distribution of obligation, their outstanding characteristic is their concern with the nature of royal power and its acquisition.[44] All texts, for example, attempt to link the text patron to preceding dynasties through complicated and often false lines of descent. Such lines, however, do not refer to insignificant predecessors but only to the most powerful and notable; the aim is not to establish a legal inherited legitimacy but a link to a source of power which in a real sense is still in existence. As Benedict Anderson has demonstrated,[45] power in Javanese thought is both concrete and constant in quantity. It follows then that later generations may acquire and utilize the power of long-dead heroes and gods. It means also that power is concentrated at the centre, in the ruler, so that central government is essentially an extension of the ruler's personal household. The ideal form of temporal power is a world-empire in which all entities are combined in a coherent unity. The existence of this unity is itself defined in the proper use of power and through the proper conduct of individuals which must be in accord with *dharma*. It is no accident that the texts refer either through genealogy or by analogy to heroes whose lines illustrate the primacy of natural propriety over personal inclination.[46]

The Malayan texts also devote space to the genealogical and analogical links to power centres, although the development is much simpler than in the Javanese examples. The conception of power and of legitimate authority is, however, the same. In addition, the Malay texts contain large portions of Islamic thought which introduce an element of tension into the structure of the texts.[47] They all show an attempt to arrive at some accommodation between the precepts of Islam and the

[43] This did not of course prevent comparative jurists from 'demonstrating' that the Thai texts were 'basically Hindu law'. See Masao (1905).
[44] See, for example, Pigeaud (1960–2), Slametmuljana (1967), Moertono (1963).
[45] B. R. O'G. Anderson (1972).
[46] Jav. *pamrih*. The well-known episode from the Bratajuda-cycle in which Ardjuna and Kresna (Krishna) discuss duty and sentiment is a classic example.
[47] See Hooker (1973: 495–6).

ideas of legitimacy drawn from non-Islamic sources.[48] This is a constant source of tension throughout the Islamic world.

The religion of Islam is a whole which encompasses a social, a legal, and a political order. Its precepts are found in the Holy Qur'ān, which is the word of God revealed to the Prophet Muhammad in the seventh century A.D., and in the practice of the Prophet—the *sunna*. Muslim legal theory is concerned to reach an understanding (*fiqh*) of the law of Islam—the *Sharī'a*. The law itself, therefore, is both a divinely given law and a jurists' law. The activities of the jurists were necessary because the Qur'ān and the *sunna* in no sense constituted a comprehensive code of law. They contain a collection of rulings on particular issues which, at most, provided modifications of existing customary practices in the lands of Islam. It was open to the individual in the early days of Islam to exercise an opinion (*ra'y*) as to the applicability of divine revelation to particular circumstance. By the eighth century A.D. the tension between revelation and reason in the formulation of legal rules had hardened into a conflict of principle in Islamic jurisprudence.[49] From the tenth century onward the definitive relationship between these two ways of knowing the law became established. In building upon the work of the great ninth-century jurist, Shāfi'i, human reason was made subordinate to the principles established by divine revelation. Its function was to regulate new cases by applying to them the principles upon which divine revelation had regulated similar or parallel cases. This principle is known as reasoning by analogy—*qiyās*. A rule of law must be derived either from the Qur'ān or the *sunna* or by analogical deduction from them. But the notion of law itself is defined as the ordained and comprehensive system of God's commands. Similarly, justice as an ethical quality is identical with the terms of religious law. In the identification of such terms problems did arise, most consistently around what one may describe as the 'letter of the law' as opposed to its spirit. In particular cases, strict analogy could occasion injustice, and it was then permissible to decide an issue on *istiḥsān*, or the search for a just solution. The problem in Islamic law, as in all legal systems, is to decide what the boundaries of this or similar

[48] This is particularly apparent in the Minangkabau texts. See Liaw (1967).
[49] See Coulson (1969: 5 ff.).

principles are going to be, taking into account the requirements of consistency.[50] However, in whatever form reasoning appears, it is always subject to divine will in that its function is to seek the implementation of the purposes of God for Muslims. *Dieu propose et l'homme dispose!*

As indicated above, the *Sharīʿa* is both a code of law and a code of morality: a distinction between the two is not clearly drawn as in Western law. In the primary source of the *Sharīʿa*, the Qur'ān, there is no clear distinction between a moral and a legal rule. The Qur'ān is concerned to distinguish behaviour proper in the sight of God and to indicate the reward or penalty which such behaviour entails. Sanctions in the legal sense are of course expressed for a number of acts or omissions, such as defamation or theft, but all sanction is non-empirical in its essential effect. All human activity and social institutions are fundamentally of religious significance, and the *Sharīʿa* sets out a system of duties owed by man to his Creator and not just to other men. At the same time the *Sharīʿa* has developed a distinction between the legally enforceable and the morally desirable. Acts are classified as obligatory (*wājib*), permissible (*mubāḥ*), and prohibited (*ḥarām*). Each class contains acts which the *Sharīʿa* courts will enforce as well as actions which are only personal. Between the extremes of binding duty and absolute prohibition are acts which also have a definite value. These are two in kind, those which are recommended or praiseworthy (*mandūb*) and those which are blameworthy (*makrūh*). Neither of these values has a legal sanction. Thus it is praiseworthy for a marriage guardian to act upon the wishes of his ward, but, if he does not do so, any marriage which he concludes on her behalf against her wishes remains perfectly valid. So too, the divorce by triple *talāq* terminates a marriage irrevocably but it is still a blameworthy act. As the Prophet is alleged to have said, 'Of all things legally permissible, *talāq* is the most blameworthy.'

The religion of Islam formulates a value and purpose for all human life, and the law of Islam directs men's behaviour to the purposes of God. Law and religion are not, nor can they ever be, separate. The definition of law is not open to question as to its nature or purpose. Its application has of course varied from time to time and from place to place, but the apparent diversity

[50] Ibid. 17 ff.

of its forms and its relations to customary laws (see below) should not be allowed to blind us to its unique and unitary nature.

We turn now, finally, to the Chinese law texts. The codes of the various dynasties are known either in their original form or through treatises written in the past 1,700 years. No two dynasties had exactly the same laws, and changes appeared in judicial procedure and organization, in the system of punishment and in the compilation of the codes themselves.[51] The last of the Imperial Codes, that of the *Ch'ing*, is perhaps the best example for present purposes of a statement of law which is unique in the legal systems of the world. The *Ta Ch'ing Lü Li* is found in a number of editions and translations,[52] the best-known English translation is that made by Sir George Staunton in 1810. It is, however, incomplete.[53] The *Ta Ch'ing Lü Li* is divided into an introduction and six parts. The introduction is a directive from the Emperor to magistrates instructing them how to act when deciding an issue. The six parts are each labelled with the name of one of the six Boards that constituted the central government in Peking: The Boards of Officials, Revenue, Rites, War, Punishments, and Public Works. The Code was thus a compendium for the administration of the Empire. Its purpose was the preservation of an administrative and social system through the medium of bureaucratic regulation, the various penalties being imposed by the six Boards. Law was an aspect of administration and not something that could be classed separately. The *Ta Ch'ing Lü Li* did not purport to cover all aspects of human life, it dealt only with those matters that were felt to require punishment[54] and was intended to ensure the preservation of order in the Empire. Order was defined to include not just offences such as treason, murder, and so on, but also peculiarly Chinese offences such as parricide, sacrilege, and the wounding of relatives within certain degrees of mourning.

In that part of the Code entitled 'Revenue', attention was directed to the registration of households and the collection of

[51] See generally Ch'ü (1965) and the sources there cited.
[52] Bodde & Morris (1967).
[53] Staunton (1810).
[54] There were five classes of punishment. See Bodde & Morris (1967: 93 ff.) and Alabaster (1899).

The South-East Asian Law Texts

various taxes. This part is sometimes translated as 'civil law'[55] because to the European observer it seems to cover what one would consider to be 'civil' as opposed to 'criminal' matters. Through the medium of taxation this part deals with a wide variety of family matters such as adoption (s. 78), succession (ss. 78, 88), marriage (ss. 101–17), as well as duty and excise (ss. 141–8) and markets (ss. 152–6). It is notable that in family law the regulations in the Code are not complete; for example, sections 78, 87, and 88 prohibit the improper appointment of an heir or the improper division of family property, but the actual rules of succession are not indicated. In other words, the rules relating to succession are only law in so far as they are relevant to taxation.

The third Part, that of the 'Board of Rites', provided for the punishment of those charged with supervising the rites if this duty was not carried out properly. Its provisions included punishments for the improper performance of rites associated with funerals, the care of imperial tombs, and for dishonouring celestial spirits by unlicensed forms of worship. It might well be regarded as an article enforcing the Confucian obligations (*hsiao*), primarily the five proper relationships[56] and the duties associated with each of them.

The fifth Part, that of the 'Board of Punishments', was the largest in the Code. While it dealt with the punishment for crimes that are universal in nature, such as murder, rape, and so on, it had some features peculiar to Chinese social structure. Crimes were distinguished according to the social or familial relations of the parties. It is more serious to assault an older relative than an equal.[57] Further, a good deal of this part of the Code, while concerned with offences against government, relates directly to the Confucian ethic which regarded as essential the maintenance of government and the preservation of the social order. Offences against the state and offences against the family order were, in a very real sense, connected parts of the same legal continuum. The legal relationships in which an individual was enmeshed were not dependent upon

---

[55] See Staunton (1810: 49), Bodde & Morris (1967: 60).
[56] Superior–Inferior; Father–Son; Husband–Wife; Older Brother–Younger Brother; Friend–Friend.
[57] See the different penalties in ss. 302, 318, 319.

the exercise of will but were derived from the basic principles of the Code: the preservation of a moral order which called for the administration of the individual as a part of that order. The nature of this order is often said to be 'Confucian', by which is meant the formalization of differences between individuals in terms of their status and roles. This formalization is essentially summed up in the concept of *li*, the rules of behaviour which vary in accordance with one's status and position. *Li* implies differentiation,[58] a concept which came to 'dominate all Chinese legislation'[59] after Han times. The legislation was directed toward encouraging and enforcing the doctrines of *li*, including distinctions between superior and inferior, in giving effect to the Confucian view of the family and to filial piety. Thus: 'What is left by *li* is covered by punishment. To go beyond *li* means to enter punishment. The two are but the outside and the inside of the same thing.'[60]

Law, therefore, was primarily regulative and punitive; it was an instrument for implementing *li*. The nature of law was thus equated to punishment invoked when the doctrines of *li* were violated. Right and wrong, though defined in a system of ethics, were not absolute but relative, dependent upon one's status. Law was not thought of as general but as a highly particularized body of rules applicable on the basis just described.

The texts discussed in this brief survey—and its brevity must be emphasized—illustrate something of the range and complexity of South-East Asian law. They show the variety of reference which the term 'law' bears in South-East Asian cultures, but despite this variety the texts as a group have a number of features in common. First, they all describe both a social system and an ideal moral or ethical order conceived as a unitary whole. Second, the foundation of these orders is not the principle of legality but rather the implementation of an ethical order. Third, all texts omit a number of areas of legal obligation in whole or in part. These omissions have led some commentators to the view that the texts are not 'really law'. But to take such a view is to misunderstand the texts described above; their function is to state a set of absolute principles within which

[58] See Ch'ü (1965: 231 ff.).
[59] Escarra (1933: 251).
[60] Ch'ên Ch'ung cited in Ch'ü (1965: 279).

The South-East Asian Law Texts

a system of obligation can be formulated. Large areas of the texts do contain rules directly applicable but this is not their primary function.

II THE TEXTS AND THE REALITY OF LAW

The texts are documents descriptive of reality in the sense that they posit a relationship between man and a cosmological and natural order. They therefore explain law as an aspect of this relationship, and to deny the reality of such an explanation is to deny the texts any relevance for comparative law. Such an extreme position is unusual; more common is the objection that personal obligation is inadequately dealt with. The existence of customary laws and textually unvalidated legal institutions is often cited in support of this objection. But it does not follow that such bodies of regulation are necessarily *sui generis* or that they constitute the sole legal reality. They each have definite relations with the texts and, most important, such institutions are formulated in the light of the texts themselves.

The relationship between the Hindu *dharma* and legal reality can best be approached by asking, what is *dharma*? For the authors of the *smṛti-s*, the answer was to be found in consulting the written law as expounded with the learning of the *śāstrī-s*. The authority of the text could not be replaced by rules of any individual's invention.[61] But the texts themselves[62] often state that when one looks for the *dharma* appropriate to a particular problem, one must look outside the texts. Custom (*caritra*) is defined in *Kātyāyana* as 'all that a person practises, whether or not it conforms to *dharma*, simply because it is the constant usage of the country'. This implies some opposition between *dharma* and custom in that each may constitute a source of law for the solution of a particular problem. In the earlier *Bṛhaspati* text, again with reference to the solution of dispute, custom is but one of four sources of law, the others being royal ordinance, practice, and the *dharma* itself. On this point, Robert Lingat describes custom as a social phenomenon owing its authority to its inveterate character, whereas the laws of the *śāstras* are preconditions for the realization of the social order itself.[63] In

---

[61] Derrett (1968: 153–4) and the sources there cited.
[62] Especially the text of *Kātyāyana*; cf. Lingat (1973: 176 ff.).
[63] Lingat (1973: 176–7).

other words, custom need not in theory be hostile to the fundamentals of the Hindu socio-religious system as expounded in the *śāstra*, but this was not always the case in real life. The *śāstra* incorporated custom because it was itself the outcome of customs rationalized and set down in written form. Since the *śāstra* is based on usage, especially in its practical (*vyavahāna*) chapters, usage might be cited to explain the written law, and the customs of the Brahmins of North India were taken as the norm. Other usages were also included, but the exact method of selection remains unknown. Very little attempt was made to record or standardize commercial custom, and even in marriage only general rules were given. The peculiar customs of specialized trades and communities were referred to, though not in great detail. Customs relating to land tenure and land tenancy were given very little attention. In the matters which were dealt with there was a tendency toward limiting the legal peculiarity of customs felt to be repugnant to the general concept of the *śāstra*.[64] Thus the early custom-based forms of adoption were retained in the texts but the validity of such transactions was subjected to reforming and unifying analysis. Customary deviations were not expatiated upon, the tendency rather was to perfect the written law; and this, in view of the character of the Hindu conception of law, was to be expected.

Customs were, however, applied and enforced in a number of tribunals—such as trade and mercantile courts—without reference to the *śāstra*. It was not necessary in such cases to compare custom with *śāstric* principles, but, where there were disputes between persons of different castes or occupation, reference to *śāstra* would be made and custom might be pleaded in derogation. In such cases both are known to have been viewed together.[65] It was essentially the responsibility of the King to determine whether or not a custom was repugnant to the *śāstra* and so to cancel or approve it. The proof of custom was a matter for investigation, which might include the production of written records if available. In assessing the validity and existence of a custom the activities of the jurist trained in the *śāstra* were essential, and where a custom failed,

[64] Thus recognizing a public desire for assimilation to the Brahminical norms. See Derrett (1968: 160 and 352 ff.).
[65] Derrett (1968: 162) and the sources there cited.

The South-East Asian Law Texts

the *śāstra* was resorted to as the residual law. Customary law itself could be effectively varied by the proper bodies concerned and it was also subject to amendment by royal decree. Neither of these forms of amendment was possible in the case of the *śāstra* unless, in the case of a royal decree, the order was in conformity with the *śāstra* or where the *śāstra* was silent. As Derrett remarks: 'The source of the *śāstra*'s authority was the public's acceptance of the postulates of Hinduism,[66] and the source of the custom's factual content and applicability was the public desire not to move from the ways of ancestors. Yet in practice custom was not static, neither was the umbrella provided by the *śāstra* inelastic.'[67]

This should not be taken to imply that a principle of *śāstra* was dependent for its application upon its agreement with custom. The rule of *dharma* was an ideal system of classification providing a certain view of reality, and it was toward the attainment of this reality that individual and caste practice was directed. Thus, custom contrary to orthodoxy would not be followed, at least by the élite, and where such a custom was already in written form it could be, and was, argued out of existence. Custom was a human and social development, but the tenets of Hinduism as expressed in the *śāstras* were not directed towards the maintenance of such development but toward higher forms of existence. The law of the *śāstras* and custom have entirely different natures but they are commingled in the law governing the conduct of a Hindu.

In Islamic law, custom occupies a very different position; custom which contravenes an express text of the Qur'ān or the *sunna* is void. Customary or local principles were of course at the basis of some of the rules of *Sharīʿa*, especially those dealing with the family and inheritance.[68] In addition, the development of the different schools of law reflected not only varieties of legal thought but also cultural differences within the Muslim community.[69] The religion of Islam is the religion of the majority of the population in Asia Minor, the Middle East, North Africa and parts of East and West Africa, south and

---

[66] See above, the preceding section of this chapter.
[67] Derrett (1968: 164).
[68] See Coulson (1964: 117–18), also Mohamed El-Awa (1973).
[69] See the following sources: Schacht (1964), (1953), Coulson (1964).

south-east Asia and, historically at least, central Asia and north China. In its relationship with the indigenous cultures one of two things happened to the *Sharī'a*: it either conflicted with the indigenous laws or legal thought of such cultures, especially in family law and matters of property, or an intermingling of principle took place in which the local custom became part of or was subsumed under the rubric 'Islam'. Both reactions might even have occurred in the same territory and affected the same people over a period of time. In all situations the determining factor was the necessity to give effect to local custom that took account of the ecological and economic facts of life. It was at precisely this point that the strict rules of the *Sharī'a* often proved unworkable. In the accommodations that took place elements of tension were always discernible simply because the *Sharī'a* is both a religious and a social system. For example, no definition of Islam can proceed on any assumption other than that the family régime is ultimately a question of religion. At the same time the distribution of family property in accordance with the *Sharī'a* may make no sense agriculturally or indeed may run directly counter to local custom. Therefore, although the doctrines of Islam were absolute, its practice was highly relative.

Conflict between Islam and local custom was and is widespread throughout the Muslim world and examples are known from all areas. One of the most extreme examples occurs in the Malay peninsula and Indonesia where Islam, as a legal system, is explicitly seen to be in opposition to the local *adat* laws. Amongst the matrilineal Minangkabau not only are the rules for marriage and the distribution of property contrary to the *Sharī'a*,[70] but the basis upon which obligation is attributed to the individual is also quite different. In the *adat* the natural human being has a basic capacity to undertake legal obligations. This capacity is qualified only in so far as conduct is proper according to one's position in life. The emphasis is upon natural capacity. In Islam, on the other hand, the legal system ascribes a minimal capacity and recognition only to those persons who are Muslims.[71] The *Sharī'a* claims and exercises an exclusive jurisdiction within which the

---

[70] Cf. Hooker (1972: 207–50); see also Prins (1954) on Indonesia.
[71] For present purposes we leave aside the position of Christians and Jews which tend to qualify somewhat the validity of this generalization.

adat views are not relevant.⁷² The opposition of systems even spilt over into politics when the struggle for power to administer law and to rule was seen as a function of an adherence to one or the other of the two systems.⁷³ At the same time it is worth noting that attempts were made to reconcile the two systems; in the Minangkabau *perbilangan* (*adat* verses) the two systems are expressly seen as the creation of God and, as such, as complementary parts of one unified whole designed for the benefit and guidance of man. The source of *adat* is located in the will of God⁷⁴ and its function is to forbid wrongs just as the function of religion is to promote right behaviour.

The commingling of Islamic law and local custom can be further exemplified from South-East Asia. In the *Undang-Undang Mahkamah Melayu Sarawak* (Laws of the Sarawak Malay Court) Islamic principles and local customary rules are intermingled in a haphazard sort of way, but the laws as a whole have worked satisfactorily for over a century. The question is, in what does Islamic law consist? This is also the question in those parts of East and West Africa, North Africa, and the Sudan in which the populations are at least nominally Muslim. In such lands the crucial factor is really the extent to which Islamic law may be said to have become customary law in some locality or community or even family. In many cases it is impossible to distinguish between some law called Islamic law and native law and custom.⁷⁵ It appears that where the religion of Islam has been accepted, the indigenous customs tend to assimilate themselves to Islamic law. Such a law may approximate in part to the *Sharīʿa*, but the extent of this approximation was and is variable.

Finally, we should not omit to notice that the position in India is, as ever, unique. There are in India major communities of what have been called 'anomalous' Muslims.⁷⁶ These were originally communities whose religion was Islam but whose inheritance and succession came to be governed by Hindu law. Such were the Khojas, the Cutchi Memons, Sunni Boharas of Gujarat, Molesalam Girasias of Broach, Halai Menons of

⁷² See further Hooker (1974), Nasroen (1957) on Minangkabau in Indonesia.
⁷³ Cf. Hooker (1971).
⁷⁴ Hooker (1974: 76, 78–9).
⁷⁵ See generally J. N. D. Anderson (1970).
⁷⁶ Derrett (1968: 522).

Porbunder, and the Moplahs of Kerala. Each of these communities had its own particular rules which were by no means consistent even within the group. For example, the Moplahs were originally governed by the *Marumakkattayam* law which included all aspects of the joint family and succession, but a few families did not follow this system by custom.[77] Legislation in the states has attempted to 'Islamize' the law of these communities more thoroughly.[78]

These examples illustrate the tension between the *Sharī'a* as an ideal law and the reality of local custom. In many instances idealism has given way to some form of compromise or even outright conflict, although the latter is rare. After all, the individual Muslim has an interest both as a believer and as a member of society in minimizing conflict so far as possible. But the *Sharī'a* remains the focus of legal thought both for the jurist and for the layman to whom in particular it provides the essential standard for conduct *vis-à-vis* local practice. Islam cannot be discussed as a legal system without considering custom, and the reverse is also true in Muslim countries.

If we turn to the classical Chinese law we find that the government was not alone in exercising jurisdiction over individuals. Additional bodies each applying their own sets of rules included the *tsu* (lineage), the guild, and the village. Such rules were not in derogation of the *Ta Ch'ing Lü Li*, but were in addition to it. They constituted a substantial extension to the official legal machinery. The *tsu*[79] shared a set of obligations to common ancestors and very often owned property the income from which was applied for the upkeep of ancestral halls, the performance of rites, and for purposes of management. Most *tsu* had formal constitutions as well as rules for the management of *tsu* business and for the conduct of members.[80] The *tsu* therefore had a corporate interest in the activities of membership, and the leaders were charged with the proper administration of the rules. The rules themselves commonly had many points of contact with the laws of the state. They included, for example,[81]

[77] See generally Fyzee (1964).   [78] See Derrett (1968: 519–30).
[79] An exogamous patrilineal group of males descended from a founding ancestor plus their wives and unmarried daughters. It consisted of a number of lines of descent and members shared the same surname. See S. van der Sprenkel (1966: 17).
[80] See Liu (1959).
[81] S. van der Sprenkel (1966: 82 ff.), Liu (1959).

clauses reinforcing the penal laws of the Empire, rules relating to the upkeep of the family and the promotion of the Confucian ethic, as well as detailed rules for the allocation of *tsu* resources. *Tsu* rules generally forbade members to engage in litigation without first submitting their case to the *tsu* leaders. It was also forbidden to stir up litigation. The most common causes of serious dispute appear to have been unfilial conduct, criminal behaviour, and disputes regarding property. In such cases the *tsu* would be convened in the ancestral hall and the matter publicly debated. Punishments included beating, the imposition of fines, and, most serious, expulsion from the *tsu*.[82] A person who had been expelled could not take part in ritual or share in the material benefits during his lifetime; after death his name would not be inscribed on the genealogy nor his tablet placed in the ancestral hall. No rites would be performed for him and he would thus be lost to the community, both living and dead, of the *tsu*. The rules of the *tsu*, by the very nature of the institution, which was both religious and secular, ranged from very vague morally tinged generalities to highly specific rules for the conduct of practical matters. Sanctions were thus both supernatural and secular, and there were cases in which ritual sanctions were applied to enforce *tsu* regulations on such everyday things as land regulation.[83] The principles upon which the *tsu* leaders administered the rules have been said to be local standards of conduct,[84] but they were apparently exercised with the approval of the administrative authorities. It was only after the *tsu* procedures had been gone through that any matter was laid before the official magistrate.

The craft and merchant guilds of China possessed detailed rules and regulations for the guidance of their members. Such were necessary because the *Ch'ing* Code had only a very few sections on commercial matters and these related almost entirely to taxation. The guilds were commonly organized by craft or trade and, in the case of merchants, by trade and by place of origin. Their chief function was mutual protection, by which was meant not just protection from non-members but essentially controlling the activities of members and settling

[82] S. van der Sprenkel (1966: 85), Hu (1948).
[83] S. van der Sprenkel (1966: 87) and the sources there cited.
[84] Ibid.

disputes amongst them. Each guild had its regulations, usually publicly displayed in the premises of its members. The leadership would meet to settle disputes[85] and to impose fines and a variety of other punishments. Rules were highly formalized and, as well as providing for the constitution of the guild, they were also codes of trading practice. As such they set standards of weights and measures and provided rules for methods of payment and so on. Members were expressly forbidden to appeal to a magistrate in disputed cases without first giving the guild court a chance to adjudicate. This was undertaken with the approval of magistrates in the official service; guild regulations were quoted and regarded as authoritative in the official courts, and magistrates often referred questions to guilds for their opinion.[86]

Although both *tsu* and guild were important for the nature and extent of control which they exercised over their members,[87] they did not cover large areas of life in China. The bulk of the Chinese people were village dwellers and it was in this sphere that the final important sets of rules regulating the individual were to be found. A certain amount of organization based on the village was necessary in the economic life of all regions of China, and the leaders of the villages were held responsible for keeping order. They had power to deal with criminal offences of a petty nature and, most important, the settlement of disputes formed a large part of the function of the village leader. Settlement was undertaken by mediation and arbitration, and parties who did not receive satisfaction could appeal to the district magistrate. The basis of the process was local custom which could be varied to suit the circumstances of the case. The important point is that the *Ch'ing* Code left large areas of law, such as sale, lease, marriage, and land transactions, either unregulated or only partially regulated so that local custom was in every sense a basic source of law. To a large extent, local custom provided the only laws governing the vast mass of village transactions, the Code itself having little direct

---

[85] It is worth noting that overseas Chinese merchant associations still perform the same function. The example with which the present writer is familiar is the Singapore Chinese Chamber of Commerce.
[86] S. van der Sprenkel (1966: 95), Kotenev (1925).
[87] See Alabaster (1899: lvi) for a summary.

The South-East Asian Law Texts

relevance to the majority of the people. The importance of custom can be gauged from the mass of data compiled in the early years of the Republic (1925) and the range of the topics dealt with.[88] All classes of land transaction were included, together with marriage. Agreements were made in writing and often registered with the district magistrate.[89] It was more or less universal practice for negotiations to be undertaken by third parties or middlemen who had a legal responsibility.[90] The village leaders, who had a variety of official duties, including the registration and taxation of land, acted as the natural forum for disputes arising out of these transactions. They administered what was, in effect, a consistent and internally self-justifying body of rules which were virtually the living law of the bulk of the Chinese people.

The process of the law in the *tsu*, guild, and village was by way of negotiation, mediation, and arbitration.[91] It was only when this process was exhausted that the official courts became involved. The major form of control over the individual was vested in the authority/ies of the group to which he belonged. Where a dispute involved members of more than one group, say two *tsu*, then mediation could be effected by a village head, by the head of another *tsu*, or by some other *locally* selected person. Similarly, inter-guild disputes were usually argued out by leaders of the guilds. In all cases the process—mediation and arbitration—was the same. However, the effectiveness of a system of localized jurisdictions applying discrete bodies of rules depended very much upon local factors for its success. The official courts did not provide an institutional forum for the individual whose treatment in any of the other forums was unsatisfactory. Indeed, it was not unknown for the official court to be used as a means of attacking one's enemies.

The whole of Chinese law was a complex made up of the texts, rules specific to groups, and local customary law. Each of these types of regulation dealt with matters conceived to be of specific interest to a certain level of society or to a certain class of person in society. In all cases there were prohibitions against

---
[88] See S. van der Sprenkel (1966: 103 ff.) and the sources there cited.
[89] See Watt (1972) on the district magistrate in late Ch'ing times.
[90] See S. van der Sprenkel (1966: 107 ff.).
[91] See Lubman (1967) on the history and importance of these forms of dispute settlement in both old and new China.

actions conceived of as threatening the structure of society. The reality of the law was plural in nature but the values that it enforced were absolute and consistent. The system promoted stability within the framework of the Confucian ethic, the validity of which was accepted at all levels of society and within all groups. The texts of the *Ch'ing* and the earlier dynasties were 'really law' in this sense.

III CONCLUSION

This survey of the law texts demonstrates that they are 'texts of law' but that their nature is quite distinct from the legal texts of the modern industrial state in the nineteenth and twentieth centuries. What is the nature of the distinction? It is, as suggested in the body of this chapter, that the function of the texts is different from that of the written laws of Western culture. They provide a framework for the idea of obligation and, in so doing, they deny the distinction, common to the law of modern industrial states, between 'positive' and 'living' law as found in the work of such jurists as Ehrlich.[92] As we have seen, the texts relate to reality in a number of ways but they all posit a continuum between written law and actual practice. The key to understanding this continuum is that the individual appears in the law not as a member of the class 'individual subject to law' but as a person of certain status (of class, caste, inferior, and so on), the significance of which varies according to the implications of the status in question. This does not mean to say that the criterion for the application of law is necessarily relativist; it may of course be so, but equally the absence of positive law in an extreme sense does not of necessity imply relativism. Relevant criteria are more properly to be found in such concepts as *dharma*, the Confucian ethic, or the will of God. It is within these that the facts of particular cases take on the appropriate legal significance.

In all the codes described above, the notion of status[93] is primary; the propriety of any action which an individual may undertake is determined by reference to a natural system of obligation. 'Natural' here means principles which are self-

[92] Ehrlich (1936: 493 ff.).
[93] In the sense established by Sir Henry Maine but without emphasizing his will theory.

evident in the ecologies, social systems, and religions. They are, so to speak, given in the facts of life. The *varṇa* of the Hindu, the word of Allah, and the five proper relationships of Confucius are not just normative, they are also real descriptions of the natural order.[94] Propriety, therefore, means acting in accord with the reality of human (and extra-human) existence. The individual accepts the obligations arising out of this state of affairs, and it is only in this sense that sanctions such as outcasting, expulsion from the *tsu*, and the denial of entry to God's presence become fully explicable.

The codes contain laws which in all cases have a determinate and absolute content. Such cannot be compromised if the society is to exist. Radical change in fact means the destruction of that society. In cases of dispute, mediation was the preferred process simply because divergent interpretations of the legal complex were not possible. Even variant interpretation was limited by the propriety of the natural (and hence legal) order itself.

The South-East Asian law texts derived these characteristics from their respective models and at the same time preserved indigenous South-East Asian features. Room for the latter was found in the interstices of the imported written texts, i.e. in those areas in which the original rules were either inoperable or non-existent. These gaps were filled in with indigenous matter (most often in connection with family and property) which, when combined with the imported matter, often results in texts that are internally inconsistent. But the inconsistency is itself a part of the process of adaptation and each textual model either assumes or explicitly states a place for local rules. In no case is a multiple *source* for regulation denied in any text, although of course the idea of law itself is both absolute and immutable. The tension between an absolute conception, derived from India, China, or Islam, and local regulation gives the South-East Asian texts their unique character.

[94] See, for example, the comments of Reale (1968) and McKeon (1968).

PART II
CONTRACT

CHAPTER 5

The English Legal World: The Straits Settlements, Federated and Unfederated Malay States, British Borneo, and Burma

THE SOUTH-EAST Asian colonial possessions in which English law became the law of general application are, in order of acquisition: the Straits Settlements, the Federated and Unfederated Malay States, the British Borneo territories, and Burma. The Straits Settlements comprised Penang, Malacca, and Singapore; the last is now an independent republic whilst Penang and Malacca have been incorporated with the Federated and Unfederated Malay States and the Borneo territories (British North Borneo and Sarawak) into the state of Malaysia. Burma is now an independent ('socialist') republic. These countries all share a common heritage of English law which, in each case, has the following characteristic: the introduced English law was the law of general application and the English courts were courts of general jurisdiction. Even where native courts were established, native law was applied subject to English principles and to the overriding jurisdiction of the general courts. There was no suggestion of special 'law areas' or 'law populations' as in the Netherlands East Indies.[1] Rather, the history of the English legal world in South-East Asia is a history of the accommodation between English principles and indigenous laws, resulting in the latter being absorbed within the English legal system by way of both statute and case law. The legal history of the area is not so much a history of institutions as of the formation of special precedents[2]

---
[1] See Chapter 7.
[2] See, for example, Wee (1974) for an analysis of the judicial process in respect of Chinese family law. See also further below, pp. 130–32.

giving effect to local laws. The latter thus became a part of the whole body of the (English) common law, applicable in the territories concerned. Variations in the particular rules derived from precedent occurred, but they were a response to local conditions and not due to any overriding theory of colonial legal development.

I THE STRAITS SETTLEMENTS

Penang, Malacca, and Singapore, which together comprised the Straits Settlements were each acquired at a different date. The Straits Settlements did not become one entity in law until 1825, and the legal history of each settlement differs from that of the others.

(a) Penang. The island of Penang (Prince of Wales Island) was occupied on 12 August 1786 by virtue of an agreement between Francis Light, acting on behalf of the East India Company, and the 'King of Kedah'. The agreement did not amount to a cession of territory but only to a limited right of occupation subject to the payment of an annual sum by the Company. The subsequent Treaty with the King of Kedah of 1 May 1791 made substantially similar provisions. Difficulty arises as to the interpretation of this treaty; Kedah in 1791 does not seem to have had an independent sovereignty but to have been, in some sense, a vassal of Siam (as it then was). Thus, in the period from 1791 to 1826 when, by the Treaty of Bangkok of 20 June 1826,[3] British sovereignty over Penang was acknowledged by Siam, the status of Penang continued so far as English law was concerned, to be uncertain. The courts of the later Straits Settlements had no doubt that the law of England, suitably modified to deal with the customs and religions of the inhabitants, could have been the only applicable law. An alternative argument, that the law properly applicable was the law of the East India Company's Bengal government, has also been put,[4] but its validity is by no means fully established. The island was regarded as having been occupied and settled by British subjects,[5] and in these circumstances, as was said in *Ong Cheng Neo* v. *Yeap Cheah Neo*,[6]

[3] Maxwell & Gibson (1924: 77).   [4] Hooker (1969: 20–35).
[5] *R.* v. *Willans* (1858) 3 Ky. 16, *Fatimah* v. *Logan* (1871) 1 Ky. 255.
[6] (1872) 1 Ky. 326 at 343–44.

The English Legal World

With reference to this history [of Penang] it is really immaterial to consider whether Prince of Wales Island, or, as it is called, Penang, should be regarded as ceded or newly settled territory, for there is no trace of any laws having been established there before it was acquired by the East India Company. In either view the law of England must be taken to be the governing law, so far as it is applicable to the circumstances of the place, and modified in its application by these circumstances.

For the first twenty years or so of the settlement's existence uncertainty persisted as to the law properly applicable,[7] and in that period the 'law of nature' was generally regarded as its basic law.[8] Some regulations were issued in 1800,[9] but it was not until 1807 that a Charter of Justice for the settlement was promulgated. The Charter provided for a Court of Judicature which had the jurisdiction of the superior courts of England and ecclesiastical jurisdiction 'so far as the several religions, manners and customs of the inhabitants will admit'. This Charter has been held to admit the laws of England, as they then stood, into Penang,[10] although the administrative authorities took some time to adjust themselves to this view.[11] So far as the law itself was concerned, English law was established either by virtue of the Charter of 1807[12] or by virtue of the fact that Penang was a territory under British control analogous to a conquered or ceded territory.[13] Both alternatives were commonly cited in later cases. It is worth noting also that this was the only view of relevance to the courts, it took no account of the politically uncertain state of the sovereignty of Kedah, with whom the agreements of 1786 and 1791 were concluded. The position of this state *vis-à-vis* Siam remained uncertain and gave rise to a good deal of public controversy in later years.[14]

The Charter of 1807 was replaced by the Charter of 1826 which repeated the substantive provisions of 1807 but extended

---

[7] Hooker (1969: 23-4) and the sources there cited.
[8] See P. B. Maxwell (1859: 33), Napier (1898).
[9] See T. Braddell (1851: 114-17).
[10] *Kamoo* v. *Bassett* (1808) 1 Ky. 1, *In the Goods of Abdullah* (1835) 2 Ky. Ecc. Rs. 8 and *R.* v. *Willans* (1858) 3 Ky. 16.
[11] See Norton Kyshe (1969: 77-95).
[12] See n. 10 above.
[13] *Campbell* v. *Hall* 1 Cowp. 204 at 209 cited and applied in *R.* v. *Willans* (1858) 3 Ky. 16 at 21.
[14] See Crawfurd (1820: (ii) 404), Begbie (1834: 24-9).

the jurisdiction of the Penang Recorder's Court to Singapore and Malacca.

(b) *Singapore.* The island of Singapore was occupied by the British in January 1819. It was practically uninhabited at the time and was nominally under the control of the Dato' Temenggong of Johore, himself subject to the Sultan of Johore. Sir Stamford Raffles entered into a series of agreements and treaties with the local rulers as follows:

1. Preliminary Agreement with the Dato' Temenggong of Johore, January 1819.
2. Treaty of Friendship and Alliance between the East India Company and the Sultan of Johore, February 1819.
3. Arrangements made for the Government of Singapore between Raffles, Farquhar, and the Sultan of Johore, 1819.
4. A Treaty of Friendship and Alliance between the Company and the Sultan and the Temenggong of Johore, November 1824.
5. Memorandum by Sir Stamford Raffles (presumed 1823) on the sovereignty of the Company over Singapore.

The first three documents did not provide for a transfer of sovereignty or for cession of the island but made provision only for the establishment of a factory and for the maintenance of peace and public order. It was not until the 'Treaty of Friendship and Alliance between the Company and the Sultan and the Temenggong' of November 1824 that Singapore was actually ceded to the Company (art. 2). Article 6 provided that English law should apply to the inhabitants 'with due consideration to the habits and usages of the people'. The laws of the Malays were to be respected where not contrary to reason, justice, and humanity. In 1823, under Regulations III and IV of that year,[15] Raffles had appointed magistrates and produced a draft set of laws, based on English law, for the administration of justice. Under the regulations regard was to be had to native customs; the regulations were general and left large powers of discretion in the hands of the magistrates. This scheme was continued until March 1827 when the jurisdiction

[15] See (1968) *Malaya Law Review* 10: 248–91.

The English Legal World 127

of the Penang Recorder's Court was extended to Malacca and Singapore by virtue of the Charter of Justice of 1826.

(c) *Malacca*. Malacca was ceded to the Crown in 1824 under the terms of the Anglo-Dutch Treaty of that year. It had actually been occupied by the British in 1795–1801 but then returned to Dutch possession. In 1825 by virtue of 6 Geo. IV c. 85 s. 19 Malacca was transferred to the control of the East India Company. The same act authorized the Company to annex Singapore and Malacca to Penang, and in 1826 the Company's petition for a new Charter of Justice for the incorporated settlements was granted. Malacca had been a Dutch possession from 1641, the Dutch having succeeded the Portuguese in possession, and the question which exercised the courts in the later years was, what was the law of Malacca after 1824 and, in particular, what was the status of the pre-existing Dutch laws?[16] This question was answered in a series of reported decisions.

In *Sahrip* v. *Mitchell and Endain* Sir Benson Maxwell *C.J.* said:[17]

> The Portuguese while they held Malacca and after them the Dutch, left the Malay custom or *lex non scripta* in force. That it was in force when this Settlement was ceded to the Crown appears to be beyond dispute and that the cession left the law unaltered is equally plain on general principles. *Campbell* v. *Hall* 1 Cowp. 204, 209. It was held by Sir John Claridge in 1829 to be then in full force; and although it was decided by Sir B. Malkin in 1834 in conformity with what had been held in India, that the law of England had been introduced into the Settlement by the Charter which created the Supreme Court it seems to me clear that the law so introduced will no more supersede the custom in question than it supersedes local custom in England.

This was a case relating to Malay *custom* which was approved as being a 'good and reasonable custom', but, so far as Dutch *law* was concerned, the reverse applied. In *Rodyk* v. *Williamson*[18] the courts had to decide the rights of a Dutch widow; these were held to be governed by English law on the following reasoning:

> I refer to the case of *Rodyk* v. *Williamson* [24 May 1834] in which I expressed my opinion, that I was bound by the uniform course of

---

[16] For some details of this see Joseph (1970), W. E. Maxwell (1884: xliii–li).
[17] (1870) Leic. 466 at 469.
[18] Unreported decision of 1834 but cited at length in *In the Goods of Abdullah* (1835) 2 Ky. Ecc. Rs. 8.

authority to hold that the introduction of the King's Charter into these settlements had introduced the existing law of England also, except in some cases where it was modified by express provision, and had abrogated any law previously existing. I intimated much doubt, indeed, whether I should have agreed in such a construction of the effect of a Charter, had the question been a new one; but I felt bound by the weight of authority and decided against the continuance of the Dutch law at Malacca, accordingly.[19]

This decision was later approved in *Moraiss* v. *De Souza*[20] which defined the interest in a (lost) Dutch grant of land to be a fee simple in terms of English law. In other words, these cases were concerned, as a matter of policy, to state that the law of *general application* was English law. This appears clearly from Sir Benson Maxwell's proposition in *R.* v. *Willans*:[21]

Such a doctrine would imply that the continuance of the existing law in a ceded or conquered country, as the right, however precarious, of the late Sovereign or of the soil itself, rather than the privilege of the inhabitants. But the case of Jamaica, referred to in *Campbell* v. *Hall* 1 Cowp. 212, shows that this is not so. Though taken from the Spaniards, Spanish Law was not considered to be in force there, after all the Spaniards had left the Island.

A local custom in terms of the Charter was thus defined to exclude a pre-existing European law, and, although commentators at the time[22] objected to such an interpretation, it became well-settled law.

After 1830 the three settlements ceased to form a separate presidency and became subordinate to Fort William in Bengal. The courts continued to be ordered, however, by the Charter of 1826,[23] although some uncertainty was expressed about this in 1830–1.[24] The Charter of 1855 replaced that of 1826 and was concerned to recognize the court into two divisions, although its substantive law content was much as in the earlier Charter of 1826. In the period 1851–67 the settlements were administered

[19] *In the Goods of Abdullah* (1835) 2 Ky. Ecc. Rs. 8 at 9–10.
[20] (1838) 1 Ky. 27.
[21] (1858) 3 Ky. 16 at 21.
[22] See Napier (1898: 22).
[23] For a reprint of the Regulations of P.O.W.I. Singapore and Malacca 1825–33 see (1971) *Malaya Law Review* 13: (2) 294–400.
[24] The court even suspended itself for a year, wrongly as it turned out. See *Caunter* v. *E.I. Co.* (1830) 4 Ky. 12.

by the Government of India, and from 1867 onwards the Colony of the Straits Settlements was administered by the Colonial Office from London. The law applicable in the colony thus had a number of sources which were stated in *Ismail bin Savoosah* v. *Madinasah Maricar*[25] to be the law of England as at 1826 (i.e. from the Charter of 1826), Indian acts having reference to the Colony, Ordinances of the Colony, and English statutes of general application.[26] English statutes were not automatically applicable.[27]

There was universal agreement that English law was introduced into the Straits Settlements by the Charters of Justice but doubt existed as to the modifications necessary on account of religion and local custom. Sir Edward Stanley, the first Recorder, thought that the effect of the Charter of 1807 was to guarantee the free exercise of religion and custom.[28] On the other hand, the court in *In the Goods of Abdullah*[29] and in *R.* v. *Willans*[30] thought that the Charter did not sanction local law but merely admitted it as an exception—mainly in ecclesiastical jurisdiction—to the general English law. It is the latter view that later became accepted.[31]

The subsequent history of colonial English law in the Straits Settlements is mainly a history of an accommodation of the law to local circumstances. The most important factors were the variety of races (Malay, Chinese, Indian) and of religions (Islam, Hinduism, and an undifferentiated mass of Chinese religious custom) which were characteristic of the territories. They gave rise to the development of 'personal laws',[32] i.e. laws which were administered to persons of a named religion or race as part of the general common law of the territories. For the legal historian the interesting feature is the judicial reasoning that developed the personal laws. As we shall see in a moment,

---

[25] (1887) 4 Ky. 133 overruling *Jemalah* v. *Mohamed Ali* (1875) 1 Ky. 368.
[26] See *R.* v. *Rodriguez* (1887) 4 Ky. 323, *Mahomed Meera Nachair* v. *Inche Khatijah* (1890) 4 Ky. 608.
[27] *R.* v. *Till* (1809) 2 Ky. Crim. Rs. 1, *R.* v. *Adam Singh* (1822) 2 Ky. Crim. Rs. 12, *Re Khoo Chow Sew* (1872) 2 Ky. Ecc. Rs. 22.
[28] See the Proclamation read by Sir Edward Stanley on 30 May 1808 reprinted in (1973) *Malaya Law Review* 15: (1) 55–9 at 56.
[29] (1835) 2 Ky. Ecc. Rs. 8 at 11.
[30] (1858) 3 Ky. 16 at 32.
[31] See *Chulas* v. *Kolson* (1867) Leic. 462 at 462–3.
[32] See Hooker (1975) for an outline.

the sorts of reasoning adopted were largely conditioned by the complex history of the three settlements.

Not surprisingly, the multiplicity of laws applicable in the Straits Settlements suggested to the judiciary that the principles of conflict of laws had a part to play. This was first expressed in *Chulas* v. *Kolson*,[33] where, in upholding a principle of native law, the court recognized such 'on the same principles and with the same limitations as foreign law is applied by our courts to foreigners and foreign transactions'. In other words, parties to a law which was not English law were to be deemed to be of foreign domicile. Now while it is true that in 1867 many of the inhabitants were not domiciled in the settlements or, at best, domicile was difficult to establish, the problems which this principle entailed were great. It amounted to saying that in matters of private law the courts would recognize a number of distinct laws applicable on the basis of private international law. This view was never accepted, as it was, for example, in the Netherlands East Indies,[34] and only ten years later in *Khoo Tiang Bee* v. *Tan Beng Guat*[35] the court doubted whether such a principle was sound for the affairs of the Straits Settlements. Later cases which established the basic principles of the personal laws never proceeded on such a basis except where a truly foreign element was in fact present. Instead, the courts proceeded by way of the Charter of 1826 (and that of 1855) or *ex comitate*.[36] The question was not just the admission of non-English principles but, once admitted, their implementation within the framework of English law as the law of general application. It was at this point that English statute often made its mark. Thus, in *Cheo Eng Choon's* case the judge admitted the validity of polygamous marriages and the legitimacy of heirs arising out of such marriages but determined the shares in the estate according to the Statute of Distributions.[37] The reason given was that the personal estate of a deceased person *domiciled* in the Straits Settlements must be distributed according to the law of the colony, that is to say, according to the Statute. But

[33] (1867) Leic. 462.
[34] See below, Chapter 7.
[35] (1877) 1 Ky. 413 at 417.
[36] *In the Estate of Choo Eng Choon decd. Choo Ang Chee* v. *Neo Chan Neo* (1908) 12 S.S.L.R. 120 and the cases there cited.
[37] *Re Choo Eng Choon decd.* (1911) 12 S.S.L.R. 120.

why the Statute of Distributions and not some local custom (in this case of the Chinese)? There were three reasons. First, the principle was accepted in earlier judgments[38] because, in the case of polygamous unions, the courts would not differentiate between different grades of wife (i.e. primary or secondary) but ordered an equal division of property among heirs as the Statute directed. It thus had the sanction of past application behind it. Second, and possibly more significant, the judges could point to English authority which clearly stated that the Statute could properly apply to persons of all races and religions and could operate in favour of a person 'legitimate by the law of another country though not legitimate by the law of England'.[39] Thus the Statute was properly applicable to the circumstances of the settlement. Finally, and perhaps most important of all, the court in the late nineteenth century was no longer applying 'foreign' law to Chinese, Hindus, or Muslims. Those parts of their laws which applied were by that time part of and incorporated into the common law of the Straits Settlements. Where conflict did arise with principles of 'English law' (i.e. law which was unaffected by local circumstance), it was a conflict *within* the newly developed common law of the colony.

This can be demonstrated by later cases again involving Chinese polygamous marriages. In *Isaac Penhas* v. *Tan Soo Eng*[40] the court found a valid common-law marriage to exist between a Jewish man and a Chinese woman on the basis of proof of consensus to enter into marriage. In respect of marriages between two Chinese, on the other hand, it was long held that elements of intent, cohabitation, and repute were necessary to establish a valid marriage. Thus, where one party only is Chinese, the common-law doctrine of consensus applies; if both parties are Chinese, three requirements are necessary. However, in *Yeow Kian Kee decd: Er Gek Cheng* v. *Ho Ying Seng*[41] a Chinese *secondary* marriage was found to exist solely on the basis of consensus. Confusion was prominent in the field of Chinese marriage, as witness the scathing comments of Sir Roland Braddell[42] when, in discussing the decision in *Khoo Hooi Leong* v.

---

[38] *In the goods of Lao Leong An* (1877) Leic. 418, (1893) 1 S.S.L.R. 1, *Lee Joo Neo* v. *Lee Eng Swee* (1887) 4 Ky. 325, *Khoo Tiang Bee* v. *Tan Beng Gwat* (1877) 1 Ky. 413.
[39] *Re Goodman's Trusts* 50 L.J. 425.   [40] [1953] A.C. 304.
[41] [1949] S.L.R. 78, [1949] M.L.J. 171.   [42] R. St. J. Braddell (1931: (i) 79).

Khoo Chong Yeok,⁴³ he pointed out not just misunderstandings of Straits Settlements precedent but also that the Privy Council dissented from its own earlier *ratio decidendi* in the same suit! It is interesting also to note that, although legitimation by subsequent marriage was recognized by the courts, legitimation by subsequent recognition was not, the reason being that it was unknown and repugnant to the common law of England.⁴⁴ We return to these issues later when we deal with conflict of laws.

In the case of the large Muslim population of the Straits Settlements, marriage and divorce according to Islamic law were held valid from the very earliest days.⁴⁵ However, the courts experienced difficulty in deciding suits which involved rules from different schools of Islamic law. For example, in *Salmah & Fatimah* v. *Soolong*⁴⁶ the guardian of a Shāfiī female obtained an injunction preventing a marriage between her and a Hanafī male. The court refused to disallow the injunction on the application of the girl until she had become a Hanafī, whereupon she was at liberty to marry.⁴⁷ More serious, however, were the limitations placed upon the court's jurisdiction by virtue of the terms of the Charters of Justice. The court refused jurisdiction, on its civil side, to recognize suits for the restitution of conjugal rights⁴⁸ and suits involving the validity or otherwise of Muslim divorce.⁴⁹ The Mahomedan Marriage Ordinance was introduced in 1880;⁵⁰ it was intended to define how much of Islamic law was to be recognized by the courts.⁵¹ It provided for the voluntary registration of Muslim marriage and divorce, the recognition of 'Kalis', and the regulation of married women's property. It did not enact the substantive law of Islam, nor did it prescribe authoritative texts, but in subsequent amendments⁵² parts of the substantive Islamic law on family matters were progressively introduced. The ordin-

---

⁴³ [1926] A.C. 529, [1930] A.C. 346.
⁴⁴ *Khoo Hooi Leong* v. *Khoo Chong Yeok* [1930] A.C. 346.
⁴⁵ *In the Matter of Inche Lebedrecha* a decision given in 1797 and reported in Norton Kyshe (1969: 42–3). The leading case is *Hawah* v. *Daud* (1865) Leic. 253.
⁴⁶ (1878) 1 Ky. 421.
⁴⁷ See also *Syed Abdullah al-Shatiri* v. *Shariffa Salmah* [1959] M.L.J. 137.
⁴⁸ *Shaik Madar* v. *Jaharrah* (1874) 1 Ky. 385.
⁴⁹ *Adoomeh Kakah* v. *Lebby Dain* (1878) 1 Ky. 438.
⁵⁰ No. 5 of 1880.
⁵¹ See R. St. J. Braddell (1915: 91).
⁵² Mahomedan Marriage (Amendment) Ordinances 1894, 1902, 1908, 1909, 1917.

ance and its amendments were re-enacted as Ordinance No. 26 (Mahomedans) of 1923, amended in 1934, and finally included as cap. 57 in the revised laws of the Straits Settlements, 1936, under the title of the Mohammedans Ordinance. It remained in force in Penang and Malacca until 1959.

In some areas it is difficult to ascertain the application of the provisions of this ordinance; in *Noordin M.M.* v. *Shaikh Mohd. Meah Noordin*,[53] Islamic law was preferred to English law in determining the age of majority for marriage, but in *Mong* v. *Daing Mokkah*[54] a Muslim woman was held entitled to bring an action in the civil court for breach of promise to marry. English law principles were expressly applied to prevent injustice. On the other hand, the *talak* (Muslim method of divorce) was recognized by the courts.[55] Equally serious were jurisdictional shortcomings in the ordinance. For example, section 18 of the Mohammedans Ordinance of 1936 provided for *fasah* (annulment) divorce, but in *Rokiah* v. *Abu Bakar*[56] the husband refused his consent despite a direction by a Kathi who ordered and registered a divorce by *khula* (self-redemption) upon repayment of the *mas kahwin* (marriage payment). It was held by the Registrar of Penang that a divorce by *khula* could not dispense with the consent of the husband. This resulted in a deadlock, the marriage subsisted in law and the wife had no further remedy.[57]

Similar difficulties arose in respect of property; in *In The Goods of Abdullah*[58] decided in 1835, it was held that a Muslim could alienate the whole of his property by will, a decision contrary to the law of Islam. The reason for this was that the court supposed the law of England to be in force to the exclusion of Islamic law in the matter of wills. It is only fair to add that this decision was harshly criticized in contemporary cases.[59] However, as early as 1865 the courts held that the property of a Muslim woman was her own separate property in which her husband took no interest either during coverture or at death.[60] But a married

[53] (1908) 10 S.S.L.R. 72.   [54] [1935] M.L.J. 147.
[55] *Syed Mohamed Yassin* v. *Syed Abdulrahman* (1921) 15 S.S.L.R. 199.
[56] Taylor (1948: 10).
[57] See also *Syed Ahmad* v. *Fatimah* Taylor (1948: 14).
[58] (1835) 2 Ky. Ecc. Rs. 8.
[59] Cf. *R.* v. *Willans* (1858) 3 Ky. 16.
[60] *Hawah* v. *Daud* (1865) Leic. 253, *Haleemah* v. *Bradford* (1877) Leic. 383.

woman's conveyance was not valid prior to the 1880 ordinance unless acknowledged on the principle of *lex loci regit actum* as required by Indian Act XXVI of 1854. Under section 5 of this act no deed executed by a married woman was valid unless her husband's concurrence had been obtained and the deed acknowledged before a judge or an appointed commissioner.[61] Section 27 of the Mahomedan Marriage Ordinance 1880 provided for the separate property of a married woman, and this was continued in later legislation. However, it was not until 1929 that a Muslim woman could take proceedings against her husband for the protection and security of her own property.[62]

The Islamic law of inheritance was recognized only in so far as expressly enacted in section 27 of the Ordinance of 1880. This was interpreted to restrict 'inheritance' to property and not to include an office, so that a claim to succeed as an imam failed.[63] It was open to any Muslim to direct inheritance by will and this was subjected to Islamic law on the topic. However, on an intestacy the rules of English law were to apply. This meant in effect that the Statute of Distributions[64] would determine shares in an estate subject to the qualification that where there was more than one widow then each would receive an equal share. It was not until 1923 that the estate of a Muslim intestate fell to be distributed according to Islamic law with the qualification that Islamic law could not override any local custom having the force of law prior to 1 January 1924.[65] A provision was also made for non-Muslim next of kin to inherit, contrary to express provisions of Islamic law.

The question of joint earnings (*harta sapencharian*) by husband and wife during coverture was not dealt with by legislation but was left to the courts. There is only one case from the Straits Settlements on this point and that is almost certainly incorrect. In *Tijah* v. *Mat Alli*[66] a wife sued her husband for a half share of joint earnings consisting of the profits derived from the sale of

[61] See *Chulas* v. *Kolson* (1867) Wood's Oriental Cases 30, *Kader Mydin* v. *Shatomah* (1868) Leic. 260, *Fatimah* v. *Armootah Pillay* (1887) 4 Ky. 225.
[62] *Nurud-din* v. *Siti Aminah* [1929] S.S.L.R. 146 reversing the decision in *R.* v. *Ojir & anor.* (1886) 4 Ky. 122 and declaring s. 10 (3) of the Married Women's Property Ordinance 1902 inapplicable.
[63] *Jamaludin* v. *Hajee Abdullah* (1881) 1 Ky. 503.
[64] 22 & 23 Car. II c. 10.
[65] S. 27 Mahomedans Ordinance No. 26 of 1923. See also Withers Payne (1932).
[66] (1890) 4 Ky. 124. See also Taylor (1937: 15), Hooker (1972: 228 f.).

produce grown upon land jointly rented during coverture. A Kathi gave evidence that according to Islamic law the wife was entitled to such a share. This is quite wrong because Islamic law does not recognize jointly acquired property as a special category; the Kathi was reporting a Malay *adat* rule. The court gave judgment for the wife, but on appeal this was reversed on the basis that the Mahomedan Marriage Ordinance of 1880 did not provide for the joint earnings of husband and wife.[67] The judge, therefore, applied English law.

English law has also been held to exclude Islamic law in respect of charities. In *Fatimah* v. *Logan*[68] a gift for *kandoories* (funeral feasts) was held not to be charitable, but this was later reversed in *Estate of Haji Daing Tahira*.[69] A gift to persons reading the Qur'ān in the testator's name has been held not to be charitable,[70] in accordance with the principle established in *Re Syed Shaik Alkaff's* case,[71] i.e. that purposes regarded by a Muslim as religious are not prima facie charitable.

The courts have never seriously questioned the application of Hindu law in the Straits Settlements. In the earliest reported case, *Pootoo* v. *Valee Uta Taven & anor*,[72] the court assumed the relevance of Hindu law without argument, and in the later case of *Karpen Tandil* v. *Karpen*[73] Hindu law was recognized on the grounds of equity and natural justice.[74] In both cases decisions from the Indian jurisdictions as to the substance of Hindu law were relied upon. Recognition was also extended to local custom,[75] which was admitted so long as it was reasonable, definite, and not contrary to natural justice. Hindu law as administered in India might also be applied if the parties were domiciled in the Indian jurisdiction.[76] Certain features of Hindu law, however, were not given effect to: for example, marriage brokerage contracts were held invalid as being against public morality.[77] Caste also was never a central issue, and in

[67] This is not surprising because the ordinance is concerned with Islam and not with Malay *adat*.
[68] (1871) 1 Ky. 259.
[69] [1948] M.L.J. 62.
[70] *Re Alsagoff's Trusts* [1956] M.L.J. 244.
[71] (1923) M.C. 38.
[72] (1883) 1 Ky. 622.
[73] (1895) 3 S.S.L.R. 58.
[74] Relying upon the judgment of Sir Peter Benson Maxwell in *Choa Cheow Neoh* v. *Spottiswoode* (1869) 1 Ky. 216 at 221.
[75] See *Nagammal* v. *Suppiah* [1940] M.L.J. 119 on 'Straits Settlements Tamil custom'.
[76] See *Soundara Achi* v. *Kalyani Achi* [1953] M.L.J. 147.
[77] *Karpen Tandil* v. *Karpen* (1895) 3 S.S.L.R. 58.

the only reported case,[78] an action for libel and slander arising out of expulsion from a caste failed. The main institutions of Hindu law as adopted in the Straits Settlements are described elsewhere,[79] but it is worth noting here that difficulty occasionally arose in marriages involving conversion from or conversion to the Hindu religion. In *R.* v. *Devendra*[80] the court held that a change of one's religion did not necessarily change one's personal law.

So far as Malay customary laws were concerned, the only changes which took place, apart from the cases cited earlier on jointly acquired property, concerned the rights of native proprietors in Malacca. These changes grew out of the history of the Dutch and English occupation of Malacca and the difficulties which arose on the formal transfer of the state to the East India Company in 1825.

At that time there were apparently three classes of landholders:

(i) Holders of land in the town and suburbs of Malacca with or without certificates of title from the (Dutch) Court of Justice.[81]

(ii) Proprietors of concessions, in the nature of zamindari rights, over country lands.[82] This system operated in the following manner. Lots of land upon which cultivation was taking place were subject to a levy of one-tenth of their total produce per year. The rights to collect the tenth were often awarded by Government to certain persons known as zamindars. The latter rarely, if ever, visited these lands and the amount collected through the agency of a Malay chief or a Chinese collector was very small.[83]

(iii) Native cultivators holding proprietary rights under an *adat* which was supposed to be based on the Malacca Digest. The Digest had two important provisions. First, rights to land were proprietary rights only and ceased to exist when land was no longer cultivated. Second, the ruler of the state had the right to levy a tax of one-tenth on all produce from this land.

[78] *Coopang Chetty* v. *Veera Padiachee & ors.* (1888) 4 Ky. 364.
[79] See Hooker (1975).
[80] (1939) 1 M.C. 51.
[81] W. E. Maxwell (1884: 213–15) for examples.
[82] Ibid. 152.
[83] Ibid. 97–103.

The English Legal World 137

The issue facing the Company was the nature of titles to land in Malacca. It was decided that land under cultivation in 1830 should continue under 'native tenure', which was defined as peasant cultivation. An attempt was made, in Regulation IX of 1830, to organize native tenures by issuing titles on the English fee simple model but without success.[84] The courts, however, had recognized customary land tenure in Malacca,[85] including the native rules on ejectment for non-cultivation.[86] The Regulation of 1830 was repealed by Indian Act XVI of 1839 which continued to recognize the customary forms of land tenure.[87] Attention was then turned to the issue of fee simple titles, and in 1861 the Malacca Lands Ordinance[88] vested all land in the Crown in fee simple. It was held[89] that the ordinance successfully introduced the fee simple title and also preserved native rights.

The result of this legislative history was simply the recognition of two forms of land tenure, that is, customary tenure, though as yet there was no serious attempt to legislate for the working of these tenures. This came about in 1886 when the Malacca Land Customary Rights Ordinance was passed.[90] The Act, which is the end point of the historical situation just described, provides for a customary tenure based on occupation and cultivation, though with statutory exceptions. It is this total body of regulation plus judicial decisions interpreting the Act which make up Malaccan 'statutory *adat*'. The salient points of the 1886 Act have been described elsewhere.[91] This example is typical of the confusion that existed in the land laws of the

[84] In any case Regulation IX was probably invalid, cf. Mills (1960: 128).
[85] *Abdullatif* v. *Mahomed Meera Lebe* (1829) 4 Ky. 249, Maxwell (1884: 205).
[86] The period for paddy being three years; for fruit trees three years; for gambier trees one year; for pepper trees one year. Cf. W. E. Maxwell (1884: 205).
[87] By section 12. Judically examined and approved in *Sahrip* v. *Mitchell & Endain* (Maxwell (1884: 205–11 esp. at 209–10)). Cf. also *R.* v. *Willans* (1858) 3 Ky. 16 which was to the effect that local custom and usage is to be upheld.
[88] Indian Act XXVI 1861, sections 1, 2, and 13 of which are now to be found in sections 2, 3, and 4 of the Malacca Lands Ordinance (1861) cap. 127 revised laws of the Straits Settlements, 1936. The remaining sections of the original Act have been repealed: sections 9 and 10 by Act No. 33/1907; sections 3, 8, and 11 by Act No. 4/1870.
[89] *Sahrip* v. *Mitchell & Endain*. Cf. note 87 above.
[90] Now cap. 125, revised laws of the Straits Settlements, 1936. It incorporates the following amendments: 1/1890, 7/1901, 24/1902, 22/1905, 30/1906, 33/1907, 2/1914, 27/1917, 16/1922, 7/1931, 10/1952, and 5/1956. None of these amendments affects its provisions in respect of customary land tenure.
[91] Hooker (1972: 105–8), Joseph (1970).

Straits Settlements.[92] It was not until 1884-6 that the tenure system of the Straits Settlements was put upon a sound basis.

11 THE FEDERATED AND UNFEDERATED MALAY STATES

Unlike the Straits Settlements, the Malay states were not colonies in the formal sense, they were protectorates whose rulers continued to exercise power in formal terms although effective authority was exercised by British Residents. Between 1873 and 1874 Perak and Selangor accepted Residents, the states of the Negri Sembilan were unified in 1889, and Pahang accepted a British Resident in 1888. In 1895 the four were united into the Federated Malay States.[93] Johore did not accept a Resident until 1914, and the Unfederated States came under British protection in 1910 (Kelantan and Trengganu), 1923 (Kedah), and 1930 (Perlis). Before the Treaty of Bangkok in 1910, the four Unfederated States were dependencies—perhaps *de jure* dependencies in international law—of Siam, but under the treaty Siam relinquished all rights to Britain. By later treaties between Britain and the individual states[94] the residency system was established. The effect of the treaties was described by Braddell as follows:

> The right to administer these states which Great Britain undoubtedly possesses as suzerain [i.e. consequent upon the Treaty of Bangkok of 1910 with Siam] has been exchanged by her for the right to advise and she has thus conferred a degree of internal independence upon the ... states, which is an indulgence by a suzerain power that is quite familiar to the jurist.[95]

The precise nature of the relationship was discussed in a number of cases. In *Mighell* v. *Sultan of Johore*[96] the status of the Sultan as an independent sovereign was raised in the English courts. Although the Sultan had bound himself by treaty[97] not to exercise some of the attributes of sovereignty, he was nevertheless held to be an independent sovereign. A similar result was reached in *Duff Development Company* v. *Kelantan*

---

[92] See Ahmad Ibrahim (1970: 39-43) for a brief outline.
[93] For the historical background see Loh (1969). See also Maxwell & Gibson (1924) on the treaties.
[94] See Maxwell & Gibson (1924). [95] R. St. J. Braddell (1931a: 30).
[96] [1894] 1 Q.B. 149.
[97] The treaty of 1885 between Johore and Great Britain.

Government,[98] where a letter from the Under-Secretary of State for the Colonies stated that Kelantan was an independent state and the Sultan was the sovereign ruler in that state. It was held that this statement was in no way qualified by the relevant treaties between Kelantan and Great Britain. The same principles were even held to apply in the case of Pahang, one of the Federated Malay States. In *Pahang Consolidated Company Ltd* v. *State of Pahang*[99] the sovereign powers of the ruler were held to be untouched within the confines of the state by any treaty with Great Britain, or by membership of the Federated Malay States, or by the Sultan's membership of the Federal Council. The same principle held good even from 1927 onwards, when, by a further agreement, the Sultan no longer sat on the Federal Council but was represented by the British Resident.

Even where a sovereign had apparently divested himself of some attributes of sovereignty, it by no means followed that he was no longer a sovereign.[1] The position of sovereign independence continued into the post-war years.[2]

The judicial organization of the states took place in a piecemeal fashion. For the Federated Malay States, Judicial Commissioners' Regulations and Orders in Council came into force in 1896 and provided for a Judicial Commissioner appointed by the Sultans. He took appeals from Senior Magistrates who had an unlimited jurisdiction. The Senior Magistrate system was introduced at different times in the four states of the Federated Malay States. It was abolished in 1906, and the Courts Enactment of 1905 provided for a Supreme Court, appeals from which lay to the Privy Council. Later legislation in 1921 and 1923 provided that judges in the Federated Malay States, Straits Settlements, and Johore were *ex officio* judges in each of the other areas. Each of the Malay states, upon the advice of the Resident, began to adopt and publish legislation which applied only within the state but much of which was taken from Straits Settlements and Indian models.

The law applicable in the states was not English law *simpliciter*; in fact in the Unfederated, as in the Federated Malay

---

[98] [1924] A.C. 797.   [99] [1933] M.L.J. 247.
[1] See *Anchom* v. *Public Prosecutor* [1940] M.L.J. 22.
[2] *Sultan of Johore* v. *Tengku Abubakar* [1952] M.L.J. 115 at 119.

States, the determination of what law applied was laid on the courts. In the earliest reported case, *Ong Cheng Neo* v. *Yap Kwan Seng*,[3] the question was what law was applicable to the distribution of the intestate estate of a Chinese who died in Selangor. In the event it was held that the deceased had never lost his Chinese domicile so that the law of China applied, but in the course of his judgment, Jackson J.C.[4] said that English law did not necessarily prevail even in so far as it had been adopted. It is noticeable that the principle of domicile was applied without question in order to establish the jurisdiction of the court. So far as Malays were concerned, they were subject to Islamic law and Malay *adat*.[5] Islamic law was not a foreign law but a local law of which the court must take judicial notice.[6] The four states of the Federated Malay States each had legislation regulating the administration of Islamic law.[7] In addition, Negri Sembilan had its own Customary Tenure Enactment 1910, amended in 1926 and 1930. In each of the Unfederated States provision was also made for the registration of marriage and divorce.[8]

Chinese family law also received legislative expression. In the Perak Order in Council No. 23/1893 certain principles of custom were made applicable to the Chinese of the state. Although this order applied only in Perak, its provisions were taken as setting broad principles applicable to Chinese elsewhere,[9] though subject to local variation. The Order was repealed in 1929 when the Distribution Enactment came into force and introduced the main provisions of the (English) Statute of Distributions which applied to all locally domiciled persons except Muslims.[10] The general recognition of Chinese customs in the Federated Malay States was a matter for the courts in which they relied upon their inherent jurisdiction to

[3] (1897) 1 F.M.S.L.R. Supp. 1.
[4] *J.C.* = Judicial Commissioner.
[5] See the principle stated in *Shaik Abdul & ors.* v. *Shaik Elias Bux* (1915) 1 F.M.S.L.R. 204 at 214.
[6] *Ramah* v. *Laton* (1927) 6 F.M.S.L.R. 128.
[7] Perak—Registration of Muhammadan Marriages and Divorce Enactment 1885. Selangor, Pahang, and Negri Sembilan—Muhammadan Marriage and Divorce Registration Enactment, 1900.
[8] See Hooker (1975).
[9] *Yap Tham Thai* v. *Low Hup Neo* (1909) 1 F.M.S.L.R. 383 (Selangor).
[10] On the enactment see *Re Tan Soh Sim decd.* [1951] M.L.J. 21 at 24–6.

The English Legal World

do justice between the parties.[11] In Selangor,[12] for example, the rule against perpetuities was applied, the age of majority was put at twenty-one,[13] and English rules of equity were applied.[14] Contemporary reports are full of warnings by the judiciary against the over-enthusiastic application of English principles,[15] and in *Hj. Abdul Rahman* v. *Mohamed Hassan*[16] the Privy Council itself had to caution the local bench on this matter. So far as Hindu law was concerned it may be considered on a par with Chinese law. The courts recognized institutions of Hindu law, or local variations of such, on substantially the same grounds as Chinese law.[17]

English law was introduced into the Federated Malay States by the Civil Law Enactment No. 3 of 1937 and extended to the Unfederated States by the Civil Law (Extension) Ordinance of 1951. This was later replaced by the Civil Law Ordinance 1956, section 3 (i) of which repeats the provision appearing in the earlier Acts providing for the application of English law 'subject to such qualification as local circumstances render necessary'. It thus gave legislative effect to past judicial practice.

The legal history of the Malay states is substantially similar in its development of personal laws to that of the Straits Settlements. Although these jurisdictions are now combined—with the exception of Singapore, which is an independent republic—precedent from each jurisdiction is freely citable in modern Malaysia, subject only to later legislative amendment.

III THE BORNEO STATES (SABAH AND SARAWAK)

Sabah and Sarawak were British protectorate states from 1888 to 1946. There was no statutory reception of English law until comparatively late. In Sarawak, section 32, Order L-4 of 1928, introduced English law subject to modification by the Raja of Sarawak and as applicable to local conditions. In North Borneo (as it then was) sections 2 and 3 of the Civil Law Ordinance of

---

[11] See the statement of Terrell J. in *Woon Ngee Yew* v. *Ng Yoon Thai* [1941] M.L.J. 37 at 42–3.
[12] *Re the Will of Yap Kim Seng* (1924) 4 F.M.S.L.R. 313.
[13] *Kandusamy* v. *Suppiah* (1919) 1 F.M.S.L.R. 381.
[14] *Motor Emporium* v. *Arumugam* [1933] M.L.J. 276.
[15] *Leonard* v. *Nachiappa Chettiar* (1923) 4 F.M.S.L.R. 265 at 267.
[16] [1917] A.C. 209.
[17] See Hooker (1976: 147–71) for a summary of the cases.

1938 provided for the introduction of English law subject to local conditions and customs.

Hitherto the written laws of the Borneo states had, not unnaturally, been based upon legislation in force in the Straits Settlements, the Malay states, and India. The early laws of Sarawak took the form of Orders issued by the Raja and, although most of them repeated existing colonial legislation in force elsewhere, many were specifically designed to deal with local conditions. Such, for example, was Order IX of June 1911 establishing a Chinese court which was to apply local Chinese law and custom. The Chinese court did not function after 1919, and in the Courts Order of 1922 which established a Supreme Court, Residents Courts, District Courts, Magistrates Courts, and Native Courts, its functions would seem to have been taken over by the Residents Courts. The system established by the Order of 1922 was eventually replaced by a unified system of jurisdiction for Sarawak, North Borneo, and Brunei in 1951; the latter system was amended again by the incorporation of Sabah and Sarawak into Malaysia in 1963. However, the Chinese Marriage Ordinance (c. 74 revised laws of 1946) of Sarawak is unique in the legal history of Malaysia as the only legislation still effective in this matter.

The sources of law in Sarawak were judicially stated to be as follows:[18]

1. Orders and other written laws enacted by or with the authority of His Highness the Rajah.
2. English law in so far as it is not modified by the law comprised in (1) and in so far as it is applicable to Sarawak, having regard to native customs and local conditions.
3. Certain law and custom of races indigenous to Sarawak, including Mohammedan law and other native law or custom in so far as it is reasonable.

The law comprised under the third heading includes Mohammedan and Dayak and other customs concerning marriage and inheritance and also certain customs by which criminal sanctions are imposed, e.g., for adultery and incestuous relations as understood by Malay and Dayak custom. The customs of certain other races are also to some extent followed... I do not mean to imply that it follows directly that English law must be applied when a question of choice of

[18] *Kho Leng Guan* v. *Kho Eng Guan* [1936] S.C.R. 60 at 61–2.

The English Legal World

law arises but that by English law rules are laid down to determine what law must be applied.[19]

Under the last heading, the laws recognized include Chinese, Islamic, and Malay and Dayak *adats*.[20]

IV BURMA

The territories which now comprise the state of Burma came under British Indian administration within the period 1824–86 as a result of the Anglo-Burmese wars. The administrative and judicial system which followed was based directly upon the Indian model.[21] Legislation for British Burma was provided from India until, in 1897, a Legislative Council was established in Burma. In 1922 a High Court of Judicature was established at Rangoon, replacing the former Chief Court of Lower Burma and the Court of the Judicial Commissioner of Upper Burma.[22] The Government of Burma Act, 1935 provided for appeals to be carried to the Privy Council.

The proper development of Burmese law was not put on a sound basis until 1898[23] when section 13 of the Burma Laws Act provided:

(1) Where in any suit or other proceeding in Burma it is necessary for the Court to decide any questions regarding succession, inheritance, marriage or caste of any religious usage or institution, [the Court shall apply]
   (a) the Buddhist law in cases where the parties are Buddhists,
   (b) the Mohammedan law in cases where the parties are Mohammedans,
   (c) the Hindu law where the parties are Hindus shall form the rule of decision, except in so far as such law has by enactment been altered or abolished, or is opposed to custom having the force of law.

(2) ...

---

[19] See also the Sarawak Application of Law Ordinance, 1949 and the North Borneo Application of Law Ordinance, 1951.
[20] For material on these laws see above, n. 17. See also Richards (1961) (1963) (1964) and the *Undang-undang Mahkamah Melayu Sarawak* which is administered as subsidiary legislation by authority of the Native Customary Laws Ordinance, c. 51 revised laws of Sarawak 1958. See also Knaup (1970).
[21] See Furnivall (1939) (1956), Donnison (1953).
[22] See Sinha (1973).
[23] For the earlier period see Furnivall (1939: 6 ff.), Hla Aung (1968: 68–9), Sinha (1973).

(3) In cases not provided for by sub-section (1), or by any other enactment for the time being in force, the decision shall be according to justice, equity and good conscience.

The purpose of the Act was to specify the sources of law for private law matters involving those persons who were Buddhist, Hindu, and Muslim by religion. Its effect was to establish three personal laws, and, in the case of Hindus and Muslims, development of their personal laws by way of precedent proceeded with little difficulty.[24] This was not so in the case of the 'Buddhist law' mentioned in sub-section (1) (a) because no such law exists. This did not prevent the Privy Council from defining the *Dhammathats* as 'the institutional Buddhist law',[25] something which neither Jardine nor Forchhammer had ever claimed. Despite the obvious error in this definition, of which the *local* judges were well aware,[26] the equation of *Dhammathat* with 'Buddhist law' remained a constant feature of judicial decision. The history of the law applicable to the mass of the Burmese Buddhist population is therefore a history of the interpretation of the *Dhammathats*, although the courts were always careful to give effect to contrary custom if such could be satisfactorily proved.[27]

A typical example of the way in which Burmese law developed is provided in the judicial administration of community property. The courts rejected ('obsolete') texts vesting management in the husband because in the traditional *Dhammathats* the object of procedure in execution was to induce the debtor to pay,[28] but the procedural law in the Anglo-Burmese courts empowered a creditor to levy execution over the debtor's total assets. In some cases of claims arising out of the action of one spouse, the court held that spouses were in the position of partners and so agents for each other,[29] but refused to

[24] See Daw Khin Khin (1954) and the cases in the following series of Burmese law reports: Upper Burma Reports, Selected Judgements of Lower Burma, Burma Law Reports, I.L.R. Reps. Rangoon. Customary laws of other ethnic groups were also recognized: see Maung Tet Pyo (1884), Aung Than Tun (1967).
[25] *U Pe* v. *Maung Maung Kha* (1932) 10 I.L.R. Ran. 261.
[26] See, for example, *Tan Ma Shwe Zin* v. *Tan Ma Ngwe Zin* (1932) I.L.R. 10 Ran. 97 esp. at 103 (Page C.J.).
[27] See Mootham (1939) for a summary of the cases. See also Rigg (1931), E Maung (1970), Lahiri (1939).
[28] See E Maung (1951) on insolvency jurisdiction in early Burmese law.
[29] *R.M.M.S.* Soobramonian Chetty (1889) P.J.L.B. 568.

The English Legal World 145

apply this either to an alienation of immovables[30] or to an alienation by the husband of a wife's pre-nuptial property.[31] In other cases, however, the court held that the interest of a spouse could be taken in execution of his or her separate debt.[32] A general principle became established that each spouse had an attachable and alienable interest in the property of the marriage equal to that which he or she would receive on divorce by mutual consent. An interesting application and extension in the context of divorce by mutual consent arises as follows. A text in the *Manugye*[33] provides that where neither of the parties has been married before and one brings much property and the other little to the marriage, a relationship of *Nissaya* (supporter) and *Nissita* (dependant) exists. On divorce, the property brought to the marriage is divisible in the proportion of two to one, the supporter taking the larger share. The rule was applied in cases in which the husband had been previously married and was wealthy. The wife had not previously been married and was poor. The justification of this was said by the court[34] to be that the *intent* of the *Nissaya* rule was to make provision for a wife who brings no property to the marriage. This clearly amounts to a judicial extension of and exception to the rule.

The *Dhammathats* insisted that partition of property was essential to divorce, so that, if one party remarried before partition, he or she forfeited all interest in the property of the marriage. The Anglo-Burmese courts early decided that divorce and partition were two distinct causes of action.[35]

The examples quoted above, and many others, led to eventual judicial recognition that the *Dhammathat* did not possess the force of a statute. The following passage states this firmly and sets out the position of customary law:

The time has come when some Judge should be courageous enough to point out, albeit with diffidence, the utmost respect, that while great value is attached in Burma to the rulings in the *Manugye*, Burmese

[30] *Mg Twe* (1899) 1 L.B.R. 11.
[31] *Ma Pyu U* (1907) 1 B.L.T. 49.
[32] *Ma Me* (1892–6) II U.B.R. 45.
[33] A translation is given in *Mi Myin* v. *Nga Twe* (1906) II U.B.R. 19. See also Mootham (1939: 43–4).
[34] *Ma Ngwe Hnit* (1921) II L.B.R. 52.
[35] *Ma Gyan* (1897–1901) II U.B.R. 28; cf. Mootham (1939: 43–8) on the rules relating to partition.

jurists do not regard this *Dhammathat* as sacrosanct and that from time to time some embarrassment has been created as the result of following the *Manugye* in the teeth of what has been laid down in the *Dhammathats*. One not insignificant reason why this *Dhammathat* is so frequently cited is because the *Manugye* was the first, if it is not the only *Dhammathat*, to be wholly translated into English and thus it is the authority to which those unversed in the Burmese tongue must readily, if not inevitably, turn.

Where, therefore, a certain rule of Burmese law is to be found in the *Dhammathats* and also in decided cases and in the modern practice and views of Burmans, the Court is not only at liberty but is bound to decide the case in accordance with Burmese Customary Law as it obtains today, rather than to perpetuate the outworn shibboleths of bygone ages, notwithstanding that some sanction for their continuance may be found in extracts from the *Manugye Dhammathat*. Burmans are not to be doomed to live for ever under the rulings and customs by which they were governed in the days of King Alompra.[36]

The application of this principle was embarked upon perhaps over-enthusiastically. A convenient example is provided in the treatment by the courts of the rules of *Vinaya*, the text which governed the conduct of Burmese Buddhist monks. One of the fundamental rules of the *Vinaya* is the prohibition on a monk of possessing property other than that given as a religious gift. This had been accepted by the courts,[37] but in 1929 the following question came before the High Court: 'Is the sale of immovable property to a Burman Buddhist monk void on the ground that a monk is prohibited by the rule of the *Vinaya* from entering into such pecuniary transactions?'[38] In the event, the Full Bench decided the question in the negative; the following passage sets out the *ratio*:[39]

The definition of the word 'laws' in its juridical sense is that 'laws' are rules of civil conduct enforced by the State. From this it follows that the rules of conduct as laid in *Vinaya* for the guidance of Buddhist monks cannot be deemed to be 'laws' unless they are enforced by the

[36] *Ma Hnin Zan* v. *Ma Myain* 1936 A.I.R. Ran. 31 at 34. This dictum was followed in *Dr Tha Mya* v. *Daw Khin Pu* (1951) B.L.R. 108 (S.C.).
[37] See *U Tilawka* v. *Shwe Kan* (1915) 29 I.C. 613, *U Teza* v. *Ma E Gywe* 1928 A.I.R. Ran. 3. The basis of both decisions was that the ownership of property was void as being against the *Vinaya* and hence 'immoral' within the meaning of the Indian Contract Act, s. 23.
[38] *U Pyinnya* v. *Maung Law* 1929 A.I.R. Ran. 354, (1929) I.L.R. 7 Ran. 677.
[39] 1929 A.I.R. Ran. at 362.

State. According to section 13 (1), Burma Laws Act, they are not enforced by the State except in cases in which questions regarding any religious usage or institution arise. A sale being a pure matter of contract is not 'a question regarding any religious usage or institution'. A Buddhist monk therefore is not disqualified from contracting by law within the meaning of s. 11, Contract Act.

We turn now to another and related provision of Section 13 (3) of the Burma Laws Act, 1898: 'In cases not provided for by sub-section (1), or by any other enactment for the time being in force, the decision shall be according to justice, equity and good conscience.' As in India, the phrase has generally come to mean 'English law if applicable to the society and circumstances of Burma'.[40] This, however, has been comparatively rare in the form just quoted, but the phrase did fall to be considered in *Ma Kyin Mya* v. *Maung Sit Han*,[41] where the question was the validity of a marriage between a Burmese Buddhist woman and a Chinese Confucian. Section 13 (1) of the Burma Laws Act did not apply because one of the parties was not a Buddhist. The question was therefore discussed under Section 13 (3), and two systems of law, English law and Chinese custom, were considered. Both were found inapplicable, the latter because it was a foreign law and hence not in accordance with justice, equity, and good conscience. The report is not clear as to why this should be so. The marriage was eventually held valid by the application of Burmese *customary law* as the *lex loci*.

The principles established in the colonial period seem to have persisted relatively unchanged into the present.[42] The succession of the new republic[43] to the former colony has left the private laws relatively unchanged although data have been scarce in the past decade.

V CONFLICT OF LAW

In the process of adapting English law to the demands presented by indigenous laws over a period of two centuries, elements of strain and conflict have never been absent.

[40] *Dr Tha Mya* v. *Ma Khin Pu* 1941 A.I.R. Ran. 81.
[41] (1937) R.L.R. 103.
[42] See Gledhill (1968), Khetarpal (1966–7), Maung Maung (1963), Hla Aung (1965).
[43] See Maung Maung (1961: 208–9) for constitutional references to state succession.

However, conflict between systems of law, i.e. on questions of basic principle, should not be over-emphasized. Much so-called conflict is a matter of inconsistency of internal precedent which, though it has its origins in cultural disparities between different rules of obligation, nevertheless is solvable within the terms of precedent itself.

Conflict on questions of basic principle does, however, arise in the following areas.

(i) *Islamic law (Malaysia and Singapore)*

This law ascribes rights and obligations to the individual on the basis of religious adherence. The legal systems of Malaysia and Singapore, being based upon principles of English law, look to such factors as domicile and nationality. Despite the fact that Islamic principles of law, especially family law, were always admitted in colonial courts and continued to be applied (though now contained in statute), the distinct ways of ascribing obligations are, or can be, fundamentally opposed. This was illustrated in Re *Maria Huberdina Hertogh: Mansor Adabi v. A. P. Hertogh & anor.*[44] Maria Hertogh had been left in Indonesia during the Japanese advance of 1941 where she had been cared for and brought up as a Muslim by a servant of the respondent. The respondent's attempt to regain custody of his daughter after the war had been resisted by the girl's foster-parent and resulted in an action in the Singapore High Court in which the respondent was successful. Simultaneously the girl was married to the appellant in a ceremony that was valid according to Islamic law. The court was asked to decide upon the validity of this marriage. It was held that the marriage was invalid because according to the law of her domicile—the Netherlands—she was below the age of consent. The application of a well-known principle of English law was in flat contradiction to Islamic principles which regarded the marriage as a valid contract. In this sort of situation the two systems of law are in fundamental opposition. The situation of the Muslim is made more complicated by legislation so far as Singapore is concerned. The 'Women's Charter', Ordinance No. 18 of 1961, was designed to reform the marriage and divorce laws of Singapore. It was based largely upon English

[44] [1950] M.L.J. 214, [1951] M.L.J. 12 & 164.

The English Legal World

legislation and so incorporated principles such as domicile and residence. The ordinance excluded Muslims from its terms (s. 3 (3) amended by s. 3 (e) of Ordinance No. 9 of 1967), but problems in its interpretation remain[45] simply because the methods of attaching a person to a law—religion or domicile/nationality—are so different.

A second aspect of conflict concerns cases involving 'conversion'. These are cases in which an individual has contracted a second marriage after conversion to Islam while the first marriage is still in existence. In *P.P.* v. *White*[46] an Englishman (probably) domiciled in the Federated Malay States married his first wife under the Christian Marriage Enactment and then took a second wife under Islamic law after both he and his partner to this marriage had become Muslim. It was held that a husband could not divest himself of a prior marriage by changing his personal law. Islamic doctrine of course is flatly to the contrary. However, in 1965 the Privy Council in *A.G. for Ceylon* v. *Reid*[47] found differently. It allowed a change of personal law so as to permit a plurality of wives. This is of doubtful authority in Malaysia and not just because the respective statutes of the two states differ, but also because the policy of the courts is clearly against such a proposition.

Finally it is as well to notice that the jurisdiction of the religious courts in Malaysia and Singapore is subject to the overriding jurisdiction of the secular courts.

(ii) *Adat and Islam (Malaysia)*

This is the only example of a conflict between two local systems of law, as distinct from conflict between a local law and the national legal system based on English law. The conflict between *adat* and Islam occurs in all the states of Malaysia and is essentially concerned with the distribution of property arising out of death or divorce. The Islamic law on the distribution of property is clear and is obligatory on the individual Muslim as a matter of conscience. The state enactments providing for the administration of Islamic law also give effect to the rules of the Sharīʻa. However, throughout the Malay states local *adat*

---

[45] See the following sources: Hooker (1968a), Daw (1972), Rajah (1974).
[46] [1940] M.L.J. 214. See also *R.* v. *Devendra* (1939) 1 M.C. 51.
[47] [1965] A.C. 720.

(customary law) law require different forms of distribution. In cases of conflict, the courts will apply *adat* in preference to Islamic law basically on the ground that this is the custom actually followed. In addition, where an Islamic court orders a certain distribution this may be overruled by the secular courts.[48]

In Negri Sembilan this basic conflict is rather sharper than in the other states both because property relationships are ordered on matrilineal lines and because they have political overtones. But the principle remains the same: the secular law is the determining law in case of conflict.[49]

(iii) *Chinese Law (Malaysia and Singapore)*

The conflict which arises in this case is not so much a conflict of principle between systems of law but between the precedent on Chinese law in one field—marriage—and legislation which attempts to reform the marriage and divorce laws of both Malaysia and Singapore. It is essential to remember that the modern legislation is itself a copy of English statute—a fact that explains a good deal of the conflict.[50]

(iv) *Burmese 'Buddhist law'*

As with the preceding laws the main difficulties arose in the field of family law, particularly in what were called 'inter-religious marriages'. In establishing the validity of marriage the courts proceeded directly upon English conflict of laws principles, i.e. validity would be determined on (*a*) capacity of the parties according to the *lex domicilii* immediately prior to marriage and (*b*) on celebration in due form which was subject to the *lex loci contractus*. This is simply enough stated, but the principles upon which the courts have acted in applying the rule are somewhat obscure. There appear to be three alternatives. First, that the rule is applied in accordance with Section 13 (2) of the Burma Laws Act as being the law for the time being administered by the High Court in the exercise of its original jurisdiction. There is no authority for this. Second, that the rule is applied by virtue of the provisions of Section 13 (3) of

---

[48] See Hooker (1972: 228–50) and the cases there cited.
[49] Ibid. 51–70, 207–27.
[50] See n. 45 above for references and also the following: Wee (1972), (1973), Dickstein (1973).

The English Legal World

the Act as being in accordance with (*a*) either 'justice, equity and good conscience' *simpliciter* or, third, (*b*) the same phrase where it means the rules of English law.[51]

In the case of Muslims, marriage with a non-Muslim was held to be invalid, since the personal law of those Muslims domiciled in Burma admitted a capacity to marry only on the basis of religious adherence. Similarly, Hindus were held to have no capacity to marry outside their own caste, so that marriage with a Burmese Buddhist[52] was not possible except in the case of a *Sudra*.[53] A Chinese Confucian was under no personal incapacity to marry a Burmese Buddhist, and, if the marriage took place in Burma and conformed to Burmese Buddhist law, it was valid. In *Ma Kyin Mya* v. *Maung Sit Han*[54] such a marriage was recognized on the principle of Section 13 (3) of the Act where, in the interests of justice, equity, and good conscience, Burmese Buddhist law applied as the *lex loci contractus*. So far as Christian marriage was concerned, the parties could not marry, save in accordance with Section 5 of the Christian Marriage Act, 1872.[55]

The really thorny problems in conflict of laws, however, arose in the case of marriage between two *Chinese Buddhists*, or between a *Chinese Buddhist* and a *Burmese Buddhist*. The complicating factor is the provision of Section 13 (1) (a) of the Burma Laws Act referring to 'Buddhist Law', which means the personal law of the community to which the Buddhist belongs and hence, in the case of a Chinese Buddhist, is prima facie Chinese customary law. The general rule, therefore, became that validity of marriage (capacity being assumed) should not be determined by the *lex loci contractus* when both parties were Chinese Buddhists, but that the question should be settled by reference to Chinese customary law.[56] However, in *In Re Ma Yin Mya* v. *Tan Yauk Pu*[57] the Full Bench held that Burmese customary law regarding marriage is prima facie applicable to Chinese Buddhists as the *lex loci contractus*. To escape such an

---

[51] *Khan Bahadur Mehrban Khan* v. *Makna* (1930) 34 C.W.N. 529 (P.C.).
[52] *Mg. Man* v. *Doramo* (1906) 3 L.B.R. 244.
[53] *S. Anamalay Pillay* v. *Po Lan* (1906) 3 L.B.R. 228.
[54] [1937] R.L.R. 103.
[55] Act XV of 1872.
[56] Cf. *Ma Kyin Hlaing* v. *Maung Kyin Swi* [1937] Ran. 90 at 94.
[57] (1927) I.L.R. 5 Ran. 406.

application a Chinese must show that he is subject to a custom having the force of law in Burma and that the application of such custom would not tend to inflict an injustice on the Burmese woman involved in such marriage. This decision cannot be regarded as good law for two reasons. First, the decision clearly states that the only Buddhist law that the courts will allow is Burmese customary law; this has been expressly dissented from in a later case[58] and is not in accordance with earlier precedent.[59] Second, the marriage in question involved a Chinese Buddhist man and a Burmese Buddhist woman, and the court was concerned to protect the position of the woman.[60] The contradictions just described eventually had to be solved by legislation, and in 1940 the Buddhist Women's Special Marriage and Succession Act came into force.[61] This was replaced in 1954, and a new Act of the same name and substantially the same provisions was passed by the parliament of independent Burma.[62] The Act applies to all Burmese Buddhist women and to non-Buddhist husbands of such women whatever the nationality of the husband. It provides for marriage by way of signed declaration in the presence of two witnesses and the local Registrar of Marriages. Such a marriage must be dissolved according to Burmese Buddhist law, and any question of inheritance, succession or ownership of property must also be decided by the Burmese Buddhist law.

The experience of these various laws has resulted in the creation of two categories of law which we may call respectively the 'general' and the 'special'. The former is the introduced English law comprising both general principles of law and a state-wide system of legal administration. 'Special' laws are the partial exceptions to the general law and comprise the principles of indigenous laws that are permitted to continue and are administered through the forms and structure of the general laws. The result is a plurality of sources for law, an idea in itself not unfamiliar in South-East Asia or, for that matter, to English law itself.[63]

[58] *Tan Ma Shwe Zin* v. *Tan Ma Ngwe Zin* (1932) I.L.R. 10 Ran. 97.
[59] *Chan Pyu* v. *Saw Sin* (1928) I.L.R. 6 Ran. 623 & 631.
[60] The position is unclear; see Mootham (1939: 15–16), Fitzgerald (1934: 116–18), and Hla Aung (1958).
[61] Act XXIV of 1939.   [62] See XI *Burma Code* 1958, Parts 22–3.
[63] See A. W. B. Simpson (1973).

CHAPTER 6

The French Legal World: French Indo-China and Thailand (Siam)

THE FRENCH legal world comprises French Indo-China, the area of French colonial dominance proper, and Thailand, or Siam as it was then called. Thailand was never a colony, the only South-East Asian nation to escape direct European rule, but from the point of view of its legal history in the nineteenth and twentieth centuries it can only be classified as belonging to the civil law world. The Indo-Chinese and the Thai situations must, however, be treated separately.

The French occupation of Indo-China spanned a little over a century and took place comparatively late[1] in French colonial history when the main principles of legal practice in the overseas territories had already been established.[2] However, the legal system which developed in Indo-China was unique for two reasons; first, the legal cultures of the area were highly developed both in practice and in theory.[3] The French, therefore, were not dealing with an undifferentiated mass of native custom but with a highly sophisticated legal system, derived from that of the Chinese,[4] which, in fact, had a history longer than their own. They had perforce to deal with a literate bureaucracy of ancient lineage administering laws whose nature was not fully understood or, indeed, assimilable into civil-law categories. Second, the progress of French control was unequal throughout the territories of Indo-China. The whole of lower Cochin-China was occupied in 1861, Cambodia came under French protection in 1863, the three provinces of western

[1] Beginning with the capture of Saigon in Feb. 1859, see Osborne (1969).
[2] For North Africa see Estoublon & Lefébure (1896), Pouyanne (1895); for Africa south of the Sahara see Salacuse (1969); for India see Jain (1970). See generally Antonelli (1926), Dareste (1915), Dislère (1914), Petit (1894).
[3] See above, Chapter 3.
[4] See Woodside (1971).

Cochin-China in 1866, and the territories of the Court of Hué followed in 1884. In October 1887 Cambodia, Cochin-China, Annam and Tonkin were brought together to form the Union Indochinoise headed by a civilian governor-general. Cochin-China had a lieutenant-governor, Annam and Tongkin shared a resident-general, and Cambodia had its own resident-general.[5] The French presence was not established without continual fighting, and local revolts were endemic in the area for many years. In these circumstances administration was difficult, and the differing statuses of the territories— protectorate or colony proper—demanded different forms of legal organization. It was not until 1919 that French Indo-China had a properly established legal system for the whole territory.[6] For these reasons the component parts of Indo-China have to be looked at separately. They fall naturally into two groups: the *pays de souveraineté française*, i.e. Cochin-China and Laos, and the *pays de protectorat*, i.e. Cambodia, Annam, and Tonkin (see below, section III of this chapter).[7]

I PAYS DE SOUVERAINETÉ FRANÇAISE[8]

The two territories in which French sovereignty was directly exercised, Cochin-China and Laos, had quite distinct types of administration, the former providing for single and the latter for a mixed form.

(i) *Cochin-China*

This territory was ceded to France by the treaties of 5 June 1862 and 5 March 1874 and became a French colony whose status was determined by Art. 18 of the *Sénatus-Consulte* of 3 May 1854. The development of a formal judicial organization began with the decree of 25 July 1864 providing for a Tribunal of First Instance, a Tribunal of Commerce, and a Superior Tribunal having appellate jurisdiction. Article 37 of the decree ordered the immediate promulgation of French law in Cochin-China and was given effect to by the *arrêté* of the governor of Cochin-

---

[5] For the history of this period see the following sources: Thompson (1942), Osborne (1969), Nguyên-Ái-Quôc (1946).

[6] See Morché (1931).

[7] It is as well to point out here that this distinction is made on the classifications of French colonial law and *not* on the basis of political theory as to dependent status.

[8] For a general outline of material see Levasseur (1939).

The French Legal World

China of 21 December 1864 promulgating the *Code Napoléon*. The decree maintained indigenous tribunals, which retained competence in civil matters involving the indigenous inhabitants or Asiatic *assimilés*. It was, however, open to such persons to enter into obligations under civil law, in which case civil law applied. The jurisdiction of the Tribunals was limited to civil and commercial matters involving Europeans, Eurasians and indigenous or Asiatic persons, or, where the parties chose civil law, between indigenous and Asiatic persons. In criminal matters all persons were subject to French criminal law.

A second decree of 7 March 1868 substituted a Court of Appeal for the Superior Tribunal; the decree was implemented by an *arrêté* of 16 March 1869. The Tribunal was empowered to exercise cassation for the decisions of French tribunals in civil and commercial matters. The *arrêté* set out the competence of the Superior Tribunal by reference to metropolitan legislation comprising the Royal Ordinance of 9 February 1827 on the powers of the Procurator-General, and Arts. 64 and 65 of the Law of 20 April 1810 on the organization and administration of justice. Its competence was extended in 1881 to take appeals from the Consular Courts of Japan, China, and Siam. This basic system continued in the period 1881–95 although with an increase in the number of courts, including a Court of Appeal at Hanoi.[9] In criminal matters involving indigenous persons, local assessors sat with the judge and French criminal law was applied with some modifications which took account of local conditions. Staffing always remained a problem, however, and in the period after 1895 some of the Tribunals of the First Instance were suppressed and replaced by courts of the *Justice de Paix* with an extended jurisdiction.[10] The Court of Appeal of Tonkin sitting at Hanoi was also abolished for the same reason by the decree of 9 August 1898, and the Court of Appeal at Saigon was given sole jurisdiction over Indo-China as the 'Court of Appeal of Indo-China' with chambers at Saigon and Hanoi. A later decree, of 19 May 1919, however, reversed this, and two distinct Courts of Appeal were re-established at Saigon and Hanoi with an organization almost exactly the same as in metropolitan France. Further reforms of the judicial service of

[9] See Garrigues (1931: 44–8).   [10] *Décret* 16 Oct. 1896.

an administrative nature followed.[11] In addition to the *Justice de Paix* with extended jurisdiction there was a *Justice de Paix française* whose function and competence were the same as in metropolitan France.[12]

The most important local innovation in the Cochin-Chinese judicial organization was the office of *Justice de Paix Indigène* created by the decree of 16 February 1921. The office was intended to provide for the direct and effective participation of the local people in the administration of justice, but it was not introduced as an effective working system until 1923.[13] Even then the system remained provisional. The office-holders were drawn from 'Annamite' officers of the administrative service who had completed twenty years of service and were at least forty years old. Graduates in law from Saigon and Hanoi who had completed fifteen years service were also eligible. They were appointed by the governor-general on the recommendation of the director of the judicial service. An *arrêté* of 7 March 1924 provided a code of usage and procedure and fixed the extent of their jurisdiction. These provisions were closely modelled on Arts. 92–106 of the Organic Decree of 16 February 1921 relating to the powers of metropolitan magistrates.

The *Justices de Paix Indigène* were competent only when both parties to a cause were Annamites or assimilated persons. The parties had to present themselves in person or be represented by close relatives; a minor by his guardian and a married woman by her husband. Representation by an advocate was not permissible. However, the *Procureur-général* and the *Procureur de la République du Tribunal* were able to give written submissions on any matter which fell within their jurisdiction. All executions of the *Justice*'s decision were carried out by village notables since this tribunal had no staff of court officers (*huissiers*)[14] charged with such a task. In civil matters the jurisdiction of the *Justices* was the same as that of the French *Juges de Paix* as established in the Law of 1905. In criminal matters they applied the modified Penal Code applicable to Annamites as established by the decree of 31 December 1912. They had the same function as the metropolitan magistrate

[11] See Garrigues (1931: 53).   [12] Law of 12 July 1905.
[13] *Arrêté* 25 July 1923 modified by *arrêté* 5 July 1928.
[14] See Garrigues (1931: 64–5).

relative to the personal status of the indigenous Cochin-Chinese as French subjects. Appeals could be taken to the Tribunal of the First Instance in civil and criminal matters, and in the case of decisions of last resort (*dernier ressort*) appeals might be made for annulment to the Court of Appeal at Saigon.

Four such *Justices* were appointed by *arrêté* of 30 September 1924 and a further three by *arrêté* of 16 July 1928. One was also established for Saigon–Cholon by *arrêté* of 20 August 1929. The chief advantage of the institution was its function in conciliation and its ability to involve the village heads in judicial administration. It must be remembered, however, that in colonial legal thought there was a unity of judicial organization: as Garrigues says, 'The indigenous Tribunals are but an emanation from French authority which has delegated one part of its jurisdiction. The Tribunals function under the control of superior French courts and their judgments of either first or last resort are susceptible to appeal or annulment.'[15]

Although the inhabitants of Cochin-China were subject without exception to French Tribunals, at least in the last instance, the same was not true of legislation. As in other French colonies,[16] there were two classes: on the one hand, French law (*statut français*) applied to French citizens, to Europeans, and to persons of those nations whose laws were substantially similar to those of France. On the other hand, the *statut annamite* applied to indigenous persons, to *asiatiques assimilés*, and to others, such as the Cambodians, Chinese, Siamese, Malays of Chaudoc, etc., as specified in the *arrêté* of the *Chef du Pouvoir exécutif de la République française* of 23 August 1871. French law applied in cases of dispute between French and *assimilés* on the one hand, and between the indigenous population and *asiatiques assimilés* on the other. Individuals subject to the *statut annamite* might opt for French law, but such an option was not open to Cambodians or inhabitants of Annam proper unless the Royal Ordinances of these territories expressly authorized it.

The law codes of France as they stood in 1864 were promulgated *en bloc* in Cochin-China by the *arrêté* of the Governor of 21 December 1864, and later laws and decrees modifying the codes were also promulgated in the colony. Under the terms of the *Sénatus-Consulte* of 3 May 1854 laws (*lois*)

[15] Ibid. 66.   [16] See above, n. 2.

of France had to be declared in force in Cochin-China by a decree of the Minister of Colonies. Where such laws dealt with civil, penal, or commercial matters the decree had to be countersigned by the Minister of Justice. Parliament might declare its laws (*lois*) applicable, and an *arrêté* of the Governor-General of Indo-China or the Governor of Cochin-China was sufficient to put them into force. By the decree of 6 March 1877 the Governor-General could, by *arrêté*, sanction the administration and execution of laws, decrees, or regulations promulgated in the colony under pain of imprisonment or fine, but such an *arrêté* had to be converted into a *décret* within four months or it became void. The laws (*lois*) of France were regularly extended to Cochin-China except where they conflicted with the local judicial and administrative organization. In that case the laws were modified by decree, and modifications to the Civil Code were made applicable to the colony by the same means. Thus, the *statut personnel* of a French citizen was exactly the same in France and in Cochin-China. On the other hand, the codes of commerce and civil procedure were adopted without change because in their spheres they needed no modification. In the case of commerce, for example, French law applied to all persons largely because there was no Annamite law suitable for a modern economy. Thus, Art. 114 of the decree of 16 February 1921 set out the principle of the unity of commercial legislation although the earlier decree of 27 February 1892 regulating Asian commerce remained in force. The unity of commercial legislation in the former decree was itself a realization of the law (*loi*) of 18 March 1919 (modified by the law of 26 June 1920) setting up a Register of Commerce open to all inhabitants of the colony.

In criminal matters, the indigenous penal laws of Cochin-China survived until 1877 when the government intervened to abolish a number of penalties such as death by strangulation and methods of procedure such as torture. The decree of 16 March 1880 rendered the French Penal Code applicable to the indigenous population and *assimilés* but with certain modifications judged necessary for its adaptation to local manners. The code remained in force until 1912, at which time, by decree of 31 December 1912, the modifications were reformulated for the purpose of making the repression of offences against the state

The French Legal World 159

and public order (*bon ordre et securité publique*) more effective.[17] The investigation of crimes and delicts committed by indigenous persons was governed by the code of criminal investigation as in France. The decree of 18 December 1906 on the organization of the rights of defence gave effect to the law (*loi*) of 8 December 1897 on preliminary investigation. In addition, the law (*loi*) of 12 December 1917 relating to provisional liberty was applicable. Judgments given in criminal matters were susceptible to cassation, and simple police matters were susceptible to annulment.

In civil matters the local legislator concentrated upon codifying the *statut personnel* of the Annamites. This was the object of the decree of 3 October 1883 which regulated the following matters 'on the basis of certain customs': civil status, domicile, absence, formalities, conditions of marriage,[18] divorce, paternity, filiation, adoption, paternal power, minority and guardianship, and emancipation. The decree, however, in doing this relied upon jurisprudence[19] of the previous years and, thus, imported somewhat novel notions into the law. The principle of equal shares between male and female in inheritance, and the admission of natural children to a share in an estate with legitimate children were examples of such.[20] Other rights, for example of the widow of the first rank to usufruct,[21] of the widow of the second rank to support, and so on, were also included. Decisions of family councils were controlled.[22] In addition a number of *arrêtés* were promulgated regulating the payment of interest and contracts and obligations.[23]

So far as civil procedure was concerned, it was felt that the French Civil Code itself was too complex, and by *arrêtés* of 20 November 1877 and 16 March 1910 a simplified procedure was established. It was designed to be speedy and cheap, the judge supervising all submissions and directing procedure. Although the parties should ideally appear in person, they could be represented by near kinsmen or by professional advocates. The cost of an advocate was half that charged in cases in which

---

[17] Cf. Garrigues (1931: 74–5).
[18] See Van-hô-lê (1932), Nguyen-Huy-Lai (1934), Bui-tuong-chieu (1933), and, more generally, Tran-Van-Trai (1942), Phan Thi Dac (1966).
[19] See Lasserre (1884). [20] See Masse (1941), Lu-Van-Li (1939).
[21] See Vu-Van-Mau (1940), Lustéguy (1935).
[22] For a full discussion see Lasserre (1884a). [23] Cf. Garrigue (1931: 77–8).

French procedure operated—*arrêté* of 31 August 1911. The judgment could be appealed from and was subject to cassation and annulment, the latter for matters of last resort, and was taken by a panel of five judges in the Court of Appeal. Finally the *arrêté* of 16 March 1910 allowed the *requête civile*, the procedure to investigate the possibility of a serious miscarriage of justice.

The different systems of land law—Annamite and French—caused grave difficulty. A particular problem, as in all colonial territories, was the question of mortgage (*hypothèque*) or land-pledging in general. Article 3 of the decree of 30 October 1883 attempted to apply the French *hypothèque* to Annamite land. The decree of 31 July 1925, modified by the decree of 23 November 1926, dealt with the problems caused by simplifying and extending to Annamites a number of the provisions of the Civil Code on servitudes, habitation, contracts relative to the acquisition and transmission of rights in immovable property, and a modified *hypothèque*. However, probably the most important provision of the decrees was the establishment of a land registry based upon survey and inspired by the Torrens system. The system (*les registres 'dia-bô'*) provided an absolute protection for third parties, and Art. 363 of the decree declared inadmissible any action claiming a right not revealed in the inquiry preceding the establishment of a title to land. To provide for the inevitable errors on the first establishment of the registers, an indemnity fund was set up. The decrees were put into application province by province as the necessary cadastral surveys were completed.[24]

Finally, the colonial government made extensive provision for the naturalization of indigenous persons,[25] and regulated the rights and claims that could be invoked by Annamites who spoke and wrote French to be 'elevated' to the status of French citizens. The decree of 4 November 1928 provided for the recognition as French citizens of illegitimate Franco-Indo-Chinese children. This was done by way of proceedings before a French court at which the person might represent himself if he was over the age of majority or be represented by a Children's Protective Society or a public Ministry.

[24] See Camouilly (1886) on the survey question in Cochin-China.
[25] *Décrets* of 25 May 1881, 7 Feb. 1877, 26 May and 25 Nov. 1913, and 18 May 1915.

It is interesting that, in the later years of the colonial legal administration, jurists[26] were looking forward to a fusion of the laws of Cochin-China in both procedure and in substance. It did not in fact take place.

(ii) *Laos*

French intervention in Laos was formalized by the Treaty of 30 October 1893. Laos became a *pays de souveraineté française* but unlike Cochin-China it had separate judicial administrations. The *arrêté* of the Governor-General of Indo-China of 30 September 1895 retained the laws of Laos in all civil and criminal matters concerning the natives and preserved indigenous tribunals (art. 1). The sole exception was crime of a serious nature, for which the penalties might include death or forced labour, which was reserved for the *Tribunal du Commissaire du Gouvernement* (art. 5). This tribunal was composed of a French Commissaire, a Laotian officer, and a *Greffier*[27] (art. 3) and where capital punishment was ordered it had to be approved by the Governor-General of Indo-China. The French Penal Code might be substituted for local customs if thought desirable. There was a right of appeal from the indigenous tribunals to the *Tribunal du Commissaire*. An *arrêté* of the Governor-General of 30 November 1896 provided a more detailed procedure for the native courts, limited their jurisdiction to suits between natives, and provided (art. 17) that indigenous judges who abused their position in matters of crime or delict were to be tried by the *Tribunal Supérieur*. Article 17 did not, however, apply in civil matters.

The system established by the *arrêtés* of 1895 and 1896 did not continue long in force; in December 1905 a commission was constituted by the *Résident Supérieur* to consider: '[how] to bring the Codes of Vientiane and Luang-Prabang into line with our rules of procedure as much as possible and especially to make their application easier and more flexible, then to revise them according to our principles of humanity and justice which necessitate the abolition of corporal punishment and slavery....'[28]

On 5 November 1906 the Commission recommended a

---

[26] See, for example, Garrigues (1931).
[27] Registrar/Clerk (French).
[28] Cited in Cressent (1931: 86).

project for the reform of the indigenous judicial administration, and on 14 December 1906 a project for the codification of Laotian law as well. Both projects were put in hand by two *arrêtés* of the Governor-General of Indo-China given on 2 May 1908.

So far as the administration of justice was concerned, village tribunals under a Laotian officer, called the *Phoban*, were established for small causes not exceeding 3 piastres in value. In the canton, the tribunal of the *Tassèng* had jurisdiction up to 6 piastres, and in the chief town of each *Muong* (district) the court of the *Chaomuong* had jurisdiction in all civil, commercial, and criminal matters. The law applied in each case was Laotian law (see below, on the Codes). Appeals could be taken to the *Tribunal Provincial* located in each *Commissariat du Gouvernement* and presided over by the *Commissaire du Gouvernement* assisted by a Laotian assessor and administered by a *Greffier*. Finally, a *Tribunal Supérieur* located at Vientiane and presided over by the *Résident Supérieur*, assisted by a Laotian functionary, took appeals for the annulment of decisions of the *Tribunal Provincial* on the grounds of a misunderstanding of Laotian law, an excess of jurisdiction, or incompetence. The *Tribunal Supérieur* reviewed all cases of crime for which the penalty imposed was death, forced labour, or imprisonment for ten years or more.

The codification of Laotian law was accomplished in 1908 with the promulgation (*arrêté* 2 May 1908) of Civil, Procedural, and Penal Codes. Laotian legal concepts were retained so far as possible although the law was arranged in terms of the classes and divisions of the French codes. The major changes included the abolition of slavery and debt slavery[29] and the regulation of master–servant contracts in terms of the *arrêtés* of 1896 and 1900.[30] Article 2 of the Civil Code allowed the judges in civil and commercial matters to use their discretion when an issue was not regulated. The Penal Code, apart from forbidding ordeals, slavery, and various forms of corporal punishment, forbade judges to impose a penalty except for an offence specified in the Code and provided that all fines must be paid into the Treasury. The Code of Civil Procedure had only 63 articles and provided

---

[29] Articles 3, 171, 322–6 of the Civil Code; Arts. 20, 23–4 Penal Code, and Arts. 52–60 Civil Procedure Code.
[30] Applied by s. III, Ch. XVII of the Civil Code 1908.

The French Legal World 163

only minimal rules relating mainly to the necessity for keeping written records. Costs of actions were regulated by separate *arrêtés*.[31] This attempt at codification was no more successful than the earlier one. Criticism was very soon directed against the Code of Procedure which was rudimentary to the point of uselessness. The Civil Code was obscure on important points of law, and the Penal Code contained strange provisions; for example, it punished theft by forced labour for a period of 15–20 years, while imposing a fine of only 50 piastres for assault on a wife or 14 piastres for rape. The *arrêtés* of the Governor-General of Indo-China of 6 September 1917, 18 October 1918, and 30 August 1923, appointing a number of officials to judicial posts in Laos, included an instruction to them to 'reform the judicial organization in Laos and to codify the customs of the Laotians and other peoples of the territory'. Thus began the third Laotian codification: five codes were drafted in the period 1917–22 and were put into effect by *arrêté* of 20 November 1922 before they were translated into Laotian; the date of coming into effect was fixed for 1 January 1923. However, difficulties of application immediately arose: there was an insufficient native cadre, the codes were in French, and so on. In the event, a translation commission began work[32] but this did not solve the administrative problem. Dates of application of the codes were delayed several times while the codes were revised and simplified so as to 'better adapt [them] to the degree of intellectual development of the Laotian populations and to the administrative organization of the country'.[33] The Codes of 1922, revised and reduced by 214 articles, were finally promulgated by the *arrêté* of the Governor-General of 5 September 1927 to come into force in Luang Prabang by Royal Ordinance of 15 October 1927. They consisted of the following:

(a) *The Code of Judicial Organization*. This code came into force on 1 June 1928 by *arrêté* of 5 September 1927. It provided basically for the organization of indigenous tribunals. The Code maintained the *Tribunal Supérieur* and the provincial tribunals in each province, but replaced the *Muong* tribunals with a

[31] 2 May 1908, 10 July 1912, 18 Feb. 1914.
[32] For the difficulties of which see Cressent (1931: 91).
[33] Cited ibid. 92.

'Tribunal of First Degree', officers of which were nominated by *arrêtés* of the *Résident Supérieur* who also fixed the numbers of such tribunals. The *Résident Supérieur* was the head of indigenous justice in Laos (arts. 1 & 14 of the Code). The officers of this tribunal continued to be recruited from civil servants (art. 14). The old *Tribunal Supérieur* became the *Tribunal Supérieur d'appel et d'annulation* (art. 23) staffed by French officers and Laotian assessors with equal votes. The *Tribunaux Provinciaux* (arts. 17 & 19), or Tribunals of Second Degree, had similar staffing arrangements although the Laotian assessors were chosen from amongst the *Chaomuongs* and *Oupahats* working in the provinces. The vote of the President of the court was overriding. Special assessors were appointed for criminal cases.

The new Tribunal of the First Degree had competence in civil matters in both first and last resort where the sum involved was 50 piastres or less. In penal matters it had competence to 5 piastres only. In civil matters above 50 piastres in value it had jurisdiction of the first resort only. More serious crime was taken by the Tribunal of the Second Degree.

(b) The Civil and Commercial Code. This Code consisted of 345 articles dealing with the law of persons, capacity, marriage, divorce, filiation, rights of the family, minority, tutelage, and so on. An important function of the Code was to retain as much of Laotian law[34] as was compatible with an efficient administration. Thus the capacity to marry and the form of marriage remained governed by Laotian law although the Code now required the completion of a written form or certificate of marriage. On the other hand, those customs in civil and penal matters which were based upon indigenous concepts of status and hierarchy were abolished so far as possible. Polygamy was permitted to continue and the status of primary and secondary wives was formalized, especially in matters affecting community property. The code also made possible legitimation by subsequent recognition. Adoption to continue a family line was permitted subject to contract, but the adopted person retained rights to the property of his former family. Divorce by mutual consent was permitted to continue although subject to supervision.

[34] See Lingat (1952–5: (ii) 58 f., 73 ff., 101 ff., 106 ff., 112 f., 143 f., 165 ff.).

The Code retained indigenous classifications in property—notably the distinction between animate and inanimate things; it was not felt necessary to introduce the civil-law classes of movable and immovable. The principle that ownership depended upon occupation was continued. However, the practice of squatting was regulated by the letter of the Governor-General of Indo-China to the *Résident Supérieur* dated 15 January 1925, No. 97-SA. Article 79 of the Code was drafted in accordance with this letter and provided that indigenous modes of acquisition and ownership were to continue so long as the property in question was not already held under the terms of the Cochin-Chinese *décret* of 21 July 1925.

Oral contracts were reformed. Contracts above the value of 100 piastres had to be in writing and would be given effect to except in the case of fraud. Oaths as proof of contract were abolished. Contracts of service governed by indigenous laws were reformed both as to terms of service and as to payment. Usury was suppressed in terms of the *arrêté* of the Governor-General of 14 July 1914.

(c) *The Penal Code.* This Code consisted of 237 articles and in its provisions it introduced ideas of criminal liability which did not correspond to indigenous law. Perhaps the most fundamental change was the distinction, which the Code made clear, between civil and criminal liability. This was not made clear in the Code of 1908 and was perhaps the main reason for its failure to be properly applied. The Code did, however, retain the indigenous table of fines for damages. Acquittal for criminal charges did not necessarily absolve an accused of civil liability. Offences against public order were defined in terms of the French Penal Code, especially so far as secret societies were concerned. The new Code also abolished certain customary features, for example, the right of a husband to kill his wife for specified reasons was forbidden and, if it did occur, was treated as murder.

(d) *The Code of Civil and Commercial Procedure (156 arts.) and the Code of Criminal Procedure (143 arts.).* Both codes were drafted in the light of the experience of the quarter-century of judicial administration preceding their introduction. The main effort in both codes was to avoid any conflict of jurisdiction and to provide detailed rules of procedure for the lower courts. In this they succeeded, as witnessed by the fact that in essentials these codes remain today in Laos.[35]

II LES PAYS DE PROTECTORAT

We turn now to the three protectorates, Cambodia, Annam, and Tonkin. The distinction between these and Cochin-China and Laos was that judicial power was exercised indirectly in the former. To a large extent, indigenous tribunals were kept, although amended in function and scope, and laws were promulgated in the names of the rulers. Codification was attempted, and in this sphere of activity the state of affairs was similar to that in the two areas of direct sovereignty (Cochin and Laos).

(i) *Cambodia*

Although France exercised a protectorate over Cambodia from 1863, it was not until the convention of 1884 between the King of Cambodia and France that the administration of justice was affected. In fact, apart from a Royal Ordinance of October 1890 relating to public order, nothing was done until 1902. In that year the Royal Ordinance of 7 February provided for a Tribunal of First Degree (*Sala-Khet*) based upon an indigenous administration, and a Court of Appeal (*Sala-Outor*) sitting at Phnom-Penh. A Royal Ordinance of 26 June 1903 added a Court of Cassation. The laws applied were the indigenous laws of Cambodia and the judicial officers were the various grades of mandarin,[36] who, as in all Indo-China, were not especially trained in law. The system was organized under the control of the French Resident. The Royal Ordinance of 7 September 1910 established courses in Cambodian law for judicial officials. Commissions for the codification of the law were instituted by Royal Ordinances of 11 August 1901, 5 May 1905, and *arrêtés* of 3 September and 21 October 1908, and 4 and 27 October 1911. By Royal Ordinance of 20 November 1911, the King gave approval to the Code of Criminal Instruction and Judicial Organization, Book I of the Civil Code, and the Penal Code, all of which came into force on 1 July 1912. The first-named Code established a series of courts, including tribunals of first

---

[35] See Lyfoung (1969), Suryadhay (1969). The effect of recent political changes on the codes remains unknown.   [36] See Nicholas (1931: 119–21) for details.

instance, a court of appeal with civil and criminal chambers, and a court of cassation with overriding jurisdiction.[37] This system was not a success because of the ignorance of the judges as to the nature of the new system and the absence of written laws sufficiently certain to be applied in such a system. In 1915, therefore, the control of the judicial organization in Cambodia was delegated to a French officer by *arrêté* of 25 December of that year. Under his influence and at his direction a number of texts were promulgated—a Civil Code in 1920,[38] texts on Judicial Organization, the *Statut Personnel*, and a law on the Control of the Judiciary.[39]

The judicial organization resulting from the reforms of 1920–2 included a court of the *Justice de Paix* (*Sala-Lehuk*) with competence in civil and criminal matters, a Court of First Instance (*Sala-Dambaung* and *Sala-Lukhun* at Phnom-Penh), a Court of Appeal (*Sala-Outor*) with civil and criminal chambers, and a Court of Annulment (*Sala-Vinichhay*) with overriding jurisdiction. The province of Stung-Treng had its own special judicial organization.[40]

The substantive reform of the laws of Cambodia had been attempted in a piecemeal way from the early years of this century. Initial work on the codification of criminal law was authorized by Royal Ordinance of 11 August 1901 although, as mentioned earlier, the Code was not applied until 1 July 1912. A new Penal Code was promulgated on 25 August 1924; it was based on the metropolitan code as amended in Cochin-China on its introduction there in 1880. It was made up of 283 articles of which 253 reproduce the French text.[41] The law, therefore, was quite inappropriate, although it was claimed to introduce 'les principes civilisateurs du droit public moderne'.[42]

In civil and commercial matters the legislation was again piecemeal; by Royal Ordinance of 2 March 1897 women of whatever rank or position were relieved of depositing security in any action although the requirement remained for all other

---

[37] Governed by Royal Ordinance of 23 Mar. 1913 and Arts. 185 & 187 Code of Criminal Instruction.
[38] By Royal Ordinance 25 Feb. 1920.
[39] Royal Ordinance 14 Sept. 1922, *arrêté* 3 Oct. 1922.
[40] See Nicholas (1931: 137–8).
[41] With some minor amendments on penalties, e.g. the replacement of banishment by forced labour. See Nicholas (1931: 146–7). [42] Ibid. 146.

168   Contract

persons.[43] Other Royal Ordinances dealt with debits[44] and imprisonment for debt.[45] The project of codification was begun in 1901 (see above), and Book I of the Civil Code was promulgated on 9 April 1913. A project for revision and codification was started in 1918 with the formation of a commission by *arrêtés* of 19 July 1918 and 29 January 1919. Book I, originally promulgated in 1911, was inserted into the new codification which was promulgated by Royal Ordinance of 25 February 1920 and came into force on 1 July 1920. The classification adopted did not conform to indigenous Cambodian law. The code was divided into four books: Persons, Property, Obligations, and Procedure. Book I on Persons was divided into six chapters treating of civil rights, domicile, absentees, family, persons incapable, patrimonial rights and obligations in the family. Book II on Property had four chapters treating of the forms and types of property, ownership, possession, and securities on real property. Book III on obligations had four chapters on general provisions as to sources and validity, the forms and effects of obligations, proof, and contracts of loan and guarantee. Book IV on procedure had seven titles dealing *inter alia* with judgments and execution as well as with documentation in civil matters. The Code introduced a number of important changes in the law, of which we may mention here the question of definition of property, securities, mortgages, usufruct, and the rights of widows to an estate.[46]

(ii) *Annam*

Annam was unique in the Indo-Chinese Territories because it preserved its original form of judicial administration and laws right up to 1930. The laws in general were comprised in:[47]

---

[43] Royal Ordinance 8 Oct. 1897.
[44] 29 Dec. 1897.
[45] 8 Mar. 1897, 30 July 1899, 7 July 1908, 29 Dec. 1897, 27 Dec. 1913, applying Art. 39 of the Penal Code, later regulated by the Civil Code, Arts. 1707 ff.
[46] See the following sources which also illustrate the persistence into the modern period of the model then imposed: Den & Decheix (1969), Sieuv (1972), Chhouk (1972), Ang (1972), Kantol Norodom (1956), Phy-thien-Lay & Allaire (1969), Pompei (1943), Prunières (1970), Youran & Pfister (1969).
[47] See generally above, Chapter 3 on the Vietnamese texts.

The French Legal World   169

the non-codified precepts contained in the Book of Rites, the Constitutional Edicts of the Emperor, the Regulations of the Six Ministries, the Laws and Decrees dealing with punishments.

The French protectorate was established on 6 June 1884 by treaty of that date. In 1885 French Residents were installed in the provinces of Annam, but the intervention of the French did not extend to the drafting and promulgation of regulations. This was a matter which remained solely in Annamite competence as a part of the retention of legal administration in Annamite hands.

The administration of justice was comprised in three degrees of jurisdiction: the tribunals of the *Phủ* (prefecture) and *Huyên* (district); the provincial tribunal; and the appropriate Ministry (of the Interior, Rites, Finance, Public Works, Justice, and War). Annam was divided into provinces, subdivided into districts called *Phủ* or *Huyên* depending upon their importance. At the head of each province was a *Tổng-Đốc* or *Tuân-Phủ*. There were also village councils.

(a) *The Phủ and Huyên.* These tribunals had competence in all matters. Process was either oral or written, if oral a note was taken including name, profession, domicile, statement of claim, and decision.[48] Witnesses were called in crime and delicts but the responsibility for public order lay with local village heads.

(b) *The Provincial Tribunal.* These tribunals were composed of mandarins of the following rank:

(i) For the major provinces, *Tổng-Đốc* (district commissioners), *Quản-Bố* (collector), and *Quản-Án* (magistrate);
(ii) For the important provinces, *Tuân-Phủ* and *Quản-Án*;
(iii) For the third-rank provinces, *Quản-Bố* and *Quản-Án*;
(iv) For the minor provinces, *Quản-Đạo* (administrator) alone.

The mandarinate as a whole did not discuss the judgments of *phủ* and *huyên*. The officers called *Quản-Án* and *Quản-Bố* revised or approved such judgments. Any revision was put in

[48] See Bonhomme (1931: 158–9).

writing and had to be submitted to the other mandarins. In case of disagreement the *Tổng-Đốc* prevailed but all opinions had to be recorded. The *Quản-Án* and *Quản-Bố* had to advise the *Tổng-Đốc* of their cases. The main function of the *Quản-Án* was to take criminal matters transmitted from the *Phù* and *Huyên*; he also controlled public order. All cases came to the *Quản-Án* through the *Phù* and *Huyên* levels (art. 301 Annamite Code (Gia-Long)), and he might also replace and discipline officers at the lower levels.

The *Quản-Bố* was concerned with finance, public works, and so on; his procedure and competence were the same as that of the *Quản-Án*. His judgments were written and might proceed to the *Tổng-Đốc* or *Tuần-Phù*.

The *Tổng-Đốc* or *Tuần-Phù* represented royal power in his province. His function was administrative and he had the right of direct correspondence with the Royal Court. He might override the *Quản-Án* and *Quản-Bố*, but he might not dispense with their services. All judgments were written, and any officer who had an interest in a suit had to declare it and this was recorded in the judgment. Judgments were sent to the relevant ministers for execution (see below) and a copy also went to the French *Résident chef de province* who, though not directly involved in the administration of justice, could report any matter to the *Résident Supérieur*, who had power to investigate abuse or error. Judgments which involved imprisonment or physical punishment could not be enforced without the approval of the *Résident*, but this rule did not apply where there was a difference of opinion between *Résident* and provincial mandarins or where the Annamite government was involved. The function of the *Résident*, therefore, was to exercise some control over the administration of justice.

Judgments given by the mandarins were directed to the competent ministry: to Justice for criminal matters; to Finance for property and foodstuffs; to Interior for administration; to War; to Rites; and to Public Works. Each ministry had three superior mandarins, the *Tham-tri* (technical adviser), the *Thi-lang* (assessor), and the *Tá-lý* (assistant judge), and a secretarial office. There was a Council of Ministers—the *Cơ-Mật*, which had competence to examine judgments involving superior mandarins, penalties of death, and judgments in especially serious matters. Full transcripts of such judgments were provided and, after French intervention, the decision had to be approved by the *Résident Supérieur* 'à qui sa qualité de haut Protecteur du Pays vaut d'être l'arbitre suprême en matière de justice'![49] It was only then that execution was directed. In addition, there were a number of special jurisdictions.[50]

The system of traditional judicial administration was thus continued under the supervision of French officers at provincial and central levels. Criticism was always directed toward the concentration of powers in the jurisdiction of the mandarin and the apparent French acquiescence in this situation. On the other hand, the system worked reasonably well for the populations. Articles 7 and 10 of the Treaty of 6 June 1884 gave the Residents an indirect power in administration and justice through their supervision of the actions of the mandarinate and also by the issue of circular letters of instruction on judicial administration. Decisions of the Council of Ministers (*Cơ-Mật*) of 1896, 1898, and 1901 regulated and agreed the function of the French officers of the *Résident Supérieur*'s office.

The main effort of the protectorate authority in law was directed toward the abolition of certain punishments in the Annamite (*Gia-Long*) Code; decapitation, torture, and a number of other punishments were all abolished by Royal Ordinances of 2 February 1912 and 5 January and 3 February 1913. Occasionally the *Résident Supérieur* would issue an *arrêté*, but to be effective it had to be approved by the Council of Ministers. In addition, modifications to the competence of the judicial organs were made by Royal Ordinance of 11 September 1914 which limited the power of the provincial mandarins and required the transmission of most judgments to the Council of Ministers for approval. Special provisions were also made for the tribal peoples of the Annamite Chain.[51]

The laws applied by the courts (see above in this section) were set out in a Chinese-derived form in the Code of *Gia-Long*,[52] commonly known as the Annamite Code, although it

[49] Ibid. 165.   [50] Ibid. 165–6.
[51] See ibid. 172. See also: Guilleminet (1938) (1952), Sabatier (1940), Tran-Chanh-Thanh (1942).
[52] See also above, Chapter 3.

was open to the inhabitants to opt for French law in certain circumstances.[53]

(iii) *Tonkin*

The French protectorate was established by the Treaty of Hué of 6 June 1884. The legal system of Tonkin was in all essentials the same as in Annam[54] but the influence of the protecting power was exercised far more directly in judicial administration and in the reform of substantive law. The decree of 27 January 1886 stated quite bluntly that France aimed at the reform of the law. The Royal Ordinances of 3 June 1886 and 17 January 1889 between them devised a mixed French–Tonkinese system of jurisdiction for matters of public security and crimes and delicts; it is also distributed legislative and administrative power between French delegates and Tonkinese ministers. Over-all control was exercised by the *Résident général*. Apart from these provisions, indigenous administration of justice continued, but by Royal Ordinance of 26 July 1897 and *arrêté* of the *Résident Supérieur* of 1 March 1900, the over-all control of all indigenous justice was transferred to the *Résident Supérieur*.

The *décret* of 1 November 1901 transferred jurisdiction over indigenous justice from the *Résident Supérieur* to a Commission of Appeal which was constituted a Court of Appeal for Tonkin. The Commission was composed of three councils drawn from the Court of Appeal of Indo-China and two mandarins. Its orders were executed by the *Procureur général* of Indo-China. The *décret* of 31 August 1905 constituted this Commission as the Fourth Chamber of the Court of Appeal of Indo-China sitting at Hanoi. Subject to this *décret* it was composed of the Vice-President of the Court of Appeal, two Councillors, and two mandarins. It took appeals from all jurisdictions. The *décret* was a prelude to the complete judicial reorganization of Tonkin and was followed in 1913 by the formation of Codification Commissions for the indigenous laws of Tonkin. On 16 July 1917 a Royal Ordinance established four codes for the Protectorate: Code of Indigenous Judicial Organization, Code of Civil and Commercial Procedure, Code of Penal Procedure,

[53] See Camerlynck (1937).
[54] See Habert (1931: 176–8).

and a Code of Penal Law. It should be noticed that there was no code of civil law. An *arrêté* of the Governor-General of 16 July 1917 executed these codes so that they came into force on 1 January 1918. The texts of the codes were revised by Royal Ordinances of 2 July 1920 and 16 June and 5 August 1921, and executed by the *arrêté* of 2 December 1921, coming into force on 1 May 1922.

The necessity to take steps to ensure the successful implementation of the codes was recognized. The mandarinate was not competent to apply them, so French judges had to be employed. Of the two tribunals established, First and Second, the latter, which was of the same status as the Tribunal of First Degree in metropolitan France, was constituted as a mixed tribunal presided over by a French judge assisted by a mandarin.[55] This arrangement was provisional; the mandarins continued to exercise their judicial functions outside this system, but in cooperation with judges of the First Degree. The mandarin appointed to the Tribunal of the Second Degree was the highest native functionary of the province. From 1921 the latter could also exercise the functions of a judge of the First Degree. In 1923 a corps of judicial mandarins was created, and the ordinance of 7 June 1923 provided that a member of this corps could exercise the functions of a *Juge d'instruction* and a *Juge enquêteur civil*. This remained something of a dead letter although in the same and following years attempts to create a complete cadre of native judges were made.[56]

The main Codes promulgated were as follows:

(a) *Code of Organization of Indigenous Justice*. This Code provided that indigenous jurisdiction could be applied only to natives; if a Frenchman or a foreigner was a party to a cause, the indigenous tribunal had no jurisdiction. The Code provided for a Tribunal of the First Degree for each administrative district (*phù, huyên*), staffed by a judge from the ranks of the legally qualified mandarins. It had competence of the First and Last resort in civil and criminal matters limited to a sum of 30 piastres, and simple crimes, the punishment for which did not exceed imprisonment. Appeals were taken to the Tribunal of

---

[55] Royal Ordinance 7 June 1923 and *arrêté* of *Résident Supérieur* 20 Sept. 1929 and Convention 6 Nov. 1925.
[56] See Habert (1931: 188–9).

174   Contract

Second Degree which, subject to the comments made above, was staffed by a judge drawn from mandarins of the grades *Án-Sát* or *Tri-Phù*. It had civil jurisdiction in First and Last resort up to 100 piastres. In criminal matters it could order punishment extending to capital punishment, but such power was exercised under the control of the Second Chamber of the Court of Appeal (of Indo-China) at Hanoi, which took appeals on civil and criminal matters. The latter court exercised the functions of appeal and cassation in respect of indigenous justice.

The Code also laid down general rules of competence, discipline, procedure, enforcement of judgments and their execution in other territories.[57]

(*b*) *Code of Criminal Procedure and the Criminal Code*. These Codes contained/continued in force a large number of the provisions of the *Gia-Long* Code.[58] In the Code of Procedure, the rules on proof, the execution of judgment, and the investigation of crime and delicts were taken from the traditional text. Some archaic principles were abolished, but any revision was kept to a minimum.

The Criminal Code was a severely modified adaptation of the *Gia-Long* text. Crimes were classified according to the nature of the offence as this was understood in French criminal theory. Particular forms of punishment, such as beating and various forms of torture, were abolished.

(*c*) *Code of Civil and Commercial Procedure*. This was the last of the Tonkinese codes and was not promulgated until 1931. Hitherto, civil and commercial matters had been regulated by the *Gia-Long* text, by the *Hội-Điển* or Royal Ordinances available in a collected volume compiled in 1851, by later Royal Ordinances, and by local practice or (unwritten) customary laws.[59] A basic text (*corps d'instructions*), ratified by an *arrêté* of the Governor-General of 25 January 1912, which contained a set of rules selected from these sources, was promulgated as the authoritative statement of Annamite law in civil and commercial matters. In addition, a Commission of Appeal established in 1901 and later absorbed into the *Cour*

[57] *Décret* 16 Sept. 1922.
[58] See above, Chapter 3.
[59] These sources were known to the French legal administration primarily in the translations of Aubaret (1865) and Philastre (1876).

The French Legal World 175

d'Appel of Indo-China in 1905 began to formulate an authoritative jurisprudence basing itself on the sources just outlined. The work of the Court was utilized by the *Comité Consultatif de Jurisprudence Annamite*, established by the *arrêté* of the *Résident Supérieur* of 30 August 1927, whose task was to extract the basic principles of Annamite law for codification. The report of the *Comité* was published in 1930,[60] and in 1931 the Civil Code for Tonkin was promulgated.[61]

III THE CONFLICT OF LAWS

The laws in the various territories of French Indo-China were peculiar to each part of the Union although there were of course underlying similarities. Much more striking are the issues of conflict that the Union itself brought about. The different statuses of the territories contributed in no little measure to this; the Union was made up of the *colony* of Cochin-China and the *protectorates* of Laos, Cambodia, Annam, and Tonkin. The legal implications of the terms 'colony' and 'protectorate' were never clear, and in the literature of French Indo-China they evoked constant controversy.[62] For example, the divisions *pays de souveraineté–pays de protectorat* are valid from the point of view of judicial organization, but the distinction *colonie–protectorat* is equally valid from the political point of view. The two sets of distinctions are by no means mutually compatible. As Paul Couzinet has shown,[63] the theoretical propositions of French international law were not sufficient to explain the full legal significance of classes such as *sujet*, *protégé*, and *citoyen*. The difficulties are apparent from the three main classes of colonial conflicts of law.

(i) *The Conflict between Metropolitan Law and Indo-Chinese Law applicable to French citizens in Indo-China*

French law applied (*a*) in relations between French or between French and indigenous—this is the colonial conflict proper; (*b*) French law might also apply in the relationship

---
[60] The report naturally concentrated largely on matters of family and succession. For a valuable review of this subject for the period 1921–41 see 'H.G.' (1942).
[61] For the particular problems to which codification gave rise in respect of obligations and property see Caratini (1938) on obligations and (1938a) (1939) (1939a) on the proof of proprietary rights.
[62] See Couzinet (1938) (1939).　　[63] Couzinet (1938).

176   Contract

between natives, exclusively where they opt for the French civil and commercial law, or where the indigenous law is silent. The latter (*b*) posed no problems, it is (*a*) that caused difficulty because the foreign element which private international law deals with might be a transaction which had a connection with the law of metropolitan France; for example, a contract executed in Indo-China and performed in France. The usual private international law recourse to nationality is of no use in this case. The question was, what was 'French' law? Different legislative provisions could and did apply.[64] This was a consequence of the principle *de spécialité de la législation coloniale*.[65] In cases of dispute the principles of (French) private international law were applied by analogy. In addition, the idea of inter-provincial conflicts (as in Alsace-Lorraine) were also applied.[66] No satisfactory solution to this area of conflict was ever worked out.

(ii) *Conflict of Laws and Jurisdictions within the* Union Indochinoise

This was a problem that arose out of the different jurisdictions, French and indigenous, in Indo-China. The issue was not made any easier by the different legislative histories of the components of the Union; and the confusion as to the implications of a common political, as opposed to legislative or judicial, status added yet a further complication. The discussion of these difficulties was also obscured by undue theorizing by some authors on the place of the principles of private international law in the colony.[67] The problem essentially reduced itself to two issues:

(*a* Conflicts between the various legislative regimes. Article 112 of the decree of 16 February 1921 provided as follows: 'in civil matters French law will regulate 'conventions' between French and between French and assimilated or natives or non-assimilated.' This is a badly drafted provision primarily because the meaning of 'convention' remained vague.[68] The question was the significance of this proposition in cases between natives

[64] See Dennery (1939: 361 ff.) for examples.
[65] See Camerlynck (1937a) on marriage between French and Annamites.
[66] Ibid. for the jurisprudence.
[67] Notably the work of Solus (1927).
[68] See Dennery (1939a: 511 n.).

of different statuses. Article 112 is at the head of a chapter entitled 'Legislation applicable in French Jurisdiction' and it seems to impose Annamite laws where the individual involved is not subject to French law. However, this interpretation would lead to absurd results. For example, if there was a case in Cambodia between a Cambodian and a Laotian and such falls within the French jurisdiction, then Article 112 would require the application of Annamite law, to which neither party was subject. Thus it seems that the article confuses the situation where a Frenchman is involved with one where no Frenchman is involved. The article is in fact a direct reproduction of Article 11 of the decree of 25 July 1864 drafted for Cochin-China at a time when the French possessions did not extend to Cambodia or Laos! The decree of 1921 should have substituted 'native' for 'Annamite' in Article 112, since by 1921 the Annamite law was not the only 'other' law. Even here the 'Annamite' laws of Cochin-China and Tonkin might and did vary. The distinctions between the different legal statuses of Cambodians and Laotians on the one hand, and Annamites who are either *sujet* or *protégé* on the other, had a direct bearing in this situation.

In the case of Cambodians, a distinction can be drawn according to whether they appeared before the French jurisdiction within Cambodia or outside Cambodia. In the latter case Article 21 of the Cambodian Civil Code revised in 1934, which refers to the French protectorate, states that Cambodian nationality was only relevant in internal matters. Such a person was a French subject 'outside Cambodia in foreign territory, i.e. in the other countries of the Indo-China Union, where he was assimilated in all matters to the natives, French subjects'. Thus, the question now becomes What was the extent of legal assimilation to French subjects? The answer is that outside his own country the Cambodian was subject to the Annamite law of Cochin-China as a French subject. However, the 1883 (civil law) Précis of Cochin-China did not cover all civil-law matters and thus a new and unfamiliar law could easily apply. If the suit was between a Cambodian and a French '*protégé* Annamite' (i.e. a person from Annam or Tonkin), the conflict was not between Cambodian and Cochin-Chinese law but between the law of Cochin-China and the 'Annamite' law of Annam and/or Tonkin.

On the other hand, litigation within Cambodia between Cambodians and non-Cambodians was subject exclusively to French jurisdiction. It was once thought that the native law of Cochin-China must apply in such cases by virtue of the *décret* of 6 May 1898. This *décret* regulated procedure and law before the setting-up of the 'Tribunal of the First Degree and *Justice de Paix* with extended jurisdiction in Cambodia'. This interpretation, however, was not correct. The *decret* of 16 February 1921 (art. 112) established the legislation applicable in French jurisdictions. Further, the *décret* of 6 May 1898 only extended the *décret* of 25 July 1864 and presidential *arrêté* of 23 August 1871. The two last-mentioned declared Annamite law applicable to natives and assimilated Asians, but the Cambodians did not fall within these groups.[69] Thus it could be argued the Cambodian law should apply where one party only was Cambodian.

The situation of the Laotians was the same. Outside Laos they could not invoke Laotian law. Article 1 of the Laos Civil Code states its provisions 'to be applicable in civil and commercial matters to [French] subjects and *protégés* in *all the territory of French Laos*'. Outside Laos such dispositions were inapplicable.

So far as Annamite *sujets* or *protégés français* were concerned, they retained the right to the application of their own laws in foreign countries, i.e. Laos or Cambodia. Where Annamites of different states were concerned the question was less complex; French subjects, e.g. Cochin-Chinese, retained their own law in Tonkin. They were never assimilated to the laws of a protectorate, i.e. they were not *protégés français*. But the law of Cochin-China was not always applied: there were conflicts between Cochin-Chinese law and the laws of Annam and Tonkin to which Article 112 of the *décret* of 1921 applied. Article 21 of the Cambodian Civil Code declared that a Cambodian subject was, in other regions of Indo-China, assimilated to French subjects, but no such text existed for Annamites or Tonkinese. Thus there was no assimilation for them in Cochin-China.

No overriding texts existed for the solution of conflicts of laws. Legislation, where it did exist, was contained in particular codes or in special rules relating to various categories of law (see

[69] Ibid.

The French Legal World 179

below). In Tonkin and Annam, Article 2 of the respective Civil Codes provided that 'the laws concerning status and capacity continue to regulate Annamite subjects [of Tonkin and Annam] even whilst they reside outside the territories of these countries'. In Cochin-China and the French possessions, Article 3 of the *Précis* of 1887 merely replaced Article 3 of the Civil Code (of France). Thus both sets of legislation are prima facie applicable in cases of internal conflict. So far as special laws were concerned, apart from the texts just cited, the *décret* of 21 July 1925 on property provided for the application of the 'personal law of the individual'. The texts are insufficient, covering as they do only personal status and immovable property. In such cases recourse to French law was often made[70] but this was not satisfactory, as the fields of law described below illustrate.

First, status and capacity: these were governed by Article 2 of the Civil Codes of Tonkin and Annam and Article 3 of the *Précis* of 1883 (art. 3, *Code Civil Français*) for Cochin-China. The definitions of the Codes applied to all classes of Annamite (*protégé* or *sujet*) in colonial or protectorate territory. Despite Article 21 of the Cambodian Civil Code, the same rule seems to have been enforced. The Court of Appeal, Hanoi, on 1 July 1938 decided that the personal capacity of an Annamite married woman resident in a French concession was governed by her personal law, i.e. by the Civil Code of Tonkin or of Annam.[71] Article 189 of the *décret* of 21 July 1925 provided that capacity to contract was subject to Annamite law for 'Annamite and Asiatic *assimilés* [Chinese]'. This law applied to both French *protégés* and *sujets*, i.e. it must be taken to include a reference to the Civil Codes of Tonkin and Annam after these were promulgated.

Second, property: the *lex situs* generally applied, so that in any part of the Union a foreigner was subject to the local law.

Third, succession: this was governed by the law which established personal status not, as in private international law, by the law of domicile or *situs*. So far as immovable property was concerned, the *décret* of 1925 and Article 169 of the *décret* of 21 July 1935 of Cochin-China applied the personal law (loi personnelle).[72]

[70] See Dennery (1938: 106) and Caratini (1939) (1939a).
[71] See Dennery (1939a: 520 n. 1) for a number of decided cases. [72] See ibid.

Finally, juridical acts: so far as the formal validity of juridical acts was concerned, the courts developed the principle of *lex loci regit actum*. For example, the *Cour d' Appel*, Hanoi, in its *arrêté* of 8 January 1937 approved a customary contract of adoption between a Tonkinese *sujet* and a (French) *sujet* of Cochin-China. Similarly, the court at Phnom-Penh admitted as valid a marriage between two (French) *sujets* of Cochin-China (a Cambodian woman and a Catholic Chinese) celebrated according to Cambodian custom.[73] So far as the substance of the law was concerned, the French private international law principle of reliance upon intention (*autonomie de la volonté*) applied. The law was that chosen by the parties, and, if no choice was made, then the court would make the choice for them, relying upon evidence of nationality, place of execution, and completion of juridical activity. This principle applied particularly in the case of conflict of native laws, a situation with which the provisions of Article 112 of the *décret* of 10 February 1921 did not deal. The principle also applied where the act in question was illegal according to the laws of the court of one of the parties involved.

(b) Competence of Tribunals in the Execution of Judgments. The conflict between indigenous and French jurisdictions was regulated by Article 108 of the *décret* of 16 February 1921 which provided:

> In the regions of Indo-China other than Cochin-China [French] tribunals only are competent in civil and commercial matters involving Frenchmen and *assimilés*, French subjects, Annamites originating in French concessions, French protected persons foreign to the territory and other foreigners. The same applies where one of the parties is an indigenous person.

The reason for this provision was that indigenous tribunals could not apply other than local laws. As a result of Article 108 the indigenous tribunals of Annam and Tonkin were incompetent to deal with suits involving foreign indigenous persons—Article 108 (2) provided: 'French tribunals in Annam–Tonkin only are competent to take suits between Annamites and Tonkinese, and Cambodians or Laotians.'

The same principle applied to French *sujets* originating in

---

[73] Ibid. 523 n. 3 for references. But see Herchenroder (1936) on 'native Christians'.

Cochin-China and in the concessions of Haiphong and Tourane. However, indigenous tribunals remained competent to the exclusion of French tribunals so far as subjects of the Emperor of Annam were concerned, even though they were *domiciled* in another part of the Union.[74]

In Cambodia and Laos, Article 108 established the competence of French jurisdiction 'to deal with suits between Cambodians and Annamites or Laotians'. The competence of indigenous tribunals in Cambodia was limited to suits between Cambodians. The Cambodian Royal Ordinance of 14 September 1922 provided that the persons subject to indigenous jurisdiction must be Cambodian subjects as enumerated in Articles 23–5 of the Cambodian Civil Code. Such comprised 'Cambodians who originate in Cambodia, other persons born in Cambodia who are members of autochthonous groups,[75] and mixed Sino-Cambodians who are nationals of Cambodia (or who have formally applied for naturalization)'.

The competence of the indigenous tribunals in relation to Cambodians domiciled in Cochin-China was affirmed by the *arrêté* of 26 December 1924 given by the *Cour d'annulation* of the Kingdom of Cambodia. The *arrêté* was in accordance with the later decision of the *Cour de Saigon* of 22 November 1925 recognizing the competence of the indigenous tribunals of Annam to deal with suits involving Annamites domiciled in Cochin-China. Thus the Cambodians were in the same position as the Tonkinese (*protégés française*) in Cochin-China, although for the latter not even domicile was required. However, Cambodians born and domiciled in Cochin-China during the annexation of Cochin-China to France had the status of 'foreigners assimilated to indigenous' and were thus French subjects.

The status of the Muslim Cham was never clear; the tribunal of Phnom-Penh and the *Cour de Saigon* both affirmed the competence of French tribunals on the ground that the Cham were 'foreign Asiatics'. On the other hand, the *Cour de Cassation de Saigon* pronounced in favour of indigenous tribunals, thus reversing the *arrêté* of 22 July 1905.

[74] Dennery (1939a: 527 n. 1), citing jurisprudence.
[75] This is primarily a reference to the Muslim Cham community. See Ner (1941: 154 ff.).

In Laos, Article 108 of the *décret* of 16 February 1921 was complemented by the Code of Judicial Organization of 1922, which provided that indigenous tribunals had jurisdiction over persons born or settled in Laos and over those enrolled on the tax lists who had no foreign nationality.

In Cochin-China the French tribunals had exclusive jurisdiction until the *décret* of 16 February 1921, Article 98 of which established a court of the *Justice de Paix Indigène* with competence in civil and simple police matters involving 'Annamites' and '*assimilés*'. This phrase meant French subjects of Cochin-China, and French *protégés* of Annam and Tonkin. Article 98 was an exception to the general rule that an indigenous tribunal could not deal with suits involving foreign *indigènes*. The exception did not apply in the case of Cambodians originating in Cambodia or Laotians who were not Annamite *assimilés*.

Despite the complexity of the rules just described, they did not succeed in determining conflicts of jurisdiction. For example, where the subject-matter of a suit involved immovable property, that fact alone tended to determine jurisdiction, particularly if the property was situated in different parts of the Union.[76]

The execution of judgments given by an indigenous tribunal in other parts of the Union raised the issue of enforcing a foreign judgment. In this case, the ordinary principles of French private international law applied.[77] This meant a recourse to French jurisdiction in the territory in which the judgment was to be enforced and was so specified in the codes of procedure of each territory.

(iii) *The Position of the Chinese*

Before 1930 the Chinese in Indo-China were subject to local law. The *décret* of 25 July 1864[78] and the *arrêté* of 23 April 1871 defined the Chinese as *asiatiques assimilés*, which was interpreted as excluding any law other than local law. Even in the case of

---

[76] See Dennery (1939a: 531-5) for the jurisprudence.

[77] See the *arrêté* of the *Cour d'Appel Indochine* of 7 May 1902 reported in the *Journ. Judicaire* (1902: 158).

[78] Promulgated in Cochin-China by *arrêté* of the Governor 28 Oct. 1871, in Cambodia by Art. 4 of the *décret* of 6 May 1898 and *arrêté* of the Governor-General of 26 June 1898, and in the whole of Indo-China by Art. 112 of *décret* of 16 Feb. 1921.

The French Legal World 183

Chinese registered as foreign subjects, e.g. British subjects, the same rule applied.[79] However, as a result of the Treaty of Nanking, signed on 16 May 1930, between France and the Republic of China, the Chinese became entitled to the benefit of the laws of the Republic of China as foreign nationals.[80] The result of the Treaty was thus to create a private international law problem where none had previously existed.[81]

IV THAILAND

The laws of Thailand (or Siam as it then was) form part of the French legal world of South-East Asia because the Civil Codes were taken as models for the reorganization of Thai law in the early years of this century. This is attributable to the presence of Franco-Belgian advisers in the Thai court at the time of the reorganization and afterwards.[82] The kings of Thailand themselves took a close interest in law reform,[83] both as an element of modernization and as an important means of getting rid of extraterritorial privileges imposed by European powers in the nineteenth century.[84] The two motives, cesser of extraterritoriality and modernization, between them resulted in a specifically Thai use of the Civil Code model.

The first set of codes were produced at the turn of the century during the reign of King Chulalongkorn (Rama V 1868-1910). They comprised a law of the Courts of Justice promulgated on 5 April 1908, a Code of Civil Procedure promulgated in 1908, and a Criminal Code promulgated on 1 June 1908. Each of these codes was the end product of legal changes made in the later nineteenth century, all of which were of a public-law character.[85] In his preface to the new Criminal Code, the King pointed out that reform was necessary because of the confused state of existing laws and in order to deal with the problem of extraterritoriality. He referred to the example of Japan where

---

[79] See Levasseur (1937b: 45-6) for the jurisprudence.
[80] See Levasseur (1937) for a detailed description of the Nanking agreement.
[81] See Levasseur (1937) (1937b) for details.
[82] See Guyon (1919), Saint-Hubert (1965).
[83] See Seni Pramoj (1950), Wichiencharoen & Luang Chamroon Netisastra (1968).
[84] See Thornely (1923: App.) for detailed rules and Sayre (1928) on the passing of extraterritoriality.
[85] For an excellent summary see Engel (1975: 59-76).

the employment of foreign legal advisers, in conjunction with local officials, resulted in the promulgation of new laws. The changes made in Thai law are apparent in each code; in the Criminal Code, drafted by M. Padoux, the French legal adviser at the time,[86] the principle of conditional sentencing was included on the lines specified in the Belgian and French laws. Similarly, a fourfold classification of recidivism was adopted on lines similar to those known in the European codes. The system of maximum and minimum punishments was also a modified form of the French system. The Code of Civil Procedure and the Law of the Courts of Justice between them established a system of judicial administration which in its detail and precision was unparalleled in Thai legal history. Its European derivation is obvious. The effect of the reforms was to create a unified Thai judiciary under the authority of a Minister of Justice directly responsible to the King. The jurisdiction of each court was clearly defined and a standard procedure eliminated former differences between the Bangkok and provincial courts. Judges from the lowest to the highest level were appointed by the Minister of Justice. The most significant change was the distinction between civil and criminal law established by the reforms. It was in effect a new definition of law, in that the distinction needed no reference to the rules (*Thamma*) of the moral universe. The codes had begun a process by which laws were no longer legitimated by reference to *Thammasat* or *Rajasat*[87] but by new ideas of state sovereignty. It was the introduction of the latter which finally ended extraterritoriality.[88] In this connection it is significant that the codes of this period were all in the area of *public* law.

The new definition of law was extended to private law in the promulgation of the Civil and Commercial Code of 1935 which changed substantive principles of traditional Thai law, especially in family law. Polygamy was abolished and the validity of marriage was made dependent upon registration.[89] On the other hand, parts of the traditional law were retained, e.g.

---

[86] See generally Padoux (1909) on the drafting, and for an outline description in English see Masao (1908).
[87] See above, Chapter 1.
[88] See Sayre (1928).
[89] The implementation of these principles leaves a lot to be desired even now. See H. E. Smith (1973).

The French Legal World 185

property rights as between spouses[90] and the right to divorce by mutual consent. The Civil Code did not require any change in the structure of the Thai family.[91] In the same period the opportunity was taken to revise the earlier laws on civil procedure[92] and the criminal law[93] consequent upon the promulgation of the new Constitution in 1932.[94] In 1936 Book IV of the Civil and Commercial Code was promulgated with reference to land and property matters in general. Its provisions so far as land titles are concerned have been replaced by the Land Code of 1 December 1954 and accompanying regulations.

With the promulgation of the Civil and Commercial Code, and the revisions of the other codes outlined above, Thailand completed the transition from traditional law to a secular state-based system.[95] The system is French-derived or, more generally, derived from the world of the European codes. In this Thailand has followed the example of Japan and China in Asia in adopting the code form that was imposed in French Indo-China. The same conflict of laws did not arise as in the French territories because of the unity of jurisdiction and the exclusive application of the codes to all nationals and residents within the state. The Thai conflict of laws rules[96] deal solely with private international law, and internal conflict is not, in theory, possible. In contrast, the development of personal laws in the English legal world implies an internal conflict. In Thailand, on the other hand, the issue is the application of the codes and their effectiveness as binding systems of obligation among the mass of the population. The issue is not only the limited application of traditional law but its application within the framework of a new definition of personal obligation.

V SUMMARY

The result of the introduction of the code-formulated law into mainland South-East Asia was quite simply to redefine law as a function of the state order. The source of law was located in the sovereign nation-state, its validity was dependent upon institutions of state, and its existence was likewise limited by the

---

[90] See Lingat (1943).
[91] See H. E. Smith (1973a).
[92] See Eygout (1932).
[93] See Eygout (1938).
[94] See Eygout (1937).
[95] For an outline description see Hickling (1972).
[96] See Chin Kim (1971).

process of state government. Since the demise of the French colonial presence in the post-war years the Union Indochinoise has been broken into its component parts, Cambodia, Laos, and North and South Vietnam. This very largely ended the internal conflict of laws because each state created or unified legal jurisdiction within its own territories.[97] While political events in Vietnam may bring further changes in law, the code formulation is unlikely to be abandoned. As David and Brierley[98] point out, the socialist codes are in essence civil-law documents.

[97] For South Vietnam see the following sources: Nguyen Nhu Dung (1966), Pham Huy Ty (1956), Prosterman (1967), Derrida (1961), Nguyen, Xuan Chanh (1968), Trinh Dinh Tieu (1961), Gittinger (1959). For North Vietnam see Gittinger (1959), Ginsburgs (1973) (1975), Fall (1967: App.), Chin Kim (1971a). For Cambodia see: Norodom Kantol (1956), Chhouk Chhay Eng (1973). For Laos see: Morel (1970), Luce (1972), Insixienmai (1972), Suryadhay *et al.* (1970), Vorachack (1972).

[98] David & Brierley (1968: 207 ff.).

CHAPTER 7

The Dutch Legal World: The Netherlands East Indies

THE HISTORY of Dutch civil law in the Netherlands East Indies (N.E.I.) is a history of legal conflict to an extent not found in other South-East Asian lands. From the very earliest days of settlement, law was applied on a racial and religious basis. Civil law applied only to Europeans or to persons assimilated to European status (e.g. Japanese); in the case of the indigenous Indonesian people, local customary laws (*adat*) governed private law transactions and Islamic law also received some minimal application. The Chinese were subject to 'Chinese (customary) law' until 1929. Even Christian Indonesians were provided with special legislation. This plurality of laws was highly formalized, and Dutch jurists developed a conflict of laws theory (*intergentiel recht*) to determine choice of law, jurisdiction, and enforcement.

I COLONIAL LEGAL POLICY

The Dutch are unique in the legal history of South-East Asia in the attention they paid to the formulation of a colonial legal policy. From the very earliest days of the (Netherlands) East India Company's rule in Java the judicial administration was plural in nature with separate tribunals for Europeans and Natives. The separation of legal regimes established in the seventeenth century remained a constant feature of later legal history and may, indeed, be regarded as the single most important aspect of the Netherlands East Indies legal history.

We may best approach Dutch colonial legal policy by examining its institutional structure and its theoretical foundation in Dutch legal thought.

(*a*) *Institutional structure.*[1] The main institutions of colonial legal policy were very much a matter of administrative

[1] This summary is taken from Hooker (1975: 251–7).

organization based on the Governor-General's executive instructions. The instructions were a response to changing economic and political conditions and we may distinguish at least five separate elements spanning the nineteenth and early twentieth centuries. First, the transfer of government from the East India Company to the state at the turn of the seventeenth century gave rise to a series of reforms initiated by Governor-General Daendels in 1808. The main effect was to formalize the legal administration into separate native and European jurisdictions. This system was preserved by the British when Java came under their control in 1811. The British added an important new element: a system of land classification and control under which land was classed as state property. The result was that only the state could confer rights in land on the individual who, in turn, was expected to pay a 'land rent' to the revenue authority. In this classification the village was taken as the administrative unit (on the Indian pattern), and land distributions under the new system were based on village communities. The village and land systems thus came to form the basis of the judicial system as it affected natives.

Third, shortly after Java was returned to Netherlands control in 1814, a new Constitutional Regulation (*Regeringsreglement*) was promulgated (1815) which kept in force the British-devised land system and added to it a system of native courts (*Landraad*) which operated at Regency (i.e. District) level. A new Constitutional Regulation was promulgated in 1858 which, though it left much to be legislated for by later decree, provided that natives were to be subject only to laws drafted in accordance with the new Regulation. Among the most important subsequent legislation was the Agrarian law of 1870 which affirmed, for the first time in legal form, the principle that all land was state land. The consequence was that it became necessary to distinguish between state land free of native rights (Free land) and state land subject to native rights (Unfree land).

The next contribution to the structure of Dutch colonial legal policy took a political form with the formation of the *Volksraad* in 1916, later reconstituted in 1927, the assent of which was necessary for some legislation. It could also amend

The Dutch Legal World

draft ordinances and initiate legislation. This initiative was accompanied by some unification of law; a common police court (*landgeracht*) for all classes established in 1914, and in 1918 a common Penal Code was introduced. The (European) Civil and Commercial laws were extended to the Chinese in part in 1919 and completely by 1929. In 1920 a draft Civil Code for all elements of the population was promulgated but not, in the event, finally accepted. This code represented the high point in the trend toward the unification of law and it was defeated largely on the initiative of the 'Adat Law School' (see below).

Finally, we turn to the administrative element in the plural law system which, in keeping with administrative structures everywhere, generated its own momentum. The indigenous Indonesians were subject to *adat* law, and the Netherlands East Indies was divided into a number of law areas (*rechtskring*) based upon cultural and language classifications. While the law areas were defined in terms of the characteristics of *adats*, they overlapped to a confusing degree with two additional classifications, one judicial and executive in nature, the other political. The first of these was the distinction between 'government justice' and 'native justice', the former being pronouncements given in the name of the Netherlands sovereign and the latter pronouncements not so given. On the political side, the Indies were divided into the directly governed and indirectly governed areas. In the former there were three types of tribunals: European courts, native courts, and courts for all classes of the population. Each court was administered its own distinct type of private law. In the indirectly governed territories, which retained some autonomy, native courts applied *adat* law, but apart from this their jurisdiction did not extend to Europeans or foreign Orientals. Their jurisdiction was also severely limited in criminal matters. The following summary, taken from Ter Haar,[2] illustrates the system as it stood on the outbreak of the Second World War:

    I. In the area of direct government judicial administration:
        i. The general rule was that (substantive) *adat* law remained

[2] Ter Haar (1948: 32).

valid for natives in so far as it was not replaced by statute or by European law. Art. 131 (2) (b), 131 (6) Constitution of 1925.

　　ii. Ordinances regulating *adat* enacted prior to 1 January 1920 had to be declared applicable to natives, if necessary by amendment.

　　iii. Ordinances made after 1 January 1920 might depart from *adat* law if the public interest or social needs of the natives so required. Art. 131 (2) (b) Constitution of 1925.

　　iv. The *adat* rule might be applied even if in conflict with a generally recognized rule of equity or justice. Art. 75 of Constitution of 1854, omitted from Constitution of 1925.

II. In the area of native administration of justice in Indirectly governed territory:

　　i. *Adat* civil and procedural rules applied in so far as they had not been replaced by general ordinances. Art. 130, 131 (5) Constitution of 1925.

　　ii. The ordinance on native justice in directly governed lands determined the extent of the validity of *adat* law. Staatsblad 1932, No. 80.

　　iii. *Adat* law alone applied in the village administration of justice in directly governed territory.

III. In the area of native administration of justice in self-governing lands:

　　i. *Adat* civil and procedural law applied in so far as it was not replaced by ordinances rendered effective by treaty or agreement. Art. 21 (2) Constitution of 1925.

It is clear from this summary that the policy of the colonial authorities was based upon a legal separatism. Further, the dominant partner in the plural laws was the introduced civil law. Its dominance was expressed by the limitations imposed upon the native *adats*. Certain forms of contract, for example, had to be formalized under the Civil Code. The actual practice of the courts and the way in which native law was presented were of course based on European principles. It was also open to the native group to submit themselves voluntarily to European law in a number of ways. This was a right given in the 1925 Constitution (art. 131 (4)), although it was also available for limited purposes under an earlier ordinance of 1917. Native law of course could not apply where it offended European principles of justice or equity. The rule was first formalized in Art. 75 (3) of the 1854 Constitution; though not directly repeated in the 1925 Constitution, it was provided in Art. 121 (2b) of the latter that the courts might depart from native law 'where the public interest or the social needs of the native so require'.

(*b*) *Dutch legal thought.* The theoretical justification for the structure just outlined was a constant preoccupation of the Netherlands Indies jurists from the closing decades of the nineteenth century onwards. The issue which made some theoretical rationalization necessary was the proposal to provide a Civil Code for all elements of the population which was first put forward in the late 1880s. A draft code was eventually produced but, as we saw above, it came to nothing. However, it gave rise to an extensive debate as to whether or not codification was either practicable or desirable, and hence, by implication, to a discussion of the nature of the Netherlands East Indies system of legal pluralism.

The proponents of codification and unification argued that change was necessary because of changing economic and social conditions in the Indies. In particular they pointed to the need for a common law if the indigenous inhabitants were to take part in the increasing capitalization of agriculture and internal trade. Behind this argument there lay a view of law as deriving its validity from the will and acts of the legislator. These arguments were put most forcibly by Nederburgh over the period 1896–1933.[3] In effect, his argument was that the only possible *definition* of law suitable for a modern state was the positivist one then current in European legal thought. That is, law consists of a complex of rules arranged in a hierarchical form and validated by the sovereign power in the state. Law and the state are thus co-extensive entitites being conceptually related. Since the Netherlands East Indies was a territorial sovereign state, then it followed that the laws ought to be territorially based, i.e. common to all the inhabitants. The logical course of action was thus to codify the laws.

Whilst this argument has a certain logical consistency, it tended to ignore the cultural, linguistic, and economic fragmentation characteristic of the Netherlands East Indies. These, the so-called 'facts of life', were relied upon by the opponents of Nederburgh in combating his views. Opposition

[3] Cf. Nederburgh (1933).

was concentrated in the 'Adat Law School', a group of jurists led by van Vollenhoven, for whom the cultural relativity of law was an absolute datum. At a more fundamental level they believed that for law to be valid it must fulfil two requirements: first, it must be properly promulgated. In this they agreed with Nederburgh but, in addition, they required that it reflect the cultural characteristics of the people to whom it was addressed. Indeed, they argued that the latter was the overriding qualification and that an individual law would stand or fall on this test. Further, by making cultural relevance primary, they shifted the definition of law away from formal requirements to a sociological definition. The important elements of law thus became its function and (cultural) content rather than its formal pedigree. Given this position, it can be seen that a codification, let alone a unification, of the laws was impossible.

The latter view triumphed, the colonial authorities preferring the existing legal relativism to a juristic consistency, but it still left open the problem of defining the nature of law in such a scheme. There was of course no problem with European law, nor were the problems of internal conflict long in receiving a set of technical solutions (see below), but the problem of defining *adat* as law remained. As early as 1893 Snouck Hurgronje spoke of 'adat that has legal consequence—*adatrecht*',[4] i.e. *adat* having a relevance within the colonial legal system. This is clearly a restricted definition designed solely for the purposes of legal administration. The restricted nature of definition was a constant feature of legal thought at the time. The early work of van Vollenhoven[5] was of this nature in equating law with (legally defined) sanction, although his later definitions did attempt to state wider speculative and philosophical aspects.[6] However, even here, definition was always limited by its role, which was to provide a plain and fixed formulation of *adat* both sociologically valid and of use in executive and judicial administration. In some ways the administrative system itself determined the content of *adat* and it certainly determined the content of *adatrecht*.

[4] Snouck Hurgronje (1893: (1) 357).
[5] See the summary in de Josselin de Jong (1948: 4).
[6] van Vollenhoven (1931: 236, 400).

The Dutch Legal World

This essentially static view of *adat* is found also in the work of Ter Haar, although he attempted to define *adat* in terms of judicial process.[7] In concentrating upon judicial method in the formulation of *adat* principles, Ter Haar hoped that *adat* laws could be subsumed into the general Indies jurisprudence. He defined 'judicial' to include both the informal decisions of native authority and the formal decisions of the state courts, thus arguing for the existence of a sole criterion of validity. He even went so far as to say:

> The decisions rendered by officials, chiefs and judges can and should always be regarded not only as applying concretely in a given case but also as setting precedents for 'similar' cases—cases, that is, which in whole or in part are relevant as to the facts and in this sense similar and subject to precedent. Such decisions indicate the legal principles which are valid in the community; their concise legal forms are drawn from a multitude of less precise living patterns from conceptions and values cherished in the community.[8]

While this passage might appear unexceptional to English lawyers, it is somewhat startling coming from a civil lawyer in the pre-war Indies. There is no doctrine of precedent as such in civil law and there was certainly none such in the Netherlands East Indies. At the same time, however, compilations of judicial decisions on *adat* were made[9] with the clear aim of providing examples for later proceedings at least. Ter Haar's views are but a slight advance on this practice—from 'example' to 'precedent'.

The introduction of the idea of precedent by Ter Haar illustrates an inherent contradiction in Dutch colonial legal thought. While there was a conscious policy to preserve and administer indigenous law, this was always subject to the dominance of the European state system and legal system. The latter were sovereign so that indigenous definitions of law or definitions which relied upon indigenous cultures were

---

[7] See Ter Haar (1937: 4). For contemporary critiques see Holleman (1938: 428–40), Logemann (1938: 27–36).
[8] Ter Haar (1948: 228).
[9] The main ones are: Enthoven (1921) for the period 1849–1912; van der Meulen (1924) for the period 1912–23; Boerenbeker (1935) for the period 1923–33. The practice continues in modern Indonesia; see Subekti and Tamara (1965).

only partly valid. The truth of the matter was that colonial legal policy implied an *internal* conflict of laws to an extent not found in other South-East Asian colonial laws.

II THE CONFLICTS OF LAWS IN THE NETHERLANDS EAST INDIES

The origin of colonial conflicts lies in the early history of Dutch commercial enterprise in Indonesia when the Dutch retained their own law and provided special regulations for those Indonesians who lived in regions controlled by the *Vereenigde Oost-Indische Compagnie* (East Indies Company).[10] This situation was widely discussed amongst the jurists of the sixteenth and seventeenth centuries, and we find Grotius saying in his *Mare Liberum*:[11]

> Java, Sumatra, the Moluccas have their own kings, public institutions, laws and rights and they have had them always. One is not entitled to deprive these infidels of their will and princely power because they do not believe. Indeed it is even heresy to assume that the infidels should not be master of their goods, for it is no less theft and robbery to deprive them of their goods than it would be if a Christian were concerned.

The administrative system which made possible juristic work of this type continued, but it was not until 1847 that legal pluralism in Indonesia became formalized in the constitution of the Netherlands East Indies. In that year the *Algemene Bapalingen van Wetgeving*[12] was enacted; it classified the inhabitants of Indonesia in two groups, European and Native. The classification was supposedly adopted on religious grounds since the classes were defined respectively as Christian or non-Christian. However, inconsistency almost immediately arose with Indonesian Christians being classified as Natives. In 1855 this system was replaced by Art. 109 of the *Regeringsreglement*,[13] which confirmed the earlier arrangement but included the Chinese, Arab, and Indian inhabitants within the Native group. In practice the foreign Orientals tended to be treated separately from the Natives so that there

---

[10] See Widjojoatmodjo (1942–3) for a sample of Dutch orders.
[11] Cited in Kollewijn (1951: 309).
[12] Staatsblad 1847, No. 23.
[13] Staatsblad 1855, No. 2.

were three law groups in existence. This continued until January 1920 when Art. 109 was amended by Art. 163 of 1920. Article 163 defined the racial groups and was later incorporated unchanged into the *Indische Staatsregeling* of 1926, Art. 131 of which defined the law in force for each group.[14] All persons were classified in one of three groups: European, Native, and Foreign Orientals.

The laws for the respective groups was governed by Art. 131 paragraph 1 of the *Indische Staatsregeling* of 1926 which laid down as a matter of general principle that the civil law of Indonesia was to be written law, including the law for the Native group. However, paragraph 2 (b) provided a set of guidelines for the legislator in respect of the Native population. All written rules must, in general, be based upon *adat*, although this principle need not be adhered to if deviation was required for the 'public interest' or because of the 'special needs' of the Native population. In this event European law might apply, or a special law applicable to all groups might be promulgated.

Paragraph 2 said nothing about what law was in force for the Native group pending the promulgation of new regulations. This was regulated by Art. 131 (6), which came into force on 1 January 1920 and which preserved all Native law already in force subject to later regulations under paragraph 2 (b). In effect this referred to the *adats* and those European regulations promulgated prior to and after 1920 and declared applicable to the Native group by the Governor-General. There were relatively few European regulations so declared; the most important of them were Book II, Ch. 4 of the Commercial Code on shipping and some articles of the Civil Code concerning labour contracts and wagering.

In the period 1920–38 a number of civil and commercial regulations were promulgated exclusively for the Native group but they were not based on *adat*. Some of them, however, drastically affected the administration of *adat*; for example, the regulation on the law to be applied in the religious courts,[15] the regulation on marriage for Christian Natives in Java, Minahasa, and Ambon,[16] and the regulations

[14] Staatsblad 1925, No. 415.   [15] Staatsblad 1931, No. 53.
[16] Staatsblad 1933, No. 84.

196   Contract

on Native corporations[17] and associations.[18] An extremely important regulation is that on Indonesian mortgages (*credietverband*) promulgated in 1908[19] and still in force. This permitted Natives holding Native land to give mortgages on the land to specified European banks although no banks were actually specified until 1937. The regulation, however, clearly contemplated a relationship between corporate bodies subject to European law and land held under *adat* tenures by members of the Native group. At the present time a number of Indonesian banks which are incorporated on civil-law principles may take *adat* land as security for credit.[20] All these regulations illustrate the impossibility of preserving one law, here the Native law, as a self-contained entity.

The influence of Western law is apparent from this brief description, and it was an issue of which colonial jurists were well aware and on which they spent a good deal of energy. An early leading paper on this question and one which still has a good deal of contemporary relevance is that of Ter Haar written in 1929.[21] Ter Haar traces the means by which substantive principles of European law directly influenced the Native group, even though the greater number of the regulations are only enabling laws. First, there was the influence of European procedure, as in the courts, which formalized *adat* rules to an extent unknown in the traditional sphere. Second, specific concepts of European law were introduced via this procedure and in terms of the regulations themselves. This was a potent source of confusion, particularly where the Native institution being regulated was misunderstood. The interpretation put upon the supposed Muslim office of 'priest' and the function given to such an official in native court procedure is a well-known instance. But it is in the specifically European context of regulation that *adat* was most affected. For example, in the matter of crime, Ter Haar demonstrates that, although the same class of wrongdoing might be recognized in native and government laws, the penalties under the latter were not those which accorded with the facts of

[17] Staatsblad 1939, No. 569.   [18] Staatsblad 1939, No. 570, No. 571.
[19] Staatsblad 1908, No. 542, Staatsblad 1909, No. 584.
[20] Cf. Gautama & Harsono (1972: 87–8) for the regulations.
[21] Cf. Ter Haar (1929).

native society. The most striking example is the use of imprisonment, which was largely unknown in pre-colonial days and which had consequences for which native society had no answer. Connected with this was the introduction of the idea that fault, classified by Western jurists as penal, need not necessarily give rise to compensation; the latter is a feature of all *adats* which, in general, prescribe restitution either in the form of payment or in the form of services.

Ter Haar defined Western influence on the *adats* in the following way:

> In all cases where—owing to the presence of the Dutch group of the population in the Indies and as a result of the administration of the government over the Indonesians by Dutchmen—ready-made Western law institutions or juridical interdictions and injunctions appear to have been included in the law of the native population in such a manner that the *adat* law would not have arrived at that stage by independent development, in all those cases we can speak of Western influence on the *adat* law.[22]

This is an extremely wide definition covering situations which would now commonly be classified as administrative or executive, substantive, and procedural. It also takes account of the situation, common in Indonesia, of indigenous tribunals refusing to admit an *adat* rule on the basis, justifiable or not, that to do so would infringe some government regulation. Ter Haar discussed this possibility and proposed that any investigation into this topic should be conducted by ascertaining the methods through which Western law can (i.e. is able to) influence native law. He isolated five such for Indonesia, of which the two most important were the influence of the administrator, particularly in reducing *adat* rules to writing, and the developed body of jurisprudence (judicial decisions) which became established.

It was open to the native to enter into situations involving the rules of some other system. Such a situation, known generally as transfer, could arise in one of three main ways.

(i) *Equalization*[23]

Before independence it was possible for a Native to make

[22] Ibid. 165.   [23] *Persamaan-hak, gelijkstelling.*

application to the Governor-General[24] to become a member of the European group. In order to qualify the applicant had to show that by reason of his superior education he had become alienated from his own society and (until 1894) he had also to undergo conversion to Christianity. After the turn of the century equalization was applied for and granted on the basis of the type of legal transactions most commonly entered into by the applicant. In effect this meant the types of contract relationship known to European law. It was also possible for equalization to be attained through judicial action; the criterion for this was a combination of such factors as following a European way of life, marriage to a European, and so on.[25]

(ii) *Voluntary Submission*

This was provided for by Art. 131 (4) of the *Indische Staatsregeling* (1854) and the procedure was regulated by a Royal Decree dated 15 September 1916.[26] Of the various sorts of submission possible (total, partial, *ad hoc*, and presumptive) only two are of real significance to *adat*. These are the *ad hoc* and presumptive submissions.[27] An *ad hoc* submission was one in which the individual submitted himself to European private law for purposes of a specific legal transaction. Generally this was possible only in that area of the law known as *hukum hartabenda* (*vermogensrecht*), which, broadly, was the law relating to commercial transactions, contract, corporations and partnerships, and, in some cases, civil wrongs. It did not extend to family law, inheritance, or land law.

Presumptive submission is rather similar and occurs when a member of the Native group participates in a transaction unknown to *adat* law but found in European law. This submission was also confined to the area of *hukum hartabenda* and, further, the transaction had to be one entirely unknown to *adat*; it was not sufficient that *adat* would regulate the matter in a different way.

[24] Art. 163 (5) Indische Staatsregeling.
[25] Cf. Gautama & Hornick (1972: 16) for case references. See also Gautama (1973).
[26] Staatsblad 1917, No. 12.
[27] The other two rarely had relevance to *adat* because they involve a more or less complete separation of the individual from *adat*. Cf. Gautama & Hornick (1972: 17–18); see also Gautama (1971).

In both cases the assumption was that European law was superior to *adat*, and this opinion seems to have been based upon three factors. First, the European law provided greater scope and flexibility in taking account of transactions which were either unknown or imperfectly known to *adat* law. The area of commercial operation is the obvious example, and, indeed, the regulation specifically limited submission to this area. Second, since most of the activities involved in these submissions were matters of contract, the European law, being written, provided the certainty of terms and conditions necessary for commercial intercourse. Third, and following from the two points already made, there was a conscious policy to protect European financial interests in contracts between European and Native.

(iii) *Involuntary Submission*

This occurred when a person from one population group became subject to a law not normally applicable to him as a result of a transaction with a person from another group. This was dealt with both in legislation and through the courts. In such transactions the law applicable was, by the nature of the transaction, uncertain. Legislation was passed which provided, *inter alia*, that where persons subject to different laws married, the law of the husband governed the incidents of marriage such as property, the status of the wife, and so on.[28] This regulation applied not only to marriage between persons of different population groups but also to marriages between Natives from different law areas. There are also regulations making similar provisions for illegitimate children and regulations on labour contracts. The regulations providing for choice of law in land matters were repealed in the Agrarian Law of 1960.[29]

In addition to regulations such as these, the courts have, over the years, developed a body of jurisprudence dealing with conflict of laws problems (*hukum antargolongan*) arising out of contracts between persons of different population groups. This is considered in more detail below.

At this point it is as well to remember that, as with other

---

[28] Staatsblad 1898, No. 158.
[29] See Gautama & Harsono (1972: 24).

aspects of *adat* in Indonesia, the courts and legislature did not function in a vacuum but had the benefit of a complex body of legal theory on pluralism. This will be described briefly here because it puts what has been said already into some sort of perspective and introduces us to the complexities of the conflicts problem.[30] Conflicts of law were bound to arise, given the multiplicity of legal systems. This was particularly the case in contract, whether for the sale of goods or in contracts of marriage. In addition the existence of a number of legal systems and the conflicts of principle that arose were often considered either in terms of or as strictly analogous to principles of private international law. Toward the end of the nineteenth century there had been a marked interest in this subject within the wider international community and the existing legal pluralism in the colonial empires of the day had not escaped the attention of leading jurists. The French jurist, Arminjon, for example, described the colonial situation as 'le droit international privé *interne*' and discussed it as an integral part of private international law.[31] Other jurists such as Neumeyer and Goadby held similar views.[32] The French jurists, especially those concerned with the French North African territories, also devoted a good deal of time to the subject, and reference is made below of the work of Henry Solus whose theories attracted the attention of the Dutch jurists.

If we turn now to the position in Indonesia, a convenient starting-point is the proceedings of the Congress of the Netherlands East Indies Jurists' Association held at Batavia in 1887.[33] One of the main features of the Congress was the debate that arose as to whether a new statutory regulation regarding mixed marriage was desirable. In the event the Regulation governing Mixed Marriages of 1896[34] was pro-

---

[30] The distinction between the European private law of the Indies and that of the Netherlands is not of moment here. See Schiller (1942–3: 34–6) for brief outline and for references. The leading texts on the nineteenth century and for the first decades of the twentieth century are those of Abendanon (1891), Wagener (1932), and Kollewijn (1938).
[31] Cf. Arminjon (1925 (i)).
[32] Kollewijn (1929: 207–8, 216–19) for references.
[33] The proceedings are reported in *Handelingen der Nederlandsch-Indische Juristenvereeniging* (1887).   [34] Staatsblad 1898, No. 158.

The Dutch Legal World

mulgated and provided that in a marriage between persons from different population groups the status and incidents of the marriage were to be regulated by the law of the husband. So far as the conflicts question was concerned, this was interpreted by some commentators, notably L. W. C. van den Berg, as demonstrating a general principle that the law from one group could not apply to an individual from another without special legislation to that effect. This view of course rested upon a belief that all law is an expression of the will of the sovereign, i.e. statute. This opinion is incorrect not just because submission to European law was possible for a Native in the absence of legislation[35] but also because this was not the view of *adat* adopted in Dutch colonial legal policy. van den Berg's arguments were rejected by contemporary jurists, but they gave rise to a considerable conflicts literature.

One of the most prominent contributors was Nederburgh who, while opposing van den Berg's position,[36] pressed for a *ius constituendum*, a general law for all the population groups in the Netherlands East Indies. In the absence of express legislation establishing this, it had to be assumed that for the proper regulation of the relationships between the different legal systems there existed a 'higher' law. This was applicable not just to the formation of the laws of each of the population groups but was also the instrument by which the legal systems as a whole were defined. Since the *adat* laws were inferior to European law in utility and scientific value, the higher law could only be European law, at least until the legislator acted.[37] This position led Nederburgh to press for the codification of a law suitable for all population groups including the Indonesian and brought him into conflict with van Vollenhoven. However, as Kollewijn points out,[38] Nederburgh did not see the issue as one of existing conflict between higher and lower laws as such but as the relationship between dissimilar laws. His classification 'higher and lower' was a classification directed toward and in support of his codification thesis.

---

[35] See above, pp. 197 ff. and Kollewijn (1929: 210).
[36] Cf. the papers in *Het Recht in Ned.-Indie* 1899–1903, and the collected works in Nederburgh (1933).
[37] See also Cassutto (1936: 66–9).   [38] Kollewijn (1929: 213–14).

The actual use of the classification in the solution of conflict between the various laws in the Netherlands East Indies had to await the advent of André de la Porte.[39] He saw the situation of pluralism as being basically one of conflict. The object of his work was to discover whether the rules of private international law could be used in solving problems in interracial law; he developed the thesis that private international law was directly applicable as a matter of principle. He reached this conclusion after adopting the principle that private international law applies by virtue of a territorial connection, whereas interracial law is a matter of personal and not territorial attachment. His solution was to make use of the following fiction:

I act as though each of these laws [for the various population groups] possesses its own territorial jurisdiction in the same way as the legislations of various states have their own jurisdictions. Europeans are then presumed to have their actual place of residence in the jurisdiction of the European legislation and therefore to exercise their civil rights in that place.[40]

This has been criticized by Kollewijn[41] on the ground that it rests upon an unproved axiom that it is proper to follow or apply the rules of private international law so far as is possible. This is a valid objection because, as has been established, a reference to the *lex fori*, the *lex loci contractus*, or the *lex domicilii* settles nothing.[42] These are territorial connecting factors and are not of themselves decisive in a territory characterized by personal laws.

Kollewijn, who had been described as the 'father of interpersonal law in Indonesia', maintained successfully that European and Indonesian laws were equal in status. Neither could be applied as a higher law and the analogy of private international law could not apply because the courts of the Netherlands East Indies had to treat both systems as equal parts of the *lex fori*. On the other hand, if the needs of interracial law demanded it, there was no reason why some rules of private international law could not be utilized. It was also open for the courts to give priority to one law as against

---

[39] Cf. de la Porte (1908).
[41] Kollewijn (1929: 215–16).
[40] Ibid. 329.
[42] Bartholomew (1952: 326), Hooker (1968a).

another if the circumstances of the case demanded it. Further, if one rule was more effective than another in the same field then that might also be preferred.[43] Kollewijn also specifically rejected[44] the French doctrine of *conflit colonial*, which was most fully expressed in the work of Solus.[45] Kollewijn's position is not so much *sui generis* as an abstraction from judicial and legislative practice. The source of interracial rules is found, as described above, in a number of special forms, judicial decision, and statute, which result in a group of clearly stated rules defined for a comparatively narrow class of circumstance. In this respect Kollewijn's views are a representation of legal reality, and for this reason, if for no other, they have stood the test of time.

Two major classes of plural relationships were important for Indonesian *adats*. First, *adat* law was not (nor is it now) uniform throughout the archipelago and the *adats* were organized into law circles on the basis of cultural differentiation. The Native law group was, and is, fragmented; individual *adat* systems often recognized the existence of 'foreign' systems but did not always provide rules dealing with such systems. The social construction of *adat* was such that the issue was not the adjustment of a foreign *principle* to one's own principles but the accommodation of an individual *person* within the system. A conflict of systems did not, however, arise in the traditional *adat* world. Conflict only came into being with the imposition of European authority, the legal basis of which was entirely founded on the exclusiveness of territorially based legal systems. Once such an idea had been introduced, the issue of the conflict of principle became primary and one could even speak about inter-local conflict of laws. This involved a contradiction; thus Schiller could say that 'inter-local law depends primarily on a legal system *territorial in origin* that *attaches to the person of a member of the group*...'[46] This represents a considerable distortion of the traditional *adat* view in which a territorial exclusiveness was not primary. On the contrary, the law was personal in origin and process, but under the twin demands of a territorial

[43] Cf. Kollewijn (1929: 233–5). [44] Ibid. 223–4.
[45] Cf. Solus (1927).
[46] Schiller (1942–3: 44). Italics supplied.

administration and a territorial system of law (including lawmaking) a contradiction arose. The colonial system therefore introduced conflict as a principle into the legal process, and the courts were concerned to answer new questions such as how does one attach a person to a system?, what are the consequences of marriage or commercial contract between members of different systems?, and so on.[47]

This sort of adjudication could not be a matter for the legislature simply because it did not legislate for the number and variety of conflicts that arose. Another and more interesting reason is that the administrative system encouraged the possibility of conflict within the Native group and the legal policy of non-interference within the *adat* universes made intervention impossible. The issue arises solely in judicial decision. This raises an interesting question, to what extent was the problem of inter-local conflict a creation of the courts? This was not an issue in the traditional systems, but it might be argued that the forum, by operating on an all-or-nothing principle of adjudication, made conflicts inevitable. It is also notable that the cases commonly cited in the literature[48] concern individuals who, by reason of their profession or business, were emigrants from their own group and had considerable means. The question was therefore confined to a small minority of the Indonesian people; to some extent, then, the 'inter-local law', while prescriptively valid, lacks a full descriptive validity. It may more properly be considered as part of the whole interracial question, not least because the conflict question in issue is a European legal issue. In addition, the extent to which problems of inter-local law now exist is a function of the interracial question, given the current preoccupations with unification and legal modernization.

The second major class in Indonesian pluralism is the interracial question proper with which the rest of this chapter is concerned. As a preliminary, some attention should be paid to the term 'interracial' itself. This is a direct translation of the Dutch *intergentiel* and was first used in English by

[47] See ibid. 43–6 for references to judicial answers to these questions. See also Gautama (1973) for the more recent cases.
[48] See Gautama (1973).

Kollewijn in 1929; the term *intergentiel recht* (interracial law) came into use amongst Dutch jurists about the turn of the century and referred to the following relationship: 'These interracial juridical conflicts [arise] when subjects of the same country, within the borders of that country, are subject to different private laws...'[49]

The term has been criticized,[50] but its use is now firmly established and there seems little point in further objection. One must, however, be careful in its use, particularly when writing in English, because its reference is to a particular type of legal system: the civil-law system in its Dutch version. The two outstanding points that must be borne in mind by a common lawyer are both contained in the passage just cited. The references there are to the [political] 'subjects' of a state and to 'private' law. Neither of these classes is properly known to the common law; a political status is not essential to the common-law jurisdictions where the issue is domicile. Private law is again not a category of importance except possibly in analytical works of jurisprudence. Further, the common law is always the law of general application, it does not admit of separate legal systems in the same territory. It does of course recognize principles of personal or religious laws but these form part of the common law in precedent although confined to (judicially) defined classes, either racial or religious. For this reason principles of private international law are not properly to be used where cases of apparent conflict arise because the conflict is internal and within the territorial common-law system and is able to be solved only in terms of that system.[51] In common-law colonial and post-colonial jurisdictions, therefore, the discussion is about 'personal law', its place in and relationship with the principles of the whole common-law system. One may explain the distinction in terms of the language of normatives;[52] the Netherlands East Indies version posits two norm systems—*adat* and European— which exist separately and touch at various points. The point of contact is called interracial law. Such systems, however, are

[49] Kollewijn (1929: 204). [50] Cf. Schiller (1942–3: 37).
[51] Cf. Hooker (1976: 1–16).
[52] Cf. von Wright (1963) for a description by a leading contemporary jurist of *norm systems*.

self-contained and internally consistent. The common law in its colonial manifestations posits only one norm system which contains within itself sets of inconsistent prescriptions. According to many jurists, amongst them Kelsen and von Wright, an inconsistency could not or should not occur, but the common law is anything but consistent, especially in its personal law aspects. It is, however, an operable system in the sense that it works, although its judges are not known for their respect for either jurisprudental analysis or jurists!

It is with these points in mind that we return to interracial law,[53] i.e. to the situation in which the norms of the mutually exclusive *adat* and European laws intersect. The colonial legal system identified two processes in such a situation. First, it was necessary to establish the factors which could create the interracial law situation. Secondly, once this had been identified as an existing situation the problem was to decide what law was to apply. Both processes were a matter for the legislature and the courts though the latter were possibly more decisive in the question of choice of law.

(*a*) *The identification of an interracial issue.* Traditionally there were four primary points[54] of contact, any one of which identified a situation involving interracial law. The first and most obvious was where the parties to any transactions were from different population groups (since independence this distinction has become less important). Many regulations are put out for the citizens of Indonesia as a whole, although in some cases earlier divisions retain a functional significance.

The second point of contact was the status of land; the Agrarian Act of 1870 and later amendments created a complex system of land classifications which had reference to the division of the population into racial groups but was not wholly consistent with it. For present purposes it is sufficient to say that land was classified into 'Indonesian' and 'Western' land; these classes did not, however, arise from the racial group of the owner but from the legal system (*adat* or Civil Code) that defined the characteristics of the land. The position was further complicated by a Royal Decree of 1870[55]

---

[53] *Hukum antargolongan* in Indonesian.
[54] *Primaire aanknopingspunt*, also known as *titik taut primair*, or *titik taut pembeda*.
[55] Staatsblad 1870, No. 118.

implementing the Agrarian Act and providing in effect that all land held under *adat* rights was part of the state domain. This meant, *inter alia*, that the state could dispose of uncleared land over the *adat* rights of a village or kinship group. Indonesian land was subject to *adat* law except in the face of special legislation, and most of it was unregistered. European land was registered and was subject to the Civil Code as to ownership and possession. However, the complication was that land, whether Indonesian or European, could be possessed by individuals without reference to their population group. Europeans could acquire *adat* land by way of inheritance or mixed marriage and, once acquired, it could later be transferred to non-Natives without restriction. It was in this sort of situation that conflict problems arose. With the introduction of the Basic Agrarian Law in 1960 the status of land is no longer a decisive point of contact. This law abolishes the dual system of land rights and prescribes that the only rights which can be exercised in respect of land are those set out in the law itself.

The third method of identifying an interracial situation is where the parties to a transaction specify that a certain legal system shall govern the transaction. The point is worth emphasizing because it retains something of its importance in contemporary Indonesia. For example, it is open to Indonesian parties to a contact to specify that the agreement shall be subject to the (European) Civil Code. The court will apply European law even though in all other matters both parties are otherwise subject to *adat*.

The final point of contact in the colonial period was the forum of a suit. Briefly, there were separate courts for the different population groups prior to independence and the choice of forum depended upon the population group of the defendant. Thus, a suit brought by a Native Indonesian against a European was tried in a European court. This system was abolished under Japanese rule and there is now a unitary system of court process throughout Indonesia.

Of the four methods of identification sketched above, only the choice of law factor and, to some extent, the significance of different racial groups continue to be important. However, even with the absence of land and forum issues, the position remains complex enough, particularly in the question of choice of law. It might also be said that these so-called points of contact are juristic classes based exactly on the facts of legal pluralism in Indonesia.

(b) *Choice of Law*. This is the more interesting and complex aspect of Indonesian legal pluralism, involving as it does the circumstances determining what law should be selected from among the systems present in the interracial situation. The area of law in which these questions arose was, and remains, contract and, to a lesser extent, the law relating to 'unlawful acts'. The latter is a category not properly known to common lawyers; an 'unlawful act' (*onrechtmatige daad*) is fairly closely analogous to tort although it can also refer to public law matters arising out of state activity. For example, it was possible for the state or for a state organization to be sued by a person who did not submit to European law. The general rule in the unlawful act cases is that in an interracial suit the law of the wrongdoer applies and if, in this case, the state is the guilty party, then liability and damages will be assessed according to European law.[56] The principle that unlawful acts be judged according to the law of the wrongdoer has not, however, received a consistent application in the period of independence. For example, in a Supreme Court decision of 1957[57] the law of the Chinese defendant, which would have been the Civil Code at that time, was rejected in favour of the *adat*, which was the law of the injured party. The reason given was that the *adat* was more flexible because it made possible the apportionment of responsibility for damage done, while the relevant article of the Civil Code provided only that damage should be made good exclusively by the wrongdoer. This decision has been criticized[58] as not being in line with previous (colonial) authority and, more important, it represents a new criterion for choosing a law, which is insufficiently supported either by practical need or by juristic refinement of its implications. The decision was, however, in line with the prevailing legal climate, because at the time (1957) there was

[56] Cf. de la Porte (1908: 348 ff.), Gouwgioksiong (1965: 564–5) and the decisions there cited.
[57] In (1957) *Hukum* 7/8: 61.
[58] Gouwgioksiong (1965: 566).

a conscious and critical assessment of the suitability of the colonial legal heritage, in this case the Civil Code, for Indonesia.[59] When we turn to the major field of interracial law, contract, it is clear that the categories established in the colonial era persist. The most important determining factor was the intention of the parties with regard to the choice of law governing their relationships.[60] In determining intention the courts took account of such circumstances as the nature and form of the contract, the place of contracting, its economic and social aspects, whether one of the parties was in a dominant bargaining position, and the acceptance by one party of the law of the other.[61] These factors are known collectively as the 'secondary points of contact' or the 'determinate points of contact'[62] in contrast to the primary points of contact discussed under (a) above.

It was well established in the colonial period that labour contracts, although they did not form a special class, were usually to be governed by European law. This was particularly true where one of the parties was a limited liability company.[63] In a decision given by the Court of First Instance (*Pengadilan Negri*) of Semarang in 1951,[64] the law governing a contract between a company and an Indonesian managing director was settled at European law on the basis of the authorities just indicated. The managing director must be taken to have accepted the applicability of European law because not only was this the law governing the affairs of the company but the individual involved had voluntarily submitted himself to this law. A similar result was reached in a case involving a loan from a bank operated on European law principles.[65]

This principle has been held to apply to a commercial

[59] Cf. Wirjono Prodjodikoro (n.d.), who accepted the applicability of the Civil Code in such cases but stressed the sometimes artificial and rigid categories of fault in the Code. See also Utrecht (1955) (1959).
[60] Cf. Gouwgioksiong (1960: 50 ff.).
[61] Before 1960 the status of land was also fundamental.
[62] This is the term preferred by the Official State Committee for the Drafting of Legal Terms.
[63] Cf. Kollewijn (1934: 789).
[64] In (1952) *Hukum* 4/5: 114.
[65] Cf. Gouwgioksiong (1965: 550 and n. 21) for references to judicial decisions.

210   Contract

contract between two Native Indonesians where, prima facie, *adat* would govern. In a case decided by the Court of First Instance of Djakarta in 1956[66] the question of what law was to apply arose between two Native Indonesians concerning the sale and purchase of some trucks. It was argued, on the basis of population groupings, that *adat* should apply. This was rejected by the court, which applied the Civil Code on the following grounds. First, the objects involved in the contract were not such usually known to *adat* law[67] and were to be used for the benefit of all population groups. Second, and possibly an even stronger ground, the contract was a commercial contract concluded in Djakarta, and both parties must, therefore, have intended the law ordinarily applicable in that place to apply. It is difficult to accept this decision as a proper example of interracial law. There was no conflict of interracial law in fact because the issue was between two persons subject to *adat*. The court in effect seems really to have been looking for reasons to avoid *adat* in favour of a more advanced and commercially suitable law; it was not properly considering interracial law at all. It is difficult on the facts to show that there was a voluntary submission to the Civil Code, the concept of sale and purchase is, after all, well known to all *adat* systems.

A further illustration of the problems involved in ascertaining the intentions of the parties to a contract is provided in a Supreme Court decision of 1956[68] concerning the question of a disputed sale with right of re-purchase. This is a well-known *adat* institution[69] and it is not properly a sale but a contract of loan with a transfer of property as security, and this was recognized by the court who looked to intention and not to the form of the contract. The transferor was in fact a native Indonesian woman; intent was therefore said to be primary.[70] Difficulties sometimes arise where the existence of any contract is itself disputed. In such a case the Supreme Court has indicated[71] that it will determine the issue on circumstances

[66] In (1957) *Hukum* 1/2: 137.
[67] In passing it might be said that there is no reason why principles of *adat* could not *in theory* be extended to new objects.
[68] In (1957) *Hukum* 3/4: 73.   [69] *Jual Janji* and other terms.
[70] For other cases on this point see (1955) *Hukum* 4/5: 24.
[71] In (1950) *Hukum* 1/2: 62.

The Dutch Legal World

surrounding the agreement including place, time, and the station of the parties.

If we turn now to marriage, these points may be developed further. When persons who live under different laws marry, the law applicable for the determination of status and incidents of marriage is the Regulation on Mixed Marriages—R.G.H.[72] The basic principle in the R.G.H. is the equality of the systems of private law in Indonesia. This principle was put to the test in a well-known case decided by the Supreme Court in 1955[73] on the validity of a marriage concluded in conformity with the R.G.H. between an Indonesian Muslim female and an Indonesian Christian male. Such a marriage was of course invalid according to Islamic law, under which a woman has capacity to marry only a Muslim. The court adopted the following reasoning:[74]

Considering that it is a fact, which we cannot in any way deny, that in our country, for a long time having been living together people of different religions and cultures, and consequently of different marriage laws; and that this difference of religion is in accordance with the constitution, which admits freedom of religion.

Considering, that with regard to what will be said later, it is appropriate for the security of the people, that as a principle of all law systems, there should be a regulation determining the law applicable to marriages between people of different religions without bias.

Considering that in the interests of society there should be no prohibition of marriage between people of different religions, for such a prohibition would render a great number of children illegitimate, and consequently—besides having no protection in his right to substance and inheritance—each child would perhaps suffer throughout his life by being despised as an 'outcast' (anak gampang).

Considering that in the R.G.H. there is no provision favouring any single religion, for in article 6 (1) it is clearly stated that a mixed marriage should be celebrated according to the law of the male spouse, and this means—if the act has been influenced by the law of a religion—that according to the particular circumstances one religious law is to be applied or another.

[72] *Regeling op de Gemengde Huwelijken.* Staatsblad 1898, No. 158, but see further below on the new marriage law.   [73] In (1955) *Hukum* 3: 44.
[74] Cited in Gouwgioksiong (1965: 558-9). On Christianity and *adat* see Prins (1973).

Considering that, whilst the Supreme Court is aware that Islamic law opposes the possibility, admitted by the R.G.H., of a legal marriage between an Islamic woman and a non-Islamic, it should not be forgotten that every law in this world is intended to regulate the relationships of the human community—sociological phenomenon—and is not aimed at the well-being after death, which becomes the primary interest of every religion.

The position would of course have been different had the marriage been celebrated under the Marriage Ordinance for Christian Indonesians,[75] section 75 of which provided that when a marriage takes place between two Indonesians one of whom is Christian, then the law of the non-Christian party was not to determine validity but the on the contrary the civil (European) law was the determining law.[76]

Another contemporary case relating to the R.G.H. is the decision of the Special Court of First Instance of Djakarta given in 1956[77] concerning the guardianship of a child who was born of a mixed marriage between a Minangkabau male and a Dutch female. It was held that under section 2 of the R.G.H. the mother had lost her Dutch status and thus European law no longer applied to her. The law applicable to this marriage was therefore the Minangkabau *adat* and this would determine the issue of guardianship. Further examples in the fields of land law and civil wrongs could also be adduced.[78]

III THE UNIFICATION OF LAW

The major legal issue since the independence of Indonesia has been the unification of law. This is a political as much as a legal question given the diversity of language and culture in the state, and it has in fact been designated a question of legal politics (*politik hukum*). Despite considerable difficulties, a good deal of progress has been made. The structure of the judicial administration has been more or less standardized although newly invented courts do exist.[79] In land matters,

[75] Staatsblad 1933, No. 84. [76] See further (1959) *Hukum* 3/4: 176.
[77] In (1958) *Hukum* 9/10: 121. [78] See Gouwgioksiong (1965).
[79] See Damian & Hornick (1972) for a general survey
See also Lev (1972) on the Islamic courts and (1972a) on judicial institutions and legal culture.

the Basic Agrarian law of 1960[80] provides a unified scheme for land holding and transfer, and in mercantile and commercial law there is an effective codification in practice (though not perhaps in strict law) based upon the old Civil Code.[81] Finally, the new Indonesian Marriage Law (No. 1 of 1974)[82] revokes the earlier laws on marriage and attempts to create a unified procedure for marriage and divorce. Unfortunately, the law is not clear and the exact meaning of its provisions is open to speculation. However, a first step in this difficult area has been taken.

In all the major fields of law, the principle of unification has now received a legal formulation so that pluralism as an alternative way of organizing laws is now on the defensive.

[80] See Gautama & Harsono (1972).
[81] See Gouwgioksiong (1965).
[82] See Katz & Katz (1975) for an outline.

CHAPTER 8

The Spanish–American Legal World: The Philippines

THE LEGAL history of the Philippines is a history of four distinct groups of laws. They include the Islamic law of the south,[1] non-Muslim indigenous systems, Spanish (civil) law, and American (common) law. This plurality of laws is a result of ethnic variation and of colonial occupation. The population of the Philippines is made up of a number of different peoples distinguished from one another by language, religion, and culture.[2]

Pre-Spanish laws fell into two groups, the Islamic and the non-Islamic. The former, as indicated in Chapter three, is found in texts (of varying degree of sophistication), and recent fieldwork on its characteristics and implementation is also available.[3] It was unaffected by either Spanish or American administration and even today cannot be said to have been assimilated into the national legal process. The non-Islamic laws consisted of a mass of 'native custom', details of which were known from the Spanish times and, in some cases, are still being collected and studied.[4] For the legal historian the overwhelming impression given by this material is of legal systems which are parts of social systems. To a large extent their description and analyses have been the preserve of the social sciences.[5] So far as the formal legal administration is concerned, these indigenous laws have been of little moment either for the Spanish, the American or, indeed, for the

---
[1] See above, Ch. 3.
[2] For descriptions see Keesing (1937: 59 ff.) and Lebar (1972).
[3] See Kiefer (1972).
[4] See the entries in Blair & Robertson (1903–9: (7) 173–85; (16) 321–9; (40) 37–98) reporting the work of Spanish authors such as Juan de Plasencia, Miguel Loarca and Antonio de Morga. See also Lobingier (1910). More recent work may be found in Barton (1919), Schlegel (1970), Bacdayan (1969).
[5] See generally Hooker (1975: 6–54).

modern administrations.⁶ They are important, however, not because they represent a 'stage' in legal evolution, but because they represent a type of law with which a formal legal administration finds it difficult to come to terms. From the point of view of that administration it is hard to know what is 'law' and what is not, just as it is awkward for the official legal mind to accept that the formal law often lacks any descriptive validity amongst the adherents of indigenous law systems. The Spanish misunderstood the indigenous law and its administration⁷ and tended to replace it, where possible, by a civil law administration and/or canon law. To a large extent, however, it remained unaffected by the Spanish legal administration, especially in the more remote areas. The Americans, for their part, concentrated upon reforms of the political process and the extension of the *pax Americana* rather than upon the assimilation of indigenous laws into the national legal process. Legal separatism is still a feature of Philippine legal life (see the conclusion to this chapter) and the part played by the indigenous laws in the formal legal history of the Philippines has been minimal.

There is one exception; we know the laws of the early Philippines in two texts, both apparently of considerable antiquity. The first is the *Maragtas* text, first issued by one Datu Sumakwel of Panay Island in the early thirteenth century. It is found in a recension dated A.D. 1650 written in the Tagalog script⁸ and is very short, having only four sections. These provide that refusal to work is a sin and must be punished either by banishment or by being sold into slavery. Only those who could support a family might get married; poor families could have only two children, any more being killed. A child born out of wedlock was directed to be killed unless the parents married. If the father refused to marry then he was also directed to be killed and the mother was disinherited. Finally, robbery was punished by mutilation. It is difficult to know what to make of this text; it is not

---

⁶ Except that some attempt has recently been made to draft laws for the protection of minority peoples. See Lumaig (n.d.) and Sullano (1972).

⁷ For details see Francisco (1951: 433 ff.), who relies on Spanish sources, and Robertson (1917).

⁸ See Francisco (1951: 438) for a specimen page of the MS.

a code of law in any sense but a collection of punishments selected upon a rather haphazard basis. If the text was in fact issued in this form it may represent little more than a personal idiosyncrasy on the part of the author or text patron.

The second text, the *Keliantiaw* text, is much more satisfactory. It was supposedly issued by a Datu Keliantiaw of Panay in A.D. 1433.[9] It is known from a Spanish MS. (translated from Bisaya) dated 1837–8 written by the Spanish friar José Maria Pavón, and published in English by James Robertson.[10]

The text is in eighteen sections. The largest number of sections by far is concerned with forbidding actions which have spiritual or supernatural effects. Such include prohibitions on disturbing, or not showing the proper respect for, graves (ss. 4 & 6), damaging trees and taking certain species of fish (s. 7), singing at night while travelling, killing certain birds (s. 9),[11] eating certain flesh and breaking idols (ss. 15–17). In addition, three sections are devoted to slavery (8, 12, 14). The emphasis is upon slavery as a punishment and not, as in other South-East Asian texts (such as the Thai), upon the relations between master and slave. The subject of female behaviour is also dealt with (ss. 3, 9), and persons are warned to control the exercise of unbridled lust. Apart from these three subjects, the *Keliantiaw* text has only two sections dealing with civil liability in 'debt' and 'contract' (ss. 2 & 5). The second section concerns punishment for non-payment, and the fifth enforces the validity of contracts entered into by word of mouth.[12]

The text presents a picture of a social order in which overt legal regulation was not necessary. The matters dealt with indicate that the general concern was with a state of spiritual welfare and that contractual relations were the exception rather than the rule. The administration of day-to-day legal affairs must thus have been a matter for local customary regulation—a supposition borne out by historical accounts.[13]

[9] Ibid. 439 ff.
[10] See Robertson (1917).
[11] See Robertson (1917: 188 n.) for an explanation of this prohibition.
[12] See also Blair & Robertson (1903–9: (12) 282).
[13] See Robertson (1917: 164 ff.) on local organization.

I THE SPANISH LAWS

Spanish government was established in 1565, forty years after the historic landing of Magellan on 16 March 1521. The Spanish attempted to unify the scattered islands of the Philippines and establish Christianity as the religion of the Philippine peoples. In neither did they fully succeed; the southern Philippines remained obstinately Muslim, as they are today, and separatist tendencies still remain to plague the modern government of the Republic.

The colonial administration was highly centralized, revolving around the person of the governor and captain-general who was appointed first by the Viceroy of Mexico and later by the King of Spain. Spanish experience in Mexico influenced the establishment of local administration. After an unsuccessful experiment with the *encomienda* system,[14] the islands were divided into provinces (headed by an *alcalde-mayor*, later styled *gobernador civil*), subdivided into *pueblos* or municipalities (headed by a *gobernadorcillo* who was a native) made up of a number of *barangays* (extended families), and headed by a (local) *datu* who was also styled a *cabeza de barangay*. The governor possessed supreme executive authority and he not only enforced the laws of Spain but could also suspend them and issue decrees having the force of law.[15]

Spanish sovereignty was predicated upon a set of quite specific propositions, all of which were canvassed in the first century of Spanish rule. Spain was outstanding among the colonial powers of South-East Asia for the attention that the authorities devoted to the question of sovereignty. In so far as the question was important in English law, the ordinary principles of reception by way of settlement[16] were generally thought to be sufficient; for the French and the Dutch, to whom the issue was more important,[17] conquest and agreement by treaty were decisive; for the Spanish, however, the matter was more complicated. The issue of sovereignty arose, as it nearly always does, over the question of taxation, in the Spanish case the collection of tribute from non-Christianized natives by the King's delegate (the *encomendero* who stood

[14] See L. B. Simpson (1950).
[16] *Campbell* v. *Hall* (1774) 1 Cowp. 204.
[15] See Barrows (1917).
[17] See above, Chs. 6–7.

between the King and the natives in a semi-feudal capacity, owing obligations to both sides. Apart from the fact that economic conditions in the late sixteenth century made payment difficult to obtain, the Roman Catholic religious orders objected to the collection of taxes where the solemn duty of conversion had not been undertaken.[18] In the ensuing comments on the situation a number of theories to justify the imposition of Spanish laws, especially fiscal laws, were put forward.

Much of the discussion of sovereignty revolved round the theories propounded in the early sixteenth century by the great Dominican theologian Francisco de Vitoria, whose work had an important influence in the development of international law.[19] Vitoria located Spanish sovereignty in the Indies in (*a*) the right to travel, (*b*) the right to preach the Gospel, (*c*) the intimidation of native Christians by non-Christian rulers, (*d*) the right of the Pope to depose the pagan ruler of a Christian people, (*e*) the despotism of native rulers, (*f*) the free election of the Spanish monarch by the natives, and (*g*) native states requesting Spanish assistance. Only (*b*) had any possible application in the Philippine islands. In the Ecclesiastical Junta of A.D. 1582 the principle that Castilian sovereignty flowed from the commitment to preach the Gospel and that of the Pope's right to depose native rulers who hindered missionary activity were reaffirmed. In addition, the cultural inferiority of the Philippine peoples was stated to be a further cause for Spanish rule, the responsibility of which was to elevate the condition of indigenous peoples. At about the same time a more exact definition of the nature of royal sovereignty was put forward: it stated that the Kings of Spain were both natural and 'supernatural' sovereigns, the latter by virtue of the donation of Pope Alexander VI who made the Kings of Castile 'the universal lords of the Indies' on condition that they introduced the faith into those regions.[20] The papal grant was in theory taken to complement and not

---

[18] See Phelan (1957: 231 ff.).
[19] See Scott (1934). It is interesting to note that the slightly later work of Hugo Grotius inspired by similar Dutch colonial expansion has also had wider repercussions.
[20] See de la Costa (1950).

The Spanish–American Legal World 219

denigrate from the personal, proprietary, and political rights of the natives.

Vitoria tended to deny that the papal donation of itself transferred political sovereignty over heathen peoples. By a compromise formula developed in later years[21] it came to be accepted that the Castilian rulers were sovereign 'emperors', an analogy with the Holy Roman Emperors of Western Christendom. However, the Spanish Kings never formally styled themselves Emperor; the formula remained 'Reyes de las Indias orientales y occidentales...' primarily because reliance would thus have to be placed on the papal donation as essentially founding the political and legal jurisdictions. Instead, alternative theories, such as that jurisdiction depended upon the right of discovery, were also promulgated. The Alexandrian donation was de-emphasized as, indeed, were some of the canon-law implications of papal bulls (see further below). In the event, the taxation problem, which had sparked the debate in the Philippines, was solved by an appeal to the facts of Spanish sovereignty in the islands. Those who had received temporal or spiritual benefits from the Spanish authorities alone were justifiably taxed. From the seventeenth century onwards these questions became of less importance as effective Spanish civil and religious control increased in scope and depth, but the whole question of sovereignty had important practical repercussions in legal administration.

These appeared most clearly in the laws declared applicable in the Philippines. It is sometimes said that the Spanish colonial administration in the Indies recognized local laws provided they did not violate Spanish-Christian precepts of morality. Thus, for the Philippines, Phelan demonstrates[22] that the Tagalog usages set down by Friar Juan de Plasencia were established as law for the local people by virtue of decisions given in the *Audiencia* (Court of Final Resort) of Manila.[23] The definition of 'Spanish-Christian' precepts naturally varied; native dowry and inheritance rules received recognition, while

---

[21] See Phelan (1957: 226 ff.).
[22] Phelan (1967: 129).
[23] See generally Cunningham (1919).

220   *Contract*

bride-gift and bride-price did not.[24] Again, the papal bull *Altitudo Divini Consili* (1537) of Paul III on the subject of 'natural' marriages, in declaring that the legitimate wife was the first woman married,[25] was not effective in the Philippines because of the nature of the existing social system.[26] Spanish legal theory for colonial possessions required (*a*) the extension of Spanish laws to the overseas territories because the latter were united with the crown of Castile and (*b*) the implementation of Spanish-Christian concepts among the colonial population. These two requirements did not always sit easily together.

The laws of sixteenth-century Spain that were applied to the Philippines were as follows:

(*a*) *Fuero Juzgo*: these were laws contained in twelve books and fifty-four titles, supposedly dating from A.D. 650 and never fully repealed but continued in later laws, especially in laws dealing with ecclesiastical matters, debts, pledges, and donations. The *Fuero* has been cited in modern proceedings.[27]

(*b*) *Fuero Real*: one of the most important law texts in Spanish history, dating from A.D. 1254, it codified the laws of Spain on the Roman model. Some of its provisions, e.g. that prohibiting double jeopardy,[28] have been referred to in modern proceedings.[29]

(*c*) *Fuero Partidas*:[30] this code was started in A.D. 1256 and completed in 1265. It was divided into seven books, 182 titles, and parts have been cited in the Philippine courts.[31]

(*d*) *El Ordenamiento de Alcalá*: a collection of miscellaneous laws enacted by the *Cortes de Alcalá* in A.D. 1348, relating to contracts, procedure, crimes and wills.

(*e*) *Leyes de Toro*: promulgated in A.D. 1502 (or 1505, dates vary) by the *Cortes de Toledo* to supplement the *Fuero Real* and the *Partidas*. Some of its provisions have been cited in the Philippine courts.[32]

[24] Ordinance of *Audiencia*, 7 January 1599 cited in Phelan (1967: 64). This decision apparently relies upon the provision in the *Partidas* that in the absence of regulation custom was to be applied. This provision was, of course, carried forward into the *Novisima Recopilación*.
[25] Or in cases of doubt allowing the husband a choice to be followed by a marriage *in facie ecclesiae*.   [26] Phelan (1967: 62).
[27] *Legarda v. Valdez* 1 Phil. 148 (1902).   [28] Lib. IV T. 21 1. 13.
[29] *Kepner v. U.S.* 195 U.S. 100, 11 Phil. 669, 689.   [30] Also called *Siete Partidas*.
[31] *Benedicto v. de la Rama* 3 Phil. 34, 40, 41, 42.
[32] *Capistrano v. Iabine* 18 Phil. 135, 139 on the definition of 'natural children'.

The Spanish–American Legal World 221

Most of the above laws were included in a codification entitled *Nueva Recopilacion* promulgated by Philip II in 1567. It comprised nine books which between them dealt with all public and private laws as they stood in the middle of the sixteenth century. Colonial law was especially provided for in the *Recopilación de leyes de las Reinos de las Indias* promulgated for New Spain in 1548, and officially promulgated for all colonial territories on 18 May 1680. It was issued at Madrid in four volumes; editions of 1754, 1774, 1791, and 1841 were also produced.[33] The function of the *Recopilación* is stated in the collection itself:

Inasmuch as the Kingdoms of Castile and of the Indies are under one crown, the laws and the order of government of one should be as similar to and as much in agreement with the other as possible; our royal council, in the laws and establishments which are ordered, must strive to reduce the form and manner of their government to the style and order by which the Kingdoms of Castile and León are governed and ruled, to the extent that the diversity and difference of the lands and nations permit.[34]

The foregoing laws were extended to the Philippines in 1530 by royal decree inserted in the *Recopilación*, which provided:[35]

That in all causes, suits, and proceedings in which the laws of this compilation do not provide for the manner of their decision, and no such provision is found in special enactments passed for the Indies and still unrepealed, or those which may hereafter be so enacted, then the laws of this our kingdom of Castile shall be followed, in conformity with the law of Toro, both with respect to the procedure to be followed in such cases, suits, and proceedings and with respect to the decision of the same on the merits.[36]

Finally, a *Novisima Recopilación* was published in 1805 by Charles V and took precedence over all earlier legislation. It comprised all the law from the fifteenth century to the date of publication and continued to be the general law until the new codes of the late nineteenth century.

[33] See Cunningham (1919: 25 n. 40) for sources.
[34] Lib. II T. II 1. 13.
[35] Lib. II T. I 1. 2.
[36] Cited in judicial proceedings, see e.g. *Rubi* v. *Provincial Board of Mindoro* 39 Phil. 660, 670–1.

In addition to the civil laws just described, canon law was binding on the Church and upon the religious orders. Moreover, canon law could become part of the civil law by action of the civil authority. For example, Philip II accepted the decrees of the Council of Trent (as to marriage) by royal *cedula* of 12 July 1554, and the decrees were brought forward into the *Novisima Recopilación* as Lib. I T. 1. 13. The effect was to give the Church sole jurisdiction[37] in matters of family law until late in the nineteenth century (see further below).

The compilations of Spanish law described above tended to be confusing and obscure and as a result the codifications promulgated in nineteenth-century Spain were largely extended to the Philippines.[38] But the laws were varied from time to time by the Governor-General in the exercise of his executive jurisdiction; for example, Lib. I T. 1 of the Civil Code of 1889 which introduced civil marriage was suspended under Church pressure. In summary, the laws of the Philippines were the laws of Spain, including the laws of medieval Spain, until the end of the nineteenth century.

It was the same with respect to the judicial system. At the head of the judicial administration was the *Audiencia Real* established by royal decree of 25 May 1590.[39] The regulations for the *Audiencia* were drafted in 1582,[40] and, with minor amendments, continued in force until the reforms at the end of the nineteenth century. The *Audiencia* fulfilled the function of a court of final resort and had jurisdiction of the same quality as that exercised in the '*Audiencias* of Valladolid and Granada', i.e. as courts of final resort on the same footing as the metropolitan Spanish jurisdictions. The regulations of the *Audiencia* provided for recourse to the procedure and practice of the metropolitan tribunals (ss. 4–5) except that, in cases of extreme importance, a right of appeal to the Council of the Indies (*Consejo de las Indias*) was allowed (s. 6). The bulk of the regulations were concerned with executive matters, but sections 54–8 dealt with the ecclesiastical jurisdiction. Section 54 established the superiority of civil over ecclesiastical jurisdic-

---

[37] See also de la Costa (1954).
[38] For details see Gamboa (1969: 71), Francisco (1951: 468–71).
[39] It had also a previous existence in the Philippines. See Francisco (1951: 471 ff.).
[40] Reproduced in Blair & Robertson (1903–9: (5) 274–318).

tion and section 56 provided that the implications of any ecclesiastical appointment was subject to the decision of the *Audiencia*. In towns not populated by Spaniards no bulls were permitted to be published and the activities of the Holy Crusade were circumscribed.[41] The most important section which had an immediate practical importance was s. 55 providing that titles to landed property resting upon ecclesiastical possession should be validated by the Council of the Indies by way of reference from the *Audiencia*.

Matters involving 'Indians' were provided for in ss. 71–9 of the *Audiencia* regulations which did not, however, lay down the substantive law to be applied. The sections merely provided for a recourse to the jurisdiction of the *Audiencia*. The original jurisdiction of 1582 was maintained until 1893, when criminal appeals of the original tribunal were limited to Manila and surrounding provinces and two new *Audiencias* were established in Cebu (1886) and Vigan (1893). This was merely an administrative change following from the reforms of the 1880s.

At a lower level the courts of the *alcaldes-mayores* had executive and judicial jurisdiction on the lines laid down in the introduced Spanish laws until the reforms of the *Ley Provisional* and the *Ley Enjuiciamiento Civil* of 1866 which provided for *jueces de primera instancia* (judges of the first instance) with limited civil and criminal jurisdiction within the judicial district (*partidos*). In addition, the Royal Decree of 29 May 1885 established a court of the *juez de paz* for the municipality with limited criminal and civil jurisdiction. Ecclesiastical courts governing all matters involving the clergy and 'other things having a sacerdotal character' as defined in canon law (i.e. family law generally) continued until 1869, when by Royal Decree of 1 February ecclesiastical and civil jurisdictions were combined. However, the clergy were exempted from the jurisdiction of the civil courts by decree of the Governor-General.

The substantive law applied in these tribunals was formally the law of Spain in the various codifications produced from the seventeenth century onwards. Provision was always made

[41] See Lib. I T. 20 recording royal decrees on the Holy Crusade in the Spanish territories.

for the application of custom, and this is continued in the modern Civil Code.[42] In addition to such general provisions, the Spanish colonial executive, particularly the colonial magistracy, always acted with a substantial degree of independence. Royal ordinances which might create injustice or conflict did not have to be enforced until the Council of the Indies had been made aware of the special circumstances of the area. The formula 'I obey but do not execute' was often invoked in the Philippines; the civil and ecclesiastical authorities in Manila thus had plenty of scope for individual discretion.[43] So far as the legal administration was concerned, the *Audiencia* felt itself free to compromise with local practice.[44]

At the close of the nineteenth century the laws of the Philippines included the following: (*a*) the Spanish laws in various editions, including special colonial collections; (*b*) the largely unwritten local laws, and (*c*) the compromise decisions of the courts of all levels based on (*a*) and (*b*). The whole Spanish legacy is sometimes described as 'Romanesque'; it could perhaps more accurately be called 'baroque Roman'.

II THE AMERICAN LAWS

Sovereignty over the Philippines was transferred from Spain to the United States of America by the Treaty of Paris of 10 December 1898. Executive authority was exercised by a United States military government until 4 July 1901, when a civilian government was appointed.[45] Under the Philippine Bill of 1 July 1902 the United States Congress assumed ultimate responsibility for government. This Bill was replaced by the Philippine Autonomy Act (Jones Law) of 29 August 1916 providing for a more autonomous form of government by way of a bicameral Philippines legislature though ultimate sovereignty still rested in the United States Congress. Both acts (sometimes called 'organic acts') embodied the substantial provisions of the United States Bill of Rights in a slightly altered form.

[42] See Arts. 11, 12, 1376 and *Wassmer* v. *Velez* G.R. No. 20089, 26 Dec. 1964.
[43] See Phelan (1967: 153–5).
[44] See generally Cunningham (1919).
[45] On the transfer of sovereignty and the government of the period 1898–1901 see *In Re McCulloch Dick* 38 Phil. 41, 96.

The Spanish–American Legal World

The laws of the United States were not extended to the Philippines unless specifically enacted by the President and Congress.[46] The Spanish laws and codes continued in force, except that laws of a political nature or laws which were inconsistent with American principles and institutions of justice were not applied.[47] Thus, laws in support of religion were declared void,[48] and the prerogatives of Church officials were no longer upheld.[49] During the period of military occupation (1898–1901) the United States Military Government promulgated several General Orders of legislative character in addition to the normal executive orders that one might expect from such a government. The legislative orders made substantive changes in private law; General Orders No. 68 of 18 December 1899 instituted a form of civil marriage, which was not known in the Spanish Marriage Law of 1870 or the *Las Siete Partidas*, by defining marriage in secular terms and so by-passing the provisions of canon law.[50] It remained in force until the passing of Act No. 3613 of the Philippine legislature of 4 December 1929, which in turn was superseded by the new Civil Code of 30 August 1950. General Orders No. 58 of 23 April 1900 entitled 'Code of Criminal Procedure' replaced the Spanish law; it continued in force until replaced by the Rules of Court promulgated on 1 July 1940. A new Code of Civil Procedure promulgated on 7 August 1901 and replacing the Spanish *Ley Enjuiciamiento Civil* was modelled on precedents in general use in the United States.[51]

In the period of civil government which, from 1902 onward, was exercised under various nomenclatures,[52] further important amendments were made. A new divorce law, Act

---

[46] See *Dorr* v. *U.S.* 11 Phil. 706, *Dewnes* v. *Bidwell* 182 U.S. 244, *Kepner* v. *U.S.* 11 Phil. 669.
[47] See *Sanchez* v. *U.S.* 216 U.S. 167, *In Re Shoop* 41 Phil. 213.
[48] *P.P.I.* v. *Perfecto* 43 Phil. 887.   [49] *U.S.* v. *Smith* 39 Phil. 533.
[50] *Duarte* v. *Dade* 32 Phil. 36 (1915).
[51] See *Cuyugan* v. *Santos* 34 Phil. 100, 106–7, *People* v. *Rosal* 49 Phil. 509, 511.
[52] As follows: (*a*) the Philippine Commission 1902–7, (*b*) the Philippine Commission and the Philippine Assembly 1907–16, (*c*) the Philippine Legislature and the Commonwealth 1916–35, (*d*) the National Assembly under the Commonwealth to the proclamation of the Republic of the Philippines, 1935–4 July 1946 (excluding the Japanese interregnum (1942–5) the laws of which were declared invalid), (*e*) the Philippine Congress 1946 to the present.

No. 2710 of 11 March 1917, allowed for full divorce instead of the relative or partial divorce of the *Partidas*: it has now been replaced by the new Civil Code. A revised Penal Code, Act No. 3815, was promulgated on 1 January 1932. It is a revision of the Spanish Penal Code of 1870, which was extended to the Philippines on 14 July 1887, and retains the basic features of its predecessor. Other laws on particular subjects, also entitled Codes, followed; they include laws on land reform, revenue, customs, elections, and transport. The Spanish civil procedure was repealed by General Orders No. 58 and replaced by American models now incorporated in the Rules of Court of 1 July 1940. The Land Registration Law, Act No. 496 of 6 November 1902, introduced the Torrens system of land registration.[53] In short, the American period saw the introduction of statute drafted on Anglo-American principles. The result is a system influenced both by 'Romanesque' and 'common law'. As Laurel says:

We cannot now evade the tendency to amalgamate into one body the laws of the conquerors and the laws of the conquered... But, whatever may be the fate of the Philippine Islands, whether destined to become a power or to remain a mere colonial possession of the United States, the writer believes that she should, at least insofar as her private law in civil matters is concerned, continue to be a civil-law country. Legally and socially, the civil-law system has become so interwoven with the life and proprietary interests of the inhabitants of these Islands that to introduce an entirely new legal system would be destructive of an institution under which the Filipino people have been bred and to which they have been accustomed for a period of more than three hundred years.[54]

Again, Carson J. in *U.S.* v. *Cunha*[55] said:

Neither English nor American common law is in force in these islands; nor are the doctrines derived therefrom binding upon our courts, save only insofar as they are founded on sound principles applicable to local conditions, and are not in conflict with existing law.

But in a later decision the court said:

...nevertheless, many of the rules, principles, and doctrines of the

[53] *Sotto* v. *Sotto* 43 Phil. 688. [54] Cited in Gamboa (1969: 75).
[55] 12 Phil. 242 (1908).

common law have, to all intents and purposes, been imported into this jurisdiction, as a result of the enactment of new laws and the organization and establishment of new institutions by the Congress of the United States or under its authority; for it will be found that many of these laws can only be construed and applied through the aid of the common law from which they are derived, and that, to breathe the breath of life into many of the institutions, recourse must be had to the rules, principles, and doctrines of the common law under whose protecting *aegis* the prototypes of these institutions had their birth.[56]

Malcolm J., in the leading case of *In Re Shoop*,[57] went even further in his analysis of the impact of American law and legal ideas. He noted the reliance upon Anglo-American judicial precedent as a source of law supplementary to the then largely Spanish substantive law. The result was the formation of a 'Philippine common law' based upon Anglo-American law which together with Spanish-derived statute formed the law of the Philippines. Other commentators in the pre-war years were rather less moderate in their assessment of the relations between the two legal systems. As late as 1939 it was claimed that the common-law system was about to 'predominate'[58] in the formation of modern Philippine law. A nationalistic element was also present from the early decades of this century. The Hon. Jorge Bocobo, Chairman of the Philippine Code Commission, called for the 'nationalization of our family law' in 1923[59] on the basis of the 'customary law of the Philippines'. In short, American political supremacy resulted in the adoption of elements of common law especially in procedure,[60] in the interpretation of statute[61] and in selected principles of substantive law including equity.[62]

The most important single importation was the introduction of a judicial system modelled in all its essential characteristics on the judicial system of the United States. The *Audiencia*

[56] *Alzua* v. *Johnson* 21 Phil. 308 (1912).
[57] 41 Phil. 213 (1920).
[58] Opinion of Vice-Governor Eugene A. Gilmore reported in Gamboa (1969: 76–7).
[59] Reported in Gamboa (1969: 77).
[60] See Francisco (1951: 540), Gamboa (1969: 77–8).
[61] See Lobingier (1905) (1908) and the following cases: *U.S.* v. *Guzman 30 Phil. 416, 419, U.S.* v. *Cunha* 12 Phil. 241, *Cerezo* v. *Atlantic Gulf and Pacific Co.* 38 Phil. 245, 248, 249.
[62] *In Re Shoop* 41 Phil. 213 although the court has denied an equitable jurisdiction, *Cuyugan* v. *Santos* 34 Phil. 100, 106–7, *Repide* v. *Afzelius* 39 Phil. 190, 195.

228 *Contract*

and the courts of first instance were abolished,[63] and Act No. 136 of 11 June 1901, the 'Judiciary Act', passed by the Philippine Commission established the new system. The new system of Supreme Court, Courts of First Instance, Municipal Courts, and Courts of the Justice of the Peace abrogated the entire Spanish system.[64] Trial by jury was not, however, introduced because it was not part of a basic civil-law system and because it was thought that the population was not ready for it.[65]

III THE DIVERSE NATURE OF PHILIPPINE LAW

The Philippines became independent on 4 July 1946, and almost immediately a movement for the revision and codification of the laws began. A Code Commission was set up in 1947 and produced a Civil Code promulgated as Act No. 368 of 18 June 1949 to replace the Spanish *Codigo Civil* of 1889. The Code includes material from the codes of Spain, France, Germany, Mexico, Italy, Switzerland, and the Argentine and from the laws of the United States (especially California and Louisiana) and Britain; indigenous Philippine elements are also included.[66]

The Code is divided into a preliminary section and four books, as follows: Book I (16 titles) Persons, Book II (9 titles) Property, Ownership, and its Modifications, Book III (5 titles) Different Modes of Acquiring Ownership, Book IV (19 titles) Obligations and Contracts. It is impossible in the space available to describe the legal sources of the different articles in the new Code, but a random selection from each Book will illustrate the diverse nature of Philippine law.

(i) *Persons*

Civil personality is defined in Book I T. I arts. 37–47. Of these articles only one (art. 37) is wholly new. The rest are either amended versions of the Spanish Civil Code or exact

---

[63] Criminal jurisdiction was suspended as from 13 August 1898, civil jurisdiction from 13 January 1899, by the U.S. Military Government. The *Audiencia*, now known as the Supreme Court, was re-established on 29 May 1899 with all its former jurisdiction and the lower courts also re-created from 5 June 1899. This system persisted until June 1901.
[64] *Alzua v. Johnson* 21 Phil. 308 (1912) 231 U.S. 106 (1913). See generally Pugh (1965).
[65] See *Dorr v. U.S.* 11 Phil. 706. See also Pugh (1965: 12 ff.).
[66] For other enactments, see generally Francisco (1951: 542 ff.), Gamboa (1969).

reproductions of that Code. However, in the case of marriage, Art. 52 of the Civil Code provides that marriage is not a mere contract between individuals but 'an inviolable social institution'. This is a new article and puts into code form what had already been expressed as principle in judicial decisions given in the first decades of the American administration.[67] The history of the law governing marriage illustrates its plurality of source: Arts. 47 and 48 of the Spanish Marriage Law of 1870 were extended to the Philippines by Royal Decree of 13 April 1883, but later superseded by Arts. 42–107 of Lib. I T. IV of the Spanish Civil Code when the latter became operative in the Philippines on 7 December 1889. The application of these articles was immediately superseded by a Decree of the Governor-General (29 December 1889), which thus revived the provisions of the law of 1870 that recognized only religious or canonical marriage. General Orders No. 68 of the U.S. Military Government of 18 December 1899 repealed the then Spanish law on the subject and instituted civil marriage without, however, prejudice to religious marriages which fulfilled the requisites laid down for a valid marriage. This order was repealed by the Revised Marriage Law Act No. 3613 of 4 December 1929 dealing with the requisites and formalities of marriage. It was itself amended, and the subject is now governed by T. III of Book I of the Civil Code which preserves the provisions of Act No. 3613 with minor amendments. Special provisions are made by Art. 78 for the marriage of Muslims and non-Christians when the application of local customs is sanctioned; in the case of mixed marriages (art. 79), where the male party is Christian, the general provisions of the Code apply, but where the male party is Muslim or pagan then Art. 78 may apply. The definition of marriage is, with the exception of procedural regulations, Hispano-Christian. For example, the grounds for annulment are clearly derived from canon law, although it is notable that the presumptions as to physical incapacity and potency were established by judicial decision.[68] Further, the Code has introduced a new definition 'natural children by

[67] *Goitia* v. *Campos Rueda* 35 Phil. 252 (1916), *Ramirez* v. *Gmur* 42 Phil. 855 (1918), *Adong* v. *Cheong Seng Gee* 43 Phil. 43 (1922).
[68] *Jimenez* v. *Cañizares* G.R. No. 12790, 31 Aug. 1960.

legal fiction' (art. 89) to legitimate children of void and voidable marriages.

This brief account of the marriage laws demonstrates a contradiction in the laws between religious and secular definitions of status. The Civil Code has come down in favour of the former with some minor exceptions such as Art. 89. The emphasis upon the religious definition is clear in the rules relating to separation simply because absolute divorce is not permitted. The Code speaks only of legal separation (T. IV Book I), although from 11 March 1917, when the Divorce Law (Act No. 2710) came into effect, until 30 August 1950, when the Civil Code took effect, absolute divorce was possible. Act No. 2710 was interpreted[69] as having abolished the suspension of cohabitation, which was all that was allowed under the *Siete Partidas*, in favour of absolute divorce. The matter is now governed by T. IV of Book I where again the religious element derived from Spanish Christendom has prevailed. This is the explanation for Art. 15 of the Civil Code, which provides that the Code is binding upon the Philippine citizen abroad in matters of status, condition, and legal capacity.[70] Foreign divorce is, therefore, not recognized, at least where a foreign *domicile* has not been attained by one of the parties.[71] Attempted agreements between spouses to renounce their respective rights and obligations and authorize remarriage are both illegal and immoral.[72]

The remainder of Book I deals with the family in the widest sense, including rights and obligations between husband and wife, the family as an institution, paternity and filiation, parental authority (T. XI), and emancipation and majority. In general these provisions are based heavily on the Spanish Code provisions either in amended or original form. The wife has a duty to live with her husband (art. 109, an amended version of art. 56 of the Spanish Code),[73] but a husband cannot compel his wife to live with her mother-in-law if the two 'cannot get along together'.[74] This is a judicial gloss on

[69] *Valdez* v. *Tuason* 40 Phil. 943 (1920).
[70] Repeating Art. 9 of the Spanish Code of 1889.
[71] See *Hix* v. *Fluemer* 55 Phil. 851 (1931), *Arca* v. *Javier* 95 Phil. 579 (1951).
[72] *Biton* v. *Momongan* 62 Phil. 7 (1935).
[73] See also *Ching Huat* v. *Co Heong* 77 Phil. 988 (1947).
[74] *Del Rosario* v. *Del Rosario* G.R. No. 1870-R, 8 Jan. 1949.

the effects of the Philippine family system which, though not defined in the Code, clearly consists of a wider group than the nuclear family. Thus Chapter 3 of T. VII (arts. 252–4) provides for a 'family council' made up of close relatives who are to consult on important family questions. These articles are new and reflect the peculiar structure of the Philippine family. On the other hand, property relationships between husband and wife (T. VI) follow the Spanish provisions, although the definition of 'property' has fallen to be determined by the courts.[75] Another local feature is that the fund of the conjugal partnership includes things acquired by means of occupations such as fishing or hunting (art. 155).

Presumptions as to legitimacy (T. VIII, Ch. 1) are governed by new rules reflecting the advancement of science rather than presumptions of canon law. The weight given to presumptions in this field, however, tends to be the same as in the Anglo-American common-law doctrine.[76] The rules relating to adoption are a mixture of Spanish law and local practice, but the objective of the adoption laws has been judicially laid down as 'the welfare of the child', a common-law doctrine.[77] In addition, a new class of authority called 'substitute parental authority' has also been included in the Code (arts. 349–55).

(ii) *Property, Ownership, and its Modifications*

Property is classified as immovable and movable (T. I, Book II), a civil-law classification taken from the Spanish Civil Code, but the Philippine Code adds a further classification of its own (art. 416). The Code also talks about 'real' and 'personal' property, a common-law classification, apparently meaning respectively 'immovable' and 'movable'.[78] Generally, the topics of ownership, co-ownership, possession, usufruct, and servitudes (also called 'easements') are based upon original or amended sections of the Spanish Civil Code.

[75] *Osorio* v. *Posadas* 56 Phil. 748 (1929), *Bismorte* v. *Aldecoa* 17 Phil. 480 (1910), *Santos* v. *Bartolome* 44 Phil. 76 (1922). These are all cases on the interpretation of the Spanish Code.
[76] *Borres* v. *Municipality of Panay* 42 Phil. 647 (1922).
[77] *Santos* v. *Aranzanso* G.R. No. 23828, 28 Feb. 1966.
[78] For example, Art. 414 defines the objects of appropriation as either '(1) Immovable or real property or (2) Movable or personal property'.

Title V of Book II, on the kinds of possession, distinguishes between good and bad faiths (arts. 526–8 repeating in slightly amended form arts. 433–5 of the Spanish Code) as the basis of possession. Good faith is always presumed and is defined not as a mistake in law but simply as a belief in rightful possession.[79]

The civil-law basis of the Code is most apparent in those sections dealing with the acquisition and extinction of ownership. For example, in acquisition by donation the court in *Balaqui* v. *Dongso*[80] cited the Supreme Court of Spain on the distinction between *donatio mortis causa* and *donatio inter vivos*. Again, acquisition by prescription was governed by the Spanish Code until repealed by the new Code of Civil Procedure, Act No. 190 of 1 October 1901, which was based largely on the Californian Code of Civil Procedure. The Act of 1901 was itself repealed in 1950, and the present Civil Code incorporates the former Spanish Code provisions with some amendments, none of which greatly alter Spanish law. A common-law influence is sometimes apparent in terminology, as when 'easement' is used in place of 'servitude'; the latter term is used only to denote praedial servitudes, i.e. where it serves another's property.

(iii) *Different Modes of Acquiring Ownership*

This is the subject of Book III, the smallest book of the Code, which deals with gifts, testate and intestate succession, and prescription. Like Book II, it is based wholly in the Spanish Civil Code, although the subject was regulated for a time by Act No. 190 mentioned above. Parts are also governed by the Rules of Court of 1940 (amended 1971). The extent of its derivation from Spanish law is striking; thus Art. 716 even deals with the ownership of swarming bees, an evergreen in Roman-law examination papers! There are, however, some deviations from the Spanish model, most notably in the definitions of 'heir', 'legatee', and 'succession'.[81] In addition, illegitimate children are now granted certain rights as 'compulsory heirs'.[82] A right of representation,

---

[79] *Kasilag* v. *Rodriguez* 69 Phil. 217 (1939).   [80] 53 Phil. 673 (1929).
[81] See Gamboa (1969: 193–4). On the canon-law influence in law relating to wills see Palma (1965) and in succession Reyes (1975).   [82] Art. 887.

i.e. standing in the place of a deceased person who was entitled to inherit, is a new provision in the Civil Code.[83]

(iv) *Obligations and Contracts*
Book IV, the largest book in the Civil Code, consists of nineteen titles dealing with obligations in general, contracts of various classes, pledge and mortgage, and damages. As in the other books, the Spanish derivation is strong, but in certain respects Anglo-American law provided the source for the Civil Code rules. In the earlier books the Spanish and Anglo-American elements were applied to the same subjects in an attempt to synthesize legal principle. In the present case the topics are governed by laws drawn from different sources and are kept quite separate. There is no suggestion that a 'Philippine common law' is about to emerge in the topics of Book IV, with one exception. In the form required of contracts (arts. 1356 ff.), the English Statute of Frauds (1677) is in force in the Philippines. It was introduced in the Code of Civil Procedure, Act No. 190 of 1901 and is now embodied in the Civil Code in a modified form. It is set out in Art. 1403 (2) as follows:

(2) Those [contracts] that do not comply with the Statute of Frauds as set forth in this number. In the following cases an agreement hereafter made shall be unenforceable by action, unless the same, or some note or memorandum thereof, be in writing, and subscribed by the party charged, or by his agent; evidence, therefore, of the agreement cannot be received without the writing, or a secondary evidence of its contents:

(a) An agreement that by its terms is not to be performed within a year from the making thereof;[84]
(b) A special promise to answer for the debt, default, or miscarriage of another;[85]
(c) An agreement made in consideration of marriage, other than a mutal promise to marry;[86]
(d) An agreement for the sale of goods, chattels or things in action, at a price not less than five hundred pesos, unless the buyer accept and receive part of such goods and chattels, or the

[83] Art. 1025.
[84] *National Bank* v. *Philippine Vegetable Oil Co.* 49 Phil. 857 (1927).
[85] *Reiss* v. *Memije* 15 Phil. 350 (1910).
[86] *Atienza* v. *Castillo* 72 Phil. 589 (1941).

evidences, or some of them, of such things in action, or pay at the time some part of the purchase money; but when a sale is made by auction and entry is made by the auctioneer in his sales book, at the time of the sale, of the amount and kind of property sold, terms of sale, price, names of the purchasers and person on whose account the sale is made, it is a sufficient memorandum;[87]

(e) An agreement for the leasing for a longer period than one year, or for the sale of real property or of an interest therein;[88]

(f) A representation as to the credit of a third person.

The Statute of Frauds applies only to executory contracts, not to those which are either partially or completely executed.[89]

Anglo-American law finds a direct and quite distinct place in T. V of Book IV (arts. 1440–57) providing for trusts. The articles establish only a rudimentary outline of the law of trusts but this is perhaps compensated for by Art. 1442, which adopts 'the principles of the general law of trusts in so far as they are not in conflict with this Code' and other laws. The remaining articles define express trusts (Ch. 2) and state the circumstances in which a trust will be implied (Ch. 3). The substantive law as to the administration of trusts is, therefore, contained in judicial decisions.[90] For the most part they state Anglo-American principles of trust, but there is one rather peculiar early decision; this is *Government* v. *Abadilla*,[91] where the Anglo-American equity jurisprudence is described as being derived from the *fideicommissa* of Roman law and thus as essentially based on civil principles. This is a wild overstatement, probably arising from the fact that the original equity jurisdiction was the preserve of the Chancellor and was a court of conscience rather than common law. A trust is not identical with, nor derived from, *fideicommissum*.

Another importation of Anglo-American legal principle is to be found in the Code articles dealing with sale (arts. 1458–1641) which incorporate many provisions taken from the Uniform Sales Acts of the United States. The contract of sale is still basically a civil-law matter, but the respective obli-

---

[87] *Robles* v. *Lizarraga Hermanos* 50 Phil. 387 (1927).
[88] *Gorospe* v. *Ilayat* 29 Phil. 21 (1924).
[89] *Hernandez* v. *Andal* 78 Phil. 196 (1947).
[90] See the cases in Gamboa (1969: 248–52).   [91] 46 Phil. 642 (1924).

gations of vendor and vendee are taken from the United States legislation. This is essentially true of negotiable instruments (art. 1508), delivery (art. 1522), lien (art. 1534), conditions and warranties (art. 1545), and actions for breach of contract (arts. 1594 ff.). On the other hand, although a valid contract of sale has been completed, the title to the thing sold is not transferred until actual or constructive delivery.[92] This of course is a result of retaining the civil law definition of contract—'A contract is a meeting of minds between two persons whereby one binds himself, with respect to the other, to give something or to render some service' (art. 1305, formerly art. 1254 of the Spanish Code). The result was expressed by the Supreme Court as follows:[93] '... our law does not admit the doctrine of the transfer of ownership by mere consent...' This principle does not, however, hold good in the case of the sale of land where registration (under a modified Torrens system) gives title.[94] Nor does it apply in the sale of large cattle, which is subject to special legislation.[95] Where there is a change in the nature of the thing sold (either of improvement or deterioration) there is a contradiction in the Code as to liability. Articles 1189, 1262, 1480, and 1538 (from the Spanish Code) tend to suggest that the seller's obligation to deliver is extinguished, while Art. 1504 places the risk on the buyer subject to certain exceptions. The question is still unsettled.[96] An interesting provision is Art. 1601 preserving the right to re-purchase the thing sold where such a right is reserved at the time of the initial contract. This was a feature of the Spanish Civil Code (art. 1507) and is known also in most South-East Asian states. The courts do not look with favour on such contracts (*pacto de retro*) and will not enforce them to the detriment of the vendor.[97] The Civil Code itself presumes such contracts to be *equitable mortgages* where the real intention of the parties is to secure the payment of a debt on the performance of some other obligation (arts. 1602–3). This is an interesting example of the extension of equity to a

[92] Arts. 1477, 1496–1501.
[93] *Fidelity and Deposit Co.* v. *Wilson* 8 Phil. 51 (1904).
[94] See Saddam & Balbastro (1962) for a review of the cases.
[95] The Cattle Registration Act.
[96] See Gamboa (1969: 261) for the cases and references to the literature.
[97] *Padilla* v. *Linsangan* 19 Phil. 65 (1911).

particular institution recognized both by the civil law and by local custom.[98]

In two areas of law, labour relations and damages, the law is almost wholly American derived. The Spanish Civil Code did not deal with the former[99] at all, and dealt only briefly with the latter.[1]

After this outline of the Anglo-American influence in Book IV it must be re-emphasized that the bulk of this book is Spanish derived. The definitions of obligation, of contract (see above), of mortgage (*hipoteca*), and of pledge are firmly rooted in civil-law notions. The articles on antichresis[2] (arts. 2132–9) are, without much exception, the Spanish principles derived from Arts. 1881–6 of the old Civil Code.

(v) *Commercial Law*

The original commercial law in the Philippines was the 'Code of Commerce for the Philippine Islands', based on the Spanish Code of Commerce (1885) extended to the Philippines by Royal Decree of 6 August 1888. Those parts which remain in force are now confined to the definition of merchants, acts of commerce, some special commercial contracts, and parts of maritime commerce. The rest of the original code has been overtaken by modern legislation.[3] In addition, parts of the Civil Code, e.g. those relating to individual capacity, such as Art. 117 which provides that a wife may engage in business, now have to be read in the interpretation of the Code of Commerce. One of the most important changes in the commercial law was the abolition of the Spanish *sociedad anonima* by the Corporation Law, Act No. 1459 of 1 April 1906, which introduced the American concept of corporate entity.[4] The Corporation Law has been amended from time to time but this part of the commercial law remains noticeably American.

[98] For the application of equitable principles to the same institution in Malaysia see Wong (1973).
[99] Now regulated in legislation see Gamboa (1969: 287–98).
[1] Now T. XVIII of Bk. IV.
[2] A contract in which the creditor acquires the right to receive the fruits of an immovable property of his debtor, with the obligation to apply them to the payments of the interest (if any) and to principal.
[3] See Gamboa (1969: 369) for an outline.
[4] See *Harden* v. *Benguet Consolidated Mining Co.* 58 Phil. 141 (1933).

The Spanish–American Legal World 237

Finally, Philippine procedure is, like the court system, closely modelled on the American pattern. The courts administer both 'law and equity'[5] and procedure is governed by the Rules of Court of 1940, revised 1964 and amended 1971. Special actions include *certiorari, mandamus,* and *quo warranto.* Throughout the middle and later portions of this chapter, judicial decisions have been cited as authority on various propositions of law. This does not mean that the doctrine of *stare decisis* obtains in the same way in the Philippines as it does in the common-law world, although the Civil Code provides that 'judicial decisions applying or interpreting the laws or the Constitution shall form a part of the legal system of the Philippines'.[6] This provision refers only to decisions in respect of already existing laws, so that judicial decisions do not form an independent source of law. In other words, decisions are evidence of existing law but do not themselves constitute that law.[7] Only the Supreme Court may establish jurisprudence,[8] which serves as a guide for the inferior courts.

IV THE REALITY OF PHILIPPINE LAW

The system of law inherited by the Philippines is plural in nature but there is also a further dimension of legal pluralism arising out of the composition of Philippine society itself. The ethnic and cultural backgrounds of the population are diverse,[9] as are their languages,[10] their being about twelve major ethnic-linguistic groups. In addition, something like 75 per cent of the population live in a variety of different rural economic and agricultural environments. The principal settlement form is the *barrio* which is both a territorial[11] and administrative[12] unit. These differences are reflected in the administration of law. In some areas, notably in the Muslim south and the Kalinga region of north Luzon, indigenous laws

[5] *Villavicencio* v. *Dimaano* G.R. No. 47087, 19 June 1940, *U.S.* v. *Tamparong* 31 Phil. 321 (1915).
[6] Art. 8.
[7] *Caltex (Phil.) Inc.* v. *Palomar* G.R. No. 19650, 29 Sept. 1966.
[8] *Miranda* v. *Imperial* 77 Phil. 1066 (1947).
[9] See Wernstedt & Spencer (1967: 149 ff.).
[10] Ibid. 153–6.
[11] Ibid. 165 ff.
[12] Romani (1956).

238 *Contract*

persist to the virtual exclusion of the national legal system.[13] In addition, the agricultural and land reforms introduced by the Americans in 1903 in an attempt to dispose of the public domain (i.e. former Spanish Crown lands) on the lines of the United States Homestead Acts of the later nineteenth century created such serious difficulties in the regulation of land[14] that the land regulations became inoperative. The reforms of the new Philippine Land Reform Code of 1963[15] and accompanying regulations have not greatly improved matters.[16] There is a serious lack in the administration of the national law in areas outside the larger urban centres. As in other South-East Asian nations a pluralism of source and fragmentation of administration are the rule rather than the exception. The unique Philippine contribution to South-East Asian legal history lies in the relationship it demonstrates between civil- and common-law systems. Although this relationship exists in other non-European surroundings,[17] the closest parallel to the Philippines is to be found in the state of Louisiana in the United States. In South-East Asia the relationship is unique, but the code form nevertheless has certain disadvantages. Chief among these is its rigidity where non-code laws are concerned. The Civil Code makes some attempt to recognize Islamic law[18] but only in a minimal fashion. Native laws are left to regulation outside the Civil and Commercial Codes and outside the regulations on procedure stated in the Rules of Court. The result is fragmentation of legal effort which makes legal administration difficult and the assimilation of laws impossible. In the absence of a coherent native law policy, this situation is bound to persist. The Spanish-American law of the Philippines is thus only partly valid as a working system.

[13] For the Muslim areas see: Kiefer (1972), Saber (1967), Dimaampao (1966); for Luzon see Bacdayan (1969), Fürer-Haimendorf (1970).
[14] See McDiarmid (1953), Krinks (1974: 2–3).
[15] Republic Act No. 3844.
[16] See Cabacungan (1969).
[17] Ceylon and South Africa with Roman–Dutch and English laws.
[18] Since this chapter was written a new Code of Muslim Personal Law has been promulgated (Presidential Decree No. 1083 of 4th February 1977) which codifies the law applicable to Muslims.

Bibliography

ABENDANON, J. H. (1891) *Publiek-en Privaatrechtlijke verhoudingen tusschen Nederland en de Nederlandsche Kolonien*. Leiden: E. J. Brill.
ADAMS, JOHN & HANCOCK, NANCY. (1970) Land and Economy in Traditional Vietnam. *Journal of Southeast Asian Studies* 1: (2) 90–8.
AHMAD IBRAHIM. (1970) *Towards a History of Law in Malaysia and Singapore*. Singapore: Stamford College Press.
ALABASTER, E. (1899) *Notes and Commentaries on Chinese Criminal Law*. London: Luzac & Co.
ALEXANDROWICZ, C. H. (1967) *An Introduction to the History of the Law of Nations in the East Indies*. Oxford: The Clarendon Press.
ANDERSON, BENEDICT R. O'G. (1972) The Idea of Power in Javanese Culture *in* Claire Holt *et al.* (eds.), *Culture and Politics in Indonesia*: 1–70. Ithaca, N.Y.: Cornell University Press.
ANDERSON, J. N. D. (1959) Conflict of Laws in Northern Nigeria. *International and Comparative Law Quarterly* 8: 442–56.
—— (1965) The Adaptation of Muslim Law in Sub-Saharan Africa *in* Kuper & Kuper (eds.), *African Law*: 149–64. Berkeley & Los Angeles: University of California Press.
—— (1970) *Islamic Law in Africa* (new imp.), London: Frank Cass & Co. Ltd.
ANG, BUNTHAI. (1972) Réserve héréditaire en droit Khmer. *Revue Juridique et Politique, Indépendance et Coopération* 26: 979–84.
ANTONELLI, ÉTIENNE. (1926) *Manuel de Législation Coloniale*. Paris: Presses Universitaires de France.
ARCHER, WILLIAM J. (1885) *The Siamese Law on Debts*. Bangkok: Printed at S. J. Smith's Office.
—— (1886) *The Siamese Law on Disputes & Assault*. Bangkok: Printed at S. J. Smith's Office.
ARMINJON, PIERRE. (1925) *Précis de Droit International Privé*. Paris: Dalloz.
AUBARET, G. (1865) *Code Annamite, Lois et Règlements du Royaume d'Annam*. 2 vols. Paris: Imprimerie Impériale.
AUNG THAN TUN. (1967) The Chin customary law (civil). *Guardian* 14: 33–4.
BACDAYAN, ALBERT S. (1969) Peace Pact Celebrations: The revitalization of Kalinga intervillage law. *Law & Society Review* 4: (1) 61–78.

BARROWS, DAVID P. (1917) The Governor-General of the Philippines under Spain and the United States *in* H. M. Stephens & H. E. Bolton (eds.), *The Pacific Ocean in History*: 238–65. New York: Macmillan & Company.

BARTHOLOMEW, G. W. (1952) Private Inter-Personal Law. *International and Comparative Law Quarterly* 1: 325–44.

—— (1960) The Ancient Codes and Modern Science. *Tasmanian University Law Review* 1: 429–45.

BARTON, R. F. (1919) *Ifugao Law*. Berkeley, Calif.: University of California Press (reprinted 1969).

BASTIN, J. (1960) The Working of the early land rent system. *Bijdragen tot de Taal-, Land- en Volkenkunde* 116: 301–12.

BEGBIE, P. J. (1834) *The Malayan Peninsula*. Madras (?): privately published.

BENDA, HARRY J. (1965–6) The Pattern of Administrative Reforms in the Closing Years of Dutch Rule in Indonesia. *Journal of Asian Studies* 25: 589–606.

BERGAIGNE, A. (1893) *Inscriptions sanscrites de Campâ et du Cambodge*. Paris: Académie des Inscriptions et Belles-Lettres.

BISSCHOP, W. R. (1934) Adat Law in Indonesia. *Journal of Comparative Legislation and International Law* (3rd ser.) 16: 304–7.

BLAIR, EMMA HELEN & ROBERTSON, JAMES ALEXANDER (eds.). (1903–9) *The Philippine Islands 1493–1898*. Cleveland: A. H. Clark Co.

BODDE, DERK & MORRIS, CLARENCE. (1967) *Law in Imperial China*. Cambridge, Mass.: Harvard University Press.

BOERENBEKER, E. A. (1935) *Het Adatrecht der Inlanders in de Jurisprudentie 1924–1935*. Leiden: E. J. Brill.

BONHOMME, ALBERT. (1931) L'Annam *in* H. Morché, *La Justice en Indochine*: 155–74. Hanoi: Imprimerie d'Extrême-Orient.

BRADDELL, R. ST. J. (1915) *The Law of the Straits Settlements*. Singapore: Kelly & Walsh.

—— (1931) *The Law of the Straits Settlements: A Commentary*. 2 vols. 2nd ed. Singapore: Kelly & Walsh.

—— (1931a) *The Legal Status of the Malay States*. Singapore: Malaya Publishing House.

BRADDELL, THOMAS. (1851) Notices of Penang. *Journal of the Indian Archipelago and East Asia* 5: 1–14, 93–119, 155–72, 189–210, 292–305, 354–66, 400–29.

BUI-TUONG-CHIEU. (1933) *La Polygamie dans le droit annamite*. Paris: Rousseau.

BUTTINGER, JOSEPH. (1958) *Viet Nam: The Smaller Dragon*. New York: Frederick A. Praeger Inc.

Bibliography

CABACUNGAN, EDISON, I. (1969) 'A Study of the Philippine Land Reform Code of 1963'. Virginia State University, unpublished Ph.D. dissertation.

CALDECOTT, A. (1918) Jelebu Customary Songs and Sayings. *Journal of the Royal Asiatic Society—Straits Branch* 78: 3-41.

CAMERLYNCK, G. H. (1937) L'Option en faveur de la loi française par des contractants annamites. *La Revue Indochinoise* 1: 100-23.

—— (1937a) Le Mariage entre Française et Annamites. *La Revue Indochinoise* 3: 51-95.

CAMOUILLY, M. (1886) The Survey Question in Cochin-China (trans. W. E. Maxwell). *Journal of the Royal Asiatic Society—Straits Branch* 18: 273-91.

CARATINI, MARCEL. (1938) La Preuve des obligations et des droits réels mobiliers en droit annamite. *La Revue Indochinoise* 6: 220-65.

—— (1938a) La Prescription acquisitive immobilière en droit annamite. *La Revue Indochinoise* 8: 720-47.

—— (1939) La Preuve de la propriété et des droits réels immobiliers en pays annamites. *La Revue Indochinoise* 10: 273-328.

—— (1939a) La Preuve de la propriété et des droits réels immobiliers en pays annamite (II-Annam-Tonkin). *La Revue Indochinoise* 11: 543-82.

—— (1942) A propos du régime des loyers en Indochine. *La Revue Indochinoise* 18: 258-88.

CARON, L. J. J. (1937) *Het handels- en zeerecht in de adat-rechtsregelen van de rechtskring Zuid-Celebes.* Utrecht: Proefschrift.

CARREON, MANUEL L. (1957) Maragtas. The Datus from Borneo. *Sarawak Museum Journal* 8: 51-99.

CASSUTTO, I. (1936) *Handleiding tot de Studie van het Adatrecht van Neder-Indië.* Haarlem: Derven F. Bohn N.V.

CHATTERJEE, BIJAN RAJ. (1964) *Indian Cultural Influences in Cambodia* 2nd ed. Calcutta: University of Calcutta.

CHHOUK, CHHAY ENG. (1972) La Dévolution successorale en droit Khmer: détermination des héritiers. *Revue Juridique et Politique, Indépendance et Coopération* 26: 969-78.

—— (1973) Les Institutions étaiques de la République Khmère. *Revue Juridique et Politique, Indépendance et Coopération* 27: 395-430.

CHIN KIM. (1971) The Thai choice-of-law Rules. *International Lawyer* 5: 709-21.

—— (1973) Marriage and Family Law of North Vietnam. *International Lawyer* 7: (2) 440-50.

CHOMCHAI, PRACHOOM. (1965) The Nature and Significance of Thai Political Philosophy. *Journal of Social Sciences* 3: (i) 51-8.

242 *Bibliography*

CH'Ü, T'UNG-TSU. (1965) *Law and Society in Traditional China*. Paris: Mouton & Co.

COEDÈS, GEORGE. (1962) *The Making of South East Asia* (trans. H. M. Wright). London: Routledge & Kegan Paul.

—— (1964) Some Problems in the Ancient History of the Hinduized States of South-East Asia. *Journal of South-east Asian History* 5: (2) 1–14.

—— (1968) *The Indianized States of Southeast Asia* (trans. Cowing). Kuala Lumpur: University of Malaya Press.

COHEN STUART, A. B. (1875) *Kawi oorkonden in Facsimile met Inleiding en Transcriptie*. Leiden: E. J. Brill.

COULSON, NOEL J. (1964) *History of Islamic Law*. Edinburgh: University of Edinburgh Press.

—— (1969) *Conflicts and Tensions in Islamic Jurisprudence*. Chicago: University of Chicago Press.

COUZINET, PAUL. (1938) La Structure juridique de l'Union indochinoise (I). *La Revue Indochinoise* 7: 426–75.

—— (1939) La Structure juridique de l'Union indochinoise (II). *La Revue Indochinoise* 10: 329–54.

CRAWFURD, JOHN. (1820) *History of the Indian Archipelago*. Edinburgh: Archibald Constable & Co.

CRESSENT, M. P. E. (1931) Le Laos *in* H. Morché *et al.*, *La Justice en Indochine*: 82–112. Hanoi: Imprimerie d'Extrême-Orient.

CUNNINGHAM, CHARLES H. (1919) *The Audiencia in the Spanish Colonies as Illustrated by the Audiencia of Manilla 1583–1800*. Berkeley, Calif.: University of California Press.

DAMIAN, EDDY & HORNICK, ROBERT. (1972) Indonesia's Formal Legal System: An Introduction. *American Journal of Comparative Law* 20: (2) 492–530.

DARESTE, F. R. (1915) *Recueil de législation et de jurisprudence coloniales*. Paris: Librairie des jurisclasseurs.

DARLING, F. C. (1970) The Evolution of law in Thailand. *Review of Politics* 32: 197–218.

DAVID, RENÉ & BRIERLEY, J. E. C. (1968) *Major Legal Systems in the World Today*. London: Stevens & Sons.

DAW, ROWENA. (1972) Some Problems of Conflict of Laws in West Malaysia and Singapore Family Law. *Malaya Law Review* 14: (2) 179–208.

DAW KHIN KHIN, U. (1954) Marriage Institutions of the Burmese Moslem Community. *Journal of the Burma Research Society* 37: (2) 24–34.

Bibliography

DE CASPARIS, J. G. (1956) *Selected Inscriptions from the Seventh to the Ninth Century A.D.* Bandung: Dinas Purbakala Republik Indonesia.

DE HOLLANDER, J. J. (1893) *Handleiding bij de Beoefening der Maleische Taal en Letterkunde.* Breda: Zesde Druk.

DE JOSSELIN DE JONG, J. P. B. (1948) Customary Law: A Confusing Fiction. Amsterdam: *Koninklijke Vereeniging Indisch Instituut Mededeling* No. lxxx, *Afd. Volkenkunde* No. 29.

DE LA COSTA, HORACIO. (1950) Church and State in the Philippines during the Administration of Bishop Salazar. *Hispanic American Historical Review* 30: (3) 314–36.

—— (1954) Episcopal Jurisdiction in the Philippines in the Seventeenth Century. *Philippine Studies* 2: 197–217.

DE LA PORTE, ANDRÉ. (1908) Beschouwingen over quasi-international privaatrecht. *Indisch Tijdschrift van het Recht* 91: 1-33.

DELOUSTAL, RAYMOND. (1909) *La Justice dans l'ancien Annam.* Hanoi: Imprimerie Nationale.

DEN, C. and DECHEIX, PIERRE. (1969) Organisation judicaire du Cambodge en matière pénale. *Revue Juridique et Politique, Indépendance et Coopération* 23: 845–58.

DENNERY, ROBERT. (1938) Reports of the Cour d'Appel de Hanoi of 8th January 1937. *La Revue Indochinoise* 5: 106–18.

—— (1939) Du conflit entre la Loi Métropolitaine et la loi applicable aux Français en Indochine. *La Revue Indochinoise* 10: 355–82.

—— (1939a) Les Conflits de lois et de juridictions intéressant les indigènes à l'intérieur de l'Union indochinoise. *La Revue Indochinoise* 11: 507–42.

DERRETT, J. DUNCAN M. (1968) *Religion, Law and the State in India.* London: Faber & Faber.

DERRIDA, F. (1961) Un Code de la famille au Sud-Vietnam. *Revue Internationale de Droit Comparé* 13: 57–77.

DHANI NIVAT, PRINCE. (1947) The Old Siamese Conception of the Monarchy. *Journal of the Siam Society* 36: (2) 91–106.

DIAMOND, A. S. (1935) *Primitive Law.* London: Watts & Co.

—— (1951) *The Evolution of Law and Order.* London: Watts & Co.

—— (1971) *Primitive Laws, Past and Present.* London: Methuen & Co.

DICKSTEIN, H. L. (1973) Radwan v. Radwan and the 1972 Malaysian Law Reform (Marriage & Divorce) Bill 1972. *Malayan Law Journal*: xv–xvii.

DIMAAMPAO, P. D. (1966) Agama Courts of the Muslim Philippines. *Lyceum Law Review*: 22–30.
DISLÈRE, P. (1914) *Traité de législation coloniale*. 4th ed. Paris: Dupont.
DONNISON, F. S. V. (1953) *Public Administration in Burma*. London: Royal Institute of International Affairs.
DRIVER, G. R. & MILES, J. C. (1955–6) *The Babylonian Laws*. Oxford: The Clarendon Press.
DULAURIER, E. (1845) *Institutions maritimes de l'Archipel d'Asie*. Paris: Benjamin Dupont.
DUPLATRE, LOUIS. (1922) *Essai sur la condition de la femme au Siam*. Thèse, Faculté de Droit, Université de Grenoble. Lyon: A. Rey.
DURKHEIM, E. (1893) *De la division du travail social* (trans. G. Simpson). Glencoe, Ill.: Free Press (1964).
E MAUNG. (1951) Insolvency jurisdiction in early Burmese law. *Journal of the Burma Research Society* 34: 1–6.
—— (1970) *Burmese Buddhist Law*. Rangoon: Daw Than Tint Mya Sapay.
EHRLICH, EUGEN. (1922) Sociology of Law. *Harvard Law Review* 36: 130–45.
—— (1936) *The Fundamental Principles of the Sociology of law* (trans. W. L. Moll). Cambridge, Mass.: Harvard Studies in Jurisprudence vol. 5.
ENGEL, DAVID M. (1975) *Law and Kingship in Thailand during the reign of King Chulalongkorn*. Ann Arbor, Mich. Michigan Papers on South and Southeast Asia, No. 9.
ENTHOVEN, K. L. J. (1912) *Het Adatrecht der Inlanders in de Jurisprudentie 1849–1912*. Leiden: E. J. Brill.
ESCARRA, JEAN. (1933) Law, Chinese. *Encyclopedia of Social Sciences* 9: 249–54.
ESTOUBLON, R. & LEFÉBURE, A. (1896) *Code de l'Algérie annoté*. Algiers: A. Jourdan.
EYGOUT, HENRY. (1932) The New Laws on Civil Procedure. *Journal of the Siam Society* 25: (2) 109–26.
—— (1937) La Nouvelle Constitution siamoise. *La Revue Indochinoise* 3: 150–61.
—— (1938) Le Droit pénal siamois. *La Revue Indochinoise* 5: 29–57.
FALL, BERNARD B. (1967) *The Two Viet-Nams*. New York: Frederick A. Praeger.
FITZGERALD, S. G. VESEY. (1934) Indian and Far Eastern Cases on the Conflict of Laws 1928–33. *Journal of Comparative Legislation and International Law* (3rd ser.) 16: 116–30.

Bibliography

FORCHHAMMER, EMIL. (1885) *The Jardine Prize: An Essay on the Sources and Development of Burmese Law.* Rangoon: Govt. Press.

FRANCISCO, VINCENTE J. (1951) *Legal History.* Manila: East Publishing.

FÜRER-HAIMENDORF, CHRISTOPH VON. (1970) Culture Change and the Conduct of Conflicts among Filipino Tribesmen. *Modern Asian Studies* 4: (3) 193–209.

FURNIVALL, J. S. (1939) The Fashioning of Leviathan. *Journal of the Burma Research Society* 29: 1–137.

——— (1940) Manu in Burma. *Journal of the Burma Research Society* 30: (2) 351–70.

——— (1944) *Netherlands India: a study of plural economy.* Cambridge: Cambridge University Press.

——— (1956) *Colonial Policy and Practice.* New York: New York University Press.

FYZEE, ASAF A. A. (1964) *Outlines of Muhammadan Law* (3rd ed.). London: Oxford University Press.

GAMBOA, MELQUIADES J. (1969) *An Introduction to Philippine Law* (7th ed.). Quezon City, Phila.: Central Lawbook Publishing Co.

——— (1974) Meeting of the Roman law and the Common law in the Philippines. *Philippine Law Journal* 49: 304–14.

GARCIA, EXCELSO. (1973) Particular Discipline on Marriage in the Philippines during the Spanish Regime. *Philippiniana Sacra* 7: (2) 7–85.

GARRIGUES, E. A. F. (1930) *Rapport sur le fonctionnement de la justice en Cochinchine.* Saigon: Imprimerie Moderne J. Testelin.

——— (1931) La Cochinchine *in* H. Morché *et al., La Justice en Cochinchine:* 41–81. Hanoi. Imprimerie d'Extrême-Orient.

GAUNG, KINWUN MINGYI U. (1908) *A Digest of the Burmese Buddhist Law.* 2 vols. Rangoon: Govt. Press.

GAUTAMA, SUDARGO. (1971) *Hukum Antargolongan.* Djakarta: Ichtiar.

——— 1973 *Himpunan Keputusan-Keputusan Hukum Antar Golongan.* Bandung: Alumni.

——— & Harsono, Budi. (1972) *Agrarian Law: Survey of Indonesian Economic Law.* Bandung: Padjadjaran University Law School.

——— & HORNICK, ROBERT N. (1972) *An Introduction to Indonesian Law: Unity in Diversity.* Djakarta: privately published in mimeo by the authors.

GERINI, G.-E. (1895) Trial by Ordeal in Siam and the Siamese Law of Ordeals. *Asiatic Quarterly Review* n.s. 9: 415–24, 10: 156–75.

——— (1909) *Researches on Ptolemy's Geography of Eastern Asia.* London: Royal Asiatic Society Monographs No. 1.

GIBB, H. A. R. (1945) *Modern Trends in Islam*. Chicago: University of Chicago Press.

GINSBURGS, GEORGE. (1973) Soviet Sources on the Law of North Vietnam. *Asian Survey* 13: 659–76, 980–8.

—— (1975) The Role of Law in the Emancipation of Women in the Democratic Republic of Vietnam. *American Journal of Comparative Law* 23: 613–52.

GITTINGER, J. P. (1959) *Studies on Land Tenure in Viet Nam*. United States Operations Mission to Vietnam, Division of Agriculture and National Resources.

GLEDHILL, ALAN. (1960) Fundamental Rights in Burma. *Burma Law Institute Journal* 2: 3–12.

—— (1962–3) Burmese Law in the Nineteenth Century. *Cahiers d'Histoire Mondiale* 7: 172–94.

—— (1968) Community of Property in the Marriage Law of Burma in Anderson (ed.), *Family Law in Asia and Africa*: 205–17. London: George Allen & Unwin Ltd.

GLUCKMAN, MAX (1967) *The Judicial Process among the Barotse of Northern Rhodesia* (2nd ed.). Manchester: Manchester University Press.

GONDA, JAN. (1952) *Sanskrit in Indonesia*. Nagapura: Academy of Indian Culture.

GOUWGIOKSIONG. (1960) *Hukum Antargolongan* (2nd ed.). Djakarta: Penerbit Alumni.

—— (1965) Interpersonal law in Indonesia. *Rabels Zeitschrift* 29: 545–73.

GOWING, PETER G. and MCAMIS, ROBERT D. (eds.) (1974) *The Muslim Filipinos*. Manila: Solidaridad Publishing House.

GRISWOLD, A. B. & PRASERT ṆA NAGARA. (1969) A Law Promulgated by the King of Ayudhyā in 1397 A.D. *Journal of the Siam Society* 57: (1) 109–48.

GUILLEMINET, PAUL. (1938) Une Forme originale d'organisation commerciale. *Les Démarcheurs bahnars. La Revue Indochinoise* 8: 704–19.

—— (1952) *Coutumier de la Tribu Bahnar des Sedang et des Jarai de la Province de Kontum*. 2 vols, Hanoi: École Française d'Extrême-Orient Publications vol. xxxii.

GULLICK, J. M. (1965) *Indigenous Political Systems of Western Malaya*. London: Athlone Press.

GUTTERIDGE, H. C. (1949) *Comparative Law* (2nd ed.). London: Cambridge University Press.

GUYON, RENÉ. (1919) *L'Oeuvre de codification au Siam*. Paris: Imprimerie Nationale.

Bibliography 247

HABERT, L. A. (1931) LE TONKIN *in* H. Morché *et al.*, *La Justice en Indochine*: 175–210. Hanoi: Imprimerie d'Extrême-Orient.

HALE, A. (1898) Folklore and the Minangkabau Code in the Negri Sembilan. *Journal of the Royal Asiatic Society—Straits Branch* 31: 43–61.

HALL, D. G. E. (1968) *A History of South-East Asia* (3rd ed.) London: Macmillan.

HARRISON, JUDY F. (1964) Wrongful Treatment of Prisoners: A Case Study of Ch'ing Legal Practice. *Journal of Asian Studies* 23: 227–44.

HART, H. L. A. (1954) Definition and Theory in Jurisprudence. *Law Quarterly Review* 70: 37–60.

—— (1961) *The Concept of Law*. Oxford: The Clarendon Press.

HAZEU, G. A. J. (1905) *Tjeribonsch Wetboek*... Batavia: Verhandelingen van het Koninklijk Bataviaasch Genootschap van Kunsten en Wetenschappen v. 55 No. 2.

HEINE-GELDERN, R. (1942–3) Conceptions of State and Kingship in Southeast Asia. *Far Eastern Quarterly* 2: 15–30.

HERCHENRODER, M. F. P. (1936) Study of the Law applicable to Native Christians in the French Dependencies and in India. *Journal of Comparative Legislation and International Law* (series 3) 18: 186–94.

'H.G.' (1942) L'Évolution des institutions communales au Tonkin (1921–41). *La Revue Indochinoise* 18: 244–57.

HICKLING, R. H. (1972) The Legal System of Thailand. *Hong Kong Law Journal* 2: 8–53.

HINLOOPEN LABBERTON, D. VAN. (1933) *Dictionnaire de termes de droit coutumier indonésien*. Amsterdam: Les Soins de l'Academie Royale des Sciences d'Amsterdam.

HLA AUNG. (1958) Sino-Burmese Marriages and the Conflict of Laws. *Burma Law Institute Journal* 1: 25–55.

—— (1965) Some Aspects of Marriage under Burmese Buddhist Law and Malayan Muslim Law. *Journal of the Burma Research Society* 48: 1–15.

—— (1968) The Effect of Anglo-Indian Legislation on Burmese Customary Law *in* Buxbaum (ed.), *Family Law and Customary Law in Asia*: 67–88. The Hague: Nijhoff.

—— (1969) The Burmese Concept of Law. *Journal of the Burma Research Society* 52: (2) 27–41.

HOADLEY, MASON C. (1971) Continuity and Change in Javanese Legal Tradition: The Evidence of the Jayapattra. *Indonesia* 11: 95–109.

HOLLEMAN, F. D. (1938) Het Adatprivaatrecht van Nederlandsche-Indië in Wetenschap, Praktijk en Onderwijs. *Indisch Tijdschrift van het Recht* 147: 428–40.

HOOKER, M. B. (1967) *A Sourcebook of Adat, Chinese Law and the History of Common Law in the Malayan Peninsula*. Singapore: Malaya Law Review Monograph No. 1. Faculty of Law, University of Singapore.

—— (1968) A Note on the Malayan Legal Digests. *Journal of the Royal Asiatic Society—Malaysian Branch* 41: (1) 157–70.

—— (1968a) Private International Laws and Personal Laws. *Malaya Law Review* 10: 55–67.

—— (1969) The East India Company and the Crown 1773–1858. *Malaya Law Review* 11: (1) 1–37.

—— (1970) *Readings in Malay Adat Laws*. Singapore: Singapore University Press.

—— (1971) Law, Religion and Bureaucracy in a Malay State. *American Journal of Comparative Law* 19: 264–86.

—— (1972) *Adat Laws in Modern Malaya*. Kuala Lumpur: Oxford University Press.

—— (1973) The Challenge of Malay Adat Law in the Realm of Comparative Law. *International and Comparative Law Quarterly* 22: 492–514.

—— (1973a) A Note on the Malaysian Petition Writer. *Journal of Asian Studies* 32: (4) 661–2.

—— (1974) Adat and Islam in Malaya. *Bijdragen tot de taal-, Land en Volkenkunde* 130: 69–90.

—— (1975) *Legal Pluralism: An Introduction to Colonial & Neo-colonial Laws*. Oxford: The Clarendon Press.

—— (1976) *Personal Laws of Malaysia*. Kuala Lumpur: Oxford University Press.

—— (1976a) The Trengganu Inscription in Malayan Legal History. *Journal of the Royal Asiatic Society—Malaysian Branch* 49: (2). 127–31.

HU, HSIEN-CHIN. (1948) *The Common Descent Group in China and its Functions*. New York: Viking Fund Publications in Anthropology No. 10.

HUEBNER, R. (1908) *History of Germanic Private Law* (trans. F. S. Philbrick 1918). Boston: Little, Brown & Co.

HUNGER, F. W. T. (1935) Het erfrecht op Bali als een vraagstuk voor Hindoes en Christenen. *Kolonial Studeën* 19: 405–29.

INSIXIENMAI, S. (1972) Testaments et la protection de la famille laotienne contre les libéralités du défunt (réserve héréditaire). *Revue Juridique et Politique, Indépendance et Coopération* 26: 1013–20.

Bibliography 249

Ismail Bakti. (1960) *Bunga Mas*: Golden Flowers. *Malaya in History* 6: (1) 40–2.
Jackson, Bernard S. (1972) Book Review. *Law Quarterly Review* 88: 266–70.
—— (1975) From Dharma to Law. *American Journal of Comparative Law* 23: 490–512.
Jain, Subhash C. (1970) French Legal System in Pondicherry. *Journal of the Indian Law Institute* 12: 573–608.
Jardine, Sir John. (1882) *Notes on Buddhist Law*. Rangoon: Court of the Judicial Commissioner, British Burma.
Jayaswal, K. P. (1920) A Judgement of Hindu Court in Sanskrit. *Journal of the Bihar & Orissa Research Society* 6: 246–58.
Jolly, Julius. (1921) Note on the Judgement of a Hindu Court: a Javanese Jayapattra. *Journal of the Bihar & Orissa Research Society* 7: 117–20.
—— (1928) *Hindu Law and Custom* (trans. Batakrishna Ghosh), Calcutta: Greater India Soc.
Jones, William C. (1974) Studying the Ch'ing Code: The Ta Ch'ing Lü Li. *American Journal of Comparative Law* 22: (2) 330–64.
Jonker, J. C. G. (1885) *Een Oud-Javaansch Wetboek*. Leiden: E. J. Brill.
Joseph, K. T. (1970) The Malacca Land Laws. *Federation Museums Journal* n.s. 15: 129–80.
Juynboll, H. H. (1899) *Catalogus van de Maleische en Sundaneesche Handschriften de Leidsche Universiteits-Bibliotheek*. Leiden: E. J. Brill.
Kāne, P. V. (1930–62) *History of the Dharmasastra*. (5 vols.) Poona: Bandarkar Oriental Research Institute.
Kantol Norodom, H. R. H. (1956) Comments on the Law and Practice in Cambodia *in*: *Studies in the Law of the Far East and Southeast Asia*: 75–83. Washington: The Washington Foreign Law Society.
Katz, June S. & Katz, Ronald S. (1975) The New Indonesian Marriage Law. *American Journal of Comparative Law* 23: 653–81.
Keesing, Felix M. (1937) *The Philippines: A Nation in the Making*. Hong Kong: Kelly & Walsh.
Kempe, J. E. & Winstedt, R. O. (1948) A Malay Legal Digest of Pahang. *Journal of the Royal Asiatic Society—Malayan Branch* 21: (1) 1–24.
—— (1952) A Malay Legal Miscellany. *Journal of the Royal Asiatic Society—Malayan Branch* 25: (1) 1–19.
Kern, R. A. (1927) Javaansche Rechtsbedeeling. Een bijdrage tot de kennis der geschiedenis van Java. *Bijdragen tot de Taal-, Land- en Volkenkunde* 83: 316–445.

KHETARPAL, S. P. (1966-7) Property of the Marriage: Burmese Law. *American Journal of Comparative Law* 15: 754-71.

—— (1968) The Debt of Burmese Jurists to Hindu Law. *Jaipur Law Journal* 8: 6-25.

KIEFER, THOMAS M. (1972) *The Tausug: Violence and Law in a Philippine Moslem Society.* New York: Holt, Rinehart & Winston Inc.

KNAUP, KATHIANNE. (1970) Native Family Law in Sabah: A Study of Customary Law within a Common Law State. *Saint Louis University Law Journal* 15: 255-82.

KOLLEWIJN, R. D. (1929) Interracial Private Law *in* B. Schreike (ed.), *The Effect of Western Influence on Native Civilizations in the Malay Archipelago.* Batavia: Royal Batavia Society of Arts and Sciences.

—— (1934) Het op arbeidsovereenkomsten toe te passenrecht. *Indisch Tijdschrift van het Recht* 139: 789-806.

—— (1938) *Interregional en Internationaal Privaatrecht.* Bandung: W. van Hoeve.

—— (1939) *Intergentiel Recht in Nederlands Indie.* Bandung: W. van Hoeve.

—— (1951) Conflicts of Western & non-Western law. *International Law Quarterly* 4: 307-26.

KORN, V. E. (1960) The Village Republic of Těnganan Pěgěringsingan in *Bali: Studies in Life, Thought & Ritual*: 301-61. The Hague: W. van Hoeve.

KOTENEV, A. M. (1925) *Shanghai: its Mixed Court and Council.* Shanghai: North-China Daily News and Herald Ltd.

KRINKS, PETER. (1974) Old Wine in a New Bottle: Land Settlement and Agrarian Problems in the Philippines. *Journal of Southeast Asian Studies* 5: 1-17.

LAFFEY, ELLA. (1969) The Content of the Sino-Vietnamese Tributary Relationship in the late 19th Century *in* E. Wickberg (comp.), *Historical Interaction of China and Vietnam*: 25-35. University of Kansas Center for East Asian Studies, Research Publication No. 4.

LAHIRI, S. C. (1939) *Principles of Modern Burmese Buddhist Law.* Calcutta: Eastern Law House.

LAM, TRUONG-BUU. (1969) Comments and Generalities on Sino-Vietnamese Relations *in* E. Wickberg (comp.), *Historical Interaction of China and Vietnam*: 36-49. Universtiy of Kansas Center for East Asian Studies, Research Publication No. 4.

Bibliography

LANGLET, PHILIPPE. (1970) *La Tradition vietnamienne: Un État national au sein de la civilisation chinoise.* Saigon: Bulletin de la Société des Études Indochinoises, tome XLV.

LASSERRE, F. (1884) *Cochinchine française: Recueil de jurisprudence en matière indigène, années 1880–1885.* Saigon: Imprimerie Nationale.

—— (1884a) *Cochinchine française: Projet de Code Civil à l'usage des Annamites.* Saigon: Imprimerie Nationale.

LEBAR, FRANK M. (ed.) (1972) *Ethnic Groups of Insular Southeast Asia (I).* New Haven, Conn.: HRAF Press.

—— *et al.* (1964) *Ethnic Groups of Mainland Southeast Asia.* New Haven, Conn.: HRAF Press.

LECLÈRE, A. (1894) *Recherches sur le droit public des Cambodgiens.* Paris: A. Challamel.

LEKKERKERKER, C. (1938) *Land en Volk van Java.* Groningen: J. B. Wolters.

LEKKERKERKER, T. C. (1918) *Hindoe-Recht in Indonesië.* Amsterdam: J. H. de Bussy.

LEV, DANIEL S. (1972) *Islamic Courts in Indonesia.* Berkeley, Calif.: University of California Press.

—— (1972a) Judicial Institutions and Legal Culture in Indonesia *in* Holt *et al.* (eds.), *Culture and Politics in Indonesia*: 246–318. Ithaca: Cornell University Press.

LEVASSEUR, GEORGES, (1937) Les Répercussions des Accords de Nankin. *La Revue Indochinoise* 1: 57–99, 2: 83–118.

—— (1937a) La Situation des Chinois en Indochine. *La Revue Indochinoise* 3: 96–149.

—— (1937b) Les Conflits de Lois et de juridictions intéressant les Chinois en Indochine. *La Revue Indochinoise* 4: 42–134.

—— (1939) Contribution à l'établissement d'une bibliographie du droit Indochinois. *La Revue Indochinoise* 9: 139–75.

LIAW, YOCK FANG. (1967) Undang2 Luhak Tiga Laras. *Nanyang University Journal* 1: 107–18.

—— (1976) *Undang Undang Melaka.* The Hague: B. V. Nederlandsche Boek-en Steendrukkerij V/H H. L. Smits.

LINEHAN, W. H. (1936) History of Pahang. *Journal of the Royal Asiatic Society—Malayan Branch* 14: (ii).

LINGAT, ROBERT. (1929–30) Note sur la révision des lois siamoise en 1805. *Journal of the Siam Society* 23: (i) 19–27.

—— (1936) La Responsabilité collective au Siam. *Revue Historique de Droit Français et Étranger* (4th series): 523–39.

—— (1937) Vinaya et Droit Laïque. *B.É.F.E.O.* 37: 415–77.

—— (1943) Le Régime des biens entre époux en Thailande. *La Revue Indochinoise* 19: 347–409.

—— (1949) L'Influence juridique de l'Inde au Champa et au Cambodge. *Journal Asiatique* 137: 273–90.
—— (1949a) The Buddhist Manu or the Propagation of Hindu Law in Hinayanist Indochina. *Annals of Bandarka Oriental Research Institute* 30: 284–97.
—— (1950) Evolution of the Conception of Law in Burma and Siam. *Journal of the Siam Society* 38: (1) 9–31.
—— (1951) La Conception du droit dans l'Indochine hinayâniste. *B.É.F.E.O.* 44: 163–87.
—— (1952–5) *Les Régimes matrimoniaux du Sud-Est de l'Asie*. 2 vols. Saigon: École Française d'Extrême-Orient.
—— (1973) *The Classical Law of India* (trans. J. Duncan M. Derrett). Berkeley, Calif.: University of California Press.
LIU, HUI-CHEN (WANG). (1959) *The Traditional Chinese Clan Rules*. New York: J. J. Augustin for the Association of Asian Studies.
LOBINGIER, C. S. (1905) Blending Legal Systems in the Philippines. *Law Quarterly Review* 21: 401–7.
—— (1908) Civil Law Rights through Common Law Remedies. *Juridical Review* 20: 97–108.
—— (1910) The Primitive Malay Marriage Law. *American Anthropologist* 12: 250–6.
LOGAN, J. R. (1855) A Translation of the Malayan Laws of the Principality of Johore. *Journal of the Indian Archipelago and East Asia* 9: 71–95.
LOGEMANN, J. H. A. (1938) Om de taak van de Rechter. *Indisch Tijdschrift van het Recht* 148: 27–36.
LOH, PHILIP F. S. (1969) *The Malay States 1877–1895*. Kuala Lumpur: Oxford University Press.
LOW, JAMES. (1839) On the Government of Siam. *Transactions of the Asiatic Society of Bengal* 20: (2) 245–84.
—— (1847) The Laws of Muung Thai or Siam. *Journal of the Indian Archipelago and Eastern Asia* 1: 327–429.
LUBMAN, STANLEY. (1967) Mao & Mediation: Politics and Dispute Settlement in Communist China. *California Law Review* 55: 1284–1359.
LUCE, E.-P. (1972) Institut Royal de Droit et d'Administration du Laos. *Revue Juridique et Politique, Indépéndance et Coopération* 26: 201–32.
LUMAIG, ROMULO B. (n.d.) *Laws Affecting the National Cultural Minorities of the Philippines*. Manila: n.p.
LUSTÉGUY, PIERRE. (1935) *La Femme annamite du Tonkin dans l'institution des biens cultuels*. Paris: Nizet Et Bastard.

Lu-Van-Li. (1939) *La Propriété Foncière en Cochinchine.* Paris: Éditions Domat-Montchrestien.

Lyfoung, T. 1969 Organisation judicaire en matière pénale au Laos. *Revue Juridique et Politique Indépendance et Coopération* 23: 859–64.

Mabbett, I. W. (1977) *Varnas* in Angkor and the Indian Caste System. *Journal of Asian Studies* 36: (3) 429–42.

McAleavy, Henry. (1958) Dien in China and Vietnam. *Journal of Asian Studies* 17: 403–15.

—— (1958a) Varieties of Hu'o'ng-hỏa: A problem in Vietnamese Law. *Bulletin School of Oriental & African Studies* 21: 608–19.

McDiarmid, A. M. (1953) Agricultural Public Land Policy in the Philippines during the American Period. *Philippine Law Journal* 26: 851–88.

McKeon, Richard. (1968) The Individual in East and West *in* Moore (ed.), *The Status of the Individual in East and West*: 535–46. Honolulu: University of Hawaii Press.

MacCormack, Geoffrey. (1971) Roman and African Litigation. *Tijdschrift voor Rechtsgeschiedenis* 39: 221–55.

Mäding, Klaus. (1967) Suzerainty over Annam. A Legal Discussion of China's Traditional Concept *in* F. S. Drake (ed.), *Historical, Archaeological & Linguistic Studies*: 150–2. Hong Kong: Hong Kong University Press.

Maine, Sir Henry. (1861) *Ancient Law.* London: Murray. (Edition published in the Everyman Series by J. M. Dent & Sons, 1917).

—— (1875) *Lectures on the early history of institutions.* London: John Murray.

—— (1883) *Dissertations on early law and custom.* London: John Murray.

—— (1895) *Village Communities in the East and West* 7th ed. London: John Murray.

Majul, Cesar Adib. (1973) *Muslims in the Philippines.* Quezon City, Philippines: published for the Asian Centre by the University of Philippines Press.

Majumdar, R. C. (1930) *Ancient Indian Colonies in the Far East—I Champa.* Lahore: Punjab Sanskrit Book Depot.

Malström, Å. (1969) Systems of Legal Systems. *Scandinavian Studies in Law* 13: 129–49.

Marrison, G. E. (1951) The Coming of Islam to the East Indies. *Journal of the Royal Asiatic Society—Malayan Branch* 24: (1) 28–37.

Masao, T. (1905) Researches into Indigenous Law of Siam as a Study of Comparative Jurisprudence. *Journal of the Siam Society* 2: (1) 14–18; *Yale Law Journal* 15: 28–32.

—— (1908) The New Penal Code of Siam. *J. Siam Society* 5: (2) 1–14. (1908–9) *Yale Law Journal* 18: 85–100.

MASSE, FLEURY. (1941) *De quelques institutions propres à la famille annamite*. Paris: Recueil Sirey.

MAUNG HTIN AUNG. (1962) *Burmese Law Tales*. London: Oxford University Press.

MAUNG KYIN SWI. (1966) The Origin and Development of the Dhammathats. *Journal of the Burma Research Society* 49: 173–205.

MAUNG MAUNG. (1961) *Burma's Constitution*. The Hague: Martinus Nijhoff.

—— (1963) *Law & Custom in Burma and the Burmese Family*. The Hague: Nijhoff.

MAUNG TET PYO. (1884) *Customary Law of the Chin Tribe*. Rangoon: Govt. Press.

MAXWELL, Sir PETER BENSON (1859) The Law of England in Penang, Malacca and Singapore. *Journal of the Indian Archipelago and East Asia* N.S. 3: 26–55.

MAXWELL, W. E. (1884) The Law and Customs of the Malays with Reference to the Tenure of Land. *Journal of the Royal Asiatic Society—Straits Branch* 13: 75–220.

MAXWELL, W. G. & GIBSON, W. S. (1924) *Treaties and Engagements Affecting the Malay States and Borneo*. London: J. Truscott.

MAYNE, J. D. (1885) Review of the Patriarchal Theory by J. F. McLennan. *Law Quarterly Review* 1: 485–95.

—— (1887) Hindu Law in Madras. *Law Quarterly Review* 3: 446–59.

MILLS, L. A. (1960) British Malaya. *Journal of the Royal Asiatic Society—Malayan Branch* 33: (3).

MOCHTAR NAIM (ed.). (1968) *Menggali Hukum Tanah dan Hukum Waris Minangkabau*. Padang: Center for Minangkabau Studies Press.

MOERTONO, SOEMARSAID. (1963) *State and Statecraft in Old Java*. Ithaca: Cornell Modern Indonesia Project.

MOHAMED EL-AWA. (1973) The Place of Custom (*'Urf*) in Islamic Legal Theory. *Islamic Quarterly* 17: 177–82.

MOORE, CHARLES A. (ed.) (1968) *The Status of the Individual in East & West*. Honolulu: University of Hawaii Press.

MOORE, SALLY F. (1969) 'Introduction" to 'Comparative Studies' *in* Laura Nader (ed.), *Law in Culture and Society*: 337–48. Chicago: Aldine Press.

MOOTHAM, O. H. (1939) *Burmese Buddhist Law*. London: Oxford University Press.

Bibliography 255

MORCHÉ, H. (1931) Organisation judicaire de l'Indochine *in* H. Morché *et al.*, *La Justice en Indochine*: 9–38. Hanoi: Imprimerie d'Extrême-Orient.

—— *et al.* (1931a) *La Justice en Indochine*. Hanoi: Imprimerie d'Extrême-Orient.

MOREL, P. (1970) Aperçus sur la constitution du Laos. *Revue Juridique et Politique, Indépendance et Coopération* 24: 65–80.

MORELAND, W. H. (1920) The Shahbandar in the Eastern Seas. *Journal of the Royal Asiatic Society*: 517–33.

MOYER, DAVID SPENCER. (1975) *The Logic of the Laws: A Structural Analysis of Malay Language Legal Codes from Bengkulu*. The Hague: B.V. De Nederlandsche Boek-en Steendrukkerij V/H L. Smits.

SYED MUHAMMAD NAGUIB AL-ATTAS. (1972) *Islam dalam Sejarah dan Kebudayaan Melayu*. Kuala Lumpur: Penerbit Universiti Kebangsaan Malaysia.

MULDER, J. A. NIELS. (1970) A Comparative Note on the Thai and the Javanese Worldview as expressed by Religious Practice & Belief. *Journal of the Siam Society* 58: (2) 79–85.

MUSTAFFA TAM. (1960) The Last Kedah Bunga Mas. *Malaya in History* 6: (i) 42–3.

MYA SEIN, Daw. (1973) *The Administration of Burma*. Kuala Lumpur: Oxford University Press (Oxford in Asia Historical Reprints). .

NAPIER, WALTER. (1869[?]) *Independence of the Judges in the Straits Settlements*. London: W. Dawson & Sons.

—— 1898 *Introduction to the Study of the Law Administered in Colony of the Straits Settlements*. Singapore: Fraser & Neave, reprinted in (1974) *Malaya Law Review* 16: (1) 1–51.

NASROEN, M. (1957) *Dasar Falfsafah Adat Minangkabau*. Djakarta: Bulan Bintang.

NEDERBURGH, I. A. (1933) *Hoofdstukken over Adatrecht...* 'S-Gravenhague: N. V. Boekhandel vh. Gebr. Belinfante.

NER, MARCEL. (1941) Les Musulmans de l'Indochine française. *B.É.F.E.O.* 41: 151–200.

NEWBOLD, T. J. (1839) *British Settlements in the Straits of Malacca*. 2 vols. London: John Murray.

NGUYEN, VAN KHUONG-HOAI (1975) 'Assimilating the Distant Lands in the Administrative Statutes and Precedents of Dai-Nam'. Unpublished M.A. dissertation, University of Kent at Canterbury, South East Asian Studies.

NGUYEN, XUAN CHANH. (1968) The Widow's Statute in Vietnamese Customary Law *in* Buxbaum (ed.), *Family Law and Customary Law in Asia*: 252–61. The Hague: Martinus Nijhoff.

NGUYÊN-AÎ-QUÔC. (1946) *Le Procès de la colonisation française*. Hanoi: Vietnam Quoc Gia Awn Thu Cuc.
NGUYEN-HUY-LAI. (1934) *Les Régimes matrimoniaux en droit annamite*. Paris: Les Éditions Domat Montchrestien.
NGUYEN, NHU DUNG, (1966) Vietnamese Law. *Quarterly Journal of the Library of Congress* 23: 337-9.
NICHOLAS, L. P. (1931) Le Cambodge *in* H. Morché *et al.*, *La Justice en Indochine*: 113-54. Hanoi: Imprimerie d'Extrême-Orient.
Nimmanahaeminda, Kraisri. (1965) The Irrigation Laws of King Mengrai *in* L. M. Hanks *et al.* (eds.), *Ethnographic Notes on Northern Thailand*: 1-5. Ithaca: Cornell University Southeast Asia Programme Data Paper No. 58.
NOORDUYN, J. (1956) De Islamerising van Makasar. *Bijdragen tot de Taal- land- en Volkenkunde* 112: 247-66.
NORODOM KANTOL. (1956) Comments on the Law and Practice in Cambodia *in Studies in the Law of the Far-East and Southeast Asia*: 75-83. Washington, D.C.: Foreign Law Society.
NORTHROP, F. S. C. (1960) The Comparative Philosophy of Comparative Law. *Cornell Law Quarterly* 45: 617-58.
NORTON KYSHE, J. W. (1969) A Judicial History of the Straits Settlements. *Malaya Law Review* 11: (1) 38-179; reprinted from J. W. Norton Kyshe (1890) *Cases Heard and Determined in Her Majesty's Supreme Court of the Straits Settlements 1808-1884 with a Judical and Historical Preface 1786-1885 (vol. 1) in Four Volumes*. Singapore: Singapore and Straits Printing Office.
OSBORNE, MILTON E. (1969) *The French Presence in Cochinchina and Cambodia*. Ithaca: Cornell University Press.
—— (1969a) The Debate on a Legal Code for Colonial Cochin China. *Journal of South-east Asian History* 10: (2) 224-35.
OVERBECK, H. (1926) Malay Manuscripts. *Journal of the Royal Asiatic Society—Malayan Branch* 4: (2) 233-59.
PADOUX, GEORGES. (1909) *Code pénal du Royaume de Siam*. Paris: Imprimerie Nationale.
PALMA, FELICIANO M. Jnr. (1965) 'A Comparative Study of Wills in Canon Law and in the Civil Code of the Philippines'. The Catholic University of America. Unpublished J.C.D. dissertation.
PETIT, E. (1894) *Organisation des colonies françaises et des Pays de Protectorat*. 2 vols. Paris: Berger-Levrault.
PHAM HUY TY. (1956) Law and Society in Vietnam *in*: *Studies in the Law of the Far East and Southeast Asia*: 70-4. Washington, D.C.: The Washington Foreign Law Society.
PHAN THI DAC. (1966) *Situation de la personne au Viet-Nam*. Paris: Éditions du Centre National de la Recherche Scientifique.

PHELAN, JOHN L. (1957) Some Ideological Aspects of the Conquests of the Philippines. *The Americas* 13: 221–39.
—— (1967) *The Hispanization of the Philippines.* Madison: University of Wisconsin Press.
PHILASTRE, P.-L.-F. (1876) *Le Code annamite.* 2 vols. Paris: Ernest Leroux.
PHY-THIEN-LAY & ALLAIRE, F. (1969) Organisation judicaire cambodgienne en matière civile. *Revue Juridique et Politique, Indépendance et Coopération* 23: 633–40.
PIGEAUD, TH. G. (1967) *The Literature of Java* (3 vols.) The Hague: Martinus Nijhoff.
PIGEAUD, THEODORE G. TH. (1960–2) *Java in the 14th Century: A Study in Cultural History* (3rd ed.). 5 vols. The Hague: Martinus Nijhoff.
POLLOCK, FREDERICK. (1883) *The Land Laws.* London: Macmillan.
POMPEI, P. (1940) Petit précis de procédure pénale annamite. *La Revue Indochinoise* 13: 5–83.
—— (1943) La notion de propriété foncière au Cambodge. *La Revue Indochinoise* 19: 430–48.
POST, ALBERT HERMANN. (1891) Ethnological Jurisprudence. *Monist* 2: 31–40.
—— (1894–5) *Grundriss der ethnologischen Jurisprudenz.* 2 vols. Leipzig: Schulzesche Hof-Buchhandlung und Hof-Buchdruckeri.
POUND, ROSCOE. (1921) *The Spirit of the Common Law.* Boston, Mass.: Beacon Press (reprint 1963).
POUYANNE, MAURICE-ALEXANDRE. (1895) *La Propriété foncière en Algérie.* Paris: Édouard Duchemin.
PRINS, JAN. (1954) *Adat en Islamietische Plichtenleer in Indonesië.* The Hague: W. van Hoeve.
—— (1973) *Pengaruh Kristen Terhadap Hukum Adat.* Djakarta: Bhratara.
PROSTERMAN, ROY L. (1967) Land Reform in South Vietnam: A proposal for turning the tables on the Viet Cong. *Cornell Law Quarterly* 53: 26–44.
PRUNIÈRES, BERNARD. (1970) L'Organisation des jurisdictions administratives au Cambodge. *Revue Juridique et Politique, Indépendance et Coopération* 24: 81–92.
PUGH, G. W. (1965) Aspects of the Administration of Justice in the Philippines. *Louisiana Law Review* 26: 1–24.
PURI, BAJ NATH. (1956) Administrative System of the Kambuja Rulers. *Journal of the Greater India Society* 15: (1) 60–70.
QUARITCH WALES, H. G. (1934) *Ancient Siamese Government and Administration.* London: Bernard Quaritch.

258 *Bibliography*

RABIBHADANA, AKIN. (1969) *The Organization of Thai Society in the early Bangkok Period 1782–1873*. Ithaca, N.Y.: Cornell University, Dept. of Asian Studies, data paper number 74.
RAFFLES, Sir THOMAS S. (1817) *The History of Java*. Kuala Lumpur: Oxford University Press, Historical Reprint 1965.
RAJAH, K. S. (1974) The Women's Charter and Customary Marriages. *Malayan Law Journal*: xlvi–lv.
RAS, J. J. (1968) *Hikayat Bandjar*. The Hague: Martinus Nijhoff.
RAZ, J. (1970) *The Concept of a Legal System*. Oxford: The Clarendon Press.
REALE, MIGUEL. (1968) Legal Status of Individuals *in* C. A. Moore (ed.), *The Status of the Individual in East and West*: 449–52. Honolulu: University of Hawaii Press.
'Regulations of Prince of Wales Island, Singapore and Malacca 1825–1833.' (1971) *Malaya Law Review* 13: (2) 294–400.
REYES, JOSE. (1975) Reflections on the Reform of Hereditary Succession. *Philippine Law Journal* 50: 277–93.
RHYS DAVIDS, T. W. (1932) Buddhist Law. *Encyclopedia of Religion and Ethics* 7: 827–8.
RICHARDS, A. J. N. (1961) *Land Law and Adat*. Government of Sarawak: Printed by Order of the Chief Secretary.
—— (1963) *Dayak Adat Law in the Second Division*. Government of Sarawak: Printed by Order of the Chief Secretary.
—— (1964) *Dayak Adat Law in the First Division*. Government of Sarawak: Printed by Order of the Chief Secretary.
RICHARDSON, D. (1896) *The Damathat or the Laws of Menoo* (1st ed. 1847; 4th ed.) Rangoon: Hanthawaddy Press.
RICKETT, W. ALLYN. (1971) Voluntary Surrender and Confession in Chinese Law: The Problem of Continuity. *Journal of Asian Studies* 30: 797–814.
RICKLEFFS, M. C. (1967) Land and Law in the Epigraphy of Tenth-Century Cambodia. *Journal of Asian Studies* 26: (3) 411–20.
RIGBY, J. (1908) The Ninety Nine Laws of Perak *in* R. J. Wilkinson (ed.), *Papers on Malay Subjects—Law Part II*: 1–88. Kuala Lumpur: Govt. Printer.
RIGG, A. E. (1931) The Buddhist Law of Succession in Burma. *Journal of Comparative Legislation & International Law* 13 (ser. 3): 43–55.
ROBERTSON, JAMES ALEXANDER. (1917) The Social Structure of, and idea of law among, early Philippine Peoples: and a recently-discovered pre-Hispanic Criminal Code of the Philippine Islands *in* H. M. Stephens & H. E. Bolton (eds.), *The Pacific Ocean in History*: 160–91. New York: Macmillan & Co.

ROBERTSON, JAMES ALEXANDER. (1917) The Social Structure of, and idea of law among, early Philippine Peoples: and a recently-discovered pre-Hispanic Criminal Code of the Philippine Islands *in* H. M. Stephens & H. E. Bolton (eds.), *The Pacific Ocean in History*: 160–91. New York: Macmillan & Co.

ROMANI, J. H. (1956) The Philippine barrio. *Far Eastern Quarterly* 15: 229–37.

SABATIER, LÉOPOLD (ed.). (1940) *Recueil des coutumes rhadées du Darlac*. Hanoi: Imprimerie d'Extrême-Orient.

SABER, MAMITUA DESARIP. (1967) 'The Transition from a Traditional to a Legal Authority System: A Philippine Case'. University of Kansas. Unpublished Ph.D. Dissertation.

SADDAM, A. S. & BALBASTRO, F. R. (1962) Land Registration. *Philippine Law Journal* 37: 99–119.

SAHAI, SACHCHIDANAND. (1970) *Les Institutions politiques et l'organisation administrative du Cambodge ancien VI–XIII siècles*. Paris: Publications de L'Ecole Française d'Extrême-Orient (vol. LXXV).

SAINT-HUBERT, CHRISTIAN DE. (1965) Rolin Jaequemyns (Chao Phya Aphay Raja) and the Belgian Legal Advisers in Siam at the Turn of the Century. *Journal of the Siam Society* 53: (2) 181–90.

SALACUSE, JESWALD W. (1969) *An Introduction to Law in French-Speaking Africa*. Charlottesville, Va.: The Michie Company.

SALEEBY, N. (1905) *Studies in Moro History, Law and Religion*. Manila: Bureau of Public Printing.

SANDHU, KERNIAL SINGH. (1973) *Early Malaysia*. Singapore: University Education Press.

SAVIGNY, FREIDRICH KARL VON. (1814) *On the Vocation of our Age for Legislation and Jurisprudence* (trans. A. Hayward, 1831). London: Littlewood & Co.

SAYRE, FRANCIS B. (1928) The Passing of Extraterritoriality in Siam. *American Journal of International Law* 22: 70–88.

SCHACHT, JOSEPH. (1953) *The Origins of Muhammadan Jurisprudence* (2nd ed.). Oxford: The Clarendon Press.

—— (1964) *An Introduction to Islamic Law*. Oxford: The Clarendon Press.

SCHILLER, A. A. (1942–3) Conflict of Laws in Indonesia. *Far Eastern Quarterly* 2: 31–47.

SCHLEGEL, STUART A. (1970) *Tiruray Justice*. Berkeley, Calif.: University of California Press.

SCHREINER, ALFRED. (1900) *Les Institutions annamites en Basse-Cochinchine avant la conquête française* 3 vols. Saigon: Claude & Cie.

SCHRIEKE, B. (1957) *Indonesian Sociological Studies, Part II: Ruler & Realm in Early Java*. The Hague, Bandung: W. van Hoeve.
SCHULZ, FRITZ. (1946) *History of Roman Legal Science*. Oxford: The Clarendon Press.
SCOTT, JAMES B. (1934) *The Spanish Origin of International Law*. Oxford: The Clarendon Press.
SENI PRAMOJ, M. R. (1950) King Mongkut as a Legislator. *Journal of the Siam Society* 38: (1) 32–66.
SHWE BAW. U. (1955) 'The Origin and Development of Burmese Legal Literature'. University of London: Institute of Advanced Legal Studies. Unpublished Ph.D. thesis.
SIBULO, E. A. (1974) Islamic laws of Marriage and Divorce as affected by Philippine Legislation. *Philippine Law Journal* 49: 406–20.
SIEUV, SAPHON. (1972) Étude de la liquidation successorale en droit Khmer. *Revue Juridique et Politique, Indépendance et Coopération* 26: 985–96.
SIMPSON, A. W. B. (1973) The Common Law and Legal Theory *in* Simpson (ed.), *Oxford Essays in Jurisprudence*: 77–99. Oxford: The Clarendon Press.
SIMPSON, LESLYE B. (1950) *The Encomienda in New Spain*. Berkeley, Calif.: University of California Press.
SINGARAVELU, S. (1968) A Comparative Study of the Sanskrit, Tamil, Thai & Malay Versions of the story of Rāma with special reference to the process of Acculturation in the Southeast Aisan versions. *Journal of the Siam Society* 56: (2) 137–85.
SINHA, C. (1973) Evolution of the Judicial Administration in British Burma 1826–1922. *Journal of the Indian Law Institute* 15: 295–300.
SLAMETMULJANA. (1967) *Per-Undang2-an Madjapahit*. Djakarta: Bhratara.
SMITH, HAROLD E. (1973) Polygyny and Marriage Registration in Thailand. *Southeast Asia* 2: (3) 291–9.
—— (1973a) The Thai Family: Nuclear or Extended. *Journal of Marriage & the Family* 35: (1) 136–41.
SMITH, SAMUEL J. (1880) *Siamese Domestic Institutions, Old and New Laws on Slavery*. Bangkok: Printed at S. J. Smith's Office.
SNOUCK HURGRONJE, C. (1893) *De Atjehers* 2 vols. Leiden: E. J. Brill.
SOLUS, H. (1927) *Traité de la condition des indigènes en droit privé*. Paris: Sirey.
STAUNTON, Sir GEORGE THOMAS. (1810) *Ta Tsing Leu Lee*. London: T. Cadell & W. Davies.

SUBEKTI, R. & TAMARA, J. (1965) *Kumpulan putusan Mahkamah Agung mengenai Hukum Adat*. Djakarta: Gunung Agung.

SULLANO, MAGDALENA. (1972) 'A Study of the Land Problems of our Indigenous Ethnic Communities'. Manila, University of Santo Tomas: unpublished Ph.D. dissertation.

SURYADHAY, I. (1969) Organisation judicaire en matière civile au Laos. *Revue Juridique et Politique, Indépendance et Coopération* 23: 641-8.

—— *et al.* (1970) Propriété foncière selon les pratiques coutumiéres lao. *Revue Juridique et Politique, Indépendance et Coopération* 24: 1215-22.

TABOULET, GEORGES. (1955) *La Geste française en Indochine.* Paris: Adrienne Maisonneuve.

TAYLOR, E. N. (1937) Malay Family Law. *Journal of the Royal Asiatic Society—Malayan Branch* 15: (1) 1-78.

—— (1948) Mohammedan Divorce by Khula. *Journal of the Royal Asiatic Society—Malayan Branch* 21: (2) 3-39.

TER HAAR, B. (1929) *Het Adatprivaatrecht van Nederlandsch Indië in Wetenschap, Practijk en Onderwijs*. Batavia: J. B. Wolters.

—— (1948) *Adat Law in Indonesia* (trans. Haas & Hordyk). New York: Institute of Pacific Relations.

THOMPSON, VIRGINEA MCLEAN. (1942) *French Indo-China*. New York: McMillan & Co.

THORNELY, P. W. (1923) *The History of a Transition*. Bangkok: Siam Observer Press.

TOMOSUGI, TAKASHI. (1969) The Land System in Central Thailand. *The Developing Economies* 7: 284-309.

TRAN-CHANH-THANH. (1942) Statut politique et juridique des Plateaux Mois du Sud-Annam. *La Revue Indochinoise* 17: 118-32.

—— (1943) Organisation actuelle et compétance des jurisdictions mandarinales de l'Annam. *La Revue Indochinoise* 19: 449-502.

TRAN-VAN-TRAI. (1942) *La Famille patriarcale annamite*. Paris: P. Lapagesse.

TRINH DINH TIEU. (1961) Adoption dans la loi vietnamienne du 2 janvier 1959 'sur la famille'. *Revue Internationale de Droit Comparé* 13: 602-15.

UTRECHT, E. (1955) Resepsi Hukum Belanda. *Hukum dan Masjarakat* 1: (2) 6-27.

—— (1959) *Pengantar dalam Hukum Indonesia*. Djakarta: Ichtiar.

VANDENBOSCH, A. (1932) Customary Law in the Dutch East Indies. *Journal of Comparative Legislation and International Law* (3rd ser.) 14: 30-44.

VAN DER MEULEN, J. C. (1924) *Het Adatrecht der Inlanders in de Jurisprudentie 1912–1923*. Leiden: E. J. Brill.
VAN DER SPRENKEL, O. (1964) Max Weber on China. *History & Theory* 3: 348–70.
VAN DER SPRENKEL, SYBILLE. (1966) *Legal Institutions in Manchu China*. London: The Athlone Press.
VAN-HÔ-LÊ. (1932) *La Mère de famille annamite*. Paris: Éditions Domat-Montchrestien.
VAN LEUR, J. C. (1967) *Indonesian Trade and Society*. The Hague: W. van Hoeve.
VAN NAERSSEN, F. H. (1933) De Saptopapatti: Naar Aanleiding van een tekstverbetering in den Nagarakrtagama. *Bijdragen tot de Taal-, Land- en Volkenkunde* 90: 239–58.
—— (1956) The Aṣṭādaçavyavahâra in Old Javanese. *Journal of the Greater Indian Society* 15: (2) 111–132.
VAN NIEL, R. (1964) The function of land rent under the cultivation system in Java. *Journal of Asian Studies* 23: 357–76.
VAN RONKEL, PH. S. (1919) *Risalat Hoekdem Kanoen*. Leiden: E. J. Brill.
—— (1921) *Maleische en Minangkabausche Handschriften Leidsche Universiteits, Supplement—Catalogus—Bibliotheek*. Leiden: E. J. Brill.
VANSINA, JAN. (1965) *Oral Tradition*. London: Routledge & Kegan Paul.
VAN VOLLENHOVEN, C. (1918) *Het Adatrecht van Nederlandsch Indië*, vol. I. Leiden: E. J. Brill.
—— (1919) The Study of Indonesian Customary Law. *Illinois Law Review* 13: 58–62.
—— (1921) Families of Language and Families of Law. *Illinois Law Review* 15: 417–23.
—— (1931) *Het Adatrecht van Nederlandsch Indië*, vol. II. Leiden: E. J. Brill.
—— (1933) *Het Adatrecht van Nederlandsch Indië*, vol. III. Leiden: E. J. Brill.
VARASIRI, S. (1929) 'La Succession ab intestat dans le droit siamois'. Unpublished thèse, Faculté de Droit, Université de Poitiers.
VINOGRADOFF, PAUL. (1920) *Outlines of Historical Jurisprudence*. 2 vols. London: Oxford University Press.
—— (1925) *Custom and Right*. Oslo: Institutt för Sammenlignende Kulturforskring.
VON WRIGHT, G. H. (1963) *Norm and Action*. London: Routledge & Kegan Paul.
VORACHACK, P. (1972) Dévolution successorale en droit lao. *Revue Juridique et Politique, Indépendance et Coopération* 26: 997–1012.

VREEDE, F. (1941) Hindu Tradition and Islamic Culture in Javanese Civilization. *Journal of the University of Bombay* 9 N.S.: (4) 127–36.

VU VAN HIEN. (1940) Les Institutions annamites depuis l'arrivée des Français. *La Revue Indochinoise* 13: 84–107.

VU-VAN-MAU. (1940) Le Dien Mai et le nantissement immobilier dans le droit annamite moderne. *La Revue Indochinoise* 14: 259–86.

—— (1964) The Humanistic Conception of Law or the Conception of Law in the Countries of the Far-East before the impact of Western Ideas. *Revue Asienne de Droit Comparé* 2: 274–97.

WAGENER, J. H. (1932) *De Verhouding tusschen het Nederlandsche en het Nederlandsche-Indisch Privaatrecht*. Utrecht: Lekkerkerk.

WAKE, CHRISTOPHER. (1964) Malacca's Early Kings and the Reception of Islam. *Journal of South-east Asian History* 5: (2) 104–28.

WAN IBRAHIM. (1968) Senior Titular Chiefs and their Functions in the Courts of Malay Sultans. *Kedah in History* 3: (1) 22–6.

WANG GUNGWU. (1960) An Early Chinese Visitor to Kelantan. *Malaya in History* 6: (1) 31–5.

WATT, JOHN R. (1972) *The District Magistrate in Late Imperial China*. New York: Columbia University Press.

WEBER, MAX. (1966) *Max Weber on Law and Economy in Society*, trans. from *Wirtschaft & Gesellschaft* by Shils, ed. Rheinstein. Cambridge, Mass.: Harvard University Press.

WEE, KENNETH K. S. (1972) Customary Marriages and the Women's Charter. *Malaya Law Review* 14: (1) 93–102.

—— (1973) Chinese Law and Malayan Society. *Malaya Law Review* 15: (1) 110–13.

—— (1974) English Law and Chinese Family Custom in Singapore. *Malaya Law Review* 16: (1) 52–82.

WENK, KLAUS. (1968) *The Restoration of Thailand under Rama I*. Tucson: The University of Arizona Press for the Assoc. of Asian Studies.

WERNSTEDT, FREDERICK L. & SPENCER, J. E. (1967) *The Philippine Island World*. Berkeley, Calif.: University of California Press.

WHITMORE, JOHN K. (1969) Vietnamese Adaptations to Chinese Government Structure in the Fifteenth Century *in* E. Wickberg (comp.), *Historical Interaction of China and Vietnam*: 1–10. University of Kansas Center for East Asian Studies, Research Publication No. 4.

WICHIENCHAROEN, A. & LUANG CHAMROON NETISASTRA (1968) Some main features of modernization of Ancient Family Law in Thailand *in* Buxbaum (ed.), *Family Law and Customary Law in Asia*: 89–106. The Hague: Nijhoff.

WICKBERG, EDGAR (comp.). (1969) *Historical Interaction of China and Vietnam: Institutional and Cultural Themes*. The University of Kansas: Center for East Asian Studies.

WIDJOJOATMODJO, R. A. (1942–3) Islam in the Netherlands East Indies. *Far Eastern Quarterly* 2: 48–57.

WILKINSON, R. J. (1908) Malay Law *in* Wilkinson (ed.), *Papers on Malay Subjects—Law*: 1–45. Kuala Lumpur: Government Printer.

WILLINCK, G. D. (1909) *Het Rechtsleven der Minangkabause Maleiers*. Leiden: E. J. Brill.

WINSTEDT, R. O. (1923) A Brunei Code. *Journal of the Royal Asiatic Society—Malayan Branch* 1: 251.

—— (1928) Kedah Laws. *Journal of the Royal Asiatic Society—Malayan Branch* 6: (2) 1–44.

—— (1947) Kingship and Enthronement in Malaya. *Journal of the Royal Asiatic Society—Malayan Branch* 20: (1) 129–42.

—— (1947a) *The Malays: A Cultural History*. Singapore: Kelly & Walsh.

—— (1953) An Old Minangkabau Legal Digest from Perak. *Journal of the Royal Asiatic Society—Malayan Branch* 26: (1) 1–13.

—— (1953a) The date of the Malacca Legal Codes. *Journal of the Royal Asiatic Society*: 31–3.

—— & P. E. DE JOSSELIN DE JONG. (1954) Undang2 Sungei Ujong. *Journal of the Royal Asiatic Society—Malayan Branch* 27: Part 3.

—— —— (1956) The Maritime Laws of Malacca. *Journal of the Royal Asiatic Society—Malayan Branch* 29: (3) 22–59.

—— & Wilkinson, R. J. (1934) *A History of Perak*. Singapore: Printers Ltd.

WIRJONO PRODJODIKORO. (n.d.) *Hukum Antargolongan de Indonesia*. Bandung: Sumur Bandung.

WITHERS PAYNE, C. H. (1932) *The Law of Administration of and Succession to Estates in the Straits Settlements*. Singapore: Printers Ltd.

WOLTERS, O. W. (1967) *Early Indonesian Commerce: A Study of the Origins of Srivijaya*. Ithaca, N.Y.: Cornell University Press.

—— (1969) Ayudhā and the Rearward Part of the World. *Journal of the Royal Asiatic Society*: 166–78.

—— (1970) *The Fall of Srivijaya in Malay History*. Ithaca, N.Y.: Cornell University Press.

WONG, S. Y. (1973) *Jual Janji* transactions—a question of Recognition and Equitable Intervention. *Malaya Law Review* 15: (1) 27–38.

WOODSIDE, A. B. (1971) *Vietnam and the Chinese Model*. Cambridge Mass.: Harvard University Press.

YANO, TORU. (1968) Land Tenure in Thailand. *Asian Survey* 8: (10) 853–63.

YOUNG, STEPHEN B. (1976) The Law of Property and Elite Prerogatives during Vietnam's Lê Dynasty, 1428–1788. *Journal of Asian History* 10: (1) 1–48.

YOURAN, C. (1967) Conditions de la femme dans l'ancien droit Khmer et à l'époque angkorienne. *Revue Juridique et Politique, Indépendance et Coopération* 21: 170–3.

—— & PFISTER, A. (1969) Statut de la magistrature au Cambodge. *Revue Juridique et Politique, Indépendance et Coopération* 23: 1197–1202.

Index

ABDUCTION, 26.
Abdul al-Ghafur, Sultan of Pahang (1592–1614), 52.
Abendanon, J. H., 200.
Aborigines in Perak, 57–8.
Abusive language, 87.
Accusations, 75; false, 75, 86, 87, 88, 90; unfilial, 91.
Adat (customary law): to be written down in Dutch Indies, 4, 193, 197; and contract, 36, 210; in Java, 36, 49; modern Indonesian, 44; in conflict with Islamic law, 49, 61–2, 112–13, 149–50; contains public and private law, 50; land tenure in, 50, 196, 207; property in, 50, 66; in Negri Sembilan, 60: *adat* Minangkabau, 61–2, 212; Malay *adat*, 66, 135, 140; Malacca statutory *adat*, 67, 136–7; in Sulu, 70; in Dutch Indies, 187, 189–91, 195; defined, 192–3; *adatrecht*, 192; subordinate to Dutch law, 193; modified by Dutch law, 195, 196–7; and Indonesians' submission to European law, 198; 'inferior' to European law, 199, 201; in conflict with European law, 200; varies throughout Dutch Indies, 203; has no internal conflict, 203; non-interference with, 204; a normative system, 205; and interracial law, 206; and choice of law, 208; and Christianity, 211.
'Adat Law School', 189, 192.
Administration of justice: in Singapore, 126; in Cochin-China, 156; in Laos, 162; in Annam, 169, 170, 171; in villages in Dutch Indies, 190 (*see also* Legal administration).
Administrative system and the law, 12; in Vietnam, 73, 82; in Code of Manu, 100; Burma under British Indian, 143; in Cochin-China, 158; in Annam, 171; in Dutch Indies, 187–8, 189, 192, 194, 197, 203–4; in Philippines, (a) Spanish, 214, 215, 217, (b) American, 214, 229.
Administrative units: family, in Vietnam, 83, 92; village, in Dutch Indies, 188; *barrio*, in Philippines, 237.
Adoption, 21, 107, 110, 159, 231; contract of, 164, 180.
Adultery: Burmese law on, 20; in *Âgama*, 42, 43, 44; in Malacca Digest, 63, 66; in *Hông Đưˊc* Code, 77; in *Gia-Long* Code, 88; Sarawak, 142.
Advocates, 156, 159.
Affray, 86.
Âgama, 39–46.
Agriculture, 38, 53, 58, 60, 74, 78, 112, 191, 238; offences against, 83.
Ahmad Taju'd-din Halim Shah, Sultan of Kedah (1803–43), 57–8, 59.
Alcaldes-majores in Philippines, 217, 223.
Alcohol, 56.
Amangkurat IV, King of Jogjakarta (1719–24), 72.
Ambassadors and envoys, 75, 76.
Ambon, 195.
American law in the Philippines, 6, 214, 224–8, 236, 238.
Ancestors: obligations to, 19, 114; Vietnamese Rulers' links with, 74.
Anderson, Benedict R. O'G., 103.
Anglo-American law, 231, 233, 234, 236.
Anglo-Burmese law, 22.
Annam: formerly a vassal of China, 94; a French protectorate, 154, 166, 169, 171, 175; legal system in, 168–72, 179; has its own laws till 1930, 168; indigenous tribunals in 169–71, 180; Annamite Chain, 171; Annamite law, 177, 178, 179.
'Annamite', generic term for 'Indo-Chinese', 156, 158, 160, 177.
Annamite Code, *see Gia-Long* Code.
Annamites: choice of law, 157; and marriage with French citizens, 176; status

268 Index

Annamites, contd.
 of, 177; jurisdiction over, 178–9, 181, 182.
Annulment: of court decisions, 157, 160, 162; in police matters, 159; of marriage, 229.
Antichresis, 236.
Apostasy, 54.
Appeals, 25; in *Phra Thammasat*, 27; groundless, 88; in *Gia Long* Code, 89; from guilds' orders, 116; in F.M.S., 139; to Privy Council, 139, 143; in Cochin-China, 154, 157, 160; in Laos, 161, 162; in Tonkin, 172; in Indo-China, 174; in Philippines, 222, 223.
Arabia, 68, 69; Arabs in Dutch Indies, 194.
Archer, William J., 31.
Argentine, Philippines take laws from, 228.
Arminjon, Pierre, 200.
Arrests, 88.
Asia Minor, Islam in, 111.
Asians, 155; *Asiatiques assimilés* (i.e. Chinese), 155, 157, 178, 179, 182.
Assault, 41, 42, 70, 107, 163.
Assessors, 155, 162, 164.
Assimilated persons (assimilés) in Indo-China: *Asiatiques assimilés* (i.e. Chinese), 155, 157, 178, 179, 182; under jurisdiction of indigenous tribunals in Cochin-China, 155, 156, 182; amenable to French law, 157, 158, 176, 180; Cambodian, 177, 178, 181, 182.
Assimilated persons in Dutch Indies, 9, 187.
Aubaret, G., 174.
Audiencia real, 219, 220, 222–4, 228.
Ayut'ia, 25, 26, 27, 28, 29.
BAD FAITH, 232.
Bahnar 'code', 4.
Bali Island, 35, 38, 39, 47.
Bangkok, 184.
Banishment, 20, 34, 167, 215.
Banks in Dutch Indies, 196, 209.
Batavia, 200.
Beating, as a punishment, 56, 84, 88, 90, 115, 174 (*see also* Caning: Flogging: Whipping).
Bees, ownership of, 232.
Belgian law and Thailand, 183, 184.
Bhavavarman I, King of Champa and Cambodia (acceded 550), 33.

Bocobo, Hon. Jorge, 227.
Bondmen, 55.
Bondsmen, 30, 37, 65, 66.
Borneo, in Malaysia, 48.
Borneo territories, 123, 141–3.
Boromakot, King of Ayut'ia (1733–58), 29.
Borrowing: of money, 64, 65, 66; of culture, 4–5, 73, 78, 95–6.
Braddell, Sir Roland St. J., 131–2, 138.
Brahmins, 20, 24, 29, 31, 34, 99, 110.
Breach of contract, 81, 83, 235; breach of promise, 133.
B<u>r</u>haspati legal text, 109.
Bribery and corruption, 87.
Bride-price, 45–6, 219.
British: and Penang, 124; and Singapore, 126; and Malacca, 127; Unfederated Malay States ceded to, 138.
British Colonial Office, 129, 139.
British colonies, 8, 70; colonial system, 23, 96, 124, 147.
British India, 96, 97, 127, 143 (*see also* India).
British North Borneo, 6, 123, 141–3.
British Residents, 138, 139, 142.
Brothers, Chinese relationship between, 107.
Brunei, 142; Brunei Code, 49, 51.
Buddha, 18, 102.
Buddhism: and law, 17–32, 96, 143–4; 'Burmese Buddhist law', 21–3, 96–7, 150–2; Hinduism and, 23–4, 101–2; in Siam, 53; rules governing priests in, 83–4, 88, 146–7.
Buddhists: Burmese, 144, 146, 147, 151–2; and interreligious marriage, 147, 151; Chinese, 151–2.
Bugis people, 58, 67.
Bunga mas (golden flowers) tribute, 54, 55.
Bureaucracy: in Thailand, 28; Vietnamese, 74, 89, 92–3, 98, 153; Chinese, 89, 106, 117; in Indo-China, 153 (*see also* Officials).
Burma, 1; law tales in, 3; Indian-derived law in, 6, 23, 27, 53, 101–2, 143; in English legal world, 6, 22, 123; law of, 17–32, 96, 143–7; 'Burmese Buddhist law', 21–3, 96–7, 150–2; governed from British India, 143; conflict of laws in, 150–1.
Burmese: and Thailand, 25; Buddhists, 144, 146, 147, 151–2.

Index 269

CALIFORNIA, laws of, 228, 232.
Cambodia, 1; a French protectorate, 153–4, 166, 175; legal system in, 166–8, 188; conflict of laws in, 177–8, 179; its jurisdiction over other Annamites, 177, 181; becomes independent, 186 (*see also* Champa and Cambodia).
Cambodians, jurisdiction over, 157, 177, 181–2.
Camels, fines paid with, 53.
Caning, 82, 83, 84, 90.
Canon law: in Philippines, 9, 215, 219, 222, 223, 225, 229, 231, 232; Pali Canon, 25: Buddhist Canon, 28.
Capacity, legal, 151, 179, 230, 236.
Cargo, 55–6; loss of, 64.
Case-law, 123 (*see also* Judicial decisions).
Cassation, 155, 159, 160, 174.
Caste, 99; and status, 10, 20, 42, 118; in legal texts, 19, 20, 42, 110, 111, 118; among Hindus in Burma, 20, 143, 151; in Straits Settlements, 135–6.
Castration, 88.
Cattle trespass, 54.
Cebu, Philippines, 223.
Celebes Islands, 49, 52, 58.
Central Asia, Islam in, 112.
Certiorari, writ of, 237.
Ceylon, Roman-Dutch and English laws in, 238.
Chaining, as a punishment, 74.
Cham community in Indo-China, 181.
Champa and Cambodia, 6, 32–5, 101 (*see also* Cambodia).
Charities, Muslim, 135.
Charles V, King of Spain (1519–56), 221.
Charters: in Java, 37–8, 43; for Straits Settlements, 125–9, 130, 132.
Ch'ên Ch'ung, 108.
Children: divorce and, 20; unseparated, 21; and inheritance, 21, 45, 159, 232; and father's debts, 65; surrender of, 67; punished for father's crime, 75; exempt from torture, 88; homicide of, 90; illegitimate, 159, 199, 211, 215, 232; limit on number of, 215; 'natural children' defined, 220; 'natural children by legal fiction', 229–30; common law concerns welfare of, 231.
China: custom and law in, 73, 114–19: Vietnam influenced by, 73, 92, 93–4; codes in, 74, 185; Vietnam's wars against, 78; Islam in, 112; French

consular courts in, 155; laws of Republic of China benefit Chinese in Indo-China, 183.
Chinese: in Straits Settlements, 129, 131; in F.M.S., 140; in Burma, 147, 151; in Cochin-China, 155, 157; in Indo-China, 178, 179, 180, 182–3; in Dutch Indies, 187, 189, 194; in Indonesia, 208.
Chinese custom, 73, 129, 131, 187.
Chinese law: basis of law in Vietnam, 2, 73, 95, 153; Chinese legal world, 6, 12, 73–94; texts, 73, 74, 76, 80–9, 92, 106, 114, 115, 116–18; family law, 107, 140, 150; non-governmental legal bodies, 114–17; in S. E. Asia, 119; in Straits Settlements, 130–2; marriage in, 130–1, 150; in Malay states, 140–1; in Sarawak, 142, 143; and conflict of laws, 150.
Chinese legal world, 6, 12, 73–94; Chinese-derived law, 1, 2.
Ch'ing Code (*Ta Ch'ing Lü Li*), 76, 80–9, 106, 114, 115, 116–17, 118.
Choice of law, in (a) Indo-China, 155, 172, 180 (b) Dutch Indies, 190, 199, 207–12.
Christianity: morality in, 12; Islam and, 49; and *adat*, 211; established by Spain in Philippines, 217; Spanish, 219, 220, 230.
Christians, 54, 112, 218; and interreligious marriage, 151, 180; Native in (a) Indo-China, 180, (b) Dutch Indies, 187, 194, 195, 211–13; infidels to have same rights as, 194; in mixed marriage, 211–12, 229.
Chulalongkorn (Rama V), King of Thailand (1868–1910), 183.
Citizenship, French, 175–6.
Civil law (i.e. as opposed to criminal); in Java, 35–6; in Vietnam, 78; in *Gia-Long* Code, 82–4, 89; in China, 107; in Cochin-China, 155, 156–7, 158, 177; in Laos, 162, 164, 178; in Cambodia, 167–8, 177; in Tonkin, 173, 174–5; conflict between laws of France and Indo-China, 175–6, 180; in Thailand, 184; in *Keliantiaw* text, 216.
Civil-law legal systems: and *adat*, 4; Roman, 7, 234; French, 8–9; Dutch, 9, 205, 209; Spanish, 9, 231–2; Indo-China is in Civil-law world, 153; only

270　　Index

Civil-law legal systems, contd.
  for Europeans in Dutch Indies, 187; no doctrine of precedent in, 193; banks in, 196; Spanish, in Philippines, 214, 215, 221–2, 226, 231–2, 235–6; Philippines receive most of their law from, 228; contrasted with common-law systems, 238.
Civil rights, 168, 202.
Civil wrongs, in Dutch Indies, 198, 212.
Cleansing of guilt (*patukuçawa*), 43, 44.
Clergy: Buddhist, 27, 84, 88; in Philippines, not amenable to civil courts, 223; lose their prerogatives, 225.
Cochin-China: a French colony, 153–4, 166, 175; legal system in, 154–61; French tribunals in, 155, 157, 182; native law of, 158, 159, 160, 178; and jurisdiction over other 'Annamites', 177–8, 181; conflict of laws in, 178–9.
Cochin-Chinese, jurisdiction over, 157, 182.
Codes: European, 3, 4; in Thailand, 25; Hindu, 101; in Cochin-China, 157–8; in Laos, 162–6; in Vietnam, 181; Spanish, 220–1.
Codification of law: in medieval Thailand, 25; in Laos, 162–3; in Cambodia, 166–8; in Tonkin, 172–3, 175; in modern Thailand, 183–5; delayed in Dutch Indies, 191–2, 201; in Indonesia, 213; in Spain, 221, 222; in Philippines, 228.
Colonialism: legal administration in, 3, 7–9, 23, 73, 124, 147; end of, 14; Spanish, 217, 220; Dutch, 218; U.S. and Philippines, 226.
Colonial laws: and native law, 7; British, 8; cause conflict of laws, 9, 10, 194, 204; exclusiveness in, 10, 13; Dutch legal policy in Indies, 187–94, 201, 206, 209; breed legal pluralism, 200; common law in, 205–6; Spain and, 221.
Colony distinguished from protectorate by French, 154, 175.
Commerce: Maritime Laws and, 62–3; commercial custom, 110; Cochin-China regulates Asian, 158; Dutch, 194 (*See* Trade).
Commercial law: in Cochin-China, 155, 158; in Laos, 162, 164, 178; in Cambodia, 167–8; in Tonkin, 172, 174; French, 176; confined to Frenchmen in most of Indo-China, 180; Indonesians and, 198–9; contracts under, 209–10; Indonesia's unified scheme of, 213; in Philippines, 236.
Commissaire du Gouverne, 161, 162.
Common law: basis of English law, 3–4, 124, 132, 205; in British colonies local laws have become part of, 8, 123–4, 129; in Straits Settlements, 131; colonial 'personal law' and, 205–6; inconsistent, 206; basis of American law in Philippines, 214, 226–7, 232, 233, 238; Anglo-American, 231; contrasted with equity, 234; precedent in, 237.
Comparative law, 22, 32, 86, 103, 109.
Compensation, 20, 26, 43, 61, 197.
Competence, judicial, 156, 162, 167, 174, 180–2.
Compromise (conciliation), 36, 72, 157, 224.
Concessions, French, in Indo-China, 179, 180, 181.
Concubines, 21, 83, 91.
Conflict of laws: in indigenous law, 8; in Dutch Indies, 9, 187, 192, 194–212; in Philippines, 9, 10; caused mainly by European laws, 9, 10, 194, 204; between Oriental and European laws, 13; conflict of principle, 14, 104, 200; Malacca Digest and, 56; between Islam and *adat*, 59, 60, 61, 71, 112–13, 114, 149–50; in Straits Settlements, 130, 131, 132; in English legal world, 132, 147–52; English law principles on, 150; conflict of jurisdiction, 165; in Indo-China, 175–82, 186; Thailand and, 185; French theory of *conflit colonial*, 203; not found in *adat*, 203; in common-law systems, 205 (*see also* Inconsistency).
Confucianism, 11, 12, 75, 78, 79, 90, 91, 107–8, 115, 118, 119, 147, 151.
Congress, United States, 224–5, 227.
Consent: age of, 148; whether property can be transferred by mere, 235.
Conspiracy to murder, 63.
Contraband, 84–5.
Contract: basis of Occidental law, 9–10; in *Āgama*, 44; in *Gia-Long* Code, 89; in Cochin-China, 159; in Laos, 162, 165; of adoption, 164, 180; of service, 165; in Indo-China, 176; in Dutch Indies,

190, 198; for labour, 195, 199, 209; choice of law for, 199, 208, 209–10; conflict of laws and, 200; legal pluralism and, 204; interracial law and, 209–12; in Philippines, 216, 228, 233–6; of marriage, 228; defined, 235.
Contract-based legal systems, 123–238; contrasted with status-systems, 9–14; S. E. Asia moves from status to contract, 13–14, 97, 185.
Conversion, religious, 49, 136, 149, 198, 218.
Corporal punishment, 34, 161, 162.
Corporations, 198; corporate entity, 236.
Corvée, 37–8, 92, 93.
Costs of litigation, 163.
Council of Ministers, Annam, 170, 171.
Council of the Indies, 222, 223, 224.
Counterfeiting, 87–8.
Court of Annulment, 164, 167, 181.
Court of Appeal: of Cochin-China, 155, 160; of Tonkin, 155, 172; for Indo-China, 155, 172, 174–5, 179, 180, 181; of Laos, 164; in Cambodia, 166, 167; Council of Indies as, 222; *Audiencia*, 223.
Court of Cassation, 166, 167, 181.
Courts, royal, 26, 33, 49, 56, 62, 82, 100, 154, 170.
Courts of law, 193; in Thailand, 26; discretion of, 126, 162, 202–3, 224; in Sarawak, 142; in Burma, 143; in Malaysia and Singapore secular courts can overrule religious, 149–50, 222–3; in Cochin-China, 155; consular, 155; in Laos, 161–2, 163–4; civil and criminal jurisdiction combined, 167, 173–4, 223; in Annam, 169–70; in Tonkin, 172–3; separate for each population group in Dutch Indies, 179, 189, 207; Native, 188, 196; police-court (*landgeracht*), 189; religious, 195; and conflict of laws, 204, 206; European, 207; in Indonesia, 212; in Philippines, 222–3, 228, 231, 235; ecclesiastical combined with civil, 223.
Couzinet, Paul, 175.
Crawford, John, 39.
Crime: in Champa, 34; in Sulu Codes, 70; in *Hông-Ɖu'c* Code, 74–5, 76, 80, 92; in *Gia-Long* Code, 80, 81, 86–8; distinguished by relative positions of the parties, 107; Chinese village leaders and, 116; in Sarawak, 142; in Cochin-China, 156–7; investigation of, 159, 174; in Laos, 162, 164; in Cambodia, 167; in Annam, 170; in Dutch Indies, 189, 196–7.
Criminal law; in Vietnam, 74–6, 80–1, 86–90; in Cochin-China, 155, 158–9; in Cambodia, 167; in Annam, 178; in Tonkin, 172–3, 174; in Thailand, 184, 185; in Spain, 220.
Cultivation of land, 53, 83, 136–7.
Culture: borrowing of, 4–5, 73, 78, 95–6: texts vary according to, 98; Sanskrit, 101; diverse in (a) Dutch Indies, 189, 191, 203, 211, 212, (b) Philippines, 214, 237; law must reflect, 192; 'inferiority' of Filipino, 218.
Custom: texts and, 8, 23, 101, 109; non-textual, 10; as important as texts, 23; in pre-Brahminical India, 24; offences against, 59; a source of law, 61, 62; unanimity decides questions of, 62; in Malacca Digest, 67–8; Chinese, 73, 129, 131, 140, 187; Hindu law and, 96, 109–11; British Indian law and, 96; Buddhism and, 96, 144; in Burmese texts, 97–8; unwritten, 98, 127; modified by *sunna*, 104; proof of, 110; and law, (a) Hindu, 111, (b) Islamic, 111–13, (c) Malay, 127, (d) in Straits Settlements, 129, (e) in Sarawak, 142; and 'anomalous' Muslims, 114; in Singapore, 126; in Malacca, 127; in F.M.S., 140; in Burma, 147; in Cochin-China, 159; in Indo-China, 180; in Philippines, 220, 224 (*see also* Local custom).
Customary law, 111; in Burma, 21, 146, 147, 151–2; of inheritance, 21; and money-borrowing, 66; divorce in, 66; Islam and, 105–6; texts and, 109; Malay, 136; Chinese, 147, 151; in Tonkin, 174; in Philippines, 216, 227.
Customs duties, 55, 56, 84, 226.
Cutchi Memons, 113–14.

DAENDELS, MARSHAL HERMAN W., 187.
Damage, to property or person, 42, 44, 65, 67.
Damages, payment of, 44, 84, 165, 208, 233, 236 (*see also* Compensation).
Damdupat, law of, 19.

Index

Daughters, 20; and inheritance, 45, 77, 78; hiring out, 83; in family degrees, 91.
David, René and Brierley, J.E.C., 186.
Dayak law, 70, 142–3.
Death penalty: for adultery, 20, 43, 63, 66; for burglary, 42; can be bought off, 43–4; for sorcery, 44; for apostasy, 54; for offences on shipboard, 63; by decapitation, 74, 171; for rebellion, 75; for murder of close relatives, 75; for incest, 75; for false accusation, 88; for serious crime, 161; review of, 162, 170; in Tonkin, 174.
Debt(s): in Burmese law, 19, 24, 144–5; in Thailand, 27, 31; bondsmen, 30–1; in *Âgama*, 41, 44; in Malacca Digest, 54; in Islamic law, 59; a first charge on debtor's estate, 65; in Sulu Codes, 69; in Code of Manu, 100; slavery for, 162; in Philippines, 216, 233, 235; in Spain, 220.
Decapitation, 74, 171.
Defamation, 105.
de la Porte, André, 202.
Delivery, actual and constructive, 235.
de Morga, Antonio, 214.
de Placencia, Juan, 214, 219.
Derrett, J. Duncan M., 111.
de Vitoria, Francisco, 218–19.
Dhammasattham in Thailand, 28, 29, 31, 102.
Dhammathat in Burma, 17–24, 101–2, 144–6.
Dhammavilasa in Burma, 18–22.
Dhani Nivat, Prince, 27–8.
Dharma, 24; and nature, 11, 47; Kingship a symbol of, 31, 101; in Champa and Cambodia, 33; sometimes means religious domain land, 37–8; equivalent to 'duty', 47, 103; and custom, 96; 'a rule of interdependence', 99; defined, 99, 109–10; sources of, 99; and legal reality, 109–10; and law, 118.
Dharmaśāstra, 18, 24, 26, 28, 31, 32–3, 99 (*see Śāstra*).
Dharmasutra, 24, 100.
Diet, 100.
Differentiation: of individual responsibility, by class and status, 10, 108; of compensation for adultery, by caste, 20; of punishment by rank, 32, 43; of fines by (a) rank, 34, 43 (b) caste, 42 (c) religion, 53–4; of crime by relationship of the parties, 107; *li* and, 108.
Discretion, judicial, 126, 162, 202–3, 224.
Disorderly conduct, 76.
Dispute settlement, 3, 4, 5, 109, 115–16.
Disrespect, 41, 75, 77.
Divorce: in Burma, 19–20, 21, 22; by mutual consent in (a) Burma, 20, 145, (b) Vietnam, 81, (c) Laos, 164, (d) Thailand, 185; in Thailand, 25; in *Âgama*, 42, 46; Islamic, 59, 67, 132; in Malacca Digest, 66–7; in Vietnam, 76–7, 81, 84; by triple *talaq*, 105; by annulment of marriage, 133; in Singapore, 148; in Cochin-China, 159; in Laos, 164; in Indonesia, 213; in Philippines, 225–6; absolute or partial in Philippines, 226, 230.
Djakarta, 210, 212.
Domicile: 'foreign' in (a) Straits Settlements, 130, (b) Philippines, 230; and Distribution Enactment, 140; in Malaysia and Singapore, 148, 149; in Burma, 150, 151; in Indo-China, 159, 179, 181; a principal factor in common law, 205.
Double jeopardy, 220.
Dowry, 41, 219.
Duplatre, Louis, 25.
Dutch: colonies of, 9; and Malacca, 127, 136; in Dutch Indies, 187, 197; colonial expansion of, 218.
Dutch law: in (a) S. E. Asia, 1, (b) Malacca, 127–8; Dutch legal world, 6; 'sovereignty' in, 217.
Dutch law in East Indies: and *adat*, 4, 190, 193, 195, 196–7, 199, 206, 207; primarily for Europeans, 187, 202, 207; Natives may choose to adopt, 190, 197–200, 201, 207, 209–10; dominates, 190, 192, 193; governs corporate bodies, 196, 209; whether 'superior' to indigenous law, 199, 201, 202; differs from that in Netherlands, 200; and conflict of laws, 204; a normative system, 205; and interracial suits, 208; applied in labour contracts, 209; European can lose right to be governed by, 211.
Duty in Oriental law, 3, 47, 99–100, 103.
Duty and excise, 107.

Index 273

EASEMENTS, 231–2.
East Africa, Islam in, 113.
East India Company, 124, 125, 126, 127, 136, 137.
Ecclesiastical jurisdiction, 125, 129, 220, 222–3, 224.
Ehrlich, Eugen, 118.
Elections, 226.
Emancipation, 159, 230.
English in Malacca, 127, 136.
English law: in South East Asia, 1; common law the basis of, 3–4, 8, 124, 132; and anthropological evidence, 4; English legal world, 6, 123–52; the general law in British colonies, 8, 123, 130; precedent in, 8, 193; in Penang, 125; in Singapore, 126, 148–9, 150; in Malacca, 127–8, 136–7; in Straits Settlements, 129–34, 137; and intestacy, 134; charities and, 135; and Malay states, 139–41; in Borneo territories, 141–3; in Burma, 147, 152; and conflict of laws, 149, 185; in Malaysia, 150; 'sovereignty' in, 217; in Ceylon and South Africa, 238.
'Equalization', 197–8.
Equity: English rules of, 141; rules of justice or equity in Dutch Indies, 190; in Philippines, 227, 234, 235, 237.
Ethics: form part of Oriental law, 1, 2, 10, 11, 25, 26, 78; in Islam, 46, 68, 104; in *Hông-Đu'c* Code, 76, 78; Chinese, 94; indeterminate, 98; in *li*, 108.
European land in Dutch Indies, 206, 207.
European law: contrasted with Oriental, 2–4, 118; disappearance of oral law from, 3; and oral law, 3–4, 7–8; adapted in S. E. Asia, 4–5, 6, 8, 184; causes conflict of laws in S. E. Asia, 9; ancient codes of, 95; medieval texts of, 97; copied in Thailand, 183–5; legal theory in Europe, 191 (*see also* Dutch law in East Indies).
Europeans in Cochin-China, 155, 157.
Europeans in Dutch Indies: law applied to, 187–8, 189, 202; status of, 194–5; European banks and companies, 196, 209; Natives admitted to status of, 197–8; protected in contracts with Natives, 199.
Evidence, 4, 11, 35, 87.
Exceptions in law, 129, 152.

Execution of judgments, 144, 174, 180, 182.
Exile, 74 (*see* Banishment).
Exogamy, 114.
Exordium in Oriental texts, 2, 18, 24, 25.
Expiation, 100, 101.
Expulsion: of Buddhist priests, 84; from *tsu*, 115, 119; from caste, 136.
Extortion, 76.
Extraterritoriality in Thailand, 183, 184.

FALSE ACCUSATIONS, 75, 86, 87, 88, 90, 91.
False information, 87.
Family: Chinese view of state and, 6, 91; rebellion against, 75; administrative unit in Vietnam, 83, 92; murder of members of, 86; punishment of members of, 91, 92, 93; family worship, 92; offences against, 107; and religion, 112; *tsu* and, 115; family councils, 159, 231; and adoption in Laos, 164; extended, 217, 231.
Family law: and canon law, 9, 222, 223; administrative validity of, 13; in Burma, 22; in *Hông-Đu'c* Code, 76, 91; Islam and, 96, 111, 112, 148; Chinese, 107, 140, 150; indigenous, 119; in Tonkin, 175; in Thailand, 184–5; Indonesians have no choice of law with, 198; 'national' in Philippines, 227; in Philippines Civil Code, 230–1.
Family property, 38, 45, 78, 82, 84, 107, 112.
Fasting, 56.
Father: child killed by, 86, 90; his relationship with his son, 107.
Federated Malay States, 6, 123, 138–41, 149.
Fee simple estate, 128, 137.
Female offenders, punishment of, 89.
Ferry Charter (1358) in Java, 38.
Filial piety, 91, 108.
Filiation, 159, 164, 230.
Finance, 170; Finance Ministry, Annam, 169.
Fines: differ according to offender's (a) rank, 34, (b) caste, 42 (c) religion, 53–4; in *Āgama*, 40, 44; for theft, 42, 70; payment of, 43, 162; for adultery, 43; exacted in camels, 53–4; for trespass, 69; Sulu and Dayak lists of, 70; in *Gia-Long* Code, 82; for bribery, 87; im-

274 Index

Fines, contd.
posed by (a) village council, 93 (b) *tsu*, 115 (c) Chinese guilds, 116.
Flogging, 63–4, 93.
Forced labour, as a punishment, 74, 161, 162, 163, 167.
Forchhammer, Emil, 23, 24, 144.
Foreigners: in Straits Settlements, 130; in Tonkin, 173; in Indo-China, 179, 180, 181; foreign *indigènes*, 182; Chinese in Indo-China become foreign nationals, 183; foreign Orientals in Dutch Indies, 189, 194–5.
'Foreign' law, 130, 131, 140, 147, 176; foreign judgments, 180; *adat* and, 203.
Foreign relations, 56, 100.
Forfeiture of property, 76, 84.
Forgery, 87.
Fornication on board ship, 63–4.
Fort William in Bengal, 124, 128.
France: *Justice de Paix* in, 156; criminal investigation in, 159; reforms Tonkinese law, 172; courts in, 173; law in, 176; signs treaty with Republic of China, 183; helps reform Thailand's laws, 183–5; Philippines take some laws from, 228.
Fraud, 83, 84, 87, 165, 233.
French: colonies of, 8–9, 78, 92, 153, 157, 166, 186; as litigants in Indo-China, 157, 173, 175–6, 180; marriage of French citizens with 'Annamites', 176; Franco-Belgian advisers in Thailand, 183, 184.
French Indo-China, 153–4, 185, 186 (*see also* Indo-China).
French law: in S. E. Asia, 1; French legal world, 6, 153–86; in Cochin-China, 154–60; in Laos, 161; in Annam, 172; in Tonkin, 174; in conflict with Indo-Chinese laws, 175–82; and Thailand, 184, 185; French theory on conflict of laws, 203; 'sovereignty' in, 217.
Fruit-trees, 67, 137.
Funerals, 85, 107, 135.

GAMBIER, 137.
Gambling, 38, 56, 88.
Genealogies, 103, 115.
Gerini, G.-E., 25.
Germany: private law in, 98; Philippines take laws from, 228.

Gia-Long (Nguyễn Phúc Ánh), Emperor of Vietnam (1802–20), 80, 82, 91.
Gia-Long Code (*Hoàng Việt*: The Annamite Code), 80–93, 95, 171, 174.
Gifts: in Burma, 20–1; Islamic law of, 53; in Sulu, 69; in Code of Manu, 100; to Buddhist monks, 146; in Spanish law, 220, 232.
God: Islam and, 6, 48, 50, 55, 56, 104, 105, 119; a Sultan is the representative of, 50, 72; a source of Minangkabau *adat*, 58, 113; in Malacca Digest, 62, 64, 68; in Sulu Codes, 70; and law, 118.
Good faith, 232.
Government of India, 128–9.
Governor-General: of Indo-China, 154, 158, 161, 162, 163, 165, 172; of Dutch Indies, 188, 195, 198.
Graves, 85, 86, 216.
Great Britain, Philippines take some laws from, 228.
Grotius, Hugo, 194, 218.
Guardian: and marriage of ward, 22, 66, 105, 132, 212; legal representative of minor in Cochin-China, 156.
Guilds and Chinese law, 114, 115–17.
Guilleminet, Paul, 4.
Gujarat, 113–14.

HAIPHONG, French concession in, 181.
Halai Memons of Porbunder, 113–14.
Hall, D. G. E., 17, 40.
Hanafi school of Islamic law, 132.
Hanoi, 155, 156, 172, 174, 179, 180.
Harivarman IV, King of Champa, 33.
Hart, H. L. A., 12.
Harta sapencharian, 46, 66, 67, 134–5.
Hermits, 100, 102.
Hierarchy: in Thailand, 27, 30; in Vietnam, 93; in India, 99; in Laos, 164; of law, 191.
High Court of Rangoon, 143.
Hinduism: Hindu world view, 6; in S. E. Asia, 17; and Muslim custom, 50; and Malacca Digest, 52–3; idea of kings in, 72; unity of, 101; public's acceptance of, 111; *śāstras* the basis of, 111; the goal of, 111; and Muslims in India, 113–14; and natural order, 119; in Straits Settlements, 129.
Hindu law: *śāstras* differ from custom, 9; morality in, 12; in S.E. Asia, 17, 47;

Index

damdupat in, 19; and Burmese law, 21–4, 101, 143; and Thailand, 28, 32; and Champa, 33; in Java, 36–47; Hindu-derived law in Malacca, 52–3; sustains Indian world's unity, 101; *dharma* in, 109–11; conception of law in, 110; in Straits Settlements, 135; in F.M.S., 141 (*see also* Indian-derived law: Manu, Code of).
Hindus, 32, 131, 143, 151.
Historical jurisprudence, 5, 8, 22–3, 32.
Homicide, 40, 86, 89, 90.
Hông Đu'c Code, 74–80, 91, 92.
Hooker, M. B., 124, 136, 137, 187.
Hué, Court of, 154.
Hukum Qanun Dato' Star, 52, 54.
Husband and wife: in Burmese law, 19–20, 144–5; in Code of Manu, 19, 100; and inheritance, 21, 45–6; in Thailand, 27, 185; property of, 78–9, 133–4, 144–5, 164, 185, 199, 231; assault by wife on husband, 87; duties of, 99, 100, 230; Chinese relationship of, 107; husband represents wife in Cochin-Chinese courts, 156; husband's right to kill wife in Laos, 165; in mixed marriages, 199, 200–1, 211; cannot renounce rights in Philippines, 230.

IDOLS, 216.
Ifugao people, Philippines, 4.
Illiteracy, 3, 4–5.
Immovable property, 145, 146, 165, 179, 182, 231.
Imprisonment: in *Gia-Long* Code, 88; review of sentences of, 162, 170; for Debt, 168; for simple crimes in Tonkin, 173; *adat* and, 196–7.
Incapacity, physical, 229.
Incest, 75, 87, 142.
Inconsistency: in Oriental texts, 2, 12, 43, 54, 59, 71, 119; in European codes, 2; in hybrid laws, 14; in *Hông-Đu'c*, 79; *Gia-Long* Code and, 91; in common law, 206; in a normative system, 206; in Philippine Civil Code, 235.
Indemnity, 64.
Independence, law after, 14, 147, 166, 186.
India: and Islam, 48; custom in, 110; 'anomalous' Muslims in, 113–14; 'Justice, equity and good conscience', 147; French India, 153; village is the administrative unit in, 188 (*see also* British India).
Indian Acts: in Straits Settlements, 129; in F.M.S., 139; law in Borneo territories based on, 142.
Indian-derived law, 1, 95; Indian legal world, 6, 17–47, 93, 99, 101; in Champa, 32–5; in Java, 35–46 (*see also* Hindu law: Manu, Code of).
Indians: in Straits Settlements, 129; in Dutch Indies, 194.
Indictment, 87.
Indigenous law: colonial powers and, 8; in conflict with Spanish law in Philippines, 9; Indian law and, 17; Islam and, 112; and texts, 119; and English principles, 123–4; in British S.E. Asia, 147; in Burma, 152; in Indo-China, 153, 174, 175, 176, 177–8, 179; in Cochin-China, 158; in Laos, 164; in Cambodia, 166–8; in Annam, 169, 171; in Tonkin, 172–4; in Dutch Indies, 193; in Philippines, 228, 237–8.
Indigenous tribunals, 9; in Cochin-China, 155; in Laos, 161–2, 164; in Cambodia, 166; in Annam, 169–71; in Tonkin, 172; in Dutch Indies, 187, 189, 207.
Individual: state claims absolute authority over, 9; contrasted in contract- and status-systems, 10–11; responsibility of, 31; defined, 71, 83, 98, 118; duties of, 92, 99, 119; morality of, 99; Islam and, 104; and legal reality, 111; choice of law for, 198, 204; *adat* and, 203.
Indo-China (Union Indochinoise), 153–4; French law in, 6; has highly-developed system of indigenous law, 153; mandarins in, 166; conflict of laws in, 175–82, 186 (*see also* French Indo-China: Vietnam).
Indonesia, 1; *adat* in, 4, 44, 112–13, 193; Islam in, 46, 48, 49; legal texts in, 47, 49–51, 103; conflict between Islamic law and *adat* in, 112–13; Japanese occupation of, 148; legal pluralism in, 194, 202, 204; Dutch arrival in, 194; mortgages of *adat* land in, 196; land in, 196, 207; conflict of laws in, 202, 204; equal status of all laws in, 202; choice of law in, 207 (*see also* Java; Netherlands East Indies: Sumatra).

276　Index

Indravarman I, King of Champa, 33.
'Inferior' and 'superior': status, 30–1, 75, 91, 92, 107, 108, 118; officials, 86; and law in Dutch Indies, 199, 201, 202.
Infidels, Muslims and, 54, 56, 194.
Information: given to a criminal, 41; about crimes, 87.
Inherent jurisdiction, 141.
Inheritance: in Burma, 19, 20–1, 143, 152; in Thailand, 27; children and, 45, 159, 211; Islamic, 59, 61, 111, 134; in Sulu Codes, 69, 70; in Vietnam, 76, 77, 78, 89, 91; in Code of Manu, 100; among 'anomalous' Muslims, 113–14; in Sarawak, 142; male and female share equally, 159; in Dutch Indies, 198; in Philippines, 219.
Injury caused by accident, 69.
Insanity, 46.
Insolvency, 144.
Inscriptions: in Champa, 33–4; in Java, 35–6.
Insults, 41.
Intelligence, Minangkabau system of, 59.
Intention, 32, 43, 44, 89, 180, 235.
Interest: payment of, 19, 30, 159, 236; rate of, 64.
Interest in a case must be declared, 170.
Interior Ministry, Annam, 169, 170.
Interlocal law, 203–4.
International law, 138, 175, 218.
International law, private: courts in Straits Settlements do not admit personal laws as, 130; used in Dutch Indies (a) to admit personal laws, 130 (b) to deal with conflict of principles, 200; foreign element in, 176; applies law of domicile, 179; French, 180, 182; for Chinese in Indo-China, 183; in Thailand, 185; and conflict of laws, 202–3, 205.
Interpersonal law, 202.
Interracial law, 202–3, 204–12.
Interreligious marriages, 147, 150, 180, 229.
Intestacy, 134, 140.
Islam: and morality, 12, 105; reaches Indonesia, 46, 63; in Malacca, 49, 51; king's position in, 50 72; and Malacca Digest, 67–8; and Sulu Codes, 68–9; in Java, 72; principles of, 104–5, 119; in Africa, 113; in Straits Settlements, 129.
Islamic law: laws based on, 1; Islamic legal world, 6, 48–72, 93; theoretically exclusive, 9; may come to terms with non-Islamic ideas, 9, 96, 103–4; in conflict with *adat*, 49, 60, 61–2, 112–13, 149–50; in Malay texts, 52–6, 103; and laws of Perak, 59–60; and custom, 71, 105–6, 111–13, 134; Schools of, 132; in Straits Settlements, 132–5, 143; overruled by legislation, 134; inheritance, in, 134; in F.M.S., 140; in Sarawak, 143; in Burma, 143; and conflict of laws, 148–9; distribution of property under, 149–50; in Dutch Indies, 187; and mixed marriages, 211–12; in Philippines, 214, 238.
Island South East Asia, 6, 49, 57, 62, 63, 70, 72.
Italy, Philippines take some laws from, 228.

JAMAL AL-BADR-AL-MUNIR, Sultan of Acheh (1703–26), 54.
Japan: overruns Indonesia, 148, 207; French consular courts in, 155; laws codified in, 185; overruns Philippines, 225.
Japanese in Dutch Indies, 187.
Jardine, Sir John, 21–3, 144.
Java, 62, 63; and law in, 3; Indian-derived law in, 6, 35–47, 72; *adat* and Islam in, 49; status in, 72; sovereignty in, 96, 194; texts in, 103; Dutch in, 187, 188; British control of, 188; Native Christians in, 195.
Jaya Indravarman II, King of Champa, 33.
Jaya Indravarman IV, King of Champa, 33.
Jayapattra (note of victory), 35–6, 38; *jayasong*, 36–7, 46, 72.
Jews, 54, 112, 131.
Johore, 52, 58, 65, 138, 139; Dato' Temenggong of, 126; Sultan of, 126.
Joint family, 114.
Judges: common law made by, 4, 22, 206; Javanese, 36; a married woman's conveyance to be acknowledged before, 134; of F.M.S., Straits Settlements and Johore have ex officio jurisdiction in all three areas, 139; in Burma, 144; assessors sit with, 155; in Cochin-China, 159; Appellate, 160; indigenous in (a) Laos, 161 (b) Cambodia, 167 (c)

Tonkin, 173–4; in Tonkin, mandarins assist French, 173; in Thailand, 184; in Dutch Indies, 193; in Philippines, 223.
Judicial Commissioners: in Upper Burma, 21, 143; in F.M.S., 139.
Judicial decisions: as precedents in (a) Dutch Indies, 193, 197 (b) Philippines, 237; on interracial law, 203; conflict of laws arises only in, 204; on labour contracts, 209; based on compromise, 224; on marriage, 229; on adoption, 231; on trusts, 234.
Judicial discretion, 126, 162, 202–3, 224.
Judicial notice, 140.
Judgments: in Annam, 169–71; execution or enforcement of, 144, 170, 174, 180–2.
Jurisdiction of courts: general courts in English colonies have overriding, 123; in Penang, 125; ecclesiastical, 125, 129, 220, 222–3, 224; domicile and, 140, 180–1; inherent, 140–1; in insolvency, 144; of religious courts, 149; High Court's original, 150; of Indo-Chinese indigenous courts, 155, 162, 164, 169–70, 180; of *Justices de Paix*, 155–6; in Laos, 161, 162, 164; conflict of, 165, 176–82; in Cambodia, 167; in Annam, 169, 171; in Tonkin, 172, 173, 174; in Thailand, 184, 185; in independent Indo-China, 186; of indigenous courts in Dutch Indies, 187, 189, 207; territorial, 202–3; in common law, 205; of civil courts superior to ecclesiastical, 222–3; of *Audiencia*, 223, 228.
Jurisprudence: in sense of legal science, 98, 193, 205, 206; in sense of case-law, 175, 181, 182, 183, 197, 237.
Jurists, 138; and *adat*, 4; and conflict of laws, 9; and Islamic law, 104; and legal separatism in Dutch Indies, 194; on whether compensation must follow penal fault, 197; and private international law, 200; and interracial law, 205; and inconsistency in common law, 206.
Jury, trial by, 228.
Justice, in Islamic law, 59, 104.
Justice, Ministry of; in, Annam, 169, 170; in Thailand, 184.
Justice of the Peace, 228; *Justice de Paix*, 155–7, 167, 178; *Justice de Paix indigène*, 156, 182; *Juez de paz*, 223.
'Justice, equity and good conscience', 144, 147, 151.

KALINGA, LUZON, 237.
Kasim, Raja (Sultan Muzaffar Shah), Sultan of Malacca (1446–59), 62.
Kedah, 54–5, 59, 124, 125, 138; Kedah Laws, 54–6, 64.
Kelantan, 138, 139; *Dato' Luar* of, 54.
Keliantiaw, Datu, 216; *Keliantiaw* Text, 216.
Kempe, J. E. and Winstedt, R. O., 52, 65.
Kertanegara, King of Singosari (1268–92), 37.
Khojas, 113–14.
Kidnapping, 27.
Kings, 22; in Thailand, 25–32, 102–3; in S.E. Asia, 31; in Champa, 34; in Java, 37, 44, 45, 103; Islam and, 50, 72; in Malay texts, 53; śāstra and, 99, 110; in India, 103, 110; of Cambodia, 166; and law reform in Thailand, 183–5; King of Spain and the Philippines, 217–18 (*see also* Royal decrees: Rulers: Sultans).
Kollewijn, R. D., 200, 201, 202–3, 204–5.
Kuṭara, 39–40.

LABOUR CONTRACTS, 195, 199, 209.
Labour relations, 236.
Land: in Thailand, 30, 185; mortgage of, 36, 91–2, 93; in Java, 37–8, 41, 188; granted to Hindu priests, 43; ownership of, 44, 45, 160, 165, 223; holding of, 50; laws governing, 61, 70, 198, 199, 212; use of, 67; rent for, 67, 188; in Vietnam, 73; taxed, 74, 83, 117; communal, 93, 207; tenancy, 110; *tsu* and, 115; in China, 116, 117; registration of, 117, 160, 207; in Cochin-China, 160; Free and Unfree, 188; classification of, 188, 206; becomes state property, 188; Native, 188, 196, 206–7; status of, 206–7, 209; in Indonesia, 212–13; in Philippines, 226, 238.
Land Charters in Java, 35, 37–8.
Landraad, 188.
Land tenure, 110, 136–8.
Languages, diversity of; in Indonesia, 189, 191, 212; in Philippines, 214, 237.

278　*Index*

Laos, 1, 177; under French rule, 154, 161, 175; legal system of, 161–6, 178; law codified in, 162–6; jurisdiction in, 162, 164, 165, 181, 182; conflict of laws in, 178; becomes independent, 186.
Laotians, jurisdiction over, 177, 182.
Law: complex in S.E. Asia, 1, 17, 71, 100, 108; definitions of, 1, 5, 6, 8, 9–10, 11, 12, 58–9, 62, 70, 96, 105, 108, 146–7, 184, 191, 192, 193–4, 201; ethnocentric view of, 1, 5, 32, 98; 'written', 1–3, 70, 72, 73, 79, 97, 98, 110, 118, 195, 199; Oriental and Occidental systems contrasted, 1–2, 6, 12–13; vocabulary of, 1–2, 11, 209; oral, 3–4, 7–8, 50; law tales in Burma, 3; absolute, 6, 7, 10, 11, 12, 13, 18, 50, 71, 77, 79, 118, 119; special, 8, 152, 195; immutable, 12, 18, 25, 28, 47, 119; hybrid, 14; substantive and adjective, 14, 102; and tension, 44, 104, 119; and custom, 73, 96, 97–8, 111, 127, 199; an expression of natural and moral order, 98–109; Islamic notion of, 104; part of general administration, 106; Chinese purpose of, 108; Hindu conception of, 110; 'positive' and 'living', 118; unwritten, 174; unification of, 189, 191–2, 201, 204, 212–13.
Law and order, 56.
Law-books in Java and Bali, 35, 38–47.
Lease, 116, 234.
Legal administration: Oriental and European systems contrasted, 12–14; in Burma, 22, 144, 152; in Thailand, 28, 184; in Vietnam, 74; in *Gia-Long Code*, 81–2; in Malaya, 113; in Indonesia, 113, 212; in Chinese villages, 114; in Penang, 125; in Cochin-China, 155–6, 158, 161; in Laos, 162; in Annam, 169, 171; in Tonkin, 172; in Dutch Indies, 187–8, 189, 192; in Philippines, 214, 215, 216, 219, 222–3, 237–8 (*see also* Administration of Justice).
Legality may yet be blameworthy, 105.
Legal personality, 17, 30–1, 98, 228.
Legal pluralism in S.E. Asia, 13, 14; in Chinese law, 118; in Burma, 152; in Dutch Indies, 187, 189, 190, 191, 194, 200, 202, 203, 204, 208, 213; in Philippines, 237.
Legal reality: anthropological evidence

and, 4; Oriental laws and, 6, 11, 17; oral law and, 7; in Vietnam, 79, 91, 92; texts and, 98, 118; Hinduism and, 101, 109, 111; in interpersonal law, 203; in Philippines, 237–8.
Legal separatism: in French colonies, 9; in Dutch Indies, 187–90; in Philippines, 215.
Legal universe, 10, 11.
Legislation, 25, 32, 97, 188–9, 191.
Legitimacy, 130, 231.
Legitimation, 132, 164.
Lê Thánh-tông, Emperor of Vietnam (1460–97), 73–4, 77.
Lev, Daniel S., 212.
Lex loci regit actum, 134, 180; *lex loci*, 147; *lex domicilii*, 150, 202; *lex loci contractus*, 150, 151, 202; *lex situs*, 179; *lex fori*, 202.
Li explained, 108.
Liability, civil and criminal, 165.
Liaw, Yock Fang, 65, 67.
Libel and slander, 136.
Lien, 235.
Lieutenant-Governor of Cochin-China, 155, 158.
Light, Francis, 124.
Limited liability company, 209.
Lingat, Robert, 24, 25, 29, 35, 97, 100, 101.
Literacy, 153.
Litigation, 33, 34, 100; promotion of, 87, 115; as a source of law, 102; *tsu* and, 115; costs of, 163.
Loarca, Miguel, 214.
Local custom: may be outside texts, 2; petition-writers and, 5; in Burma, 24; Ferry Charter cancels, 38; Muslim texts and, 48, 53, 60; a source of Minangkabau law, 61; Chinese, 73, 131, 142; in Vietnam, 91; Islam and, 111–14; in Chinese villages, 116–17; in Malacca, 128; in Straits Settlements, 131, 135, 137; admissibility of, 135; in Sarawak, 142; and equity, 235–6 (*see also* Custom).
Local law: in English colonies becomes part of common law, 8, 130; does not cause conflict of laws, 9; in Java, 35–7; in texts, 50, 102, 119; in ancient codes, 93; Chinese customary, 117; confirmed by precedent, 123–4; Islamic law in F.M.S. is, 140; Chinese, in Sarawak, 142; conflict in, 180; and

Index

Chinese in Indo-China, 182; in Philippines, 219 (*see also* Indigenous law).
Louisiana, U.S.A., 228, 238.
Low, James, 25.
Luang Prabang, Laos, 161, 163.
Lubman, Stanley, 117.
Luwaran Code of Magindanao, 51, 68–9, 70.
Luzon Island, Philippines, 237, 238.

MADJAPAHIT, KINGDOM OF, 39, 72.
Magellan, Ferdinand, 217.
Magic, 60, 85, 86.
Magindanao, Mindanao, 51, 68.
Magistrates: guide to Buddhist law for, 22; in Vietnam, 81, 82, 90; codes a 'manual' for, 95; in China, 106, 115, 116, 117; in Singapore, 126; in F.M.S., 139; in Sarawak, 142; in France, 158; in Annam, 169; independent in Philippines, 224.
Mahasammata, King, 18.
Mahmud Shah, Sultan of Malacca (1488–1511), 63, 68.
Maine, Sir Henry, 10, 50, 71, 95, 97, 118.
Majority, 230; age of, 10, 133, 141, 160.
Makassar, Celebes, 63.
Malacca: Islam in, 49; Dutch Governor of, 56; dynasty of, 62; one of the Straits Settlements, 123, 124; now part of Malaysia, 123; under Penang's legal jurisdiction, 126; ceded to Britain, 127; law in, 127–8; law for Muslims in, 133; landholders in, 136–7.
Malacca texts, 49–62, 71; Malacca laws, 62–8, 70, 136.
Malaya, 3, 4, 49, 103, 112–13.
Malays: in Singapore, 126; in Straits Settlements, 129; in F.M.S., 140; Sarawak recognizes Malay customs, 142–3; in Cochin-China, 157.
Malaysia, 1; Islam in, 48; composition of, 123, 142; precedent in, 141; conflict of laws in, 148–9; reform of laws on marriage and divorce in, 150; equity in, 236.
Malay States, 53, 55, 63, 123, 138–41, 142.
Malay texts, 51–68, 71, 103–4.
Mandamus, writ of, 237.

Mandarins, 90, 166, 169–70, 171, 172, 173–4.
Manila, 219, 223, 224.
Manslaughter, 43.
Manu (Manosara): (a) the author of Buddhist *dhammathats*, 18, 102, (b) the author of Hindu code, 99, 102.
Manu, Code of, 17; a source of law for (a) Buddhist *dhammathats*, 18–21, 23–4, 27, 102 (b) Thailand, 27, 29, 32, 33, 102 (c) Champa, 33–4 (d) Java, 36–7, 38, 39–43, 44, 46; and Malay texts, 52–3; analysed, 99–102.
Manugye dhammathat, 18, 22, 145–6.
Manu Reng dhammathat, 18, 22.
Manusmṛti, 23, 24, 33, 99–100.
Maragtas text, 215–16.
Maritime Code of Malacca, 62–4, 66.
Markets, regulation of, 85, 107.
Marriage: in Burma, 19–20, 22, 143; Jardine's Notes on, 21; validity of, 22, 147, 148, 150, 184; *Wagaru* and *Manu* contrasted on, 24; in *Āgama*, 41; between slave and free woman, 45; bride-price, 45–6, 219; in Islamic law, 59, 61, 105, 132, 148, 211; as a penalty, 64; in Malacca Code, 66; in Vietnam, 76–7, 81, 83–4, 91; marriage settlement, 92; land and, 93; in Code of Manu, 99; against bride's wish, 105; Chinese, 107, 116, 117, 130–2; in India, 110; *adat* and, 112; polygamy, 130–2; common-law, 131; based on consensus, 131; registration of, 132, 140, 152, 184; brokerage contracts for, 135; conversion and, 136; in Sarawak, 142; inter-religious, 147, 150, 152, 180, 229; conflict of laws over, 148, 200; in Singapore, 148; in Cochin-China, 159; in Laos, 164; mixed, 176, 198, 199, 200–1, 204, 207, 211–12; among Native Christians in Dutch Indies, 195; interracial law and, 211–12; in Indonesia, 213; in Philippines, 215, 229–30, 233; Council of Trent and, 222; civil, 225, 230; religious or canonical, 229, 230; annulment of, 229.
Master: and slave, 45, 65, 88, 216; and servant, 162.
Mataram, Kingdom of, 72.
Matriarchy and matrilineal system, 61, 78, 112, 150.

280　　Index

Maxwell, Sir Peter Benson, 125, 127, 128, 135.
Maxwell, W. E., 67; Maxwell MSS., 52, 57, 60.
Mediation, 38, 116, 117, 119.
Medicine, 85; improper administration of, 90.
Mexico, 217, 228.
Middle East, 59, 95, 111.
Minahasa, Celebes, 195.
Minangkabau people, 57–9, 61; *perbilangan* of, 3, 61; laws of, 57–61, 67–8, 71, 104; matrilineal, 61, 112; their *adat*, 61–2, 212.
Mindanao Island, Philippines, 48, 68, 69.
Ming Code, 74, 76.
Minorities, protection of, 215.
Minority, 159, 164; marriage of minors, 83.
Miscarriage of justice, 160.
Miscegeny, 147, 176, 180, 198, 199, 200–1, 204, 207, 211–12.
Missionaries, 32, 218.
Mistake, and validity of gifts, 20.
Mitigation, 81.
Modernization of law, 14, 183, 204.
Mohammedan law; in Straits Settlements, 132–3; in Sarawak, 142; in Philippines, 214, 237–8 (*see* Islamic law).
Molesalam Girasias of Broach, 113–14.
Molucca Islands, 194.
Monks, 100; monasteries, 82; rules governing Buddhist monks, 83–4, 88, 146–7.
Moplahs of Kerala, 114.
Morality: Oriental texts do not distinguish between public and private, 6; and individual responsibility, 10; contributes to law in status systems, 11, 12; not a part of contract-system law, 12; offences against, 89; moral principles in *Thammasat*, 97, 184; individual, 99; contracts offending public morality, 135; Spanish-Christian, 219.
Moro (i.e. Muslim) texts in Philippines, 49.
Mortgages, 67, 91–2, 93, 160, 196, 233, 236; equitable, 235.
Mourning: rules for, 75, 77, 83, 84, 85, 90–1; relatives within degrees of, 106.
Movable property, 165, 231.
Municipal law, 13–14.

Murder: of slaves, 65; of parents and other relatives, 75, 86, 106; of officials, 86; Chinese punishment for, 107; of wife by husband, 165.
Muslims: and infidels, 54, 56, 194; 'anomalous' Muslims in India, 113–14; in Africa, 114; in Straits Settlements, 131, 132; in Burma, 144; and marriage with non-Muslims, 151, 211–12, 229; in Indo-China, 181; 'priests' among, 196; in South Philippines, 217, 237–8.
Mutilation: as a punishment, 43, 54, 215; of females, 75.

NAGARAKṚTĀGAMA law-book, 39–40, 46.
Nang talung, 3.
Nāradasmṛti, 23, 24, 33, 34.
Nationality, 148, 149, 152, 176, 177, 180, 182.
Nationalization of family law, 227.
Native custom in Philippines, 214 (*see* Custom: Local custom).
Native law: admissibility of, 7; in Straits Settlements, 130; in Dutch Indies, 195, 203; possibility of conflict in, 203–4; in Philippines, 238 (*see also Adat*: Customary law: Indigenous law: Local law).
Natives: in Tonkin, 173; in Indo-China, 177; have separate law and status in Dutch Indies, 187–8, 189–90, 194, 195; land reserved for, 188, 196, 206–7; may choose to be governed by European law, 197–9, 207–11; Europeans protected in contracts with, 199.
Naturalization, 160, 181.
Natural justice, repugnancy to, 135.
Natural law, 12, 125.
Natural world, Oriental law and, 4, 6, 11, 12, 17, 46–7, 100, 109, 118–19.
Nederburgh, I. A., 191–2, 201.
Negligence, 41.
Negotiable instruments, 235.
Negri Sembilan, 58, 60, 61, 138, 140, 150.
Netherlands, 148, 189, 200.
Netherlands East India Company, 187–8, 194.
Netherlands East Indies: *adat* in, 3, 4, 187, 189–91, 192–3, 195, 196–7, 199, 201, 203; Dutch-derived law in, 6, 187–213; 'law areas' in, 123, 189; and

Index 281

private international law, 130; legal separatism in, 187–90; land in, 188, 196, 206–7; cultural, linguistic and economic diversity in, 189, 191–2, 203, 211, 212; direct and indirect rule in, 189–90 (*see also* Indonesia).
Newbold, T. J., 67.
New Spain, 221.
Nguyễn Phúc Anh (Gia-Long), Emperor of Vietnam (1802–20), 80, 91.
Ninety-Nine Laws of Perak, 59–60.
Nissaya and *nissita* rules, 20, 145.
Normative system of law, 4, 10, 12, 100, 205–6.
North Africa: Islam in, 111; French colonies in, 153, 200.
Northrop, F. S. C., 32.
Nushirwan the Just, of Ctesiphon, 59–60.

OATHS, 19, 54, 69, 165.
Obligation: imposed in Oriental law as part of a natural and social order, 6, 47, 98–9, 118–19; oral law proves multiple source of, 7; in Dutch Indies imposed by local laws, 9; attributed to individuals in 'status' systems, 10, 14, 17, 32, 71, 99; predictable in European law, 11; 'status' systems do not touch large areas of, 12, 108–9; in 'status' law founded on relationships of 'superior' and 'inferior', 30–1; exists in a set of pre-ordained external characteristics, 32; in pledge or mortgage, 44, 235, 236; in Malay texts, 103; Confucian, 107; in *adat*, 112; *tsu* and, 114; and conflict of laws, 148; under civil law in Cochin-China, 155; contractual, 159; family obligations in Cambodia, 168; caused difficulties in codification in Indo-China, 175; covered by codes in Thailand, 185; general Philippine rules of, 228, 233; in marriage, 230; in sales, 234–5.
Occidental laws, 1; contrasted into Oriental, 2–3, 6–13; defined, 6; origin of, 7; based on contract, 9–10 (*see* European law).
Occupation, right of, 74.
Officials, 65, 71; duty of the people to, 12; in Thailand, 26, 28; in harbours, 56; administer Vietnamese laws, 74, 89; punishments for, 75, 81–2; privileged, 76; rights and duties of, 81–2, 84; and

natural calamities, 83; formal behaviour of, 85; murder of, 86; bribery of, 87; not to consort with prostitutes or actresses, 88; homicide of, 90; Chinese Board of, 106.
Oral law, 3–4. 7–8, 12, 50, 109.
Ordeals, 19, 27, 35, 66, 162.
Ordinances in Dutch Indies, 190.
Oriental laws, 1; vagueness of language in, 2; contrasted with Occidental, 2–3, 6–13; oral law in, 3–4, 8; defined, 6; based on status, 9–10.
Outcasting, 119; outcasts, 211.
Ownership: in Oriental texts, 3; in Java, 45–6; dependent on occupation, 45, 165; acquisition of, 45, 228, 232; in Dutch Indies, 207; in Philippines, 231–2; co-ownership, 231; by consent, 235.

PADDY, 83, 137.
Padoux, Georges, 184.
Pagar Ruyong state, Sumatra, 63.
Pahang state, Malaya, 52, 138, 139; laws of, 65.
Pali language, 28: Pali canon, 25–6.
Panay Island, Philippines, 215, 216.
Paramesvara (Megat Iskandar Shah), 62.
Pardon, 81.
Parents: duty owed by their children to, 21; and their children's marriage, 22, 83, 84; inheritance by, 45; accusations against, 75, 91; murder of, 75, 86, 106; respect for, 77, 78; duties of, 81; parental authority, 230.
Parricide, 86, 90, 106.
Partition, 21, 82.
Partnership, 69, 198.
Patani, Thailand, 63.
Paternity, 159, 230.
Pavón, José Mariá, 216.
Peasants, 3, 5, 7, 43, 92–3, 137.
Penalties: differentiated by status or parties' relationship, 20, 32, 34, 42, 43, 53–4, 81, 89–91, 107, 108; classification of, 34, 74, 81, 106; fines lists, 34, 42–3, 70, 87; *Agama* basically a list of, 44; against slaves, 53; imposed by (a) village elders, 76, 93 (b) *tsu*, 115 (c) Chinese guilds, 116; vary with crime's seriousness, 87; abolition of some, 169; jurisdiction of Tonkinese courts over, 173–4; maximum and minimum, 184; Dutch introduce imprisonment into

Index

Penalties, contd.
  Indies, 196–7 (*see also* Death penalty: Fines: Imprisonment: Punishment).
Penang (Prince of Wales Island), 57, 123, 124, 127, 133; Recorder's Court in, 126, 127.
Pepper, 137.
Perak state, Malaya, 52, 57–8, 59, 138, 140: Perak Laws, 56–60, 67.
Perbilangan (customary sayings), 3, 58, 61, 113.
Performance of contract, 233.
Perlis state, Malaya, 138.
Perpetuities, rule against, 141.
Persia, 59–60.
Personal laws, 8, 202; recognised by European law, 14, 205; in Straits Settlements, 129, 141, 148–9; change of religion and, 136, 149; in F.M.S., 141; in Burma, 144; based on religion, 148–9; in Indo-China, 179; in English legal world, 185; *adat* accommodates individual, 203.
Personal responsibility, 10, 31.
Petition-writers, 5.
Philastre, P.-L.-F., 82, 89, 174.
Philip II, King of Spain (1555–98), 221, 222.
Philippines, 1; conflict of laws in, 9; Spanish law in, 16, 214, 217–24, 229; American law in, 16, 214, 224–8, 231; Islamic law in, 48, 214, 237–8; Sulu laws, 69–70; law diverse in, 214, 228–37; indigenous laws of, 215–16; modern Codes of, 228–38.
Phra Thammasat in Thailand, 26–8 (*see Thammasat*).
Pledges, 40, 41, 44, 45, 67, 220, 233, 236.
Pnom-Penh, Cambodia, 166, 180, 181.
Poisoning, 90.
Police matters, 52, 182.
Politics and law, 205, 225; in new states, 13, 14; in Malay texts, 52, 63; in Sulu Codes, 70; in Vietnam, 78, 94; in all Oriental texts, 98; in Islamic law, 104, 113; in Negri Sembilan, 150.
Pollution, 41, 100.
Polygamy, 130–2, 164, 184.
Popes: and grants of sovereignty, 218–20; Papal Bulls, 220, 223.
Port Laws in Kedah, 54, 55–6.
Portuguese and Malacca, 127.
Possession, delivery of, 20, 30, 235.

Power, in Javanese thought, 103.
Pramuan Kotmai Ratchakan thi Nung, 25.
Prayers, rules for, 55.
Precedent: in English legal world, 8, 123–4; in Malaysia, 141; in Burma, 144, 150, 152; inconsistency of internal, 148; Ter Haar on, 193; not found in civil law, 193; common law and, 205, 227, 237; in U.S.A., 225, 227; Philippines and, 227, 237.
Prescription, acquisition by, 232.
Presumptions, legal, 231, 232.
Priests, land given to Hindu, 43; rules applied to Buddhist, 83–4, 85, 88, 146–7; Catholic, 223, 225.
Principle(s): conflict of, 9, 14, 104, 200; governing gifts, 20, 87; of Buddhism, 25; Islamic, 70; *Thammasat* a set of moral, 97; Ter Haar on legal, 193; private international law to be applied as matter of, 202; in *adat*, 203; of conflict of laws, 204; attempt to extend *adat*'s, 210; of Anglo-American law, 226, 227, 234; of common law, 227; of marriage, 229; Philippines synthesize legal, 233.
Private law: neglected in Oriental texts, 2–3, 7–8, 13, 77, 89, 91; punishment for breach of, 53; in Vietnam, 73; German, 98; in Code of Manu, 100; in Straits Settlements, 130; in Burma, 147; in Thailand, 184–5; European, 200; and conflict of laws, 205; equality of Indonesian systems of, 211; in Spain, 221; in Philippines, 225, 226.
Private morality, 6.
Privileged classes: Brahmins, 20, 34; in Java, 37; in Vietnam, 76, 80, 81, 90.
Privy Council, 22, 132, 139, 141, 143, 144, 149.
Produce: levy on, 37, 136; theft of, 83.
Proof, 62, 100, 174.
Property: its distribution on divorce, 19–20, 66–7, 145, 152, in *Wagaru*, 24; in Champa, 35; in Malay texts, 61, 67; in Philippines, 69, 228, 231; in Vietnam, 73, 89, 91; royal, 75; forfeiture of, 76; women's rights in, 78, 92, 132; of husband and wife, 78–9, 133–4, 144–5, 164, 185, 199, 231; private and public, 86; in Islamic law, 96, 112; *adat* and, 112, 149–50; *tsu* and, 115; in indigenous law, 119; in Straits Settlements,

133; jointly acquired, 135; in Laos, 165; in Annam, 170; proof of title to, 175; in Thailand, 185; in mixed marriages, 199 (*see also* Family property: Immovable property).
Protectorate, distinguished from colony, 154, 175.
Protégés, 177, 178–9, 180, 181, 182; distinguished from *sujets*, 175, 177.
Public domain: in Dutch Indies, 207; in Philippines, 238.
Public interest, *adat* and, 190, 191, 193.
Public law: Oriental texts and, 3; in *Āgama*, 43; in Malay texts, 50, 53, 56; in Thailand, 183, 184; 'unlawful act' and, 208; in Spain, 221.
Public morality, 6, 135.
Public order, maintenance of: in Java, 44; in Malay texts, 56; in Vietnam, 74, 76; in China, 106; in Singapore, 126; in Cochin-China, 158; in Laos, 165; in Annam, 169–70.
Public property: theft of, 84; damage to, 86, 88, 89.
Public security, 159, 172.
Public service, evasion of, 82–3.
Public Works, 80, 81, 89, 99, 170; in China, Board of, 106; in Annam, Ministry of, 170.
Punishment: of women, 20, 89, 90; in Thailand, 32; in Champa, 34; can be bought off, 43, 44; in Java, 43–4, 70; in Malay texts, 56; of offences on board ship, 63–4; vicarious, 65, 75, 84, 91, 92, 215; in Vietnam, 74, 76, 80, 81, 84–9; by sovereign in China, 76; is basis of law in (a) Sulu, 70 (b) China, 76, 89, 108 (c) *Gia-Long* Code, 89; of officials, 81, 82, 84, 87; to fit the crime, 89; commuting of, 90; in Code of Manu, 100; Chinese Board of Punishments, 106, 107; laws of Annam dealing with, 169; in *Maragtas* text, 215–16; in *Keliantiaw* text, 216; slavery as, 216 (*see also* Penalties).

QANUN DATO' KOTA STAR, 54, 55.
Quarrelling, punishable, 27, 41, 86.
Quo warranto, writ of, 237.
Qu'rān, 11, 56, 58–9, 60, 62, 69, 104, 105, 111; reading of, whether charitable, 135.

RACE: and personal laws, 8; law in Dutch Indies applied on racial basis, 9, 187, 194–5, 205; personal obligation in status system a function of, 10; varied in Straits Settlements, 129; and land, 188, 196, 206–7; interracial law, 202–3, 204–12.
Raffles, Sir (Thomas) Stamford, 39, 126; Raffles MSS., 52, 65, 66, 67–8.
Rajasat (Royal Decree in Thailand), 28–9, 102, 184.
Rama I, King of Thailand (1782–1809), 25, 27, 28, 29–30, 31.
Rāmādhipati, King of Ayut'ia, 28.
Rāmarāja, King of Ayut'ia, 26.
Rank, 30–1; penalties vary with offender's, 32, 34, 43.
Rape, 41, 88, 107, 163.
Reason: in Islamic law, 67, 104; criminal liability not removed by absence of, 75; repugnance to 'reason, justice and humanity', 126.
Rebellion, 74–5, 81; 'grand rebellion' (disloyalty), 75; against one's family, 75.
Recidivism, 76, 184.
Reciprocity, 4.
Redemption: of pledge, 45; from death, 66.
Regencies (districts) in Dutch Indies, 188.
Register of Commerce, Cochin-China, 158.
Registrar of Marriages, Burma, 152.
Registration: of families, 82, 92; of land, 117, 160, 207, 226, 235; of Muslim marriages, 132; of divorces, 133, 140; of marriages, 140, 152, 184; of cattle, 235.
Regulation of private law, 8.
Regulations: administrative, 2, 5; in Cochin-China, 158; in Annam, 169; in Dutch Indies, 194–6, 199; in Philippines, 238.
Relatives: punished for another's acts, 44, 91, 92; and land, 45; punishment of, 75; crimes against, 75, 86–7, 106, 107; punished for arranging unlawful marriage, 84.
Religion: and law, 1, 2, 47, 50, 52, 59, 60, 62, 67, 69, 96, 97, 98; personal obligation a function of, 10; in *Manugye Dhammathat*, 18; absent from *Wagaru*, 24; in *Āgama*, 46; in Malay texts, 55; offences against, 59; separate from

284　Index

Religion, contd.
　Sulu law, 70; reform of, 74; marriage and, 77; organization of, 81; in Vietnam, 92; in China, 92; in Islam, justice identical with religious law, 104; not separated from Islamic law, 105; in Hinduism, 109–10; Sharī'a is both a religion and a social system, 112; Islamic family regime is based on, 112; function of, 113; variety of religions in Straits Settlements, 129; law in Straits Settlements modified by, 129; change of, 136, 149; basis of personal laws, 149; law in Dutch Indies applied on religious basis, 187, 194, 205; religious courts, 195; common law recognizes religious laws, 205; laws in support of, 225.
Remarriage, 24, 46, 75, 230.
Rent for land, 67, 188.
Repugnancy: to *śāstra*, 110; to reason, justice and humanity, 126; to English common law, 132; to public morality, 135; to equity and justice, 190; to American principles and institutions of justice, 225.
Re-purchase, sale with right of, 210–11.
Residence, 149, 202; joint, 21.
Résident, 161, 162, 166, 169, 170, 171; *Résident-général*, 154, 172; *Résident Supérieur*, 164, 170, 171, 172, 173, 175; *Résident chef de province*, 170.
Restitution, 44, 61, 76, 84, 197.
Restitution of conjugal rights, 132.
Retribution, 44, 61.
Revenue: in Java tax on rice the main source of, 37; penalties in Sulu intended mainly to increase Sultan's, 70; Vietnamese rules for, 84; Chinese Board of Revenue, 106–7; in Dutch Indies, land managed by revenue authority, 188; in Philippines, 226.
Riau Island, 63.
Richardson, D., 22.
'Right' in Oriental law, 3, 108.
Rites, 19, 80–1, 85, 107; Chinese Board of, 106; Annamese Book of, 169; Annamese Ministry of, 169, 170.
Ritual, 85, 99, 115.
Robbery, 86, 215.
Robertson, James Alexander, 216.
Roman Catholics, 85, 180, 218.
Roman law, 7, 224, 226, 232, 234, 238;

XII Tables, 97; Roman-Dutch law in Ceylon and South Africa, 238.
Ross, A., 12.
Royal Decrees: in Vietnam, 79; Hindu, 111; for Dutch Indies, 198, 206–7; for Philippines, 221, 222, 223, 224, 229, 236.
Royal Edicts: in Vietnam, 90, 91, 92, 93; in Annam, 169.
Royal Ordinances: in Cochin-China, 155, 157; in Laos, 163; in Cambodia, 166–8, 181; in Annam, 171.
Royal Rules, in Thailand, 28–9, 97, 102, 184.
Ruler: duties of, 12, 27–8, 44, 97; his subjects' duty to, 12, 52, 60, 98; fines paid to, 43; Islamic view of, 50, 72; rules for, 55; in Malay texts administers the law, 56; European traders and local rulers, 56; his authority enforced in Malacca, 62–3; killing a slave is offence against Raja, 65; an individual in Oriental texts, 71; offences against, 74–5, 80; identified with the state, 75, 80; and privileged persons, 75–6, 90; punishment inflicted by, 76; status in (a) *Hông-Đu'c*, 80 (b) Code of Manu, 100–1; laws protecting, 85, 86; China validates position of Vietnamese, 94; Raja of Sarawak, 141–2; in Annam, 169, 170, 181; and Dutch Indies, 189 (*see also* Kings: Sultans).

SABAH, 141–3.
Sacrilege, 85, 86, 106.
Sahai, Sachchidanand, 34.
Saigon, 153, 155, 156, 157, 181.
Sailendras of Sri Vijaya, 57–8.
Śakti-nā (dignity marks) in Siam, 26, 30, 32.
Sale, 116; to monks, 146–7; of goods, 200, 210, 233–4; with a right of repurchase, 235.
Saleeby, N., 68.
Salvage, 69.
Sanction: distinguishes law from the other forms of social control, 4; custom may suffer from lack of, 5; breach of valid prescription needs application of, 13; may be imposed by sovereign on privileged class, 76; breach of contract attracts criminal, 81; in Islamic law, 105; among *tsu*, 115, 119; in 'status'

Index

systems, 119; in Sarawak some customs carry criminal, 142; law sometimes identified with, 192.
Sanskrit, 28, 36, 41, 42, 101.
Sarawak, 70, 123, 141–3.
Śāstra: copied in Thailand, 28; copied in Champa, 32–5; fines adjusted to offender's rank in, 34; and custom, 96, 109–11; difficult for Indian Courts to interpret, 96; deals with religion, ritual and Kings' duties, 99; King enforces the rules of, 101; its law transcends the world, 102; and dharma, 109–10 (see also Dharmaśāstra).
Savigny, Friedrich Karl von, 97.
Seals, 25, 26, 35, 82, 87, 94, 102.
Secret societies, 165.
Security: for debt, 30; in civil suits, 167–8.
Sejarah Melayu, 51, 63.
Selangor state, Malaya, 65, 138, 140, 141.
Self-defence, 43.
Semang aboriginal tribe, 57.
Semarang, Java, 209.
'Senior' and 'junior' members of a family, 75, 83, 84, 86, 90, 91, 107.
Sentences: review of, 90, 162, 170; conditional, 184.
Servitudes (easements), 160, 231–2.
Sexual intercourse, 41, 42, 69, 88; gifts and, 20; pre-marital, 81; when criminal, 88.
Sexual offences, 53, 70, 88.
Shāfi'ī school of Islamic law, 53, 66, 104, 132.
Sharī'a (law of Islam), 67, 104; a code of law and morality, based on Qur'ān, 105; embodies some customs, 111; and non-Islamic laws, 112; exclusive, 112–13; and local custom, 113–14; distribution of property in, 149.
Shipping, 195; rules for ships, 63–4.
Siam, 59; French-derived law in, 6; recension of legal code in, 25–30; royal installation in, 53; suzerain of Kedah, 54, 124, 125; cedes Unfederated Malay States to Britain, 138; French consular courts in, 155 (see Thailand).
Siamese in Cochin-China, 157.
Singapore, 13, 116, 123, 124, 126–7, 141, 148–9, 150.
Slametmuljana, 39, 40.
Slander, 41.
Slavery: in Siam, 27, 30; emphasized in (a) Malay texts, 53 (b) Keliantiaw text, 216; in Islamic law, 59; in Selangor, 65; in Luwaran Code, 69; as a punishment, 74, 215, 216; abolished in Laos, 161, 162; for debt, 162.
Slaves: in Wagaru, 21; in Java, 40; classified, 42; non-payment of a fine makes the defaulter the king's Slave kawula), 43; property of, 45; marriage with a free woman, 45; sexual offences by, 53, 88; reward for capture of runaway, 64; debt-slaves, 65; master and slave, 65, 88, 90, 216; killing of, 65, 90; treated as individuals, 71; forbidden to marry, 83; and affray, 86.
Smṛti (Hindu religious text), 24, 33, 35–6, 99, 102, 109–10.
Snouck Hurgronje, C., 192.
Social order, law as a part of: in South East Asia, 4, 5, 6, 11, 12, 97, 98, 108; in Thailand, 26; in Indian-derived law, 47; Hinduism, 99, 109–10: Buddhism does not reveal a social order, 102; Chinese law, 106, 107, 117–18; custom, 111; sharī'a, 112; social needs of the people, 190, 192; social construction of adat, 203; Philippines' customary legal laws, 214; in Keliantiaw text the social order has no regular laws, 216; attitude to marriage in Philippines, 220.
Solus, Henry, 176, 200, 203.
Sons, 21, 45, 77, 86, 107; filial piety, 91, 108; unfilial behaviour, 91, 115.
Sorcery, 41, 44, 60, 86.
Source of law: the state is source of European law, 7; oral law as, 7–8; oral law supplements texts, 8; municipal laws claim a monopoly, 13; Indian-derived law, 17; in ancient Thailand, 27; in Java, 37, 38, 40; of dharma, 99; litigation as, 102; texts can be, 108–9; in Sarawak, 142; of 'Special' laws in Burma, 152; in modern Thailand, 185; of Philippines' laws, 228, 233, 238; of Philippines' marriage law, 229; in Philippines, judicial decisions are not, 237.
Sources of legal texts: of Āgama, 40; secular and sacred in Malay texts, 50; of Kedah Laws, 54; of Ninety-nine Laws of Perak, 59; in Minangkabau texts, 61; of Malacca laws, 67; of Luwaran, 68; in Vietnam, 73, 79.

286　*Index*

South Africa, 238.
South East Asia: complexity of law in, 1–2, 17, 100, 108; contrast of Oriental and Occidental laws in, 1–13; oral law in, 3–4, 7–8; ethnography and law of, 4; legal ideas in, 5; origin of its laws, 6; conflict of laws in, 9; turns from status to contract systems, 14; Islam in, 111–12, 113; texts preserved indigenous features of, 119; codification of law in, 185.
Sovereignty: state claims absolute sovereignty over individual, 9; in status systems, 12–13; in Thailand, 31, 184; Western principles of, 32; in Champa, 33; in Java, 37; Islam and, 49–50; tension between theory of absolute sovereignty and legal reality, 51; in Malay texts, 55; in Malacca, 62–3; law and, 78, 79; in Vietnam, 80, 91, 95–6; of Kedah, 124, 125; of Britain in Kedah and Penang, 124; of E.I. Company in Singapore, 126; of Johore, 138; of Kelantan and Pahang, 139; partial divestment of, 139; law and sovereign states, 185, 191, 193; of Spain in Philippines, 217–19; transfer of sovereignty in Philippines to U.S.A., 224.
Spain and the Philippines, 214, 222, 223.
Spanish-derived law, 1, 6, 9, 214–15, 217–24, 225, 226, 227–8, 229, 230–3, 235–6, 238; Spanish-American legal world, 6, 214–38.
Spanish law: in Jamaica, 128; *Fuero Juzgo*, 220; *Fuero Real*, 220; *Fuero Partidas* (*Las Siete Partidas*), 220, 225, 226, 230; *El Ordenamiento de Alcalá*, 220; *Leyes de Toro*, 220, 221.
Special laws, 8, 98, 152, 195.
Spirits, dishonouring of, 107.
Spiritual values, 6, 216.
Squatting, 165.
Sri Vijaya Kingdom, Sumatra, 57, 63.
Stanley, Sir Edward, 129.
Stare decisis, principle of, 237.
State: and family in Chinese law, 6, 91; fountain of law in European systems, 7, 9, 13, 191, 193; now creates law in South East Asia, 9, 13, 185–6; claims absolute sovereignty over individuals, 9; law in status systems is part of state order, 12, 185; family law separate from state organization, 13; offences against, 74–5, 81, 107, 158–9; and law in Vietnam, 78, 79, 89; and law in Thailand, 184; assumes the government of Dutch Indies, 188; all land in Dutch Indies belongs to, 188, 207; suits against, 208.
Status, personal: basis of Oriental law, 6, 9–11, 118; differentiation by, 10, 32, 34, 42, 43, 81, 89–90, 107, 108; obligation a function of, 10; defined, 71; limits personal freedom, 71; in Java, 72; in Confucianism, 108; *Statut personnel*, 158, 159, 160, 167; in Cochin-China, 159, 160; of wives in (a) polygamous, 164 (b) mixed marriage, 199, 200–1, 211; in Indo-China, 176–7, 179; political status unnecessary for jurisdiction in common law, 205; in Philippines, 230.
Status, public: of local rulers, 56; of Minangkabau and Bugis immigrants, 58; of French colonies in S.E. Asia, 154; of European and traditional law in Dutch Indies, 199, 201, 202; of land in Dutch Indies, 209.
Status-based legal systems, 1–119; contrasted with contract systems, 9–14; S.E. Asia moves from status to contract, 13–14, 97, 185.
Statutes, 123.
Staunton, Sir George, 106.
Straits Settlements, 123–38; English law in, 6, 123–9, 130–1, 132, 133, 134–5, 137; Chinese law in, 130–2; Muslim law in, 132–5; Hindu law in, 135–6; Judges of, 139; personal laws in, 141; Borneo territories take laws from, 142.
Strangulation, punishment by, 74, 88, 158.
Stung-Treng province, Cambodia, 167.
Submission to European law in Dutch Indies, 197–8, 201; voluntary, 198–9, 207–12; involuntary, 199.
Succession to property: in Vietnam, 76, 93; in China, 107; among 'anomalous' Muslims in India, 113–14; in Burma, 143, 152; in Tonkin, 175; in Indo-China, 179; in Philippines, 232 (*see also* Inheritance).
Sudan, Islam in, 113.
Sudras, 42, 43, 46, 151.
Sūfī mystics, 48.
Sujets in Indo-China, 178, 179, 180, 181,

182; contrasted with *protégés*, 175, 177, 178, 179.
Sukhotai, King of Siam, 31.
Sultans, 51; installation of, 53; and law, 54, 70; lists of, 57; sovereignty of Malay, 138–9 (*see* Rulers).
Sulu Island, Philippines, 48, 69; Codes of, 49, 51, 69–70, 71.
Sumakwel, Datu, 215.
Sumatra, 52, 58, 61, 194; texts in, 49.
Sumptuary laws, 52–3, 55, 85, 90.
Sungei Ujong Laws, 60–2.
Sunna (the Prophet Muhammad's practice), 104, 111.
Sunni Boharas of Gujarat, 113–14.
Supercargo, 63–4.
'Superior' and 'Inferior', *see* 'Inferior' and 'Superior'.
Supreme Court: of Straits Settlements, 127; of F.M.S., 139; of Sarawak, 142; of Indonesia, 208, 210–11; of Philippines, 228, 235, 237; of Spain, 232.
Sūryavavarman I, King of Champa, 33.
Suzerainty: Siam and Kedah, 54–5, 124; China and Vietnam, 93–4; Britain and Unfederated Malay States, 138; Siam and Unfederated Malay States, 138.
Switzerland, Philippines take laws from, 228.

TA CH'ING LÜ LI, 80–1, 95, 106, 114 (*see* Ch'ing Code).
Tagalog people, Philippines, 219; their language, 215.
Talak (divorce), 105, 133.
T'ang Codes, 74, 78, 80.
Taxation: in Oriental law, 12–13; tax on rice harvest, 37; port dues, 55, 56; of land, 74, 83, 117; in Vietnam, 92, 100; in China, 106–7, 115; in Philippines, 217–18, 219.
Tax Charters in Java, 35, 37–8.
Tembera Datu' Sri Paduka Tuan, 54, 55.
Tengah, Rajn, 51.
Tension: in Javanese legal thought, 44; between theory of absolute sovereignty and legal reality, 51; inclusion of some Islamic law in texts leads to, 103; between revelation and reason in Islam, 104; in law in S.E. Asia, 119.
Ter Haar, B., 189–90, 193, 196–7.
Territorial jurisdiction, 202–4.

Texts: important source of Oriental law, 1–3, 10; contrasted with oral law, 7; and custom, 8, 23, 96, 101, 109, 144; inconsistency in, 12; whether 'real' law, 13–14, 95, 97, 98, 101, 108, 118; Burmese, 17–25, 31, 32, 96–7, 101–2, 144–6; Hindu, 27, 102, 109–10; in Indonesia, 46–7; express natural order, 47, 109, 118–19; Islamic, 49–50; Malayan (Malaccan), 51–68, 103–4; Javanese, 62, 103; in Sulu, 68–70; Vietnamese, 73–94, 168; European medieval, 95, 97; and legal development, 95; interpretation of, 96–8; Thai, 97, 102–3; Minangkabau, 104; Chinese, 106, 108; and natural order, 109, 118–19; contrasted with Western law, 118; preserve indigenous features, 119; in Philippines, 215–16.
Thailand, 1, 48; oral law in, 3; Indian-derived law in, 6, 25–32, 100, 102; recension of the laws of, 25–6, 28, 29–30; texts of, 97, 102–3; modernized law of, 153, 183–5; and extraterritoriality, 183, 184 (*see also* Siam).
Thammasat in Thailand, 28–9, 32, 97, 184 (*see Phra Thammasat*).
Theft: in Thailand, 27; classified, 40–1, 86; punishment for, 42, 54, 70, 76, 105, 153, 163; from Royal property, 75; a ground for divorce, 77, 84; of produce, 83.
Things (*choses*) in action, 233.
Third parties, protection for, 160.
Time, efflux of, and variation of contracts, 36, 44.
Tin, 55–6.
Title: proof of, 35, 38; to property, 185, 223, 235.
Tombs, 75, 85, 107.
Tonkin, 177; a French protectorate, 154, 166, 175; Court of Appeal of, 155, 172; legal administration in, 172–5; tribunals in, 173–4, 180; conflict of laws in, 178–9.
Tonkinese, jurisdiction over, 181, 182.
Torrens system of land registration, 160, 226, 235.
Tort, 208.
Torture, 88, 158, 171, 174.
Tourane Concession, Indo-China, 181.
Trade, 52; European traders and local rulers, 34–5; sea-trade, in Maritime

288   Index

Trade, contd.
  laws, 62–4; trading rights, 64; in Malay texts, 66; specialized trades in India, 110; trade courts, 110; trade guilds in China, 115–16; in Dutch Indies, 191 (*see* Commerce).
Traditional law: preferred by many in S.E. Asia, 13; in Thailand, 184–5; no conflict in, 204.
Transport laws in Philippines, 226.
Treason, 27, 75, 81, 86, 91, 106.
Treaties, sovereignty obtained by, 217.
Treaty: of Peace and Friendship, with Kedah (1791), 124; Bangkok (1826), 124, 138; over Singapore (1824), 126; Anglo-Dutch (1824), 127; with Johore (1885), 138; with Cochin-China (1862 and 1874), 154; with Laos (1893), 161; with Annam (1884), 171; of Hué (1884), 172; of Nanking (1930), 183; of Paris (1898), 224.
Trengganu state, Malaya, 138.
Trial of cases: in Champa, 34–5; in Java, 36.
Tribal peoples, Annam, 171.
Tribunals: in Champa, 34–5; in Java, 36; in Vietnam, 100; in India, 110; in Cochin-China, 154–5; indigenous, in (a) Cochin-China, 155, 157 (b) Laos, 161, 163 (c) Cambodia, 166 (d) Tonkin, 173 (e) Indo-China, 180–2 (e) Dutch Indies, 189, 197; French, in (a) Cochin-China, 157 (b) Laos, 161 (c) Annam, 169 (d) Indo-China, 180–1; in Laotian villages, 162; divided by race in Dutch Indies, 187, 189 (*see also* Courts).
Trusts, 77, 78, 85, 234.
Tsu (lineage), 114–16, 119.

UDAYĀDITYAVARMAN, King of Champa (1049–66), 33.
Undang 2 Kerajaan, 52, 54, 57, 65, 66.
Undang-Undang Mahkamah Melayu Sarawak, 113, 143.
Unfederated Malay States, 6, 138, 139–40, 141.
Unfilial conduct, 91, 115.
Unification of law: in Sarawak, 142; in Dutch Indies, 189, 191–2, 201, 204, 212–13.
Unitary system of law, 207.

United States: and Philippines, 9, 214, 215, 224; American-derived law, 1, 6, 224–8, 229, 233–4, 236, 237–8.
'Unlawful acts' in Dutch Indies, 208.
Unlawful entry, 42, 76.
Usufruct, 92, 159, 168, 231, 236.
Usury, 85, 165.

VALIDITY: of gift, 20; of progression from status to contract law, 97; of custom in India, 110; of Muslim divorce, 132; of juridical acts, 180; of oral contracts, 216; of ecclesiastical ownership of land, 223.
Validity of law, 70; social order regulated by law finds validity in spiritual terms, 6; ensured in the west by the state, 7, 8, 12, 13–14, 185; gained by Oriental law by its place in a wider Universe, 10, 11, 12; Oriental law has no 'invalid law', 12; prescriptive and descriptive, 13, 76, 79, 96, 204, 215; European laws can be valid at two levels, 13; descriptive validity of Oriental law, 13; populace may disregard valid 'contract' law, 14, 215; Islam and, 96; of *adat* law, 190; two requirements for, 191–2; in Dutch Indies civil law's domination lessens indigenous law's validity, 193–4; of inter-local law, 204.
Validity of marriage: mutual consent necessary for, 22; bride's unwillingness and, 105; of interreligious marriages, 131, 147, 151–2, 180, 212; Chinese, 131, 150; age of consent and, 148; effect of conversion on, 149; depends on registration, 184.
van den Berg, L. W. C., 201.
van Ronkel, Ph. S., 54, 66.
van Vollenhoven, C., 4, 201.
Varasiri, S., 25.
Varṇa (status), 34, 43, 46, 99, 100, 119.
Veda, 99.
Vientiane, Laos, 161, 162.
Vietnam, 1; formal arrangement of Codes in, 2, 40; Chinese-derived Codes in, 6, 73–94, 168; China's wars with, 78; dynastic struggles in, 80; legal reality in, 91; China's suzerainty over, 93–4; divided into North and South, 186.
Vigan, Philippines, 223.

Villages: village elders in (a) Malay texts, 61 (b) Vietnam, 76, 93 (c) China, 116–17 (d) Cochin-China, 156, 157 (e) Annam, 169; administrative units in (a) Vietnam, 91–2 (b) Dutch Indies, 188; have councils in (a) Vietnam, 93 (b) Annam, 169; have tribunals in (a) China, 114, 116–17 (b) Laos, 162 (c) Dutch Indies, 190; and land in Dutch Indies, 207.
Vinaya, 146.
Vinogradoff, Sir Paul, 32, 97.
Violence, 40, 41, 61, 69, 86, 89.
Volksraad in Dutch Indies, 188–9.
'Voluntary submission', in Dutch Indies, 198–9, 207–12.
Voluntary surrender (*tzu-shou*), in China, 81.
von Wright, G. H., 205, 206.
Vyavahāra smṛti, 24.

WAGARU CODE, 18–22, 24, 101–2.
Wagener, J. H., 200.
Wagering, 195.
War Board, China, 106.
War Ministry, Annam, 169, 170.
Wayang, 3.
Weights and measures, 56, 85, 100, 116.
West Africa, 113, 153.
Whipping, 74.
Widow: and remarriage, 19; whether liable for late husband's debts, 65; inheritance by, 78, 127, 134, 168; and murder, 86; her right to usufruct, 92, 159; and maintenance, 159.
Wife: in *Wagaru*, 19, 21; inheritance by, 21, 46, 78; whether liable for husband's debts, 65, 144–5; punishable for husband's crime, 75; secondary, 78, 84, 131, 159, 164; desertion of, 78; immoral loan of, 83; fugitive, 84; assault on husband by, 87; primary, 131, 159, 164; separate property of, 133–4, 145; represented in court by husband, 156; assault on, 163; murdered by husband, 165; her status in mixed marriage, 199, 200–1, 211; in business, 236 (*see also* Husband and wife).
Wilkinson, R. J., 4, 50.
Wills, 133–4, 232.
Winstedt, R. O., 50, 57; and de Josselin de Jong, P. E., 61, 63.
Witchcraft, 41, 60.
Witnesses, 35, 100, 169; to marriage, 66.
Women: in Burmese texts, 19–20; and right to property, 92; duties of, 100; Muslim woman can sue for breach of promise, 133; and security in civil suits, 167; in *Keliantiaw*, 216.
Wounding, 32, 41, 106.

YAŚOVARMAN I, King of Angkor (889–900), 33.

ZAKAT AND *FITRAH* (charity tax), 55.
Zamindari in Malacca, 136.